Fairy T
Reimag

Fairy Tales Reimagined

Essays on New Retellings

Edited by
SUSAN REDINGTON BOBBY

Foreword by KATE BERNHEIMER

McFarland & Company, Inc., Publishers
Jefferson, North Carolina, and London

LIBRARY OF CONGRESS CATALOGUING-IN-PUBLICATION DATA

Fairy tales reimagined : essays on new retellings / edited by Susan
  Redington Bobby ; foreword by Kate Bernheimer.
      p.   cm.
  Includes bibliographical references and index.

  ISBN 978-0-7864-4115-0
  softcover : 50# alkaline paper ∞

    1. Fairy tales—Moral and ethical aspects.   2. Fairy tales—
  Social aspects.   I. Bobby, Susan Redington, 1969–
  GR550.F284   2009
  398.2 — dc22   2009019474

British Library cataloguing data are available

Cover image ©2009 Shutterstock

Manufactured in the United States of America

McFarland & Company, Inc., Publishers
  Box 611, Jefferson, North Carolina 28640
  www.mcfarlandpub.com

For Darren:
donor, helper, hero.
I love you —forever.

Acknowledgments

This book would not have come to fruition without the assistance of so very many people. I am grateful for the help of the following:

My husband, Darren, whose background in science lies completely opposite mine in literature, but who has learned more than he perhaps ever wanted to know about fairy tales as he supported my efforts to complete this collection. His patience has been extraordinary; his love is infinite.

My contributors, who enthusiastically heeded my call for papers for the NEMLA panel several years ago, and who came from both near and far to meet in Baltimore a cold weekend in February to discuss our shared interests. I'd like especially to thank those whom I could not accommodate on the panel due to size limitations but who revised their essays for me nonetheless, even before I had a contract. I am grateful for their belief and trust in me as their editor and thrilled that we could put this volume together.

Kate Bernheimer, whose letter of encouragement on the panel and packet of "gifts" arrived unexpectedly in my mailbox one day, and who kept in touch with me through the process. I am indebted to her for introducing me to two amazing writers who also became contributors. I feel blessed that such a successful author has taken her time to encourage me and offer assistance along the way, and even more humbled that she has validated my work through her brilliant foreword.

My colleagues, who have offered unending encouragement and support, and in the case of Jeffrey K. Gibson, a contribution to this collection. In particular, I'd like to acknowledge the support of my friend and colleague Linda De Roche, who took me under her wing many years ago and shepherded me through the transition from adjunct faculty member to tenured professor. Her ability to write and publish scholarly work while teaching full-time has encouraged my own professional development. I will also not forget that she assisted me in transforming my fairy tales course from a special topics course to a permanent catalog offering at Wesley College.

My students, who have kept up their interest in this material by supplying me with full classes every year. Their enthusiasm makes teaching a joy, and I know that they will carry on the tradition of telling tales, both classic and contemporary, to those with whom they come in contact for years to come. A special thank you also to Katie Beetschen and Doryann Barnhardt, who provided feedback on many portions of the book as well as unending enthusiasm for all things "fairy-tale."

My mother, Joyce Redington, who supplied me with the Disney Cinderella Halloween costume that I desired, but who also supplemented Disney with Bridget Hadaway's *Fairy Tales* book, one which contained the Brothers Grimm, Perrault, and Andersen among others. My mother's interest in reading and our trips to the public library fostered my love for the literary that would eventually grow into a career.

My sister, Kelly Redington, who read all of Shannon Hale's novels in order to give me feedback on my essay. Like my husband, Kelly's disciplinary interests and career could not be more different from my own, but our shared love of queens, fairies, mermaids, and castles forever binds us.

Lastly, I wish to thank the late Dr. Steven R. Centola of Millersville University. He was instrumental in awakening in me a desire to explore the literary world through research and analysis. To this day, I recall the spirit of adventure that he provoked in his students through discovery of new ways of looking at literary works. Though he attained scholarly success as a researcher and chronicler of the works of Arthur Miller, he was first and foremost a brilliant, though down-to-earth and kind teacher. His passion for literary discussion and inquiry lives on through the work of his former students in both the classroom and their publications.

Table of Contents

Foreword
The *Affect* of Fairy Tales

KATE BERNHEIMER*

> If methods are different, not only in the different arts but in differ-
> ent artists, we can nevertheless characterize some great monumen-
> tal types, or "varieties," of compounds of sensations: *the vibration.*
> — Gilles Deleuze and Félix Guattari, *What Is Philosophy?*

Fairy tales represent hundreds of years of stories based on thousands
of years of stories told by hundreds, thousands, perhaps even millions, of tellers. The mind reels at their influence, omnipresence, phosphorescence: like
a star or a planet, they shine, ubiquitous and necessary as gravity, as air or ice.

Almost precisely 200 years ago the Grimm Brothers published their first
edited fairy-tale volumes. Very shortly after that in cosmic time—four decades
ago—as a young girl, I lived at the edge of a fairy-tale woods less than a mile
from the village library, itself built almost precisely 200 years ago. I walked to
the library with my mother, father, sisters, and brother each Saturday and
worked my way alphabetically through the children's room — how I especially
loved any series about horses, flowers, and girls! And the adventure tales about
pirates, shipwrecks, and sleuths! I read so fast and so much that I got an early
pass to the adult room. That's where the fairy tale books were then kept, and
Reader, I found them. Witches and bears and teakettles and darkened moons.
Hedgehogs and princesses and donkeys and singing spoons.

*Kate Bernheimer is the author of two novels, The Complete Tales of Merry Gold (FC2, 2006) and
The Complete Tales of Ketzia Gold (FC2, 2001). She edited the essay collections Mirror, Mirror on
the Wall: Women Writers Explore Their Favorite Fairy Tales (Anchor/Vintage, 2002) and Brothers
& Beasts: An Anthology of Men on Fairy Tales (Wayne State University Press, 2007). Her first children's book, The Girl in the Castle Inside the Museum (Random House, 2008), was named one of
the Best Books of 2008 by Publishers Weekly, and her second children's book, The Lonely Book, is forthcoming from Random House. She founded and edits Fairy Tale Review and Fairy Tale Review Press,
and she is an associate professor in the Department of English at the University of Alabama.*

I could not get enough; I still cannot get enough.

The first versions I read were bare-bone stories about the triumphs of the weak and the humble: over and over I read them. With their gilt spines and illustrations, the books drew me in not only to the world of faeries and spells, but also into the world of The Story. It was through these endless variations that I recognized intuitively how one could live inside a story forever by reading it over and over again (and then by picking up a pencil and scribbling the poignant tales of one's own clumsily imagined toadstools and magic).

And so I was Little Red Riding Hood often. I donned my red cap and the red poncho my grandmother had made, and I set out writing fairy tales of my own. These I published in a village newspaper my best friend Diana and I typed and taped together and mimeographed at my father's office. I had a sort of fairy-tale column I kept, where I serialized a story about my Russian great-grandmother Rose, a princess who eloped with the gardener's son, Jacob — the castle where she slept, waiting for him to come, was totally covered in vines. Years later, I learned Rose was actually Latvian and had not eloped, but rather escaped Nazi sympathizers in her small town. Her real and terrifying story had collapsed into tale for my grandfather, who told it to me as a tale of enchantment. Dressed as Little Red Riding Hood, carefully I typed it. "Jacob, The Gardener's Son, A Fairy Tale, Part Three." Smudges from the typewriter ink.

So as a young writer, something drew me instinctively and matter-of-factly to fairy tales. In the fairy-tale collections I found in the library (Russian, German, Korean, Chinese, Yiddish, and more), their flatness, abstraction, everyday magic, and repetitive forms drew me in hard, shaping an obsession that figures into my work to this day as a reader, author, editor, and critic. Those early encounters with talking corpses and feather-coat girls reconfigure again and again whether I am writing a children's book, a novel, a story, or editing a volume of essays ... or writing a foreword to a scholarly collection.

And just as I love fairy-tale collections, so too do I adore fairy-tale criticism. In fact, while there are obvious differences in the modes, I don't differentiate between the two very much: fairy-tale work is the thing. It is the fairy-tale-ness of any piece of writing — be it an essay, prose poem, or play — that draws me in, and which accounts, I think, for fairy tales' mirror-like reception by readers. Fairy tales contain us like a picture or poem, and reflect back to us in language, image, and trope.

Scholars have offered a vast array of persuasive theses about why and how fairy tales continue to attract readers and writers over the centuries. These scholars[1] provide transfixing narratives about the Marxist, postmodern, psychological, feminist, and aesthetic magnets in fairy tales, which rivet audiences worldwide in music, film, television, literature, and fine art versions and inspire new versions to be produced at an immeasurable rate. As Andy Warhol is once rumored to have responded when asked "Which contemporary artists do you like?" ... "I like them all." All of the scholarly arguments about the origins of our deep and undying affection for fairy tales seem to me remarkably, beautifully sane. I respond likewise to the wide array of contemporary authors working from fairy tales, whether well-known in fairy-tale circles or not, whether they are considered literary or commercial or genre writers is no matter to me. *I like them all.*

That is why I like Susan Redington Bobby's collection, *Fairy Tales Reimagined*, so much. For it brings into the conversation — that melodious, inharmonious whole — so many voices from scholars to artists arrayed. What I admire is the inclusiveness of this volume, reflective of the inclusiveness and uncontainability of the history of fairy tales themselves.

What is it that binds this collection of essays? Professor Bobby contextualizes the collection in her elegant introduction, and in the organization of the essays themselves. But for me what also binds this essay collection, and seals it with a wax throne or flower or star, in the history of fairy-tale criticism, is how the approaches, taken together in here, can be seen to contribute not only to the very important living history and interpretation of contemporary fairy tales — so nascent and now — but to a conversation about what constitutes a "fairy tale," that monumental type of art we so know and love.

I often refer to my own method of identifying fairy tales as my sensing (through feeling and through close-reading) what I call *a fairy-tale feel.* The fairy-tale-ness of a work. The books inspected in this collection do contain elements that scholars (and I) have identified as marking a work as a fairy tale; including plot devices, aesthetic elements, and political tropes. (I ascribe to all interpretive lenses as helpful in identifying fairy-tale works, and take them together prismatically as a beautifully un-unified yet total cosmos).

So Bobby's collection confirms even more what I have been thinking about lately in light of French philosopher Gilles Deleuze's discussion of *affect.* Applying his concept of *affect* to new fairy-tale literature, one sees how these works may be identified atmospherically, scientifically, telepathically: in certain books, fairy tales are in the air. In *Gilles Deleuze*, author Claire Colebrook illustrates this concept of affect as such: "A horror film presents horror; for beyond the fear of the characters of the viewer there is just a *sense* of the horror which the film draws upon. The film is not about horror, or a representation of horror; it is a sense or feeling of horror which we may or may not enter. Before the viewer or character is actually horrified we view within the affect or milieu of horror in general."[2] This Deleuzian notion of affect is precisely on display in Bobby's collection. The works here discussed — whether a postmodern novel by Robert Coover or popular literary collection by Emma Donoghue, whether philosophical nightmare by Gaétan Soucy or a genre-inspired book by Robin McKinley — have the *affect* of fairy tales. The works are not about fairy tales, or a representation of fairy tales; it is a sense or feeling of fairy tales which we may or may not enter. In true fairy-tale fashion, I borrow Colebrook's words:

"Before the reader or characters are actually enchanted, we view within the affect or milieu of fairy tales in general."

The creation, therefore, of a new fairy tale is not merely a re-creation or variation on a fixed form, but art; for Deleuze, art creates worlds through affects. Fairy tales create fairy tales through fairy-tale affects and become *affect.* Jack Zipes aptly once wrote, "There is no such thing as *the* fairy tale. There are fairy tales."[3] When we see them we know them; we sense that they *are.* Likewise, fairy-tale scholarship enters and expands the art form itself; I believe that without fairy-tale scholarship, which seeks to identify and comprehend the fairy-tale affect, the fairy tales would not vibrate so much and with so bright an aspect. The scholarship in this volume is the thinking-aspect of the fairy-tale affect. Together it all comes alive and lives on. Of the scholarship too I would say, as Deleuze once wrote, "It sculpts and is sculpted" by fairy tales. I congratulate the writers included in here, and their humble editor, Susan Redington Bobby, for bringing our ageless anxieties and hopes once more to light through the hypnotic and clinical lens that is fairy tales.

Kudos to Professor Bobby too for here including essays on writers widely known and canonized in the field, and writers as-yet less widely known. Interpretations and formulations of diverse work across the stylistic divides are here presented in beautiful, surprising and original ways, providing not only the delight that comes from discovering a new piece of literature or critic, but the rapture that can only be provoked by hearing a story so old and familiar it is part of our very breath. Through *Fairy Tales Reimagined*, readers gain literary access and insight into the deep connection we have with fairy tales. The wild and wise conversation continues.

Notes

1. Not a comprehensive list, but many referred to in this volume, and to whom I owe so much of my thinking and writing: Cristina Bacchilega, Stephen Benson, Ruth Bottigheimer, Alan Dundes, Donald Haase, Max Lüthi, Steven Swann Jones, Maria Tatar, Marina Warner, Jack Zipes, and more.

2. Claire Colebrook, *Gilles Deleuze* (London: Routledge, 2002), 26.

3. Jack Zipes, *Fairy Tale as Myth, Myth as Fairy Tale* (Lexington: University Press of Kentucky, 1994).

Works Cited

Colebrook, Claire. *Gilles Deleuze.* London: Routledge, 2002.
Zipes, Jack. *Fairy Tale as Myth, Myth as Fairy Tale.* Lexington: University Press of Kentucky, 1994.

Introduction
Authentic Voices in Contemporary Fairy Tales

SUSAN REDINGTON BOBBY

After mother cry and gone quiet like sleeping I hold my head like apple shake it for see what sick. Sound all right. Never can tell.
— Emma Donoghue, "The Tale of the Cottage"

Of all her compelling, lyrical tales in *Kissing the Witch*, Donoghue's "The Tale of the Cottage" may be the most mystifying. My own students, strongly familiar with Disney's sanitized child-centric tales, are quick to catch on to Donoghue's reworking of 13 classic tales into a contemporary context. They are hungry for a new narrative, one that hearkens back to the old yet moves the storyline forward to reflect conditions of our modern world. They have no trouble identifying Donoghue's "The Tale of the Shoe" as a revision of Cinderella, or "The Tale of the Needle" as a refashioned Sleeping Beauty, in spite of their deviations from the familiar plots. But "The Tale of the Cottage" gives them pause. It isn't the plot that initially confounds; it is the language. Is it possible that this rudimentary syntax emerges from the first person narrator of a variant of Hansel and Gretel? Are my students reading the words of a feral child? Is she developmentally challenged? Or are her expressions stunted by the abuse, illness, and abandonment that she has suffered? As my students come to realize, these halting words are spoken by a new Gretel, one of Donoghue's 13 protagonists of her "old tales in new skins," a series of interwoven re-envisioned fairy tales that question the identities of their narrators and imagine new trajectories for each tale's finale. Indeed, some of the variants, like "The Tale of the Cottage," are so altered from their classic predecessors that their status as variants is debatable; perhaps they are more accurately new literary creations which only allude to archetypal fairy tale motifs as catalysts.

5

One of many remarkable qualities of Donoghue's work is her accuracy at providing a series of authentic voices, each teller relating her tale to the next in the collection. Gone are the typecast cloned heroines of Charles Perrault and the Brothers Grimm. Of these classic inspirations, Joyce Carol Oates contends that "characterization does not exist; of the growth, development, and evolution of human personality there is none" (252). It is the barrage of flat, one-dimensional character types and the stylized voice of the third person omniscient narrator (read: editor) which once emerged as the voice of the storyteller. But did this voice accurately depict the truth? Can a mere fairy tale suggest a rendering of the cultural conditions for men, women, and children at any point in time?

To be sure, all fairy tales reflect if only in a small way the culture from which they evolved — though most can identify which parts of the tale are reflections of true social injustices and which parts reveal fantasy wish-fulfillment. As Maria Tatar asserts, "Wish-fulfillment in fairy tales often has more to do with the stomach than with the heart.... Fairy tales often take us squarely into the household, where everyone seems to be anxious both about what's for dinner and about who's for dinner" (179). But a problem with the classic tales has consistently been that they do not provide an authentic voice. They provide an altered version of truth, for one reason more than most: their "original" tellers likely lacked the verbal finesse to tell a story on the page that would both honor the oral component of the tale and delight the reader with elegant descriptive details.

Readers of fairy tales can see in dramatic fashion what happens when an oral tale is transcribed authentically via Delarue's "The Story of Grandmother." A well-known variant of Little Red Riding Hood, "The Story of Grandmother" is often cited as an example of the oral tale that was transcribed more or less "as is" — bereft of embellishment and concise, driven by dialogue. Maria Tatar explains that "it is presumably more faithful to an oral tradition predating Perrault, in part because the folklorist recording it was not invested in producing a highly literary book of manners for aristocratic children and worked hard to capture the exact wording of the peasant raconteur..." (4). As a result, this variant is generally viewed as falling flat on the page, failing to engage the reader and only a model for the "much better" versions which followed from experienced editors who transformed the tale into a real "story."

Yet move to the year 1997 when Donoghue publishes "The Tale of the Cottage," in which the fairy tale seems to have come full-circle. In this striking piece we hear the authentic voice of a child, presumably Gretel, described as "a halfwit girl" (136). The child relates her parents' description of her: "The little one's no earthly use not right in the head" (134). Donoghue provides a version of Hansel and Gretel likely closer to the *truth* than her predecessors. Clearly her protagonist is limited in her expression yet carefully observant of what goes on around her. She communicates with painful intensity her most basic needs for food, warmth, shelter, and family: "I suck bread soft and wait for them come back. Cold. Sound like crows. Good girl. Want home. Cry" (135).

This is what happens when a skilled *writer* seizes a fairy tale motif and uses it to craft a new work of fiction. It's surprisingly more accurate and reflective of true life than we might have ever thought a fairy tale could be.

One could even say it's magical.

In 2005, Kate Bernheimer, editor and author of books for both children and adults, created *Fairy Tale Review*, a literary journal devoted to contemporary expressions of fairy tale motifs in fiction and poetry. In her editorial from "The Blue Issue," Bernheimer asserts, "Fairy tale motifs often are reflexively dismissed as clichés, reflecting a misapprehension of this art form's intricate history" (104). In her journal of creative work lies one answer to the critics who may have "dismissed" the importance of fairy tales to our world. The success of Bernheimer's journal proves the relevance of fairy tales as inspiration to the worlds of contemporary fiction and poetry. Additionally, the "intricate history" to which Bernheimer refers has been explored by many of the great minds of fairy tale scholarship. Jack Zipes, Maria Tatar, Ruth Bottigheimer, Donald Haase, Cristina Bacchilega, Marina Warner, and many others have provided us with an astounding amount of research on classic fairy tales. Their work has pioneered a field of literary criticism that is growing by the year. These scholars have also crafted brilliant interpretations of the work of those whom we might call the "classic" writers of the contemporary period: Anne Sexton, Angela Carter, Margaret Atwood, and others, the pioneers themselves of feminist postmodern contemporary fairy tale revisions. To be sure, we owe much gratitude to those scholars who have enlightened us to the authentic voices of these canonical writers—writers who have reflected the world of the late 20th–early 21st centuries through innovations in story-telling to an audience eager for a counter-movement to fairy tales' so-called "Disnification." And yet, those of us who immerse ourselves in the study of fairy tales, including my students, face some scrutiny from those outside the discipline. Some might ask, can fairy tales really be as important as Faulkner?

The answer, of course, is yes. When we bind together the study of both classic and contemporary fairy tales, we see that we can no longer dismiss such narrative forms as simplistic or irrelevant. We must recognize Bernheimer's accurate observation, that "we are experiencing an explosion of fairy tale influences in art and literature" (104), and this resurgence of works whose archetypal motifs allude to the genre has become quite diversified. Fairy tale revisionists have come into their own by embracing a wide variety of theoretical approaches in their works. While the canonical contemporaries have focused primarily on feminist concerns, the publications of the lesser-known but still critically important writers have moved into other areas entirely. Yet the truth is that most criticism does focus on a narrow portion of writers and theoretical approaches; in his preface to the 2002 edition of *Breaking the Magic Spell: Radical Theories of Folk and Fairy Tales*, Jack Zipes admits, "Despite some superb feminist analyses and social criticism, there has been a strange avoidance to discuss social class, ideological conflicts, and the false assumptions of numerous psychological approaches ... literature and art cannot be fully understood without considering the socio-political-cultural context in which they are produced" (ix). It is my contention that the reason behind the avoidance is not nearly as important as the move to correct this oversight. If our goal is to bring the relevance of fairy tales to a larger audience, then we must prove ourselves by widening the scope of our inquiry to include an even greater variety of writers and literary works.

In addressing the fairy tale revisions of the writers in my collection of essays, I have separated their work into four broad categories, recognizing, of course, that some pieces overlap every category yet primarily "fit" into one area the best. Four sections of this gathering echo theoretical differences which mirror the diversity of current fairy tale offerings: gender and sexuality, narrative forms, trauma and dystopia, culture and politics. Readers of fairy tale studies are aware that various other texts provide surveys of the theoretical underpinnings before applying them to texts— Kevin Paul Smith's *The Postmodern Fairytale: Folkloric Intertexts in Contemporary Fiction* (2007) comes to mind as a text which offers a range of illustrative definitions of postmodern techniques. By contrast, my compilation assumes the reader has an understanding of critical theory and chooses to jump right into the discussion of the tales themselves. In many cases, the conversation on certain contributions is long overdue.

In 2006, I recognized the need for heightened critical attention of contemporary fairy tale writers. I proposed a panel titled *Fairy Tale Visions and (Re) Visions* for the 2007 NEMLA convention, and I called for papers on contemporary fairy tales as invented or reinvented by critically acclaimed writers of the late 20th century to the present. I invited papers that explored contemporary fairy tales in various forms, including the novel, novella, short story, or poetry. I wanted contributors to investigate how each writer claimed the fairy tale as his or her own by reflecting concerns of the social, political, or cultural climate. I wanted to see how the "magic mirror" reflected changes in our world and how writers were keeping the fairy tale alive through continuous revision and adaptation.

Instead of receiving essays on Sexton and Carter, as I expected, I acknowledged submissions on many writers whose work was appreciated but might have been overlooked by critics. Other than the occasional positive book review or listing as a "recommended text for further reading," most of these writers had not seen their work under the microscope in extended interpretive analyses. Therefore, I saw a need to bring the work of these newest writers to the attention of others, and this collection grew from that desire. My collection addresses a wide range of writers: for one, it addresses the work of those coming into canonical contemporary status who will likely be considered as influential as Sexton or Carter, such as Byatt, Coover, or Yolen, while it also brings to light the offerings of writers known for other genres who have made outstanding but lesser-known contributions to this field, such as Gaiman or Pullman. Additionally, my compilation focuses on some of the most recent additions to the field by writers such as Soucy, Hale, Kerr, and Bernheimer. The thread that binds all of these writers and their work is their awareness of the fairy tale tradition and their innovation as each reimagined tale both reflects our time and shapes the genre for years to come.

So how do these writers reflect the social, political, and cultural climate of their age through reimagined fairy tales? Some reflect changes in identity through analysis of gender. Martine Hennard Dutheil de la Rochère begins the conversation with an insightful study of Emma Donoghue's *Kissing the Witch*, primarily focusing on her story "The Tale of the Shoe" and its lesbian feminist perspective through her clever analysis of language, metaphor, and meaning. Christa Mastrangelo Joyce continues the dialogue on gender by presenting her reading of feminist poetry which embraces Sexton's influential work and then moves beyond to identity and theme in the poems of Hay, De Ford, Yolen, and Broumas. Then, Bethany Joy Bear's essay on Peg Kerr's *The Wild Swans* brings to light adaptations of Hans Christian Andersen's work that "raise questions about gender, homosexuality, and community" by creating a socially-relevant work that exposes the plight of victims of HIV/AIDS. Next, Joanne Campbell Tidwell's essay "Found Girls" offers a critique of Jane Yolen's Nebula award-winning tale "Lost Girls" and its defiance of the enslavement of Victorian femininity; in Tidwell's words, this brings forth "a message that still bears repeating today." Lastly, Mathilda Slabbert, whose essay bridges both gender and postmodern narrative strategies, brings a male writer into the discussion with her piece on Neil Gaiman's *Stardust*, "Troll Bridge," and "Snow, Glass, Apples." According to Gaiman, "Books have genders," and each of Slabbert's choices for discussion prove his contention by breaking down issues surrounding gender, identity, and other thematic concerns relevant to our time.

In terms of postmodern narrative techniques, it could be said that every piece in this collection interprets a postmodern work that explores new methods of storytelling; however, there are four selections that stand out for their innovation in reading between the lines and uncovering metafictive qualities in contemporary fairy tales. Jeffrey K. Gibson's piece on Byatt's fairy stories introduces our discussion of postmodernism through his examination of Byatt's self-reflexive narrative style which mirrors the metafictional strategies she perfected in her prior historical fiction selections. Expanding on the techniques illustrated in Gibson's analysis, Marie C. Bouchet's essay on Robert Coover's *Briar Rose* focuses on "repetition with variation," binary rhythms, and alliteration in his ground-breaking work. Next, Maureen Torpey takes the fairy tale both backward and forward through time and space in her investigation of Jeanette Winterson's *The PowerBook*; she connects Winterson's works to Lewis Carroll's Alice books and our current age by identifying the limitless participatory facets of technology that affect methods of storytelling. Finally, Amie A. Doughty explores a range of novels by Robin McKinley, who has demonstrated her own evolution in storytelling through metatext and intertext. The self-reflexive nature of her tales shows how form is ever-changing, even from one writer's text to her next.

Additionally, contemporary writers are embracing a range of possibilities regarding narratives of trauma and dystopia. Helen Pilinovsky's essay on Kate Bernheimer's first two novels, part of a roman-fleuve, connects both metatextual and intertextual dialogue to a dystopian world view through the accounts of her two protagonists Ketzia and Merry Gold; Pilinovksy's lucid analysis unites Bernheimer's classic influences with her haunting contemporary narrative, one which will certainly gain even more depth as other introspective voices are added to Bernheimer's *Complete Tales*. Interlocking both dystopia and trauma, Margarete J. Landwehr's piece on Yolen's *Briar Rose* and Murphy's *Hansel and Gretel* suggests that fairy tales can serve as allegories of the Holocaust because they so deftly "represent the unrepresentable." Her essay connects Freudian symbolism and metaphor to current research on trauma therapy. Lauren Choplin rounds out this grouping with a similar premise as she examines "displaced pain" in Gaétan Soucy's tragic tale *The Little Girl Who Was Too Fond of Matches*, a novel whose protagonist experiences diverse forms of "ontological confinement" in which both fairy tale tropes and linguistic patterning serve to limit the heroine's narrative possibilities.

In our final section on cultural and political allegory, Mark C. Hill articulates the limitations for heroes in Bill Willingham's *Fables* series, which reflects an American mythology of hyper-masculine behavior and conservative ideology prevalent during global hostilities. Hill observes, "If *Fables* is a magic mirror held to American society, then it displays a country that glorifies war and the soldiers who fight them." Vanessa Joosen adds to the debate on social and political reflection with her compelling argument that in Philip Pullman's fairy tale *I Was a Rat!* lies a clever re-telling of the abduction and murder of James Bulger in Britain in the 1990's, shedding light on the ongoing discourse of childhood violence and exploitation in both academe and the media. Afterwards, Christopher Roman examines wartime rhetoric in his essay on Gregory Maguire's *Wicked*, a text which calls into question the very nature of the word terrorism and asks where the line should be drawn between a radical and a freedom fighter. Finally, my essay on Shannon Hale's *The Goose Girl* and *Princess Academy* argues that Hale's focus on class inequities suggests how role reversals can create empathy between members of different socioeconomic groups, leading to a pseudo–Marxist utopian vision in which relations are revolutionized and communities move towards social harmony. As one of Hale's characters admits, "It seems like the world has changed and we shouldn't still be talking about things like marrying a prince" (286).

Considering the many ways our contemporary world has expanded far beyond the quest to marry the prince paramount in classic fairy tales, we should not be satisfied that we have exhausted the potential of contemporary fairy tale analysis in this collection, although the essays contained herein span a wide range of writers and tales. In fact, one could say that we have only just opened the door to innumerable possibilities for further research. Every time we come across one new teller of tales, we inevitably find another. This is the beauty of fairy tales. They never cease being told, and the ways in which writers express their ideas seem boundless. Readers should view this collection as a point on a continuum: the contemporary fairy tale began with the revolutionary work of writers like Anne Sexton, Angela Carter, Margaret Atwood, and others, but it continues to grow with the writers of this grouping who are delving into new territories and who deserve critical examinations.

In his essay "Yours, Mine, or Ours? Perrault, the Brothers Grimm, and the Ownership of Fairy Tales," Donald Haase writes that the way to keep fairy tales alive is to take ownership over them. He notes that "teachers, librarians, parents, and powers in the culture industry" hold the ultimate power over the dissemination of tales to children (362). He also asserts that those same entities can encourage revision of existing forms, to make the power of the fairy tale implicit in all of our lives. He notes that this is a dual-sided process, for it isn't just the storytellers and professional writers who recast the archetypal motifs, but the readers, both children and adults alike, who can "reread and reinterpret" the tales, thereby "assert[ing] their own proprietary rights to meaning" (363). In an age becoming increasingly dominated by technology, with fairy tales tending to be relegated to the visual arts through animated films or products aimed at children, we must bring to the surface those cutting edge literary works that emphasize the mutability of the fairy tale as an art form. These works aren't only the "magic mirror of the imagination," as Stephen Swann Jones suggested, for in some cases, mirrors can reveal distortions of truth. Rather, these contemporary writers have given us an accurate view of ourselves; the contemporary fairy tale of the late 20th–early 21st centuries *is* the authentic voice of the people — it is a voice, like Gretel's, that simply *must* be heard.

Works Cited

Bernheimer, Kate, ed. "Editor's Note." *Fairy Tale Review.* The Blue Issue. 2005: 103–05.
Donoghue, Emma. "The Tale of the Cottage." *Kissing the Witch: Old Tales in New Skins.* New York: Harper, 1997. 133–41.

Haase, Donald. "Yours, Mine, or Ours? Perrault, the Brothers Grimm, and the Owner-ship of Fairy Tales." Rpt. in *The Classic Fairy Tales: Texts, Criticism*. Ed. Maria Tatar. New York: Norton, 1999. 353–64.

Hale, Shannon. *Princess Academy*. New York: Bloomsbury, 2005.

Oates, Joyce Carol. "In Olden Times, When Wishing Was Having: Classic and Contem-porary Fairy Tales." *Mirror, Mirror on the Wall: Women Writers Explore Their Favorite Fairy Tales*. Ed. Kate Bernheimer. New York: Anchor, 1998. 247–72.

Tatar, Maria, ed. *The Classic Fairy Tales: Texts, Criticism*. New York: Norton, 1999.

Zipes, Jack. Preface to the 2002 Edition. *Breaking the Magic Spell: Radical Theories of Folk and Fairy Tales*. 1979. Lexington: University Press of Kentucky, 2002, ix–x.

Queering the
Fairy Tale Canon
Emma Donoghue's *Kissing the Witch*

MARTINE HENNARD DUTHEIL
DE LA ROCHÈRE*

> I have come to intuit an originary queerness within which the heterosexual bond is loosely contained.
> —Gayatri Chakravorty Spivak, *Death of a Discipline*

A striking phenomenon of contemporary Anglophone fiction is the renewed interest in fairy tales which are appropriated and subverted through rewriting, parody, and other intertextual modes. The modern authors tap the extraordinary wealth of narrative forms, plots, motifs, and images of the fairy tale tradition as they reinvent its familiar stories after their own fashion since, as Angela Carter well knew, fairy tales "can be remade again and again by every person who tells them" (Introduction xi). Every retelling testifies to the endurance of such stories, but it often also expresses the need to transform these influential cultural scripts in order to voice new possibilities of being and living in the world.

Emma Donoghue, one of the talented writers to have refashioned some of the most popular tales in recent years, creates a rich and complex dialogue with Charles Perrault, the Brothers Grimm and Hans Christian Andersen in *Kissing the Witch: Old Tales in New Skins* (1997). Donoghue's retellings of Cinderella, Snow White, Rapunzel and Thumbelina, to name but a few, exemplify Adrienne Rich's definition of revisionary writing as an "act of looking back, of

*This is dedicated to Chantal and Karine, whose courageous life choices have inspired the piece. I wish to thank both Ute Heidmann and Jack Zipes for their precious expertise, generous feedback and useful advice.

13

seeing with fresh eyes, of entering an old text from a new critical direction" ("When We Dead" 90). Rich adds that far from being trivial, revision is "an act of survival," because "[u]ntil we can understand the assumptions in which we are drenched we cannot know ourselves" (90). In the same spirit, Donoghue — a self-proclaimed lesbian writer and scholar — uncovers the underlying assumptions of the classical versions as she explores "deviant" or "perverse" alternatives which challenge stereotypical representations of gender roles and sexual desire and derail the straight path of female destiny encoded in the tales. Donoghue's bold departures from the accepted plots question the authority of the "master" texts and the cultural norms that inform them from a minority position, but they also reveal the great diversity and hidden critical edge of the classic versions by exploiting their emancipatory potential. My reading of Donoghue's collection therefore seeks to initiate a set of complications that question not only the norms of heterosexuality that her revisited tales mock, but also critical commonplaces about the alleged conservatism of their sources.

As she appropriates the canonical stories from a lesbian feminist perspective, Donoghue interrogates the role played by fairy tales on the reader's sense of self, expectations and aspirations. Her literary practice derives much of its creative and playfully subversive energy through a self-conscious reclamation of some of the meanings of "queer" which, beside its current use as a synonym for homosexual or lesbian, includes "of obscure origin, the state of feeling ill or bad, not straight, obscure, perverse, eccentric." As a verb-form, "to queer" also has a history: "to quiz or ridicule, to puzzle, but also to swindle or to cheat" (Butler 176). This essay analyzes some of the forms that the queering of familiar stories takes in Donoghue's collection, and it discusses the implications of her rewriting strategies. While undoubtedly questioning the cultural impact of the fairy tale as a popular and commercially successful genre, Donoghue challenges the reader's assumptions about what fairy tales are and mean by emphasizing the uniqueness of each retelling and uncovering their equally underestimated or forgotten social critique. To demonstrate how Donoghue activates the subversive potential of her sources, I will focus on the first story in the volume, entitled "The Tale of the Shoe," which I interpret as a retelling of Cinderella that doesn't speak its (and her) name. I will relate Donoghue's tale to its main intertexts as I show how the author also aligns herself with a literary tradition which subverts the dominant myth of sexuality, love and happiness that the Cinderella story (as a cultural stereotype) supposedly perpetuates. While "The Tale of the Shoe" has been shown to illustrate the development of "lesbian genre fiction" (Palmer 139), I prefer to read it as an intervention in fairy tale discourse which celebrates the mutability of the genre and self-consciously situates itself in a long and diverse tradition which has provided the stuff from which new stories and new selves are made and remade.[1]

Alan Sinfield points out that queer reading is inseparable from an inquiry into textual and sexual politics insofar as all literary works "address contested aspects of our ideological formation" (3). But so-called minority writings, he argues, do so in a particularly urgent and compelling way because "when a part of our worldview threatens disruption by manifestly failing to cohere with the rest, then we reorganize and retell its story, trying to get it into ... a new shape if we are ... adventurous" (3–4).[2] In keeping with Sinfield's injunction, we shall see how Donoghue focuses on problematic moments in her sources to activate new possibilities for representation. To play on the image Donoghue herself uses to describe her collection, the story of Cinderella is put into a new "skin," i.e. a new form or shape which embodies the matter of the tale (and the heroine whose fate lies at its heart) in a more subjective mode and sensual style; but it also puts it into a new "skein" (if I may indulge in a not wholly gratuitous pun), as the familiar yarn is given an unexpected twist and spun anew. As a result, the story as we know it is transformed to explore original and adventurous narrative possibilities. In particular, by weaving older versions (or threads) of the tale together, Donoghue changes the cut and the very fabric of the story to make it fit as yet untold desires, decisions and denouements. As such, "The Tale of the Shoe" links the art of spinning tales to cloth-making as a metaphor for the creation of more positive identities and new types of relationships.

Unravelling Intertextual Networks
in "The Tale of the Shoe"

Kissing the Witch is composed of thirteen interlocking tales which read against the grain (and between the lines) of the fairy tale canon. The collection is structured as a series of first-person narratives shared and passed on from one anonymous female narrator to another, so that the helper, or antagonist, or minor figure of the first tale is prompted to tell her own story in the next tale. Much emphasis is put on the idea of the voice as embodied language invested with the power to create strong bonds between women as the narrators in turn speak and are listened to, confiding in their addressee while responding to the life-story of their predecessor. By linking each tale to the one which follows it in a narrative chain, the volume not only reflects the polyphonic variety of female voices, conditions, experiences and choices, but also simultaneously "creat[es] a single story and a single female genealogy" (Coppola 135). This multiple yet connected body of narratives challenges the pre-established patterns of action of its most well-known literary predecessors by exploring alternative possibilities and denouements. While the volume as a whole writes back to the predominantly male fairy tale canon, it also reclaims an alternative female tradition of women writers through intertextual references and allusions to Jane Austen, Christina Rossetti, Virginia Woolf, Anne Sexton, Angela Carter, Olga Broumas, and Adrienne Rich. In this sense, Donoghue's revisionist literary practice involves actively seeking female and feminist predecessors whose work was inspired (closely or loosely) by fairy tales.

Told by one nameless fairy tale character to another, the tales dramatize the passing of intimate experience, painful secrets and unofficial knowledge between women. As they experiment with plot structures, motifs and functions, the tellers deconstruct fairy tale stereotypes and conventions from within and expose the patriarchal, heterosexual ideology implicit in some of the most popular versions, first and foremost Disney's conservative fairy tale films. To question the still dominant representations of social relations and sexual roles, *Kissing the Witch* conflates the fairy godmother with the prince charming, fairy tale heroines fall in love with their stepmother, witches are rehabilitated, and Beauty becomes confused with the Beast. In this way, class and age divisions, fixed gender identifications and single sexual preferences are undermined, so that Donoghue's volume becomes an illustration of Eve Kosofsky Sedgwick's definition of queer reading as stressing "the open mesh of possibilities, gaps, overlaps, dissonances and resonances, lapses and excesses of meaning when the constituent elements of anyone's gender, of anyone's sexuality aren't made (or can't be) made to signify monolithically" (8).

Opening the collection, "The Tale of the Shoe" is based on Cinderella, "one of the best-known stories in the Western world" (Dundes vii). Dundes ascribes its ongoing popularity and "special appeal to women" to the centrality of "the relationships between a girl and her sisters or stepsisters, as well as a girl and her mother or stepmother" (xiii). Donoghue's placement of this tale in an inaugural position immediately announces her interest in women's relationships as they are represented in various retellings, although her aim is to recast them in a more positive light and explore new possibilities. Her retelling functions like a riddle (or a quiz, to play with one of the meanings of "queer"), so that the reader is made to identify it as a retelling of Cinderella through indirect (if tell-tale) clues. These include the story-line, significant motifs (such as the shoe) as well as verbal echoes, which heighten our enjoyment of the unusual combinations, daring innovations, and the surprising final twist introduced in the story. The tale also exemplifies the poetics and politics of Donoghue's collection by presenting itself as a dramatization of the literary project underlined in the subtitle of the volume. "The Tale of the Shoe" thus thematizes and enacts the creative process as the re-making of stories from old material, implying that all writing is rewriting. The dialogic principle which shapes the collection, whereby female speakers of different age, condition, and sexual orientation tell a story which generates the next one, extends to the intertextual dialogue established with various fairy tale authors in the individual tales.[3] Not only is Donoghue's anonymous narrator herself "an informed reader: she knows how 'Cinderella' or the fairy tale 'woman' should behave, and she tries to conform to this model" (Coppola 135), but she will learn to escape from this role with the help of her literary mothers.

Initially she is the unhappy victim of internalized voices which tell her how to behave and what to think, but with the help of a patient and loving helper figure (who looks like a witch but acts like a foster mother, a godmother, and finally a lover) who encourages her to make her own experiences and follow her desires, the girl finds the courage to change the course of her life — and of the story as we know it. This enables her to achieve a positive and distinct sense of identity and discover her own voice. Likewise, the piecing together of quotations, references and allusions to literary variations of the Cinderella story in her narrative provides her with a textual dress that will eventually "fit."

Donoghue reinterprets the story of Cinderella as a coming-of-age and a coming-out narrative which traces the emancipation of the central character from pre-written scripts, while playing with the idea of rewriting as dress-making. The girl's ability to free herself from the voices of convention is connected — if more ambivalently — to other voices that are never explicitly identified, but that the informed reader recognizes as belonging to individual versions of the tale.[4] Donoghue highlights the inherently transformative nature of the genre by situating herself in a genealogy of fairy tale writers, as she simultaneously pays homage to her literary predecessors and states her difference from them. She tropes (etym. turns, queers) the story of Cinderella into a pared-down (thread-bare?) and yet subtly lyrical narrative of emotional self-realization and erotic fulfilment: the story-line and motifs of the tale are used metaphorically to convey the subjective experience of a young woman who undergoes a process of transformation as she develops from a state of self-loathing to self-confidence. This enables her to reject the conventional marriage plot in favor of lesbian love. Although she identifies the agent of her transformation as an older, female, "stranger," the latter will point out in the next story entitled "The Tale of the Bird": "You think I have saved you, but the truth is that your need has conjured me here ... take your own life in your hands" (Donoghue 11).

In "The Tale of the Shoe," the anonymous speaker reflects her initial condition of loss and grief after her mother's death when she begins her narrative with an isolated line: "Till she came it was all cold" (Donoghue 1). An apt and concise summary of the tale, this observation documents the beneficial influence of the woman who has helped the narrator overcome her misery. Her arrival is seen in terms of warmth, suggesting both physical comfort and emotional well-being. The emphasis on subjectivity immediately connects Donoghue's tale with the Grimms' version, which emphasizes Ashputtle's emotional state. In contrast to Perrault's Cendrillon, who only cries because she is not allowed to go to the ball, Grimms' tale puts the focus on the girl's despondency after her mother's death: "Every day the girl went to the grave of her mother and wept.... She wept so hard that her tears fell to the ground and watered it" (Tatar 117–18). In Donoghue's story, the girl's despair is couched in images of social exclusion, material degradation and verbal abuse that symbolize her psychological condition; all her punishments are self-inflicted.[5] The cruel stepmother and sisters of the traditional tales are altogether absent from this version, or more exactly internalized by the narrator who hears "voices" in her head which hassle and insult her: "...nobody punished me but me. The shrill voices were all inside. Do this, do that, you lazy heap of dirt" (3). The loss of her mother has transformed the girl's perception of her surroundings and her body, so that the clothes she is wearing feel like "sackcloth chaf[ing] [her] skin" (1). The girl's "mal-être" is both psychological and physical, expressed through painful or unpleasant sensations.

Speech itself is experienced as something loathsome and repulsive: "Every word that came out of my mouth limped away like a toad" (1). This striking image is borrowed from Perrault's "Les fees" ("The Fairies," also known as "Toads and Diamonds"), where the spoiled elder sister of a victimized, Cinderella-like girl is condemned by a fairy in disguise to spit toads and serpents whenever she speaks as material evidence of her bad manners and selfishness. In "The Tale of the Shoe," the spell is used metaphorically to convey the girl's disgust with and rejection of language as something alien and abject. The implications of this intertextual reference are manifold: apart from drawing attention to the familiarity of the narrator-character with the fairy-tale tradition, it stresses her ability to transform the literal toad of Perrault's tale into a verbal one (a shift which is of course already made in the second moral attached to the tale).[6] The image of the toad-like words vomited by the girl also serves to emphasize the performative power of language that the heroine of Donoghue's tale will later learn to use in a more positive and constructive way, when she is reconciled with herself and discovers her real needs or wishes. It also signals her capacity to identify not merely with a positive fairy tale heroine, but with her negative double, and experience her terrible punishment and banishment from within. In this modern-day reinterpretation of the tale in psychological terms, the heroine is not punished for her bad character or manners, but under the only too real spell of depression. This insistence on the changeability of roles, situations and identifications ties in with the systematic challenge of binary oppositions (male and female, good and bad, beautiful and ugly, normal and deviant, etc.) in the volume as an enactment of "queerness" understood as the potential for metamorphosis and self-transformation. Before the arrival of the "stranger," then, the girl's self-imposed chores and trials not only reflect her deep sense of self-loathing but through the conflation of the heroine with negative female characters Donoghue also avoids reproducing the discourse of envy, jealousy, and rivalry between women that we find in many fairy tales (from Perrault to Disney), while eschewing their moralizing aspect. In the new story the condition of abjection of the Cinderella figure is internalized to express her feelings of rejection, alienation and loneliness, and another fairy tale character is going to help the heroine emancipate herself from the socially accepted roles and behaviors that make her miserable.

By breaking into the inner world of the miserable girl and interrupting the endlessly repeated gestures and rituals of mourning at last, the older woman initiates the narrative process.[7] The reader immediately associates this "stranger" with the "witch" in the title of volume. She is described as another, older, Cinderella figure who, the narrator speculates, "Must have come out of the fire. Her eyes had flames in their centers, and her eyebrows were silvered with ash" (Donoghue 3). While such qualities account for the spark in her eye and her warmth (hence her ability to rekindle the wish to live in the girl), the fact that her features are associated with ash suggests that on another level, she is also a literary creature born out of the Grimms' tale itself—"Aschenputtel" (in *Kinder-und Hausmärchen*).

The sudden apparition of the stranger in Donoghue's story is reminiscent of Grimms' version, but it also evokes the fairy godmother in Perrault's "Cendrillon" insofar as the woman is a fully embodied character, unlike the white dove of Grimms' tale. The female helper, in this case, combines elements from the classic versions as she introduces characteristic motifs of the German text into the story. The woman indeed brings the girl "into the garden and show[s] [her] a hazel tree [she] had never seen before" (Donoghue 3) on which a "dove" softly whispers.[8] In contrast to the Grimms' tale, however, she helps the grieving girl by telling her not to be "good and pious," as in Grimm, but by encouraging her to be kinder to herself.[9] The possibility arises that this mysterious woman is even akin to Anne Sexton's self-representation as a "middle-aged witch" in the opening lines of "The Gold Key," the poem which introduces her famous collection of revisited Grimms' tales, *Transformations*. Sexton's collection uses some of the traditional stories to explore intimate personal dramas; further, the girl's use of the word "transformations" in the passage that accounts for the positive influence of the stranger on her state of mind could be seen as textual evidence of Donoghue's homage to her predecessor. Although Sexton rewrites Cinderella as a grimly funny rags to riches story which makes bitter fun of the cheap dreams popularized by the media, she openly addresses female homosexuality in "Rapunzel," another poem from the same collection.[10] While Sexton's "Rapunzel" begins as a love poem addressed by "an old aunt" (35) to a young girl, and praises lesbian love as a way to stay young, the 'moral' that concludes Sexton's retelling of the Grimms' tale contradicts the prologue by commenting sarcastically on the union of the prince and the long-haired girl locked away in her tower (42). Donoghue thus responds to Sexton's poem by adopting the perspective of the younger woman, reversing the situation and dénouement of Sexton's "surprisingly delicate, even timid" (Harries 149) retelling of the traditional tale to explore the possibility of a stronger relationship between Rapunzel and the witch. Donoghue's heroine indeed meets the Prince thanks to the help of the older woman, and yet she freely chooses the latter, opting for lesbian love instead of the conventional heterosexual romance.

Thanks to the caring presence of this helper figure, a first transformation takes place in the girl. Struggling for words to describe the nature and effects of the profound inner change that she is undergoing, the girl resorts to the metaphor of spinning when she explains that her "old dusty self was spun new" (Donoghue 3). The importance of this moment is highlighted by the fact that it echoes the programmatic subtitle of the volume ("old tales in new skins"), initiating the process of recovery of the heroine as well as the renewal of the fairy tale tradition (by reactivating the old etymological connection between text and textile — self-fashioning — in relation to the female body). Like the wonderful metamorphoses effected by the fairy godmother in Perrault's tale and the magical gifts of the dove in Grimms', the older woman provides the girl with new, beautiful and comfortable clothes. The gifts seem to be of a different nature, however, even if they mark a first step towards the girl's achievement of a full and positive identity. The metaphor of the spun self is immediately followed by a reference to the narrator's new dress which materializes the process of spinning a new identity: "this woman sheathed my limbs in blue velvet" (3). The young woman's transformation is expressed in terms of a change of clothes fitting the body and made of sensual material which is set in strong contrast with the rough and shapeless 'sackcloth' referred to at the beginning. The emphasis placed on dress as something that symbolizes and even determines social identity is a central theme in Perrault's and Grimm's versions of the tale. In Perrault's "Cendrillon," for example, the stepsisters are obsessed with clothing: the eldest sister wears her "red velvet suit" (Lang 65) at the first ball organized by the Prince. Later on, they do not recognize the heroine at the ball, even though she gives them oranges and citrons and spends some time conversing with them, "amusing her sisters"— and of course herself at their expense (Lang 69); even the guards report that they have only seen "a young girl, very meanly dressed" (70) when she leaves the palace in a hurry after midnight, and the Prince himself is prepared to marry whoever can wear the glass shoe.[11] Reduced to a derisive nickname, Cinderella therefore entirely depends on items of clothing that determine or confirm her identity, as the full title of Perrault's tale makes clear ("Cendrillon, ou la petite pantoufle de verre"). In keeping with its psychologizing perspective, "The Tale of the Shoe" pushes this idea further to suggest that the most intimate sense of self is itself subject to transformation, just as the tales are. The well-known motif of the glass shoe is accordingly used metaphorically to suggest the girl's newly found happiness when she comments that, upon receiving the gift of the blue dress, "[she] was dancing on points of clear glass" (3).[12]

The helper then takes the girl to the ball. The self-conscious narrator addresses the reader, "Isn't that what girls are meant to ask for?" (Donoghue 3), drawing the reader's attention to the social conditioning of young women through cultural and literary discourse, including romantic stories and fairy tales.[13] At the ball, the girl is fully aware of the expectations concerning her behavior (84). She is familiar with the code of courtly etiquette and good manners, but more profoundly, she has learnt her prescribed role for those circumstances. Her remarks on how she is "meant" to behave even show her awareness of playing a part in a story she knows only too well. She smiles prettily, refuses to eat and keeps her "belly pulled in" (4), dancing with "elderly gentlemen who had nothing to say but did not let that stop them" (4). The humoristic rendering of the ball and her affirmative replies to her dancing partners draw attention to the sexist conventions underpinning the code of "etiquette" (a woman is expected to smile, be slim-waisted, and patiently humor chatty and boring old men). The social comedy and theatrical performance of gender roles and relations in Donoghue's tale in fact reworks elements already found in Perrault's "Cendrillon," which used the fairy tale genre to make fun of high society and ridicule the pride and vanity of the guests invited to the extravagantly lavish parties organized by Louis XIV. Perrault's stepsisters fast for "almost two days" and "br[eak] above a dozen of laces" in their quest for "a fine slender shape" as they preen before their mirror (Lang 66). But if Donoghue draws on Perrault's disguised satire of the world of the Court, she shifts its perspective to poke fun at the men. Her jibe against the one-sided and vacuous conversation of the gentlemen replaces Perrault's comic rendering of the stepsisters' coquetry as well as the heroine's susceptibility to flattery. Cendrillon is indeed so enraptured by the Prince's lavished compliments that she ignores the passage of time and the midnight hour (69). At first sight, Donoghue seems to have simply effected a feminist reversal of the situation found in her source. And yet, the possibility arises that Perrault's Cendrillon only feigns to be interested, and we cannot fail to notice that the Prince himself is a rather dull and passive figure, especially in contrast to the active, resourceful and cunning heroine.

As in Grimms' tale (unlike Perrault's), Donoghue's narrator attends the ball three times: the first time she is dressed in blue velvet — the second time in "green satin" (5), when she dances with the prince. But when he asks her what her favorite color and name are, she is unsurprisingly at a loss for words; another possibility is that she has forgotten what she likes and even who she is, fated as she thinks she is to be (or rather behave like) a fairy tale princess. Like her predecessors, Donoghue's heroine is thrilled by the experience of going to the ball and being courted by the prince, even though she chafes against the social pressure of conforming to the accepted plot. The jabbering voices are now barking in her head to remind her of her impending future (5). Nervously preparing for the last ball, the helper eases her tension by claiming to be a fairy who can use "her little finger" like "a magic wand" to "do spectacular things" (6). The (sexual) joke, which plays with the idea of the body as capable of wielding a very special kind of magic, is more than a queer (that is to say both funny and irreverent) reinterpretation of the traditional motif of the wand, since it celebrates lesbian love as the site of magic in the otherwise simple, ordinary and homely world of Donoghue's tale.

On the third night, the girl finds the courage to reject social and literary

conventions altogether. Her radical departure from traditional fairy tale structures is put under the aegis of Angela Carter, whose self-styled "stories about
fairy stories" have made her (after Anne Sexton) into a "modern classic" author
for a younger generation of fairy tale writers.[14] Carter, heralded as "the fairy
godmother of magic realism" (Johnson 3), "high sorceress" and "benevolent
witch-queen" (Rushdie), becomes an inspiration for Donoghue's helper when
she dresses the girl for her last ball. The young girl's "new skin was red silk"
(Donoghue 6) refers to one of Carter's lesser-known rewritings of classic tales,
titled "Ashputtle or The Mother's Ghost," published posthumously in *American Ghosts and Old World Wonders* (1993). Composed of three variations on
Grimm's "Aschenputtel," it explores the darker side of mother-daughter relationships. The motif of the blood-red/bloody dress is taken from "The Burned
Child," in the second section of the piece: "When the bird had no more blood,
the burned child got a red silk dress" (118). However, Donoghue's description
of the dress as a "new skin" of "red silk" suggests that the dress is so close-fitting
that it almost becomes a second skin (realizing her book's subtitle). More dis-
quietingly, the girl seems to be wearing her skin inside out, as if she had been
"skinned"—to explore yet another resonance of the subtitle. Unlike Carter's
harsh version of the Cinderella story, which explores the idea of the tyranny of
mothers who manipulate and dictate the destinies of their daughters, Donoghue's revision seems to represent mother-daughter relationships in a more
favorable light, although the possibility arises that the mother is not actually
dead (as in Grimms' tale) or simply replaced by another woman (as in Perrault's), but possibly estranged from her daughter, especially if we read the
story in the light of its intertextual reference to Perrault's "The Fairies." In the
absence of the mother, the only sources of comfort and consolation are provided by the girl herself, as she "told [her]self stories" and "stroked [her] own
hair" (Donoghue 2). Here again, the narrator-protagonist combines various
roles: mother and daughter, listener and storyteller, lover and beloved.

The episode of the ball is characterized by repetition and treated with
mocking irony by the narrator: the musicians play "the same tune over and
over" (Donoghue 6), and the girl herself dances "like a clockwork ballerina,"
smiling "till [her] face twisted" (6).[15] The strain of the forced smile manifest in
the twisted face announces another, even more spectacular, deviation from
social and generic conventions, in the form of a brutal physical reaction of discomfort, nervous tension and exasperation. Having dutifully "swallowed a little of everything [she] was offered" (6), the girl "thr[ows] it all up again" over
the balcony (6). In more than one sense, she is fed-up and her vomiting is
symptomatic of a more general rejection of what the ball represents. This unexpected (and most un-fairy-tale-like) visceral reaction interrupts the scene and
breaks the spell of romance, as it brings to a crisis the girl's disgust with words
expressed at the tale's beginning. With all the delicacies she has consumed out
of duty, she purges the rigid codes of good behavior and polite manners, as well

as the stifling conventions and clichés of courtship. Significantly, her body refuses to comply with the rules and constraints of heterosexual romance celebrated in fairy tales. One of the meanings of "queer," we recall, refers to the physical sensation of queasiness and sickness, and Butler's understanding of queer writing notoriously reinscribes the body as a site of resistance and contestation.

Immediately after this incident, the prince comes to propose, but the girl wryly remarks that the steps and the moon were "all very fairy-tale" (Donoghue 6), thereby showing her newly acquired ability to distance herself from the situation as she comments on the artificial décor of heterosexual romance. She describes the prince's "long moustaches" (6) — a typically masculine, if somewhat outdated and out-of-place, appendage.[16] The scene becomes even funnier when we spot the intertextual reference to Perrault's tale, in which the rat caught by Cendrillon is chosen on the grounds of its bushy whiskers, and transformed by the godmother into "a fat, jolly coachman, who had the smartest whiskers eyes ever beheld" (Lang 67). While in the classic French tale and in Disney's film adaptation the rat is caught by Cendrillon/Cinderella, in "The Tale of the Shoe" it is the other way around for the girl is trapped by the Prince's marriage proposal.[17]

At this crucial moment, another, more radical, transformation takes place: "The voices were shrieking, Yes yes yes say yes before you lose your chance you bag of nothingness" (7). The "voices" of convention urge the girl to accept the Prince's marriage proposal, in keeping with heterosexual values and norms. The voices claim that she can only achieve a sense of self through marriage, or else remain a "bag of nothingness," i.e. a nobody represented as a shapeless and empty body, where skin is just rough cloth or unfeeling dead leather. The image, which carries the same self-deprecatory implications as the "sackcloth" and the "heap of dirt" used previously by the narrator to describe herself, suggests that becoming somebody paradoxically implies conforming to the pattern established by the Cinderella story. The girl nevertheless refuses to listen to the voices she has internalized, and will similarly retain, and reclaim, her anonymity.

When she tries to speak but fails (Donoghue 7), her body again refuses to comply, and the prince's proposal is met with silence. Insofar as the girl does not know whether she should follow the conventional plot or invent a new story for herself, she exemplifies Bonnie Zimmerman's notion of the "what-if" moment in "heterotexts," which the lesbian-feminist reader seizes to rewrite the story from her own perspective, "perverting" and appropriating it as a lesbian text: "There is a certain point in a plot or character development — the 'what if' moment — when the lesbian reader refuses to assent anymore to the heterosexual imperative; a point in the narrative labyrinth where she simply cuts a hole and follows her own path" (139).

When the midnight bell begins to toll, the young woman runs away, but this time not because she is afraid of being disenchanted and losing her beautiful garments, but because she wants to get away from the Prince and all he represents. Her choice to go back to the older woman who helped her regain a sense of self-esteem redistributes the roles by bringing together the heroine and the helper figure to invent a lesbian romance which indeed "cuts a hole" in the fabric of the tale. In other words, the Prince Charming is conflated with the witch-fairy, godmother-mother substitute, so that the magic of the tale now lies with the lesbian relationship. The heroine's transgressive desire for the female "stranger" thus enables her to radically depart from the traditional plot and explore an alternative to the pre-written script while rebelling against the socially approved attitudes propounded by the dominant discourse.

The girl's beautiful dress is torn to rags as she escapes from a role and a life she no longer wants for herself. A much more powerful spell than the magic trappings and paraphernalia of the fairy-tale heroine is indeed broken here, namely the constraining discourses of social advancement and compulsory heterosexuality. When the Cinderella figure and the older woman are reunited, they remain speechless, if only because they need to invent the language that will tell the story of their love, for which there is no pre-existing narrative. In this way, Donoghue teases out the "faultline" stories circulating in the fairy tale tradition by probing what Sinfield calls "the silences of the text [which] manifest moments at which its ideological project is under special strain" (38).

When she notices that the older woman is beautiful and finally acknowledges her desire for her, the girl realizes that she "had got the story all wrong" (Donoghue 8). The new story she was looking for was in fact present all along in the old ones, which only needed to be reshaped from a different perspective. Dumbfounded, she notes that she "must have dropped all [her] words in the bushes" (8). This time, however, words give way to touch, "I reached out" (8), and the language of the body (already celebrated by Broumas) marks the realization of the lesbian romance plot as one of the forms taken by the literary project encapsulated in the subtitle: the (old) tales literally give way to (new) skin.

At last, the two women have a brief verbal exchange when the helper asks the girl three questions concerning the shoe, the prince, and herself. The girl explains that she got rid of the shoe because "it was digging into [her] heel" (Donoghue 8). The uncomfortably tight shoe (like the "sackcloth" referred to above), needs to be replaced by something that fits the girl's body, just as the tale needs to be reshaped to embody her new identity. The reference to the painful heel obviously evokes the mutilated feet of Aschenputtel's stepsisters (once again conflating the "good" and "bad" women of the tale as a way of deliberately displacing attention from moral judgement to individual choice).[18] The girl flings the shoe into the bushes, like the useless words in the previous paragraph — a symbolic gesture that marks her liberation from the narrow constraints of existing versions of the story. She answers the second question by speculating that the prince will "find someone to fit" (8), thereby using the shoe metaphorically to designate his future bride as both object and function. Finally, when the helper expresses concern about her age and worries about a possible confusion between the girl and the young woman's mother, the girl replies: "You're not my mother, I said. I'm old enough to know that" (8). This line in fact pays homage to the work of another literary mother while also reclaiming a lesbian literary tradition, since it is a quotation from Olga Broumas's "Rapunzel" in *Beginning with O*, a collection of erotic lyrics based on Greek myths and fairy tales.[19] Through this reference to Broumas's lesbian take on "Rapunzel," which itself explicitly acknowledges its debt to Sexton's bold treatment of the story in an epigraph, the girl disclaims any identification of her lover with her mother. Even though the woman was a friend of hers, and apparently belongs to the same generation, the girl suggests that their relationship has undergone yet another significant change, so that the helper is made to play several roles in the course of the story which recapitulate the functions of the magical helper in the classic versions: she is at first a mother substitute as in Grimm's tale, but has a human appearance like the godmother in Perrault's tale, and from their fusion and reinterpretation she becomes the lover herself.[20] Unlike the miserable Cinderella figure in Broumas's eponymous poem who has chosen to live among men, severed from her mother and sisters (57), regretting her ashes and her "sisters' hut" (58), Donoghue's heroine chooses to return to the helper's house and make it their own, shared, home.

Discarding the remaining shoe, the heroine encourages an open and happy homecoming. Instead of a triumphant departure for the prince's castle, the narrator offers alternative endings that are all placed on the same level, blurring agency and celebrating equality in love and language: "she took me home, or I took her home, or we were both somehow taken to the closest thing" (Donoghue 8). Thus Donoghue disrupts the normalizing patriarchal and heterosexual closure at the end of the tale. The twist in the plot exposes the status of the heterosexual norm as a socially sanctioned fantasy. Ideology is located in the very structure of literary texts and especially in the dénouement of classic tales, which often celebrate socially acceptable choices or sanction transgressive behaviors or attitudes.[21] Significantly, Donoghue's most radical queering of Cinderella (the girl as much as the tale), deliberately and self-consciously deviating from the "straight" plot, i.e. from the normative which of course includes the sexual norm, takes place at the end of the story. In this sense, the happy ending of "The Tale of the Shoe" echoes Jack Zipes's definition of the fairy tale as a form which nurtures the imagination in order to enable readers to find their true home: "This pursuit of home accounts for the utopian spirit of the tales, for the miraculous transformation does not only involve the transformation of the protagonist but also the realization of a more ideal setting in which the hero/heroine can fulfill his or her potential" ("Towards a Definition" xix).

Coda: From a Stone in the Shoe to a Story in Your Mouth

"The Tale of the Shoe" lends a new semantic content to the famous "shoe" of the traditional versions: it becomes a symbol of the literally and symbolically prescribed role that the young heroine is expected to play, and which she refuses at the end when she throws the emblematic shoe "into the brambles" (Donoghue 8), rejecting as she does so any identification with Cinderella, whether by name or by fate, to assume the decision that (paradoxically) brings the happy ending that is usually seen as one of the defining features of fairy tales. The success of the protagonist, however, leads neither to marriage nor to wealth, but simply to personal fulfilment and happiness.

This first story in Donoghue's collection thus dramatizes the difficult and often painful but also exhilarating and ultimately liberating process of "perverting" (another loaded meaning of "queer") traditional stories, codes, and conventions, so that the heroine of Donoghue's tale comes to embody the emancipation of the individual (female, lesbian, artist) from socially sanctioned roles in order to invent her own. Far from seeing "Cinderella" as a homogeneous, universal and timeless story, then, the anonymous story-teller emphasizes the diversity of its retellings and plays on their differences, and from the unexpected fusion, reinterpretation and reconfiguration of her numerous sources she simultaneously recapitulates the fairy tale tradition and creates something new and thought-provoking. Challenging the conservative aspects of her sources, Donoghue also brings out their emancipatory potential: thus, her reworking of the social comedy and patriarchal conventions of high society mocked by Perrault draws the reader's attention to the often neglected critical and subversive dimension of the classical versions.

Kissing the Witch adopts a choral structure, multiplying combinations, interactions and possibilities for identification. It gives voice to different characters, perspectives and preferences, so that the reader is interpellated by the very form of the collection, and explicitly at the end, encouraged to come up with her own story and participate in this ongoing chain of story-telling. In other words, the role of the active reader is stressed — a reader whose frame of references (socio-cultural systems, expectations, pre-conceptions and attitudes) has been revealed as socially (and discursively) constructed so that by developing a new awareness she can also develop a new creativity. Hence the importance of a subjective appropriation of the stories (which tend to posture as timeless and universal), as well as an interest in the performance of story-telling, where the interaction between storyteller and listener, or narrator and reader, contributes to produce new forms and meanings which replace conventional morality by pleas for independence, individual choices, and the respect of differences. Like other stories in the volume, "The Tale of the Shoe" uses the characteristic feature of fairy tales, namely magic and metamorphosis, as a means to question the belief in fixed social roles and stable identities, thereby challenging the binary oppositions of Western culture (male/female, hetero/ homo, natural/unnatural, and so on) in favor of what Rich has termed the lesbian continuum, i.e. a rich and diverse spectrum of love and bonding among women, which also includes female friendship, mother-daughter relationships, and women's social groups.[22]

As they narrate their own story, the various story-tellers of Donoghue's book centrally draw on the material (pun intended) of the classical tales but they also insist on the need to refashion it in order to represent painful intimate dilemmas, the courage it takes to make individual choices and the uniqueness of personal experiences. While referring to a common heritage, they all stress the creative potential of reading and reinterpretation from every point of view. Therefore, at the end of the volume, they in turn invite the reader to tell her own story, so that Donoghue's book not only centrally focuses "on the effect and power of literature on the reader, and on the reader's power on the literary text" (Coppola 129) but also enacts it in its very structure.

In the last story, "The Tale of the Kiss," the female narrator, who is also one of the witches referred to in the title of the volume, chooses to interrupt the story-telling instead of providing a neat conclusion, because "there are some tales not for the telling, whether because they are too long, too precious, too laughable, too painful, too easy to need telling or too hard to explain. After all ... my secrets are all I have to chew on in the night" (Donoghue 210–11). After drawing the reader's attention to the existence of untold tales, she ends on an invitation to the reader to add a story of her own making, in keeping with the traditional word of mouth transmission of fairy tales: "This is the story you asked for. I leave it in your own mouth" (211).

Notes

1. Palmer argues that Donoghue "subvert[s] both the ideology of heterosexual romance and the focus on female rivalry which the tale traditionally inscribes ... foreground[ing] instead the positive aspect of female relationships and explor[ing] the connections existing between mother-daughter relations and lesbian love" (146). While Palmer captures Donoghue's main intentions, I contend that a close analysis of the text and its intertexts reveals an ambiguous treatment of mother-daughter relations and a more complex and ambivalent engagement with the fairy tale tradition. See also Zipes *Why Fairy Tales Stick* (103) for an examination of Donoghue's tale alongside other recent rewritings of the story by Anglophone women writers.

2. Sinfield adds, "These I call 'faultline' stories. They address the awkward, unresolved issues; they require most assiduous and continuous reworking; they hinge upon a fundamental, unresolved ideological implication that finds its way ... into texts ... people write about faultlines ... to address aspects of their life they find hard to handle" (3–4).

3. Beside the analogies between text, cloth, skin and self Donoghue also plays with

the multifold meanings of (en) gendering, centering on the complex relationship between women of different generations as a metaphor for personal renewal and artistic regeneration. She reinterprets Cinderella as a coming to terms with the "death" of the mother which involves her daughter and a female helper who acts as a substitute mother and later the girl's lover. Donoghue places her tale explicitly under the aegis of women, marking a shift from Grimm to Perrault, and finally a daring combination of the two; the shift is paralleled on the textual level as the female narrator both learns from and emancipates herself from her literary predecessors.

4. There is no such thing as a "true," timeless and universal Cinderella story but rather an endless series of rewritings playing on repetition, transformation and innovation. See Jean-Michel Adam and Ute Heidmann "Réarranger des motifs, c'est changer le sens. Princesses et petits pois chez Andersen et Grimm." In A. Petitat, ed., *Contes: l'universel et le singulier* (Lausanne: Payot, 2002) 155–74.

5. The girl's grief and state of abjection echoes Bettelheim's interpretation of Ashputtle as a story about sibling rivalry; he also notes that ashes refer to bereavement and to the symbolic death of the mother when a female child reaches adolescence.

6. Angela Carter provides another moral: "Diamonds and pearls make powerful impressions; but kind words are more powerful still, and are infinitely more valuable" (*Sleeping Beauty and Other Favourite Fairy Tales*, 68).

7. She comes from behind; not from outside, but from within the kitchen, possibly from within the narrator-character's mind itself.

8. The hazel tree, her mother's grave, and the dove allude to the German version (see Tatar 118).

9. From Grimm's tale: "I shall look down on you from heaven and always be with you." If the stranger represents the heritage of the old tales, Donoghue seems to suggest that they exist in order to help us come to terms with pain and loss, perhaps marking Bettelheim's influence again.

10. Harries points out that Olga Broumas's sequence of fairy-tale poems in *Beginning with O* is "inspired in part by Sexton's *Transformations* [while it] also transforms them: her homage to Sexton begins earlier in the book in the poem 'Demeter,' an act of homage to all her literary 'foremothers'.... Like Sylvia Plath, Virginia Woolf, and Adrienne Rich [all evoked in Broumas's poem], Sexton has shown her a path to follow... Broumas does not frame her tales in any of the ways that Sexton does; she doesn't begin the sequence with a frame-tale or start each tale with an ironic contemporary prologue. But she consistently transposes the traditional images of the tales she chooses into a new and often unfamiliar key" (149).

11. Donoghue echoes both the "beautiful dresses" (Tatar 117) which Cinderella's stepsisters receive at the beginning of Grimm's tale, and the heroine's even more fabulous "dress of gold and silver" (119). Donoghue's use of velvet connects her heroine with one of the stepdaughters in Perrault's tale, a negative character, but this time, the magical helper is responsible for the identification.

12. This image also echoes Andersen's "Little Mermaid," suggesting the dance of the girl may in fact conceal suffering and self-mutilation in the frame of heterosexual love.

13. See Zipes *Fairy Tales and the Art of Subversion* for further discussion on how fairy tales have been used to enforce the "civilizing process" which seeks to socialize children by shaping their values, norms, expectations, and desires. According to Zipes, such traditional models of masculinity and femininity establish patterns of behavior that the socialized individual tends to assimilate, accept, and enact unquestioningly.

14. Donoghue answers Carter by exploring a possibility in which Carter apparently had no interest. As Patricia Duncker speculates, "She (Carter) could never imagine

Cinderella in bed with the Fairy Godmother" (qtd. in Simpson's Introduction to *The Bloody Chamber*, 2006, viii).

15. Possibly an allusion to Carter, to the heroine of "The Tiger's Bride," a rewriting of Beauty and the Beast in *The Bloody Chamber and Other Stories* (1979), in which Beauty sends a mechanical doll to her father and stays with the Beast before turning into an animal herself at the conclusion.

16. Her main target is presumably Disney's influential adaptation to the screen, *Cinderella* (1950). Donoghue borrows the moustaches which originally belonged to the coachman in Perrault and were later given to the Prince's superintendent in Disney's movie to the Prince himself while also poking fun at the conservative values, romantic ideals, sexist stereotypes and "infantilizing celebration of the cute" (*Oxford Companion, Wood* 133) that characterize the film.

17. Donoghue stresses the artificiality and theatricality of the climactic proposal scene by indicating that the not-so-charming prince's conventional speech sounds prepared and recited (6). This marks her distance from the action, but also reflects a typically lesbian way of seeing, according to Bonnie Zimmerman who cites Marylin Frye: "Reality is organized by men as a stage on which they are the principal actors and women the stagehands and backdrop. To maintain the fiction of this reality, no one must attend to any other movements but those of the main actors, men. Reality relies on not seeing the background, women. But lesbians construct an alternative reality by attending to, and focusing on, that background. In Frye's words, lesbians 'are in a position to see things that cannot be seen from within the system and their seeing is why they have to be excluded'" (137).

18. The emphasis on the shoe that hurts the foot harks back to Grimm's tale, but possibly echoes Sexton's emphasis on the cruelty of the double mutilation of the step-sisters in her sarcastic retelling of the story as an allegory of the condition of women under patriarchy in *Transformations*.

19. Donoghue's close familiarity with Broumas's work is evidenced in her book *Hood*, which opens with a quote from Broumas's revision of "Little Red Riding Hood" (*Beginning with O*, 68).

20. The possible confusion of the mother and the lover which is dispelled by the girl at the end may express an anxiety about theories of homosexuality that explain lesbianism as a form of fantasized return to the mother (as in H.D.'s "Letter to Freud"). This is suggested when Donoghue's Cinderella re-connects herself with her mother through the fairy godmother/dove figure, but she either rejects this identification at the end or shifts it onto the literary plane when she refers to the empowering heritage of literary mothers and lesbian role models.

21. See Blau du Plessis.

22. Significantly, Donoghue dedicates her book to her mother, Frances, and in the Acknowledgements she stresses the importance of a community of women who have contributed in different ways to the collection, by supporting, encouraging, inspiring, reading, responding, commenting, criticizing and listening to the author's readings. For Donoghue, art is made possible through various forms of female support and collaboration.

Works Cited

Blau du Plessis, Rachel. *Writing Beyond the Ending: Narrative Strategies of Twentieth Century Women Writers*. Bloomington: Indiana University Press, 1985.

Broumas, Olga. *Beginning with O.* New Haven: Yale University Press, 1977.

Butler, Judith. *Bodies that Matter: On the Discursive Limits of "Sex."* New York: Routledge, 1993.

Carter, Angela. "Ashputtle *or* The Mother's Ghost." *American Ghosts and Old World Wonders.* London: Vintage, 1993. 110–20.

_____. *The Bloody Chamber and Other Stories.* 1979. London: Penguin, 2006.

_____. Introduction. *Angela Carter's Book of Fairy Tales.* London: Virago, 2005. xi–xxiv.

_____, trans. *Sleeping Beauty and Other Favourite Fairy Tales.* Boston: Otter, 1991.

Coppola, Maria Mircea. "The Gender of Fairies: Emma Donoghue and Angela Carter as Fairy Tale Performers." *Textus* 24 (2001): 127–42.

Donoghue, Emma. *Kissing the Witch: Old Tales in New Skins.* New York: HarperCollins, 1997.

Dundes, Alan, ed. *Cinderella: A Folklore Casebook.* New York: Garland, 1982.

Harries, Elizabeth Wanning. *Twice Upon a Time: Women Writers and the History of the Fairy Tale.* Princeton, NJ: Princeton University Press, 2001.

Johnson, Daniel. "Books Barely Furnish a Room." *The Times* 16 Sept. 1992: 3.

Lang, Andrew, ed. "Cinderella; or, the Little Glass Slipper." 1889. *The Blue Fairy Book.* New York: Dover, 1965.

Palmer, Paulina. "Lesbian Transformations of Gothic and Fairy Tale." *Contemporary British Women Writers.* Ed. Emma Parker. Cambridge: D. S. Brewer, 2004. 139–53.

Rich, Adrienne. "Compulsory Heterosexuality and Lesbian Existence." *Signs* 5.4 (1980): 631–60.

_____. "When We Dead Awaken: Writing as Re-Vision." *Adrienne Rich's Poetry.* Ed. Barbara Charlesworth Gelpi and Albert Gelpi. New York: Norton, 1975. 90–98.

Rushdie, Salman. "Angela Carter, 1940–1992: A Very Good Wizard, a Very Dear Friend." *The New York Times* 8 Mar. 1992. 13 May 2008. <http://www.nytimes.com/books/98/12/27/specials/carter-rushdie.html>.

Sedgwick, Eve Kosofsky. *Tendencies.* Durham: Duke University Press, 1994.

Sexton, Anne. *Transformations.* 1971. Boston: Houghton Mifflin, 2001.

Sinfield, Alan. *Cultural Politics-Queer Reading.* Philadelphia: University of Pennsylvania Press, 1994.

Tatar, Maria, ed. "Brothers Grimm: Cinderella." Trans. Maria Tatar. *The Classic Fairy Tales.* New York: Norton, 1999. 117–22.

Zimmerman, Bonnie. "Perverse Readings." *Sexual Practice, Textual Theory: Lesbian Cultural Criticism.* Ed. Susan J. Wolfe and Julia Penelope. Cambridge, MA: Blackwell, 1993. 135–49.

Zipes, Jack. "Towards a Definition of the Literary Fairy Tale." *The Oxford Companion to Fairy Tales.* Oxford: Oxford University Press, 2000. xv–xxxii.

_____. *Why Fairy Tales Stick: The Evolution and Relevance of a Genre.* New York: Routledge, 2006.

Contemporary Women Poets and the Fairy Tale

CHRISTA MASTRANGELO JOYCE

From Perrault to the Grimms to Walt Disney, male authors of fairy tales created female characters who sleep through their lives: vain representations of real women who are cloistered and trapped, they are commonly flat, one-dimensional characters who come to life only through the actions of a male character. These tales end perfectly, each playing out the "happily ever after" stasis. Yet fairy tales actually have a history filled with women authors who created rich archetypal themes in their works. This history has drawn contemporary women poets, such as Anne Sexton, Sylvia Plath, Olga Broumas, Sara De Ford, and Sara Henderson Hay, to explore and recreate the fairy tales. These poets entered a literary genre long dominated by men and claimed it as their own, likely drawn to the tales based on an inescapable desire to explore the human characteristics inherent in them. However, they have also stretched the original boundaries of the tales, giving them a modern, feminist appearance by reversing or highlighting many of the perverse misogynistic views with which the source texts were imbued. Most importantly, they have reclaimed a literary history that once belonged to women authors whose contributions may have been overshadowed by predominantly male compilers and editors.

Though we often associate some of the first fairy tales with Perrault, women authors were responsible for very early fairy tales, accounting for nearly two-thirds of written selections historically composed in the 17th century. Elizabeth Wanning Harries explains much of this history in *Twice Upon a Time: Women Writers and the History of the Fairy Tale*:

> Marie Catherine le Jumel de Barneville, baronne d'Aulnoy, and Henriette-Julie de Castelnau, comtesse de Murat, were among the aristocratic women who began the vogue of writing fairy tales down in France at the end of the seventeenth century. In 1690 Marie-Catherine d'Aulnoy published a fairy tale, *L'ile de la felicite....* This tale ... is now considered to be the first literary fairy tale written in France [23–24].

Called conteuses, the women authors' tales differed in many ways from the better known fairy stories. For instance, the conteuses' fairy tales were never meant for children because they were based on French salon conversations, events told for and by adults. Also, the tales "tend to be long, complex, often full of digressive episodes and decorative detail" (Harries 32). The conteuses were daring in their use of narrative, too, often using self-referential techniques, in which they made "self-conscious commentaries on themselves and on the genre they [were] part of" (32).

Often the content of the conteuses' tales dealt with the struggles associated with transformations while also commenting about women's life and placement in 17th century society. Though the plots of the male authors' fairy tales were virtually the same as earlier versions written by women, the imagery and the content, particularly the endings, were altered by male authors to reflect a less socially discursive attitude.[1]

The 18th and 19th centuries put a further end to the stories written by the conteuses. According to Harries, "Stories suitable to be read in girls' schools or about girls were thought at the time to be particularly moral ... the fairy tale [became] a civilizing instrument, designed to produce women who conformed to a restrictive set of gender norms" (87). The fairy tales, even those by Perrault, were revised to reflect a more pious story to teach children, particularly young girls, morals. This trend became that much more obvious in the post–World War I era and the advent of Disney films.

The conteuses, though, beautifully depicted common human characteristics. Their tales reflected narcissism, jealousy, vanity, and oedipal relationships. They were about failures and family derision. Most of all, they illustrated transformations, and the often frightening, though natural, changes that occur through life. These themes and the conteuses' storytelling model have resurfaced through the works of the contemporary female poets.

Among contemporary authors there is a desire to expose patriarchal gender ideologies integral to male-authored fairy tales. Hilary Crew of Kean College comments on this, stating, "Criticism has focused on the passivity of young girls waiting to be rescued, the encoded binaries in a text that equate beauty with goodness ... and the closures which seal a girls' dependency on a prince." Women are represented as prizes if they are young or as fearful witches if they are old. They are pitted against each other, showing a vile interpretation of women's relationships as competitive in nature. In her article "In Olden Times, When Wishing Was Having," Joyce Carol Oates writes:

> Young, maturing girls like Snow White, Cinderella ... are the natural targets of the homicidal envy of older women; ubiquitous in the tales are "wicked stepmothers" who conspire to injure or kill their beautiful stepdaughters ... the lot of women in a patriarchal society which privileges them as valuable possessions (of men), or brands them as worthless and contemptible, made it inevitable that women should perceive other women as dangerous rivals [248–49].

Girls who came to womanhood understanding their role through the tales were bound to cut themselves off from other women in a struggle to find the prince who would save them.

Additionally, contemporary poets are revising the fairy tales to revive the stories' aesthetic edge. The conteuses often used dramatic narrative structure, frightening plot lines, and endings that were discursive or disheartening. False perfection or good cheer endings were not expected. In her essay "It Is You the Fable Is About," Rosellen Brown states, "Even among didactic tales, their true potency lies in their proximity to dream, and more particularly, to nightmare. Like deathbed conversions, last paragraph soul-saving does not convince" (56). If art is meant to imitate and heighten the experiences of life, then writers need not be consumed with "happily ever after" endings. These endings do not convince, and a storyteller's purpose should be to expose and illuminate, not to mask the truth with false expectations and twisted notions of reality.

In revising the fairy tales afresh, these poets are inspiring questions and astonishment by restoring the life blood to these stories. They are creating characters with depth, ones who embody both good and evil, as well as retelling the tales from more than one point of view and revealing the circumstances that may have influenced their characters. Sara Henderson Hay is one poet who has done this. Hay's poetry reveals the way in which forces work to bring about a character's situation. She imagines for her character a life beyond the original tales, showing what perhaps really drove this person to act. In the foreword to Hay's collection, Miller Williams writes of her work that "assuming there are two sides to all stories, [Hay] set about telling us those other sides, and in the telling made the stories marvelously ironic, even scarier than they were, sometimes surprisingly moving, and outrageously funny" (xi). She appropriates the sonnet, a form traditionally utilized by male poets, to craft her new vision for the fairy tale.[2]

Hay's sonnet "Sequel," based on *Beauty and the Beast*, begins where the original tale ends. Beast is no longer beastly; now a handsome prince, he and Beauty are destined, it seems, to live the good life. Beauty, however, is quickly deemed a token wife who performs activities that showcase Beast's accomplishments. To make matters worse, Beauty realizes this is no longer the man with whom she fell in love. Like the original tale written by Villeneuve of the loveless state that often results from marrying an image of perfection, Hay reestablishes this with the idea of change in marriage: the man who courted the woman is figuratively not the same man once the marriage vows have been uttered. Beast is handsome and well-loved now among the court; however, along with his less-than-princely exterior, the kindness and love that were his traits before seem to have disappeared. In Hay's thoughtful sequel, the Beast shines anew in the marriage state. The princess, however, wants her loving boyfriend back.

Hay reveals another character's future in her poem "The Sleeper" based on *Sleeping Beauty*. In this poem she ponders whether the "sleeping beauty," obviously a woman who had no choice in her awakening, wished her circumstances otherwise. The woken "beauty" isn't charmed by the new world into which she has awoken. She wishes for the tranquility that was hers before she arose to the chaos in the world that now surrounds her. Indeed, the woman is even angry that the prince did away with her symbol of safety and security, the brambles that surrounded her sleeping chambers. Again Hay gives voice to the aftermath. In the conclusion of this sonnet Sleeping Beauty is anything but a voiceless female who simply accepts her fate. She may have been awoken but that does not mean she has to like it or respond. Hay's princess refuses in the end to be truly awakened by this prince, knowing that kisses are cheap and can not buy her "dearest privacy" (10).

There are actually two ways to read this sonnet. In one respect, the woken princess may not be willing to fall instantly in love with this man just because he has performed an act that he perceived as saving her. However, there is also an undercurrent of rape in this poem. Hay's sleeper seems quite angry and trespassed against. Though this could be a matter of having her world invaded, it may also be a matter of having her person invaded. The woman was, it should be remembered, sleeping. She did not have a say in whether her body was touched or kissed. This theme recalls an original version of the *Sleeping Beauty* tale in Basile's *Pentamerone*, written in the 16th century. In his version, Sleeping Beauty awakes after 100 years of sleep to a prince who is already married, and she instantly gives birth to two children, Sun and Moon (Prose 293–94). In Basile's original, Sleeping Beauty was raped.

Another measure of reality comes in Hay's "Rapunzel." Hay sheds light on the motif of the tossing down of hair. This is a woman who deeply loved the man she thought would do anything for her. Yet she discovers his words are lies: though she's loosened her braided hair, it can not lift him to her any more than her complete devotion can. Rapunzel was not a woman whose hair a man could use to climb a tower, but a woman who had been wooed into believing the fantastic things her love could make a man do for her. Hay's tower is a figurative place from which the woman leans in hope of the fantastical love she has been promised. She trusts this man enough to throw over her personal treasure, her heart, and, in turn, she is used by him. Then, she is locked in the chamber of her own humility and sadness. The poem ends with Rapunzel lamenting the locked chamber in which she is trapped, knowing that she "twisted [ed] her heartstrings to a rope" (13) and that, instead of climbing up to be with her only, she was just another climb for the prince.

Many of the same themes Hay explores are revealed in Anne Sexton's book of modern poetic fairy tale renderings, *Transformations*. Sexton knew there was much under the surface themes of the tales. In her study of the stories she found thematic parallels to her own life, as well as powerful archetypal figures. In Sexton's fairy tale poems she is the primary storyteller, a modern day conteuse, driven to recreate the archetypes and to retell these fairy tales using her personal struggle with acts of violation, such as incest, alcoholism, the association of dual personalities, and a split from the human spirit.

Sexton uses the same framework as the conteuses and the same skeleton story as the Grimm's; however, she deepens the experience of the tales through highly graphic and modern images. Truly, her art is a transformation away from the stripped down tales by the Grimms and Disney, as well as a transformation into revelation by the speaker and/or characters. Using a frame based on personal experience and a modern vernacular, Sexton transforms the tales into emotionally-charged events. Harries states, "Sexton transforms the Grimms' dispassionate, nearly invisible third-person narrator into a speaker whose angry and sardonic perspective on her midcentury American world determines the shape of the whole collection" (123). "Dame Sexton," as she has prodigiously named the speaker of the poems, is a woman living the modern equivalent of the themes within the fairy tales. This is the same frame technique that the French story-telling women used in the 17th century. However, rather than a sibyl or a goddess who tells the tales, Sexton declares herself a witch, a madwoman, crazed by her ability to see into these stories, capable of vexing her audience with her visions and reminding them of the truth.

Like the conteuses, Sexton creates adult versions of the tales. Her poems reveal life as tedious and hurtful when one is trapped within the confines of any loveless state. Though many of her poems end with marriage, this does not guarantee happiness. Rather, it often signifies a mundane and cloistered life for both genders. Too, Sexton's poems are not based on a black and white version of woman or man. She creates realistic characters with a blend of goodness and evil, as well as a mix of masculine and feminine traits.

Sexton creates a prologue to frame each poem that is sardonic, witty, and often chilling. She draws on her own experience of the world while using the transformative power of literature to reveal that experience to readers. In "Briar Rose (Sleeping Beauty)" Sexton opens with a plea, asking readers to journey with her into the world of a girl who can not stay awake, stuck in a place between waking and dreaming, with memories that imply an incestuous relationship with her father, the king. This journey on which Sexton is about to lead her readers will be sickening, she reveals, one that will be "rank as honeysuckle" (24). This sleeping beauty, hypnotized, has no control over the journey she keeps making into her subconscious. Right away, Sexton has placed her readers in the poem and makes them complicit in the voyage on which they are about to embark. With her classic irony and twisted sense of word play, Sexton ends the prologue with the warning to her readers that this is going to be a twisted ride; rank, strangling sweetness will prevail.

In this poem, as in many, Sexton also uses the "once upon a time" frame in a way that highlights her intended irony. She begins the poem's twenty-fifth line, the first line after the prologue, with her "Once" set up, immediately placing her reader into the original tale. Yet from here nothing is as one would expect. She embellishes with her sarcastic commentary throughout using slang and pop culture references. For example, she describes the thirteenth, evil fairy with "eyes burnt by cigarettes, / her uterus an empty teacup" (33–34), and when the prophecy of the princess's spinning wheel death is avowed, Sexton writes that the silenced court "looked like Munch's *Scream*" (42).

Sexton then uses repetition to highlight her opening idea. Of the protective king and his daughter, Sexton revisits the image of strangling sweetness throughout, reminding readers that the princess lives in the presence of her father's "rank as honeysuckle" kind of love. She leads the reader further into this "sickeningly" too-close relationship between father and daughter when, after the prescribed hundred years of sleep, Briar Rose wakes crying out for her "daddy," terrified of sleep. In Sexton's version, Briar Rose becomes an insomniac. Henceforth, only drugs can help her sleep. The princess's sleep comes, too, with a set of stipulations: she must not know that sleep is coming because she is so fearful of "that brutal place" (111) and she must not dream because when she does she sees herself replaced by an old "crone." Briar Rose is consumed by her subconscious, where her dreams reveal her fears. Her nightmares revolve around her having grown old and dying, a state that would be the ultimate "death" for a princess whose whole life has been based on being beautiful, doted upon, and encapsulated in a youthful state.

As with other poems in this collection, Sexton ends with a return to her prologue and to her own life. She harnesses the poem using a digression and adding a final side to the original frame. The epilogue ending the poem brings readers back to the theme of incest and abuse in Sexton's own life as she is the one who slips back and forth between worlds, trapped in a prison of memories and disillusionment that involve her father and her lost youth. Too, in Sexton's version, the princess and the narrator are afraid to sleep because slumber represents a violent and violated place; their tormented memories cause them to slip into and out of consciousness.

This theme of sexually-induced sleep or unconsciousness in life is seen in the work of many women poets, among them Sara de Ford. De Ford uses sex as the catalyst to induce sleep, or rather unconsciousness, in her poetic revision of *Sleeping Beauty*. Again the relationship with a male figure "pricks" her, leaving her dormant and powerless. De Ford's "Sleeping Beauty" is the youngest child, left only with a gift from the malignant witch after her older sisters have been granted goodness and bright wit: the gift is that "the spindle prick of sex" (13) will render her life to a death-like stupor. The beauty of this poem is again vexed by the "prick" that is sexual. Her fate is predicted; she will become old within her sleeping world, without anyone who can wake her "torpid consciousness" (21). The word torpid is quite interesting here, considering its multiple meanings. Meaning both to be deprived of motion or rendered benumbed, as well as to be dormant or hibernating, it describes a woman who has been spellbound by the wound of love, and yet whose consciousness is not dead but is latent. This sleeping beauty, too, is not a young princess but a person growing older. There is a much different association with a woman beyond naiveté who is sleeping bleakly through her life. De Ford imparts even more of a sense of hopelessness. Yet like Sexton and Hay, De Ford again allows for the sleepy trance to serve as protection from the evils of a sexual relationship. It is the feared or unwanted union in all three poems that leads the women to hide in unconsciousness.

Returning to Sexton's poetry, the theme of duplicity and dueling natures is one that is woven throughout *Transformations*. In the prologue to "Red Riding Hood" Sexton begins with a look at all those who live two-faced lives. "Many are the deceivers," she writes in her opening line, going on to list the various characters: the suburban mother who, proper in public, flies off to meet her lover; the respectable looking woman who swindles an old woman; the standup comic who kills himself; and even herself, living so professionally and publicly, all the while dying inside. She uses these deceivers as a catalyst to reveal the fairy tale deception of the wolf in grandma's clothes, who in the end, is suffocated by his one heavy burden of weight. This death is symbolic of the way that living dishonestly eventually kills a person, at least figuratively, weighing her down with the burden that becomes like lead.

Sexton highlights deception again in her "Rumpelstiltskin," in which the little man is not an outside force so much as he is symbolic of the dual nature, or split personality, within most every person. Sexton reveals that inside us all resides an evil, represented by the little old man, lurking. His chilling first words let the reader know that this little man will dig into a person's psyche. He is the force that makes a person blind to his or her own actions, even as he or she tries to deny its existence. He speaks of himself as "the enemy within" (14), "kindred [of] blackness and impulse" (19). He represents the wicked desires present in most everyone.

The woman in this poem uses the little man, her alter ego, greedily. She is hungry to obtain her deepest desires and will do anything to obtain them — even make deals with her own devil. The only way she can eventually beat this Doppelganger is to understand who he really is and to recognize that he is very much a part of her. When she discovers his real identity, "he tore himself in two ... laid his two sides down on the floor, / one part soft as a woman, / one part a barbed hook" (147–51). Sexton does not allow the woman or the reader to be removed from this little man, Rumpelstiltskin. He is all facets of the human, that which is good and that which is evil. He is also the masculine, aggressive side of the woman that she tries to deny. Oates comments on Sexton's "Rumpelstiltskin," stating that "Sexton's feminism is radical enough to expose and condemn the deadly 'femininity' of women who refuse to acknowledge their masculine, aggressive selves" (257). The princess's failure to protect her own life eventually consumes her when she must protect the life of her child.

Another aspect that Sexton illuminates is a woman's inability to acknowledge her feminine side, that side that profoundly connects her to other women. Sexton criticizes the disparaging relationship between women that is often portrayed in fairy tales by showing a lack of growth in her female characters that accompanies the denial of female connections. This comes through in three of her poems: "Snow White," "Rapunzel" and "Cinderella." In betraying their sisterhood, the characters of these poems essentially betray themselves.

Sexton's Snow White begins and ends with a virgin who is mostly mindless and dumb. Sexton describes her stepmother, a once beautiful woman who has been "eaten, of course, by age" (19). Sexton reflects disdain in the older woman's description. It is always the way with fairy tales that time devours a woman's beauty. She goes on to warn the vain with a play on the Grimms' tale, that, should one's vanity lead to the condemnation of other women, she will "dance the fire dance in iron shoes" (23). Throughout the poem, as with the fairy tale, Snow White is betrayed by her step-mother with poisoned items. When Snow White is finally saved, once and for all, the older woman, invited to Snow White's wedding, has red-hot iron shoes clamped upon her feet. In the end, the stepmother is watched as she dances, her body frying, becoming a "subterranean figure" (158). The older woman is punished for her vain acts of treachery against the younger version of herself. Yet Snow White does not learn to correct these mistakes; instead, she will only continue the vicious cycle: "Meanwhile Snow White held court, / rolling her china-blue doll eyes open and shut / and sometimes referring to her mirror / as women do" (161–64). Snow White ends the poem in much the same way that she began. Sexton shows that there has been no growth as a person or as a sexual being. Vain and dependent on her beauty, she condemns her kind to death. The cycle continues; the women who harm each other continue to harm themselves.

Sexton makes this idea even more explicit in "Rapunzel." She begins with "A woman / who loves a woman / is forever young" (1–3). She establishes the nourishing aspect of the "mentor" / "student" relationship between women, showing that women can indeed give each other strength. The older woman should be viewed as a mentor, not a witch who wishes to destroy her younger complement.

The reciprocal relationship between the two women in Sexton's "Rapunzel" infuses each with a sense of beauty and strength. They have no need for a male relationship; in fact, the presence of a man in this poem causes a split between the women. When it is just the two, however, their love forms an idyllic world in which both women are able to flourish. Together, they are strong, avoiding the "cesspool" that is symbolic of a life in which greed, vanity, and competition prevail. All of the images Sexton constructs of the two women convey a sense of innocence and beauty: they are glistening clouds, "birds washing," strong, nourished "green pond weeds" (49).

The union of the women closely represents the early relationship between a mother and a daughter. The younger woman is really a "copy" of the older. Additionally, the relationship is not sexual so much as it is nourishing, a healing tie. In fact, the opening line, "A woman / who loves a woman / is forever young," is oft repeated. In the end, Sexton alludes to the fact that Rapunzel leaves her idyllic world for a prince's love; however, Sexton's sarcasm shows her lack of conviction that Rapunzel's life is necessarily better than before. It's expected, Sexton writes, that Rapunzel and her prince will live happily ever after; she leaves the relationship between the man and woman flat, though, creating a dichotomy between the beautifully described world of the women and the new life for which Rapunzel trades the old.

Finally, in Sexton's "Cinderella" she delivers, without commentary, a sarcastic and ironic tale, with which she makes apparent her distaste for the "Cinderella story" that portrays the treacherous lengths some women are willing to go for love. She begins with fantastical stories of people who "strike it rich," stories in which, out of the blue, someone goes from rags to riches, and tells readers, mockingly, that we know the story, we hear about it all of the time. It's "that story" (5). She continues for three additional stanzas with stories based on people who fall into wildly good fortune, ending each with her sarcastic "that story." Clearly, Sexton is disillusioned by these tales.

Sexton proceeds to retell the original tale of Cinderella; however, she adds her own spin to the events. She describes Cinderella sleeping on the sooty hearth as looking like Al Jolson. The infamous ball is described as a marriage market, and when Cinderella's stepmother refuses to let her attend, Sexton comments, "That's the way with stepmothers" (55). It is obvious that she means to berate the role typically given to stepmothers in the Grimms' tales. She uses many more declarative statements to show her sarcastic rendering of the plot.

The most telling part of the poem occurs when the stepsisters attempt to win the prince. Each sister in turn tries on the slipper, just as they do in the Grimms' tale; just like the sisters in the Grimms' tale, Sexton's characters do not quit when the shoe does not fit. The older sister cuts off her big toe, while the younger slices away her heel. Though each tries to hide their wounds and ride off with the prince, "amputations," Sexton tells us, "don't just heal up like a wish" (88). For these sisters, "the blood told as blood will" (90). Both women were initially willing to betray Cinderella, leaving her to remain loveless and alone at home. Now, they are willing to betray themselves. Each woman's mutilation of her body is not only gory; it represents the lengths that some women are willing to go to find "love." Again, Sexton does much with one line: "The blood told as blood will." It is impossible to deny oneself forever, Sexton warns. Indeed, it is impossible, too, to forgo the necessary relationships between women without there being repercussions.

Sexton once again comes to the finale of her poem with a bit of a twist on the typical ending. Though the prince and Cinderella marry, their happiness and perfection are not entirely believable. Sexton refers instead back to her references of "that story," reminding us that it is said that the prince and Cinderella did live happily ever after, just like "two dolls in a museum case" (103) without any of the problems or mundane affairs that plague married couples, "their darling smiles pasted on for eternity" (108). The prosaic sarcasm of "that story" returns again to end this piece, showing just how unbelievable and trivial the idea of this story is. Sexton reveals the common belief that marriage saves as a myth. Marriage does not create perfection and no one escapes the trivialities that can become part of marriage, except, perhaps, for two dolls in a museum case.

Olga Broumas is another modern woman poet who uses many of the same themes as Sexton in her poetic fairy tale revisions. Broumas, however, makes her feminist vision even more predominant. In her version of "Cinderella," Broumas extends "that story" into the future, imagining what it would be like for this woman who has denied her female sisterhood in becoming the prince's wife. Broumas' Cinderella chose to become a part of the male-dominated world represented by the castle and now suffers openly for it. Here, Cinderella laments her separation from her sisters and her mother, knowing that she is on her own in this masculine realm. This is a woman who is set apart from other women. She has no connection within this "castle." She is used by the men because she easily filled their "slipper," able to fill their needs. Broumas's Cinderella is a woman who was once glad to be knowledgeable enough to know how to gain access to this kingdom, yet now she compares herself in her lonely state to "one piece of laundry, strung on a windy clothesline" (19). These are not the words of a woman who is happy having relinquished her feminine side. Like Sexton before her, Broumas contends that when a woman chooses to forsake herself and those women to whom she is connected in order to become a part of a world where she will be cared for, a world that may seem safer and more secure, she is actually trading in her life for loneliness.

Broumas shows exactly how this Cinderella ended up in this state of isolation. She allowed herself to be enticed easily into the role she now fills; in fact, she delivered herself here by setting herself apart from her kind. She became a competitor of other women, deeming herself more beautiful, more clever, more capable and generally better suited to be the prince's wife, than all other women. This woman could be anyone who chooses the role of competitor for love. However, Broumas' Cinderella ends the poem begging to be released from her place, as if she is in a state of slavery, claiming that she will not be able to go on living for long in her present emotional state. Clearly this Cinderella was wooed by the concept of marriage, especially to a suitor who seemed so desirable; however, the death she now fears, whether literal or figurative, shows that the marriage state has left her realizing that she has exchanged her personal freedom and traded her connection to the feminine for an indentured state. Thus, Broumas establishes that marriage does not necessarily create a perfect union.

The profound difference between Sexton and Broumas and the characters they create in their revisions is articulated by Harries, who writes, "Broumas' Cinderella, like Sexton's in the last lines ... is isolated from other women in the house of the prince; but unlike Sexton's Cinderella, she is not a mechanical doll or an eternal Bobbsey twin; she can still make choices and reject her privileged and isolated status" (150). Relying on the state of entrapment that she felt in her marriage, Sexton creates female characters who, while sardonically showing the underbelly of the tales, do not find freedom or enlightenment. Broumas expands these characters, as if she has carefully taken each of Sexton's women and with a fresh, more contemporary feminist view, has allowed them a future in which they can breathe again, where they will be allowed choices that are not necessarily in line with the status quo of society, particularly the patriarchal society that created the best-known classic fairy tales.

This idea is apparent again in Broumas' "Rapunzel," in which she further extends the theme of connection to women, rejecting any societal standard of male/female marriage. Broumas begins with an epigraph from Sexton's poem of the same tale, that recurring line, "A woman / who loves a woman / is forever young." Like Sexton, Broumas again wants to show the nourishing relationship that can exist between women. Although there are similarities between the two poems in imagery, Broumas depicts the union between the two women in Rapunzel as sexual, not just sensual as Sexton did, making it clear that this relationship is not meant to be that of a mother and daughter; these women are lovers. As lovers, they have created an idyllic union, in which there is no need to "subdue their heat" (16). Instead, they both flourish and are able to revel in this sexuality fully, revel in themselves as women fully, without having to change any part of themselves. Unlike the Rapunzel of Grimms' tale, who is consumed by dark passions during pregnancy, creating her state of entrapment, and unlike the Rapunzel of Sexton's poem, who in the end is taken away from her feminine connection, in Broumas' version the women are allowed, and in fact *choose*, to maintain the union they have, a union that seems almost divine, with both women able to grow in each other's light, creating with each other "red vows like tulips" (32).

In her "Sleeping Beauty" Broumas is able to use the fairy tale allusion in order to show the power of female "marriages." Broumas finds a way to finally give Sleeping Beauty a true awakening. Unlike the women written of by Sexton, Hay or DeFord, Broumas' character is able to waken fully since the relationship, the kiss, is one that is chosen and not forced. As is standard for Broumas' fairy tale poetry, she begins by describing Beauty's extensive hours of sleep with a first person account, revealing the intimate nature of the narrative, as opposed the more removed narrative used in both Sexton's and Hay's poetry. She describes the dreamlike remembrance of a traditional love affair that clings to her, strangling like a "necklace" that is wrapped tightly. Broumas then allows the memory, this necklace, to be "snapped apart" by the awakening that follows. This awakening is not hidden away, nor is it one that happens while the choice-less woman sleeps. Rather, in this setting, Beauty is quite public, in the midst of the busy city, with the woman, Judith, who wakes her with a kiss. No longer is Beauty strangled by the confines of a traditional love affair; no longer are there brambles to cut through in order to free the chaste and hidden princess. Instead, Broumas concludes with a vitality that is very much awake: "we cross the street, kissing ... singing, *This is ... the woman that woke / me sleeping*" (50–53). This Beauty has claimed her right to awaken to her sexuality publicly, signifying the lack of any suppression. Beauty is triumphant, delighted to be stirred into living passionately, thrilled to be kissed by this "princess." Too, Beauty here is not saved by the woman, Judith, implying that she has no control over her personal happiness. This awakening happens mutually, with each character, each woman, revitalizing the other. And though she recognizes the sleep that the other poets highlighted as their main theme, Broumas focuses instead on the possibility of life, not death, for her awakened Beauty.

Though each does so a bit differently, these poets have reformed the language of the fairy tales. In her poem "Artemis" collected with her fairy tale poetry, Broumas writes that she is "a woman committed to ... transliteration" (26–28); she knows she must transform the verbiage of the tales, reminding readers that there is something more than we had come to expect, both of the fairy tales and of life in general. Harries writes, "To "transliterate" for Broumas is to invent a language for the experiences that cannot be caught in an language that already exists.... She "transliterates" or re-forms the old stories, omitting some elements, emphasizing others, to make them part of her new and dangerous vision of the world" (135). This is true of all of the poets examined. These poets are using what Harries refers to as a "memory of salient images" (136) and transforming them. By transliterating and reframing the tales, these women question the traditional framework of "that story"; they create new patterns of stories, bringing a fresh look at old words, and expose the trickery in believing there is only one way to read the tales, a way that is imbued with a masculine hierarchy. As Harries states, each poet knew that it was not the themes or motivations of the tales that needed to be dispelled, but the language that reflects only a masculine standard. In seeing these tales in a new light the contemporary female poets reveal the powerful archetypal themes inherent in the tales and create a language that reflects their true depth.

Notes

1. One example of this can be seen in a version of *Beauty and the Beast* by Catherine Bernard. Unlike male-authored versions of this tale, Bernard's depicts the princess marrying the beast, yet keeping her handsome lover on the side. When this is discovered by her gnome husband, the husband transforms the lover into an ugly gnome. The princess then lives with both men (two husbands), unable to distinguish one from the other. Bernard writes: "She lives with two husbands instead of one, and never knew who

to complain to, for fear of taking the object of her hatred for the object of her love" (Harries 38).

2. The sonnet throughout history was written by male poets. The writers discussed in this essay have shown brilliance in taking back this form for themselves while also reappropriating the form of the fairy tale. Additionally, the sonnet provides the perfect "if / then" form. In the first eight lines the argument is established; in the last six, the argument is resolved or concluded.

Works Cited

Bernheimer, Kate, ed. *Mirror, Mirror On the Wall: Women Writers Explore Their Favorite Fairy Tales*. New York: Bantam Doubleday Dell, 1998.

Broumas, Olga. *Beginning With O*. New Haven: Yale University Press, 1977.

Brown, Rosellen. "It is You the Fable is About." Bernheimer 50–63.

Crew, Hilary. "How Feminist are Fractured Fairy Tales." *Fractured Fairy Tales*. 3 pp. 2 July 2004. <http://www.scils.rutgers.edu/~kvander/Culture/crew.html>.

De Ford, Sara. "The Sleeping Beauty." *Disenchantments: An Anthology of Modern Fairy Tale Poetry*. Ed. Wolfgang Mieder. Hanover, NH: University Press of New England for the University of Vermont, 1985.

Harries, Elizabeth Wanning. *Twice Upon a Time: Women Writers and the History of the Fairy Tale*. Princeton, NJ: Princeton University Press, 2001.

Hay, Sara Henderson. *Story Hour*. Fayetteville: University of Arkansas Press, 1998.

Oates, Joyce Carol. "In Olden Times, When Wishing Was Having." Bernheimer 247–72.

Sexton, Anne. *Transformations*. Boston: Houghton Mifflin, 1971.

Struggling Sisters and Failing Spells
Re-engendering Fairy Tale Heroism
in Peg Kerr's *The Wild Swans*

Bethany Joy Bear

When an artist chooses to bring a traditional fairy tale into her writing, she transforms the story's long-standing magic with her own variety of enchantment. In doing so, she follows generations of other storytellers who have capitalized on "the detotalitive being of folklore" (Singh 122), which undermines any writer's or culture's claim that their version of a tale is authoritative. At the same time, fairy tales — ranging from unpolished folklore to literary revisions — share deep structural similarities. Since Propp and his followers earnestly catalogued narrative patterns and recurrent motifs, scholars have used the insights of structuralism to explore fairy tales as sites of subversion, examining how individual tales deviate from expected structures or archetypal characters, or how multiple versions of the same basic tale vary from one another.[1] In this tension between stability and variation, fairy tales address a question that is equally perennial and evolving: how can one be at home in the world? The answers to this question depend upon the teller's understanding of what constitutes home. Defeating a stepmother, achieving a marriage, producing a child, restoring an endangered household, gaining wealth, escaping a dangerous marriage, breaking a dehumanizing enchantment, removing the threat of a giant — these and similar victories establish identity, community, and security in a way that warrants a proclamation of "happily ever after."

For several decades, both writers and scholars have been fascinated with the role of gender and sexuality in fairy tales.[2] Terri Windling, whose Tor Books fantasy series inspired Kerr to adapt a fairy tale (Morehouse 13), describes the fairy tale as a form particularly apt for depicting the concerns of women ("Old Wives'" par. 1). Although Windling is in danger of oversimplification when she praises the "feminist subtexts" of Madame D'Aulnoy or Angela Carter in opposition to the "patriotic and patriarchal" ideals of the Grimms (par. 5), Win-

44

dling rightly emphasizes the essential importance of gender roles in literary versions of fairy tales. Altering the gender of a character, for instance, can change the vision of a happy ending. This is the case in Carter's retelling of the Bluebeard legend, "The Bloody Chamber" (1979). In Carter's version, the endangered bridge is rescued by her mother, rather than the traditional brothers. Instead of sustaining a structure in which women must wait for men to rescue them, Carter's text explores the possibilities of care within the context of female relationships.

Unlike Carter, Peg Kerr's works have remained beneath the radar of scholarly interest, but her novel *The Wild Swans* (1999) deserves attention as an important innovation in fairy-tale redaction. In *The Wild Swans*, Kerr retraces the entanglements of gender, identity, and community, re-engendering the protagonist of a popular tale. Be "re-engendering" I mean that Kerr not only changes the gender of the protagonist, but she alters the ways in which supposedly gender-specific qualities shape the function of the story's hero. Following the ironic telling of Hans Christian Andersen, Kerr destabilizes the sexual identity of several characters in *The Wild Swans*, and in doing so she significantly alters the ways in which the fairy tale constructs its vision of home and of heroism.

The fairy tale Kerr adapts (AT 451) is most familiar to American readers through Hans Christian Andersen's story "The Wild Swans" from which Kerr draws her basic plot. His text is one of several literary versions of the fairy tale which appears throughout European folklore as "The Seven Doves," "The Seven Ravens," "The Twelve Brothers," "The Six Swans," and so on. Although these titles always focus on a group of brothers, the crucial figure in all literary incarnations of AT 451 is their sister, who redeems the brothers from exile, enchantment, or both. The sister confronts her family's plight in very different ways as her story travels from century to century and from culture to culture. A medieval prototype of AT 451 shows the sister saving her brothers almost by accident,[3] while later storytellers depict a much more intentional sister-savior. For example, in "The Seven Doves," Giambattista Basile's seventeenth-century heroine treks boldly away from the safety of her home, ultimately triumphing through compassion and cleverness. The Brothers Grimm include three variants of AT 451 in their *Kinder-und Hausmärchen*, and these stories illustrate various ways of empowering the heroine. In "The Seven Ravens" she saves her brothers through an active and courageous quest, while in "The Twelve Brothers" and "The Six Swans" her success requires redemptive silence. In some of these texts, the sister's happy ending comes when the siblings return to their parents, reestablishing their childhood home, while in others, the sister marries and creates a new home with her brothers and husband. The latter ending, which appears in both the Grimms' "The Six Swans," "The Twelve Brothers," and Andersen's "The Wild Swans," comes only in the tales which depict the sister-savior as a silent redeemer. In these versions, establishing a home also means reaching sexual maturity (i.e. marriage), which may explain why these versions emphasize the sister's conformity to silence, an idealized feminine virtue.

Hans Christian Andersen, whose first volume of fairy tales appeared twenty years after the first edition of *Kinder-und Hausmärchen* (1812–1815), makes his sister-savior, Eliza, endure more than any of her literary predecessors. To redeem her brothers, Eliza must overcome silence, persecution, and the painful labor of spinning stinging nettles into shirts for her brothers. Both the Grimms and Andersen assign considerable agency to their silent sister-saviors, envisioning a distinctly feminine savior whose work is symbolized by her spindle, an ancient emblem of women's work. This is especially true for Andersen, who throughout his fairy tales associates women with the salvific powers of faith, childhood, and nature.[4] At the same time, Andersen is one of the nineteenth-century's darkest fairy-tale writers, and, even as he enhances Eliza's Christ-likeness, he makes it clear that her work is incomplete; one shirt is unfinished, leaving one brother with a swan's wing in place of his arm.

Andersen's uncertain happy ending is important to Kerr's contemporary revision. Out of the hundreds of fairy tales Andersen published, "The Wild Swans" is one of the few Andersen derived from preexisting sources. It resonates with the tone of his original stories, such as "The Steadfast Tin Soldier," which ends with the death of its namesake protagonist. Furthermore, Andersen, like many other Danish writers of his generation, was influenced by the German Romantics. This influence is manifest in Andersen's fascination with irony and the "disaffirmation" of both characters' and readers' expectations (Prickett 187). Andersen considered himself to be a serious poet, not a children's entertainer, and his willingness to use fairy tales indicates how, following the work of Goethe, Novalis, and others, the fairy tale became one of the quintessential forms of European Romanticism. The enterprise of preserving and adapting fairy tales, though it existed earlier, gained aesthetic and philosophical preeminence in the late eighteenth and nineteenth-centuries. For Novalis, the controversial poster child of Romanticism, the fairy tale was the "canon of poesy" against which all other creative works should be measured (167). While the German Romantics may have justified the form, Andersen made the fairy tale into a genre entirely his own. More than a disciple of the Romantics, Andersen wrote as one poised between the Romantic faith in *natur-poesie* and the darker concerns of literary modernism (de Mylius 166). By basing her novel on Andersen's version of a story, Kerr relies on a foundation already open to ambiguity, reversal, and irony. Furthermore, the genre Kerr claims as her own, fantasy literature (Morehouse 13–15), came into its modern form during the decades following Andersen's early works, as the stories of Lewis Carroll, George MacDonald, and others established fantasy as a form that must "reverse its ground rules time and again" (Rabkin 37). The reversal of these ground rules distinguishes fantasy from fairy tale, for a fairy tale, though filled with wonders and enchantment, always operates according to the ground rules of its enchanted world (36–37). Transforming the fairy tale into a fantasy allows Kerr to question her source tales' presuppositions about gender, home, and heroism.

Within a fairy tale, many of the "ground rules" govern the achievements of a single heroic protagonist. Kerr's re-engendering complicates both the nature of the AT 451 heroes and the rules whereby they establish homes for themselves and their brothers. While writers like Windling and Carter may hope to recreate feminist visions of heroism ("Old Wives'" par. 4–7), Kerr's re-engendering implies that fairy tales must birth entirely new concepts of heroism in order to address the concerns of the twenty-first century.

Kerr first shifts the focus away from a single hero by reincarnating Andersen's basic plot in two parallel storylines within *The Wild Swans*. One, the story of Eliza, follows the structure of Andersen's "The Wild Swans" very closely but places it in a more specific historical context — the Puritan colonization of New England. In 1689 Eliza's contented life as the fosterling of poor weavers ends when her father, the Earl of Exeter, summons her home. Expecting to find her eleven elder brothers at the Earl's manor, Eliza is dismayed to discover that her brothers vanished ten years earlier. They were exiled as traitors, and when Eliza tries to speak in her brothers' defense, the Earl disowns her. After wandering for several days, Eliza finds her brothers, who have been under their step-mother's enchantment for ten years. Swans by day and men by night, they are planning a flight from England to the New World.

Eliza's swan-brothers bear their sister across the ocean, and when they arrive in North America they take up residence in a cave. This cave, one of Andersen's additions to AT 451, intensifies the message that the brothers' disenchantment requires a distinctively feminine magic. There, a fairy reveals how Eliza can disenchant her brothers. Until she completes eleven shirts from nettle-spun yarn, Eliza must not speak. Shortly into her work, Jonathan Latham, the magistrate of a local Puritan community, finds Eliza and brings her (initially against her will) to his village. Eventually, Jonathan falls in love with Eliza and asks her to marry him. She agrees, but the minister, William, strongly objects, and he eventually frames Eliza for witchcraft. She is condemned to die by hanging, but moments before her execution her swan-brothers arrive. She throws the shirts over them, restoring all but the youngest brother to complete human form. The gallows burst into blooming roses, and she ends her tale by establishing a home with her brothers and husband.

In the novel's second storyline, Kerr adapts the sister-savior tale with far more daring, transforming the sister into Elias Latham — a young gay man living in New York City in the early 1980s. Whereas Eliza seeks to restore her fragmented family, Elias, rejected by his parents, must first discover who his family actually is. Kerr foreshadows Elias's role as a new kind of "sister" by opening the novel with a dream in which Elias sees swans "watching over someone, protecting him — or was it a her?" (3). Similarly, Elias' name — an obvious cognate of Eliza — anticipates Kerr's intriguing transposition of the traditional sister onto a *man* whose sexual identity as a gay person complicates his relationship to the roles traditionally assigned to male fairy-tale protagonists: tricksters, soldiers, princes/kings, and so on. At the same time, Elias cannot step easily into the role of Andersen's unquestionably feminine sister-savior. There is no fairy-tale type Kerr can use as a pattern for Elias; his character has no established ground rules for heroism to follow. Thus, re-engendering Eliza as Elias unsettles the ground rules of fairy-tale heroism. In Andersen's text, Elisa can only save her brothers by enacting a feminine ideal; gender identity and heroic ability are one in the same. Now, as sexual identity and gender roles become increasingly complex, the ability of a single "sister" to accomplish redemption is similarly doubtful.

Additionally, Kerr prevents her "sisters" from constructing themselves as heroes by denying them a voice in the discourse that labels their sexual identities and, consequently, affects their ability to fulfill Andersen's extremely gendered concepts of heroism. Judith Butler has famously argued that "identity categories tend to be instruments of regulatory regimes" (1514), and Kerr uses language as the primary medium of this regulation. The obstacles to Eliza's and Elias's redemption of home and family come through vocal accusations that they are violating appropriate gender roles through sexual deviance. For example, when Eliza answers her father's summons, her stepmother dresses her in a way that implies licentiousness, so that her father not only dismisses her, but calls her a "painted whore" and a "pestilent harlot" (Kerr 85). Eliza has no voice to offer an alternative definition; her stepmother administers a potion to ensure that Eliza cannot speak in her own defense. Elias also experiences voicelessness when his father learns that Elias is gay. His father immediately assumes that Elias is also a pedophile and asks "not even *if*, but *how many times*" Elias molested his young nephews, refusing to heed any of Elias's protests (56). The discourse of others labels Eliza and Elias as sexually deviant, and while other AT 451 protagonists endure false accusations, Kerr makes these accusations a greater threat to Eliza and Elias's work; both characters struggle and, in some measure, fail to complete their work as saviors. While fathers and stepmothers say that Eliza and Elias fall short of being a virtuous woman or a true man, the protagonists' silence isolates them from the discourse necessary to establish their roles as heroes. Furthermore, since their alleged deviance excludes them from the only families they have ever known, Eliza and Elias must turn to others to help them redefine the foundational concepts of home and family. Thus, as the novel progresses, Eliza's and Elias's communities must begin to participate in the function once reserved for a single hero.

The shifting emphasis from a single hero to a more communitarian vision of heroism affects all the major motifs — the objects and characters significant to the plot — and mythemes — basic units of narrative action — of AT 451. The controlling mytheme of the sister's quest immediately reveals the ways Kerr has reconstructed the sister-savior of the earlier tales. For the sister-saviors in Basile's and the Grimms' texts, the quest begins immediately after the sisters learn the condition of their enchanted or exiled brothers. All these sisters act in accordance with a clear goal of recreating or restoring unity with their brothers. In Andersen's text, the sister sets out to rescue her brothers as soon as she is expelled from her father's house, but in *The Wild Swans* neither Elias nor Eliza begin with such a clear goal. When Eliza's father disowns her, she first tries to return to her foster mother's house. Only when she finds her foster mother dead does Eliza decide to seek her brothers, whom she only vaguely remembers. For Elias, the trauma of his father's rejection shatters his conception of what his family is, and at first he does not even consider the possibility of finding kinships to replace those he has lost. He is on the verge of resorting to prostitution when he meets Sean, a writer and musician who takes Elias into his home. Eventually Sean, who is also gay, becomes Elias's partner. Sean introduces Elias to a supportive gay community, but this family quickly begins to disintegrate as Elias' friends— his metaphorical brothers— succumb to HIV/AIDS. Consequently, before Eliza and Elias can work towards their brothers' disenchantment, they must first struggle to define "family" for themselves.

As they seek to find a family, and, from there, to establish some kind of home, both Eliza and Elias first learn that their former ideas about home must change. Just as Andersen provides his Elisa with a fairy guide to her brothers' redemption, Kerr introduces various characters who help her protagonists construct new visions of family and community. Eliza's "fairy" is a Quaker woman who tells Eliza of eleven swans with "light playing around their heads like crowns of gold" (152). Although Eliza has been seeking twelve young men, the woman's description hints that Eliza's former understanding of her family's identity will not guide her rightly. Instead, the Quaker woman prepares Eliza to find her brothers in an unexpected form.

Elias encounters his own fairy guide during a weekend with Sean on Fire Island, a popular retreat among gay men. Along the way, a soft-spoken drag queen and self-proclaimed "fairy" explains to Elias that on the Island, among other gay men, he has found his "family" (Kerr 126). Like Eliza's fairy, Elias's guide suggests that Elias will find a home in an unexpected place: an island Elias' father used to call "the Sodom and Gomorrah of the East Coast" (106). This "fairy" then remarks, "We actually used to call each other 'sister,' you know," explicitly equating the "gay community" (126) with Elias's metaphorical siblings. Elias— a man, but a man who transgresses his culture's idea of masculine sexuality —finds on Fire Island his gay "sisters" who function also as his brothers in the context of the sister-savior fairy tale. Here Kerr follows a practice at work in Victorian fantasies by "queering" the portrayal of male figures. For example, Roderick McGillis has argued that George MacDonald, one of the first writers of what we might call modern fantasy, departs from traditional fairy tales by "queering" male characters. While he does not go so far as Kerr in transgressing his culture's sexual mores, MacDonald "managed to challenge the prevailing view of the sexes," especially of men, through his fairy tales (86). The ambiguity of who is a sister or brother allows Kerr to suggest that entire communities—a more flexible concept than a family, with a wider range of possible relationships—share both sibling roles, and that freedom from the deadly transformations of AIDS must be a matter of mutual salvation, rather than the work of a single hero.

For both sister-saviors in *The Wild Swans*, Kerr's reworking of another mytheme—in which a king discovers the sister while she silently labors— changes the course of their efforts to disenchant their brothers. In all variants of AT 451 which include this mytheme, the king's discovery brings the sister into a community that both facilitates and threatens her work. The sister's discovery brings her into a home, foreshadowing the hoped-for happy ending, but it is a false home, determined by the king's desire rather than by the sister's creation of a stable and complete community. Kerr elaborates this threat. For Eliza, the "king" is a Puritan magistrate, and his discovery initially disrupts Eliza's work. Like several of her predecessors, including the sister in the Grimms' "The Six Swans" and Andersen's "The Wild Swans," Kerr's Eliza resists furiously when Jonathan takes her from her cave. By removing her from a grotto overhung with creepers "like a fine veil" (Kerr 213), Jonathan violates the boundary of Eliza's safety and commits a kind of rape. His discovery does, however, bring Eliza into a place where she can work in relative safety, and her growing love for Jonathan creates the possibility of a secure home within human society. William, the minister, disrupts Jonathan's attempt to bring Eliza into the community. William sees Eliza as a wild woman, guilty of bewitching Jonathan. He insists that Eliza "is no sister, no child of ours, and has no claim upon us!" (230–31) while Jonathan demands that Eliza "will have a proper place in the community" (231). William's hostility eventually leads to Eliza's condemnation for witchcraft, turning the community into the enemy of Eliza's work.

For Elias, the mythemes of the king's discovery and the brothers' disenchantment are more complexly intertwined. Both the threat and the promise of Jonathan's discovery of Eliza are realized when Sean discovers Elias. Ironically, Sean saves Elias from potential death on the streets by bringing him into a community, but that community also infects Elias with the HIV virus that eventually kills him. Sean acts as the king when he rescues Elias from starvation and prostitution, and their subsequent relationship allows Elias to understand himself and his desires in a way he never could before. At the same time, Elias' faithfulness transforms Sean from a man who drifts from one casual sexual encounter to another into a loyal and loving partner. Like Eliza, who leaves one brother with a swan's arm, Elias works real but incomplete redemption in the lives of his brothers; neither the gay community nor the surrounding culture has fully joined with him. The curse facing his "family" is too much for a single sister/brother/lover to counter alone.

The king's discovery mytheme brings Eliza and Elias into communities, but, more importantly, it highlights their isolation from these communities. In Andersen's retelling, the king's discovery is immediately followed by another mytheme, which is a descent into an underworld of some kind. This mytheme is another of Andersen's innovations, and it heightens the story's tension by making the sister enact the accusations against her. In the same way, Eliza and Elias seem to confirm charges of deviance by making their descents. Eliza must descend to the village churchyard to gather more nettles for her brothers' shirts. The condemnation that results from this visit nearly destroys Eliza's hopes of redeeming her brothers, but when her brothers arrive before her pyre is lit, she is able to publicly demonstrate her innocence to the entire village. Kerr uses Eliza's descent mytheme to recreate the sense of Andersen's text. An unjust sentence only intensifies the sense of the hero's innocence, which then serves as a foil to Elias's descent.

Elias's crucible is the Maze, a bathhouse where gay men go for anonymous sexual contact. Elias had gone once with Sean but left quickly, sickened by the anonymity of the encounters. Later in the novel, Elias returns to the Maze to seek Sean, who has been missing for several days. Although most of *The Wild Swans* depicts Elias's introduction to a compassionate and talented gay community, the Maze represents an equally real side of New York's gay scene in the early 1980s. It is there that Elias experiences the ways in which his own community unwittingly works against the redemption he is supposed to achieve. The men in the Maze are nameless, voiceless, with no identity beyond their desire. AIDS here can be seen as a physical manifestation of a culture that reduces identity and relationships to sexual acts, a reduction of which both Sean and Elias's father are guilty. Elias's descent does not unambiguously affirm Elias's purity — for he is "at once paralyzed and horrified and incredibly aroused" (209) — but his determination to save Sean takes precedence; he visits the Maze because he wants to bring Sean out of the lifestyle the Maze represents.

For both of the sister-saviors in *The Wild Swans*, the descent mytheme suggests that transgressing their communities' norms actually contributes to redemption: Eliza gathers the nettles she needs, and Elias demonstrates the depth of his love for Sean. For the auxiliary characters, this mytheme also highlights how re-engendering undermines the sexual mores or gender roles against which the sisters are measured. For example, Kerr's treatment of William is far more interesting than her adaptation of Eliza's condemnation. After falsely accusing Eliza, William begins to examine his motives for objecting to Jonathan's marriage. With a truly Puritan horror, he realizes that his hatred of Eliza comes from his own desire for Jonathan, a thought that in his mind can only mean that, rather than being one of "the blessed elect" he is "instead one of the eternally damned" (Kerr 428). William's religious convictions force him to bear the painful irony of thinking "himself incapable of love, and then, when he finally found it, to discover that love has brought only destruction" (429). Here Kerr continues Andersen's own manipulation of certain older versions of the tale, such as the Grimms' "The Twelve Brothers" and "The Six Swans," in which jealous mothers-in-law accuse the sisters of various abominations. Andersen transforms these jealous mothers into a male archbishop, and Kerr probes this gender reversal even further through William's struggle. This transformation parallels Elias's role as the sister-savior and the male drag queen's function as a fairy godmother. If William, the main voice speaking against Eliza, violates his own categories of appropriate behavior, the categories themselves come into question. All these transformations reinforce the instability of gendered identity, invalidating categories of normative or deviant behavior that previously defined heroism.

Kerr's gender reversals are part of her more significant inversion of Andersen's apparent glorification of silence. While his tale overtly claims that a woman's power comes through meek silence and suffering, Kerr's story argues that silence ultimately results in destruction, not salvation. As the AT 451 protagonist loses rigid gender identity, Kerr has the freedom to question the qualities associated with that identity, such as silence. As one of the primary ground rules of Andersen's fairy tale, salvation-through-silence provides Kerr with a significant opportunity for reversal. This reversal, in turn, demonstrates the potential benefits of stepping beyond the traditionally gendered concepts of heroism. Andersen uses silence to reinforce his hero's self-control and dedication to her brothers, emphasizing her individual victory, but Kerr uses silence to communicate alienation from others, the opposite of the cooperation needed to break the curse of bigotry and AIDS.

William's agony over his own sexuality foreshadows Kerr's treatment of the silence mytheme, which she indicts as a source of fear and death. By refusing to voice his own struggles, William nearly destroys Eliza's life, Jonathan's happiness, and his own faith. Similarly, Elias's descent into the Maze forces Sean to examine the consequences of his own inability to voice his love. When Elias explains that Sean has been his only sexual partner, Sean realizes that he is responsible for Elias's HIV infection. Elias's visit to the Maze demonstrates his self-sacrificing faithfulness, and only after that descent does Sean say "I love you" for the first time (295). Sean, unlike William, finds a voice and escapes the guilt that William bears.

Sean's and William's struggles with expressions of love reveal how closely the mythemes of the sister's quest and silence are entwined in *The Wild Swans*. Though Eliza keeps her literal silence, she manages to communicate in ways Andersen's Elisa does not, such as through rudimentary sign language. Eliza is also more vocal during the first portion of her quest than Elias is during his, openly discussing her lost brothers with the Quaker woman. Furthermore, as soon as she learns that her brothers are captive to a spell that deprives them of their human lives, Eliza prays for a way to save them, voicing to God her need for empowerment. Elias, on the other hand, is consistently silenced by the fear of public disapproval. He admires gay men who act "like they don't give a damn what anybody thinks" but admits, "I always do. Give a damn, that is" (Kerr 128). Elias's fear is part of the larger silence that prevents the novel's gay community from understanding and preventing the rapid spread of AIDS.

As Eliza's and Elias' experiences suggest, Kerr complicates the silence mytheme considerably. The mytheme of the sister's redemptive silence is the linchpin for the Grimm and Andersen versions of AT 451, and Kerr's Eliza narrative seems to follow earlier texts' use of the silence mytheme as a necessary part of her brothers' salvation. Thus, the fairy warns Eliza that the "first word you utter will pierce through the hearts of your brothers like a dagger. Their lives hang upon your tongue" (216). Obediently, Eliza makes the eleven shirts and maintains her literal silence, apparently creating a "garden of Paradise" with her brothers and husband (438). Beneath the surface of the familiar silence mytheme, however, Kerr begins to question the source of Eliza's mandate to silence. In Andersen's version, Elisa's silence fits into the overt pattern of Christological suffering which contributes to her role as a sister-savior. Kerr has described both of the novel's protagonists as Christ figures (Morehouse 14), but within the text itself, Kerr downplays some of the idealized Christ-likeness of Andersen's Elisa. For example, as Eliza wanders through the woods after her father's rejection, she catches sight of her own reflection as the "sunlight caught glints of red in her hair, transforming them into threads of molten gold shining in a corona around her face" (112). The glorified reflection of her own face replaces the vision of "God looking down at her" that consoles Elisa (Andersen 120), suggesting that Kerr intentionally diminishes Eliza's connection to divinely-patterned redemption.

Kerr also undermines the images of unquestionable goodness which define Andersen's Elisa. To do this, Kerr adapts the scene from Andersen's tale in which Eliza's stepmother places three poisoned toads in Eliza's bath. One detail significantly alters the encounter. Kerr emphasizes that the poisoned toads do not turn into poppies until a sprig of juniper falls into the water. Eliza, remembering her foster mother's herb lore, carries this sprig with her because "juniper protects against all evil that would do thee harm" (47). Andersen's Elisa needs no such talisman because the sister herself is "so good and so innocent that evil magic could not harm her" (119). Making a bit of juniper, rather than Eliza's innate goodness, thwart the stepmother's magic indicates Kerr's reluctance to make her hero completely self-sufficient. To make Eliza perfect would leave no room for Kerr to question Eliza's success and the silence mytheme. Furthermore, the silences of Eliza's brothers and of Jonathan come from black magic or fear, and their silence actively works against Eliza. The weakening of the sister-savior is also important for Elias's story, because Kerr clearly believes that for AIDS victims the "story is not complete, for we haven't yet found a way to break the curse" (448). It is not only that Eliza herself is an insufficient hero. Breaking the curse will not come through the work of any sister-savior, no matter how powerful, but from entire communities that are willing to reevaluate how they relate to and work for the good of one another.

Silence affects Elias's tale even more insidiously than Eliza's. The "curse" of AIDS destroys Elias's brothers because of silence within and outside the gay community about the transmission of AIDS. Thus, Elias's tale indicts silence even more strongly than Eliza's does. In an epigraph to one chapter of *The Wild Swans*, Kerr includes a passage from Samuel R. Delany's *The Motion of Light in Water* that describes the complex atmosphere of New York's East Village in the 1960s, where "intensities of both guilt and of pleasure, of censure and of blindness" regarding sexuality "were grounded on a nearly absolute sanctioned public silence" (qtd. in Kerr 196). In Elias's experience, silence — manifested as ignorance, apathy, or denial towards the growing AIDS epidemic — becomes synonymous with death. *The Wild Swans* is an attempt to give a voice to the people who suffer and die from HIV/AIDS. In a way, the entire gay community becomes a sister whose silence perpetuates a fatal enchantment.

As we have seen, Eliza's supposedly redemptive silence for her brothers is not her first period of voicelessness in the novel. When she first returns to her father's estate, her stepmother casts a spell over Eliza that renders her unable to speak, associating silence not with sacrificial suffering, but with the effects of dark magic and manipulation. Furthermore, Kerr's intimate narrative voice breaks Eliza's silence continually, moving into her thoughts and struggles in a way no earlier version of AT 451 dares. Kerr is even bolder as she breaks the silence of earlier fairy tale writers, especially Andersen, on explicit questions of sexuality. Sexuality is inextricable from any discussion of AIDS and contemporary society, and Kerr's frankness on the subject of both hetero- and homosexual relationships is one of the most significant ways in which she breaks her protagonists' silence.

For example, Kerr balances the fathers' accusations of sexual perversion with explicit introductions to meaningful sexual experiences that actually define the relationships between Elias and Sean, Eliza and Jonathan. Still, Elias's father is a voice of authority deeming homosexuality deviant, and during an encounter with another socially marginal character, Elias reveals the extent to which he has internalized his culture's condemnation of deviance. Sean takes Elias to see a friend, Lizzie, who is clairvoyant, and he tells Elias that this friend can answer any question he might have. When Elias learns that Lizzie is a Wiccan, he calls her a "witch" and refuses to ask her anything because "*my* religion says a witch shouldn't be permitted to live" (284). Elias' meeting with Lizzie begins to re-enact Eliza's encounter with the fairy, but the question that Elias refuses to ask hangs heavily over the rest of the novel, as though that question might have given Elias the key to saving his brothers. Thus even Elias is guilty of the bigotry that fueled his father's rejection and of the silence that continues to trap his brothers.

Elias sees Lizzie again in the novel's Epilogue. They meet at a display of the AIDS Quilt, an event where family and friends of AIDS victims can contribute memorial squares. With Lizzie is the last of her eleven brothers, ten of whom have already died from HIV infections contracted during blood transfusions. His arm, which rests in a white sling, recalls the swan's wing which, in Andersen's tale, the youngest brother retains because Elisa could not finish his shirt in time. The brother with the swan's wing intrudes into the happy ending of the older tale, and here Kerr enlarges the sense of the sister-savior's incomplete success. Lizzie's brother apologizes that "she doesn't talk much anymore" (Kerr 445); the mytheme of silence is working backwards, and Lizzie's silence is the effect of her loss, not the secret to disenchanting her brothers. Creating a square for the public exhibition of the quilt constitutes a small break in the silence of "failures and fears" surrounding AIDS (419), but the break in silence occurs too late to save Lizzie's brothers. The quilt also provides an emblem for the kind of communal effort necessary to properly mourn, and perhaps, one day, to save, those infected with HIV/AIDS.

The AIDS Quilt also recalls the shirts Eliza uses to disenchant her brothers, but in Kerr's telling, the "shirt" that breaks the spell must come from many hands. When her brothers fly onto her pyre, Eliza clothes them in their nettle shirts, publicly dressing the swans as human beings. Following her brothers' disenchantment, Eliza's happy ending seems to bring a complete end to her silence. Unlike Andersen, Kerr shows Eliza speaking and laughing as she climbs off her pyre, not returning silently to her husband's castle. Still, the brother who is left with one swan wing troubles Eliza's success, and a careful reading reveals that Eliza's incomplete redemption has longer-lasting consequences. She marries Jonathan *Latham*, and when Elias *Latham* mentions "someone way back on the family tree who ended up condemned to death for witchcraft" (Kerr 66), the connection between Eliza and Elias becomes even more significant. The curse that threatened Eliza has revisited her family. The heirs of Eliza's supposedly happy ending include Elias's bigoted father as well as Elias himself, another beautiful and loving "sister" who cannot completely save his brothers or himself from the curse that threatens them all (244).

As Elias nears the end of his narrative and his life, he finally realizes that silence will never save his family. *The Wild Swans* closes, as it begins, with Elias dreaming of swans. Unlike the first dream, the swans are flying away instead of watching over Elias. When he meets the eyes of a young woman watching the swans, Elias feels "a tug of something, wordless and urgent, stretching over the infinite gulf between them, echoing through the centuries" (Kerr 446). He asks her, "If I can't save them, and I die for nothing, what did all the silence and suffering accomplish? What was it all *for?*" (446) Neither the young woman nor Kerr give Elias an answer to that question, and he watches as the swans fly away.

Although Elias does not receive an answer, the fact that he asks at all testifies that he has undergone a transformation of his own. By reversing the ground rules of Andersen's already-ironic tale, Kerr shows that fairy tales are complex enough to sustain multiple subversions and adaptations.[5] As fairy tales evolved into fantasy during the nineteenth-century, the new genre developed a voice that thrived on subversion, upsetting its own ground rules for the sake of creating a story that spoke truth to its readers. Thus, Kerr also challenges the assumption that modern fairy tales must follow a now-standard pattern of empowering princesses or deconstructing happy endings. Her call for a community of brothers and sisters, rather than a single hero, redacts the heroic individualism so foundational to the fairy-tale mythos, including many feminist revisions. Kerr also has the audacity to sustain a belief in happy endings, even though her story does not provide a tidy resolution. She writes that the story of AIDS victims is incomplete, not impossible, suggesting one day something will happen to finish the story, once and for all healing the cursed and reconciling the lovers. Even in the death of her characters, Kerr implies that stories of restoration, even resurrection, may have a place in a cynical age. As Elias watches Sean struggle through his final moments, he joins their friends in a tender benediction, praying, "Go forth, Sean, from this world in the name of God the Father.... May you live in peace this day, may your home be with God in Zion" (412). With these closing words, Kerr reminds us that there can be no home until the sister finds a voice, and that her voice must join with others if that home is to be safe from any future curse.

Notes

1. This essay is adapted from the last chapter of my unpublished thesis, *Wild Swans and Sister Saviors: Cultural Moments in the Life of an Indo-European Fairy Tale*, which examined how the major literary adaptations of AT 451 created images of female agents of redemption.

2. Although it is difficult to date a trend exactly, the publication of Anne Sexton's *Transformations* in 1971 is a helpful touchstone. For a sample of recent work in this vein, see the collection edited by Donald Haase, *Fairy Tales and Feminism: New Approaches* (Detroit: Wayne State University Press, 2004).

3. The medieval Latin text "Cygni" is a kind of proto–AT 451 that features many of the same characters and mythemes as the modern sister-savior tales. However, it lacks the positive emphasis on the sister's significant labor of redemption. "Cygni" is part of *Dolopathos, or The King and the Seven Wise Men* by Johannes de Alta Silva, a Cistercian monk living in the late twelfth century.

4. For more on Andersen's vision of women and salvation, see Wolfgang Lederer's psychoanalytic study, *The Kiss of the Snow Queen: Hans Christian Andersen and Man's Redemption by Woman* (Berkeley: University of California Press, 1986).

5. Fantasy writers in the last ten years have found AT 451, especially Andersen's version, particularly compelling. Since the publication of Kerr's novel, several other fantasy writers have adapted the tale: Juliet Marillier, *Daughter of the Forest* (New York: Tor, 2000); Rafe Martin, *Birdwing* (New York: Levine, 2005); and Zöe Marriott, *The Swan Kingdom* (Cambridge, MA: Candlewick, 2008).

Works Cited

Andersen, Hans Christian. "The Wild Swans." *The Complete Fairy Tales and Stories.* Trans. Erik Christian Haugaard. New York: Anchor, 1983. 117–31.

Basile, Giambattista. "The Seven Doves." *The Great Fairy Tale Tradition.* Ed. Jack Zipes. New York: Norton, 2001. 641–47.

Butler, Judith. "Imitation and Gender Insubordination." *The Critical Tradition: Classic Texts and Contemporary Trends.* 2d ed. Ed. David H. Richter. Boston: Bedford/St. Martin's, 1997. 1514–25.

Carter, Angela. "The Bloody Chamber." *The Bloody Chamber and Other Stories.* New York: Penguin, 1979. 7–41.

de Alta Silva, Johannes. *Dolopathos, or The King and the Seven Wise Men.* Trans. Brady B. Gilleland. Binghamton: Center for Medieval & Early Renaissance Studies, 1999.

de Mylius, Johan. "'Our Time Is the Time of the Fairy Tale': Hans Christian Andersen Between Traditional Craft and Literary Modernism." *Marvels and Tales* 20.2 (2006): 166–78.

Grimm, Jacob and Wilhelm. "The Seven Ravens (Die Sieben Raben)." *Children's and Household Tales (Kinder-und Hausmärchen).* Trans. D.L. Ashliman. *Folklore and Mythology Electronic Texts.* University of Pittsburgh. 16 Feb. 2005 <www.pitt.edu/ ~dash/grimm049.html>.

_____. "The Six Swans (Die sechs Schwane)." *Children's and Household Tales (Kinder-und Hausmärchen).* Trans. D.L. Ashliman. *Folklore and Mythology Electronic Texts.* University of Pittsburgh. 16 Feb. 2005 <www.pitt.edu/~dash/grimm025.html>.

_____. "The Twelve Brothers (Die zwolf Bruder)." *Children's and Household Tales (Kinder-und Hausmärchen).* Trans. D.L. Ashliman. *Folklore and Mythology Electronic Texts.* University of Pittsburgh. 16 Feb. 2005 <www.pitt.edu/~dash/grimm 009.html>.

Kerr, Peg. *The Wild Swans.* New York: Warner, 1999.

McGillis, Roderick. "'A Fairytale is Just a Fairytale': George MacDonald and the Queering of Fairy." *Marvels and Tales* 17.1 (2003): 86–99.

Morehouse, Lydia. "SFC Interview: Peg Kerr." *Science Fiction Chronicle* 207 (2000): 13–15.

Prickett, Stephen. *Victorian Fantasy.* Waco, TX: Baylor University Press, 2006.

Rabkin, Eric S. *The Fantastic in Literature.* Princeton, NJ: Princeton University Press, 1976.

Singh, Gurbhagat. *Literature and Folklore after Poststructuralism.* Delhi: Ajanta, 1991.

Windling, Terri. "Old Wives Tales: An Exhibition of Women's Fairy Tale Art, Old and New." *Endicott Studio.* 12 June 2008 http://www.endicott-studio.com/gal/galWives/ wivestales.html>.

Found Girls

J.M. Barrie's *Peter & Wendy* and Jane Yolen's "Lost Girls"

JOANNE CAMPBELL TIDWELL

Jane Yolen first published "Lost Girls," a re-imagining of *Peter Pan*, in 1997 in *Twelve Impossible Things Before Breakfast,* and the novella was subsequently reprinted in *Sister Emily's Lightship and Other Stories* in 2000. The story won the Nebula for best novelette in 1999. In this essay I analyze J.M. Barrie's *Peter Pan* in order to understand his portrayal of the feminine gender and situate my reading of Yolen's revision of Barrie's myth. Yolen brings the fairy tale into the late twentieth century by making consciousness-raising, labor relations, and equal pay for equal work the stuff of bedtime stories. She subverts a story meant to reinforce traditional gender roles and uses it to reinforce the values of feminism, giving new life to the tale for a new generation of readers.

J.M. Barrie's tale of *Peter Pan* operates as a prototypical fairy tale of the late nineteenth century. The story offers an escape from the overly mechanized, alienating world of Victorian London into a magical world of nature, while at the same time reinforcing the societal norms that produced Victorian society in the first place. Ann Wilson writes in "Hauntings: Anxiety, Technology, and Gender in *Peter Pan*" that *"Peter Pan* is a fable of modernity, anxiously negotiating industrial technologies that produced a middle class predicated on instability and which encoded impossible roles for men and women" (608). Peter attempts to escape from the life planned for him by his mother and runs away as an infant to live with the fairies in Kensington Park. When he is joined by Wendy, John, and Michael in Neverland, however, Peter recreates the world he escaped. He becomes the father, Wendy the mother, and the Lost Boys the children. At the end of the tale, all of the Lost Boys return with Wendy, John, and Michael to live with the Darlings, thus supporting the value of the Victorian family. Peter, a rebel, stays alone in Neverland.

Yolen has been a dominant writer in the field of folklore for decades. Her focus on feminism is also clearly stated. In a letter to her daughter and grand-daughters that prefaces *Not a Damsel in Distress: World Folk Tales for Strong Girls*, Yolen writes, "But this book is for you because it is important to know that anyone *can* be a hero if they have to be. Even girls. Especially girls" (xii). The collection presents both folk and historical stories about heroic women, meant to act as mythological figures for girls. In her book of essays, *Touch Magic*, Yolen argues that myth and folk literature serve very important functions in the development of children. She writes:

> These four functions of myth and folklore should establish the listening to and learning of the old tales as being among the most basic elements of our education: creating a landscape of allusion, enabling us to understand our own and other cultures from the inside out, providing an adaptable tool of therapy, and stating in symbolic or metaphoric terms the abstract truths of our common human experience [18].

Yolen argues that learning about myths and folklore gives children a connection with a larger world and enables them to connect with their own humanity as well.

Myths and fairy tales are often used to teach the young and impressionable, thus setting up traditional and often overly conservative ideas of *normal*. In *The Madwoman in the Attic*, Sandra Gilbert and Susan Gubar write, "[M]yths and fairy tales often both state and enforce culture's sentences with greater accuracy than more sophisticated literary texts" (36). As Donald Haase explains in "Feminist Fairy-Tale Scholarship," Jack Zipes illustrates that "the folktale had been appropriated and reappropriated by European and American writers as a special discourse on sociocultural values and how that fairy-tale discourse was intended to function in the socialization of children — especially in its modeling of gender-specific identity and behavior" (10). Zipes argues in *Breaking the Spell: Radical Theories of Folk and Fairy Tales* that folk tales, the historic basis for fairy tales, were originally "revolutionary and progressive, not escapist" (36). Originating in the agrarian, mostly illiterate classes under feudalism, the tales reflected the problems and concerns of the "folk." Zipes writes:

> The folk tale is part of a *pre-capitalist people's oral tradition* which expresses their wishes to attain better living conditions through a depiction of their struggles and contradictions. The term fairy tale is of *bourgeois coinage* and indicates the advent of a new literary form which appropriates elements of folklore to address and criticize the aspirations and needs of an emerging bourgeois audience [27, his emphasis].

Barrie saturates *Peter Pan* with Victorian, bourgeois ideas of gender, grounded in the separation of spheres, and he reinforces those ideas as norms for generations of children. Yolen reverses the transition from fairy tale to folk tale by returning the emancipatory, revolutionary influence of the folk tale to the story of Peter Pan.

For the purposes of this article, I will limit my analysis of Barrie's story to

Peter & Wendy, the portion of the Neverland stories most well known and the story that details the adventures of the Darling children. Yolen's revision of the Peter Pan myth concentrates almost entirely on the character of Wendy. Four female characters figure in Barrie's *Peter & Wendy*: Mrs. Darling, Wendy, Tinker Bell, and Tiger Lily. While Tinker Bell appears in Yolen's story, her role is relatively minor, and Mrs. Darling and Tiger Lily are not mentioned. Wendy's role is of primary interest for this paper's purpose, but Mrs. Darling, Tinker Bell, and Tiger Lily deserve some attention as well in order to fully understand Barrie's portrayal of women and girls.

Mrs. Darling's character operates as the prototypical mother of Victorian and Edwardian England, a model for Wendy and other subsequent Neverland mothers. Barrie's portrait of motherhood in the frame story is at turns contradictory and sympathetic. His initial description of Mrs. Darling describes her "romantic mind" as "like the tiny boxes, one within the other, that come from the puzzling East, however many you discover there is always one more" (69). She is not logical and straightforward but rather a mystery without end. However, she "loved to have everything just so," a phrase later used to describe Wendy in Neverland, and she is clearly in a position of power in her household (71). Wilson argues that Mr. Darling has been unmanned by his job as a clerk, and he is no longer the patriarchal head of the household he was supposed to be. In "The Kiss: Female Sexuality and Power in J.M. Barrie's *Peter Pan*," M. Joy Morse writes, "Mr. Darling's lack of a central role in his home, resulting from his failure as a breadwinner, is painfully evident in the fantasy games his children select" (292). His children do not play at their father's job but rather at having children and creating a home. With her power, however, comes responsibility, and Mrs. Darling must take care of her husband as she does her children, tying his tie, giving him his medicine, and shoring up his fragile male ego when he thinks that the nurse, a Newfoundland dog, does not like him.

Barrie's fickle attitude toward Mrs. Darling is particularly clear in one of the final chapters, when the children return to the nursery. The narrator is at once contemptuous and loving of Mrs. Darling: "You see, the woman had no proper spirit. I had meant to say extraordinarily nice things about her; but I despise her, and not one of them will I say now" (208). Just a little while later, the narrator declares that he likes Mrs. Darling the best and whispers to her that her children are coming home in order to comfort her. He cannot help but love Mrs. Darling, but he despises how she loves her children without limit and how she welcomes her children back with open arms, despite their heartless behavior in forgetting her. In the final chapter of *Peter & Wendy*, an addition that was only performed once as part of the play, Barrie writes, "Mrs. Darling was now dead and forgotten" (221). Despite the centrality of motherhood in this story and the supposed importance of girls, Mrs. Darling, who was "the chief one" until Wendy was born, is forgotten by the end of the story (69). Barrie's depiction of Mrs. Darling makes her both powerful and powerless; although he does love her, he cannot respect her.

Morse offers the possibility that the entire story of the Darling children's adventures in Neverland might be a dream had by Mrs. Darling. Morse argues that Wendy and Peter represent Mrs. Darling's own divided self and her discomfort with her role of wife and mother. Wendy symbolizes the part of her that wishes to grow up and be a mother, while Peter represents the portion of Mrs. Darling's self that wishes to stay young and childish. In this reading, Wendy is the proper Victorian female, welcoming her role as matriarchal center of domestic life. She wants nothing more than cooking, cleaning, mending, and otherwise caring for her brood of boys. In showing that Mrs. Darling is uncomfortable with society's expectations of her, however, Morse argues that Barrie displays an understanding of the pressures of womanhood in Victorian and Edwardian society. She posits that the lack of overt rebellion on the part of Mrs. Darling made those sympathies less intrusive to his audience. Indeed, Morse labels Barrie's work "rich, imaginative, and pro-feminist" (300). While Barrie's story does indicate an understanding of the pressures of femininity, the alternate versions of womanhood that he offers allow even less freedom and power.

Tinker Bell's position as sexualized female in the context of Neverland makes her representative of another type of womanhood, different from Mrs. Darling's position in the frame story. She represents the working class woman. Christine Roth writes in "Babes in Boy-Land: J.M. Barrie and the Edwardian Girl" that middle class women were considered pure and girlish, while working class women were immediately sexualized in Victorian culture. When she first enters the story, her sexuality is in the foreground: "It was a girl called Tinker Bell exquisitely gowned in a skeleton leaf, cut low and square, through which her figure could be seen to the best advantage" (88). Peter says of Tink, "She is quite a common fairy ... she is called Tinker Bell because she mends the pots and kettles," immediately explaining Tink's class standing to Wendy (94). Tink's use of coarse language further differentiates her from the middle-class world from which Wendy hails. She is openly jealous of Wendy, indicating a romantic, sexual desire for Peter that is quite at odds with his appearance as the little boy who never grew up. While Wendy is still a little girl, and Peter describes Tink as a girl, the narrator writes, "[Wendy] did not yet know that Tink hated her with the fierce hatred of a very woman" (111). Tink signifies a wilder, freer womanhood than Wendy has seen in the person of her mother, but Tink has only limited powers. She does not rule over the Lost Boys as Wendy does, and she is never given even the ghost of respect that Peter pays to Wendy. Therefore, Tinker Bell is displaced as a role model for female readers by her class standing and sexuality.

Tiger Lily also provides a limited portrayal of womanhood, for she is separated by her race. Princess of the "Piccaninny" tribe, she is brave and strong, but beautiful and wild: "She is the most beautiful of dusky Dianas and the belle of the Piccaninnies, coquettish, cold and amorous by turns; there is not a brave who would not have the wayward thing to wife, but she staves off the altar with a hatchet" (116). Interestingly, Tiger Lily is not interested in wifehood and motherhood at all, and her interest in Peter is less straightforward than that of Tinker Bell or Wendy. After Peter saves Tiger Lily from Captain Hook, she and her braves guard the home of Peter and the Lost Boys in repayment. At first, this regard seems to be from one warrior to another, but a conversation between Peter and Wendy further illuminates Tiger Lily's interest in Peter. Peter says, "You are so queer ... and Tiger Lily is just the same. There is something she wants to be to me, but she says it is not my mother" (162). All three girls, Tinker Bell, Tiger Lily, and Wendy, want Peter to grow up and be a romantic figure to them, but he cannot. Tinker Bell and Tiger Lily do not wish to be wives and mothers, but they are outsiders to the Victorian family recreated in Neverland, kept in the margins by their class and race. Wendy, on the other hand, occupies the strongest position for a woman, but ultimately she is ruled by her role in Neverland society, restricted by her position as mother to the Lost Boys.

Wendy, the central female character, is only able to partake in the adventures of Neverland in a limited fashion, and she is never allowed to leave her gender behind. For Barrie, the ultimate adventure for a girl child is being a pretend mother to seven little boys, rather than fighting with pirates or hunting for bears. As the Darling children settle in to their lives in Neverland, the narrator comments, "I suppose it was all especially entrancing to Wendy, because those rampagious boys of hers gave her so much to do. Really there were whole weeks when, except perhaps with a stocking in the evening, she was never above ground. The cooking, I can tell you, kept her nose to the pot" (135). Wendy's greatest adventure is going above ground while darning a sock. Even when all of the Lost Boys go swimming, Wendy watches over them, sewing while they nap.

After the children are captured by pirates, they are taken aboard their ship, the *Jolly Roger*. While the boys are tempted by the pirate life, Wendy can only see that the ship is filthy: "There was not a port-hole on the grimy glass of which you might not have written with your finger, 'Dirty pig'; and she had already written it on several" (192). Wendy is so completely taken over by her role as mother that she has forgotten how to be a little girl. She is not fascinated by the strange world she is seeing; she is only concerned about proper order and cleanliness.

Peter, of course, saves Wendy and the Lost Boys from Captain Hook. Throughout the battle, one of the Lost Boys keeps count of the dead pirates and the others rush about, helping Peter. Barrie writes, "Wendy, of course, had stood by taking no part in the fight, though watching Peter with glistening eyes; but now that all was over she became prominent again. She praised them equally, and shuddered delightfully when Michael showed her the place where he had killed one" (204–05). Michael, who has slept in a basket and pretended to be Wendy's baby, has killed a pirate, while Wendy, who is older than both John and Michael, has stood by and watched others have adventures. Her "prominence" is fleeting and takes the form of complimenting the boys on their bravery.

In a note on her story, "Lost Girls," Yolen comments that part of her inspiration stemmed from a belief that Wendy was having no fun at all in Neverland, despite the raucous adventures that the boys were having (*Sister Emily's Lightship* 292). Yolen's story begins at bedtime, with our heroine, Darla, being read *Peter Pan*. Immediately, Yolen conveys to the reader that this story is meant to be taken as a fairy tale, the sort read to children at bedtime. Darla is incensed that Wendy must cook and clean while the boys get to fight pirates, and she fumes about unfairness. Darla's complaint transports her to the world of Neverland and the Lost Boys, where she finds an entire group of Wendys, all girls who were transported to Neverland the same way she was. Almost immediately, the realities of the world of Peter Pan become evident. Darla notices some of the practical details that upset the golden vision of paradise without parents that Peter presents. The path to Peter's home smells of "moldy old leaves, " and the tree that leads to their home smells like Darla's grandmother's wardrobe, "musty and ancient" (134). The boys all smell like unwashed socks, and they're all badly behaved.

Darla is a sympathetic character who illustrates the ambivalent attitudes many women have toward their traditional role as caretaker, as well as their attitudes toward men; Darla is both attracted to and repelled by Peter. She recognizes Peter by his outfit of green tights, shirt, and hat, his smell of lavender, and his perfect, movie star lips. Contradicting the image, though, is Darla's confused reaction: "Darla wasn't sure she liked Peter. Of course, she wasn't sure she *didn't* like him" (134). Peter is charming and handsome, but there's something about him that repels Darla as well.

Her initial meeting with Peter follows the established pattern; he bows gallantly and asks for a thimble. Darla recognizes the ploy and answers that she has no thimble. Peter asks if he can give her one instead, and she does not answer, choosing instead to study her feet. The kiss, as in a marriage ceremony, symbolizes a contract, one that Darla isn't sure she wants to enter into. Her refusal to give him a thimble is also a refusal of her role as Wendy, but Peter ignores her and takes her to his home under the tree. To her surprise, Peter declares to the Lost Boys that Darla has given him a thimble, effectively cementing her place in the society in Neverland, despite the fact that she did not willingly enter the agreement. He perpetuates the myth of the happily serving Wendy through a bald-faced lie; he only wanted to make Darla think she had a choice in the matter by asking her for the thimble in the first place. Darla's protest is lost in the celebrations of the Lost Boys, and Peter calls for a Welcome Feast.

The Welcome Feast is prepared by a group of girls that Peter refers to as the Wendys. They are treated as servants, not as the worshipped Feminine. When Peter introduces Darla as a new Wendy, she declares that her name is Darla. Yolen writes, "Peter looked at her, and there was nothing nice or laughing or young about his eyes. They were dark and cold and very old. Darla shivered. '*Here* you're a Wendy,' he said" (137). The coldness of Peter's eyes is the underlying coldness of Victorian standards of gender. While Peter and the others celebrate Darla's arrival, beneath the welcome is the harsh reality that Darla cannot refuse to take up her prescribed role, anymore than a woman could refuse her place in Victorian society without considerable cost to herself. After the Feast, which ends in a food fight, Darla is left with the others to clean, her time in the spotlight over. Darla immediately protests but eventually helps the other girls clean up, doing her job after all.

Yolen's imagery of the house underground constantly recalls prisons and schools. Darla describes the clothing of the chief Wendy as similar to "a school uniform that's badly stained" (13). After cleaning up the remnants of the food fight, "the place smelled like any institution after a cleaning, like a school bathroom or a hospital corridor, Lysol-fresh with an overcast of pine" (140). The kitchen is not much better, although the girls have tried to decorate the room with signs and dolls and have filled the kitchen with the smells of baking. Instead of a haven of freedom and excitement, the home of the Lost Boys is institutional, a place of limitation and incarceration.

Darla is relieved to find that the girls do indeed have their own names; only the first girl who came to Neverland is really named Wendy. When Darla asks why Peter calls them all Wendy, the real Wendy answers, "Because he can't be bothered remembering" (142). In Barrie's original, Peter forgets that Wendy exists altogether. When Wendy reminds him of her presence, he is contrite: "I say, Wendy," he whispered to her, "always if you see me forgetting you, just keep on saying 'I'm Wendy,' and then I'll remember" (Barrie 104–05). Names are very important; each girl's name establishes her individuality and her difference from the others. However, Yolen's Peter can't be bothered to remember their names any more than he can be bothered to remember the differences among the girls. Symbolically and practically, Peter sees no difference between one girl and another; they are all commodities, able to be easily exchanged. Later in the story, when the girls leave Peter, one of the Lost Boys asks what they will do without the girls. Peter answers, "Don't worry. There are always more Wendys where they came from" (153). This attitude parallels a mind-set under patriarchy that women are all the same, all equally able to cook, clean, and bear children. Women are not individuals with distinct personalities; they are embodiments of the Eternal Feminine. In Barrie's story, Wendy is eventually replaced by her daughter, Jane, and then her granddaughter, Margaret; the switch makes no difference to Peter.

The real Wendy of Yolen's story, the first girl to come to Peter, upholds the myth of gender roles almost as strongly as Peter does. When Darla rebels against the rules, Wendy excludes her from the group, smiling all the while. Darla thinks that Wendy is "as much of a bully as Peter, only in a softer, sneakier way" (143). Darla is disgusted by the weak femininity displayed by the girls when the signal is given that the pirates are nearby. The girls grab kitchen utensils for defense and then claim that they were scared silly when the all clear is given and the boys return, at which point Darla exposes the ridiculousness of the situation by pointing out that they would not really be able to do anything to the pirates with soup ladles and sugar tongs. Everyone is stunned by the idea that Darla thought that the girls were really expected to do anything. Darla's twentieth century assumption that girls are capable of action jars the Victorian sensibilities around her, reminding readers of how Wendy stood by during the big final battle with Hook in Barrie's original story.

Over tea, Darla explains what oppression is, and the Lost Girls slowly begin to voice their complaints about their lives in Neverland. Wendy responds, "After all Peter has done for you, taking you in when no one else wanted you, when you had been tossed aside by the world, when you'd been crushed and corrupted and canceled. How *could* you?" (148). Wendy's sentiments echo the idea that women are lucky to find good husbands who will take care of them. The girls ignore Wendy's plea and organize a strike, complete with signs and a chant.

The boys return and confront the girls, who ask only to be treated as equals. Seeing one of the signs that reads, "Wendys won't work," Peter protests, "Why, Neverland counts on the Wendys working. And I count on it, too. You Wendys are the most important of what we have made here" (150), voicing sentiments used to pacify women over and over again across generations: you are valuable, and we need you. While the girls chant for equality, Tink, clearly on Peter's side, buzzes around Wendy's head "flickering on and off and on angrily" (151). Peter issues the ultimate challenge, telling the girls that Captain Hook and his entire crew wait outside, and if they want to be equal, then they can face the pirates. The girls rush up the holes to face the pirates, despite the fact that Darla thought a compromise might be reached. Peter and Darla are surprised by the conviction of the girls, who are quickly captured by the pirates and taken back to the ship.

Aside from Darla's rebellion, the most substantial change in the story regards the nature of the pirates. Contrary to Barrie's pirates, Yolen's pirates represent an ideal world. There is no one patriarchal Captain Hook; instead, a husband and wife administer the ship together. The chores are done in rotation, with everyone taking a turn at the cooking and cleaning. Mrs. Hook introduces herself by several names, including Mother Jane, Pirate Lil, and The Pirate Queen, all strong women in tales (154). She explains that "a pirate ship is a very democratic place" (155), an historically accurate assertion supported by James Nelson. In the History Channel's *True Caribbean Pirates*, Nelson comments, "A pirate ship was really a pure democracy, and it was arguably the only real democracy in all of the Western world at that time." The pirates have been snatching girls up before Peter finds them for years; apparently, girls have been arriving in Neverland continuously, but the pirates are usually able to intervene in time.

Peter is the real evil in Yolen's revision, taking young girls and enslaving them to Victorian femininity. He reinforces cultural norms under the guise of escape. The pirates are the true rebels, not Peter. Although Barrie saw Peter as one who sought to escape the confines of society, in Yolen's story, Peter is the patriarchy, the enforcer of those rigid rules. The pirates, fighting against Peter, represent equality, stealing away girls and introducing them to healthy food and shared labor. Yolen effectively hijacks Barrie's story and returns the bourgeois fairy tale meant to reinforce conservative societal norms to its folk tale origins meant to inspire change. Yolen's story is of the truly oppressed of Victorian times, girls of mostly working class origins, and it restores the revolutionary and emancipatory nature of the tale. This tale comes from the folk and represents their needs and desires, a refashioning of society to improve their lives, meeting Zipes's definition of a folk tale.

Throughout Yolen's revisioning of the tale, she shatters the ideal with the real and grounds the fairy tale in a reality familiar to many young readers, while still maintaining the fantastic nature of the original tale. She presents a fantasy world fashioned over real, everyday life, just as the original story did, and she brings feminism into that fantastical-real world as a basic right, a message that still bears repeating today.

Works Cited

Barrie, J.M. *Peter Pan in Kensington Gardens; Peter and Wendy*. Oxford: Oxford University Press, 1999.

Gilbert, Sandra M., and Susan Gubar. *The Madwoman in the Attic: The Woman Writer and the Nineteenth-Century Literary Imagination*. 2d ed. New Haven: Yale University Press, 1979.

Haase, Donald. "Feminist Fairy-Tale Scholarship." *Fairy Tales and Feminism — New Approaches*. Detroit: Wayne State University Press, 2004. 1–36.

Morse, M. Joy. "The Kiss: Female Sexuality and Power in J.M. Barrie's *Peter Pan*." *J.M. Barrie's* Peter Pan *In and Out of Time: A Children's Classic at 100*. Ed. Donna R. White and C. Anita Tarr. Lanham, MD: Scarecrow Press, 2006. 281–302.

Roth, Christine. "Babes in Boy-Land: J.M. Barrie and the Edwardian Girl." *J.M. Barrie's* Peter Pan *In and Out of Time: A Children's Classic at 100*. Ed. Donna R. White and C. Anita Tarr. Lanham, MD: Scarecrow Press, 2006. 47–67.

True Caribbean Pirates. Dir. Tim Prokop. The History Channel. 26 Sept. 2006.

Wilson, Ann. "Hauntings: Anxiety, Technology, and Gender in *Peter Pan*." *Modern Drama* 43 (2000): 595–610.

Yolen, Jane. *Not One Damsel in Distress: World Folktales for Strong Girls*. New York: Harcourt, 2000.

_____. *Sister Emily's Lightship and Other Stories*. New York: Tor, 2000.

_____. *Touch Magic: Fantasy, Faerie, and Folklore in the Literature of Childhood.* Expanded ed. New York: Philomel Books, 2000.
_____. *Twelve Impossible Things Before Breakfast.* New York: Harcourt Brace, 1997.
Zipes, Jack. *Breaking the Spell: Radical Theories of Folk and Fairy Tales.* Austin: University of Texas Press, 1979.

Inventions and Transformations
Imagining New Worlds in the
Stories of Neil Gaiman

MATHILDA SLABBERT

The fairy tale tradition and contemporary reinventions have "always been a female genre" (Renk 615). Although men such as the Grimm Brothers, Andersen and Perrault recorded and rewrote some of the "contes de fées" originally told and written by women in the French Salons, postmodernist recreations are largely the work of contemporary female writers, such as Anne Sexton, Angela Carter, A.S. Byatt, Margaret Atwood and Jeanette Winterson. The tales recorded by men like Perrault and the Grimm Brothers, the stories with which most of us are familiar since childhood, are often revisions of the oral tales that originated from various geographical and cultural sources. Because parents started reading these tales to their children, much of the content was regarded as unsuitable and the content was revised and transformed, and as Neil Gaiman observes, cleaned up with added "little morals" (*Stardust* interview) which contain particular suggestions about gender roles, focusing especially on how women should behave sexually in a patriarchal society. In *The Fiction of Rushdie, Barnes, Winterson and Carter*, Gregory Rubinson clarifies this point in his discussion of Angela Carter's pioneering contribution to the genre and her re-visioning of fairy tale conventions for feminist purposes: "Because written literary traditions historically have been shaped and institutionalized by men, women writers have had to respond to literary forms that carry an androcentric bias— forms that have traditionally, often subtly, helped subordinate women to men" (149).

The strategy to rewrite and retell stories from any genre and to address cultural practices and issues in contemporary society is of course not limited to fairy tale revisions or to female writers. Many male authors such as Gregory Maguire, Donald Barthelme, Robert Coover, Kurt Vonnegut and Robert Bly have produced reinventions that contribute to the postmodern fairy tale genre, and many postmodernist authors have reworked fairy tale plots, settings, characters and motifs (Smith, *The Postmodern Fairytale*). Additionally, Neil Gaiman's creative contributions to the postmodern fairy tale genre warrant some attention. In his introduction to *Hanging Out with the Dream King*, Joseph McCabe writes:

> Neil Gaiman's stories have always crossed boundaries. The boundaries between life and death, between reality and dream, between male and female, and between humans and gods. And the forms these stories take refuse to adhere to any strict boundaries of genre or medium. If an idea doesn't quite work in one medium, Gaiman does not abandon it like an unwanted child, but instead lifts it up and carefully examines it to see if it could work in another — be it a comic book, a movie, a novel, a short story, a poem, or a song [1].

Because of his wide range of mediums and the overlapping of these with various genres, I have selected only three texts for the purpose of this discussion. The aim is to establish and validate Gaiman's contribution to the postmodern fairy tale genre which was previously regarded as the domain of women writers and the platform for feminist commentary. Gaiman's narratives transcend previous conventions and subtly enhance contemporary concerns that are not only linked to female "liberation and metamorphosis" and "the histories of women's lives" (Renk 616) but without ignoring these. He incorporates, invents and reinvents folklore[1] motifs in his work, often linking mysterious worlds and settings through the device of fantasy.

Neil Gaiman began his career as a journalist and then proceeded to write comics and graphic novels, a genre in which he is most known for the brilliant *The Sandman* series. In 1990 he collaborated with Terry Pratchett and they produced the mirthful and entertaining novel *Good Omens*. *Neverwhere* (1996) was Gaiman's first independent novel and was soon followed by *Stardust* (1999), the epic meta-mythology[2] *American Gods* (2001) and *Anansi Boys* (2005). He has won numerous awards, including the Hugo Award for his children's book *Coraline*. *The Day I Swapped My Dad for Two Goldfish* and *The Wolves in the Wall* reached the *New York Times* best selling list for children's books. Gaiman also wrote the film script for *Mirror Mask*, co-wrote the screenplay for *Beowulf* with Roger Avary and published two short story collections, *Smoke and Mirrors* (1999) and *Fragile Things* (2006).

My reading proceeds from Gaiman's novella, *Stardust*, to two selected short stories from *Smoke and Mirrors* for two reasons: a tale set in Faerie should be the obvious starting point, and these texts deal more directly with fables or fairy tale revisions than other selections by Gaiman. In an interview in *Stardust*, Gaiman observes that "Faerie is the perfect metaphor for a lot of places, and for a lot of things and a lot of ideas"; describing fairy tales as "transmissible," he suggests that "you can catch them, or be infected by them. They are the currency that we share with those who walked the world before ever we were here."[3] I shall investigate the manner in which Gaiman adheres to or subverts original models to reconstruct and deconstruct attitudes surrounding a sense of identity, gender roles, concepts of good and evil, commodification, loneliness and isolation.

Stardust *and the Quest Myth*

Stardust, also available as an illustrated novel,[4] is set in the late nineteenth century and draws fundamentally on the Arthurian legend of Tristan, one of the Knights of the Round Table, to convey Tristan Thorn's quest to locate a falling star for the girl he falls in love with, ironically called Victoria Forester (although she never ventures outside the confines of Wall). Gaiman harnesses the conventional journey motif and quest tale to transport Tristan from the realistic Victorian setting of the village Wall to the enchanted and magical world of Faerie with its range of fairy tale characters such as witches, spirits of dead lords, a unicorn, gnomes, and the star girl Yvaine. Although the novella deals with a hero's quest, it is the female characters and their experiences that propel the action forward. Besides Victoria who sends Tristan on his quest and the fallen star, Yvaine, who is the metaphorical grail, events are guided by the wicked witches and their desire to obtain Yvaine's heart for rejuvenation and longevity. Included in the range of female characters is Tristan's biological mother from Faerie who was transformed into a bird by Madame Semele (18) and is later revealed to be Lady Una of Stormhold (187). Together these female characters are representative of the virgin, the mother and the old crone, prominent in many ancient mythologies and representative of the three feminine stages.

The structure and action of the narrative adhere to the main functions of the folktale as identified by Vladimir Propp in *The Morphology of the Folktale* and the stages associated with the rites of passage constructed by Joseph Campbell which parallel the stages of life, namely "leaving home, benefiting from supernatural help, overcoming obstacles as a sort of initiation, acquiring magical powers and strength, and returning home" (qtd. in Meletinsky 49), or as is the case in many fairy tales, living somewhere new. Although the reader is conscious of Tristan's origins after Dunstan's (his father's) brief relationship with the dark-haired girl at the Faerie Market, his journey reveals his true identity to him — hybrid, half-human and half-faerie, he is the heir to the throne of Stormhold who eventually marries the star which he ventured out to locate for Victoria.

In true postmodern idiom, Gaiman does not leave the reader satisfied with a traditional "and-they-lived-happily-ever-after" ending and neither does he present Tristan as Prince Charming to whom Yvaine succumbs immediately on introduction. In the Epilogue, subtitled "In Which Several Endings May Be Discerned," he hints at the reality of life's and love's endurances with the remark

"Tristan and Yvaine were happy together. Not forever-after, for Time, the thief, eventually takes all things into his dusty storehouse..." (193); this reflects on Madame Semele's earlier remark that Tristan will break Yvaine's heart, "or waste it, or lose it. They all do that" (189). The inclusive use of "they all" seems to be a stereotypical view and criticism of male behavior, but by extension the remark reflects on women's ideals based on traditional fairy tale elements which celebrate the notion that romantic unions will last forever.

At face value, *Stardust* seems a sweet and innocent tale about a boy who falls in love, goes on a journey, realizes his folly or misplaced love, then finally settles down with his newfound love in a fantasy fairyland, but Gaiman skilfully embeds serious contemplations in the seemingly innocent tale. The Lilim's obsession with youthful appearances, beauty and longevity is a subtle reflection on women's vanity and fear of aging. The fact that their fate depends on consuming the heart of another, younger female (54), and the lack of sexual innuendos aimed at the opposite sex, suggest that their yearning for beauty and longevity is not based on male objectification, but is motivated by selfish and competitive desires among themselves. The two old "crones" are described as staring at the younger witch's "naked body" with hunger and "envy" (53–54). Both genders argue that women generally dress, apply cosmetics and go to often painful and bizarre extremes to look beautiful, young and groomed, not only to please the male gaze but rather to comply with the female gaze. Such effects are often achieved at the expense of other women and selfish and insensitive actions that figuratively "devour the heart' of another woman. Furthermore, Madame Semele's and Yvaine's ponderings on the erosive power of time on love and life commentate on women's plight when sacrificing their freedom and creative purpose for love.

Tristan first holds the injured Yvaine captive by tying her to him with a magic silver chain. The traditional subservience of the female to the male hero is underplayed by Tristan's use of a delicate silver chain, suggestive of jewellery, but yet a tool which entraps her and forces her submission. The presence of the chain and the suggestion of male dominance are ironically emphasized by Yvaine's inability to escape; even without the chain, she has broken her leg. When Tristan finally realizes that he loves Yvaine and not Victoria and discovers his true heritage, Yvaine explains that the union will "probably" be childless (184), acknowledging the physical and creative unproductiveness that will exist as a result of their unnatural union. Yvaine (in vain) can never return to her position as star in the sky and her longing is evident when in Stormhold she takes "rooms in the highest peaks of the citadel ... open to the sky, and the stars and the moon" (193). After Tristan's death we read that at night "she climbs, on foot, and limps, alone, to the highest peak of the palace, where she stands for hour after hour, seeming not to notice the cold peak winds. She says nothing at all, but simply stares upward into the dark sky and watches, with sad eyes, the slow dance of the infinite stars" (194). The dominant female agency of the story is underscored by the fact that Tristan's character is terminated with three words, "[a]fter Tristan's death," while the reader is left with Yvaine who still gleams (194) occasionally. Tristan dies, but Yvaine, the star, maintains her essence and ability to glitter.

What is most significant about the novella is the inclusion of a short story that never appeared in the illustrated novel. Entitled "*Wall*: A Prologue"[5] Gaiman adds a seemingly disconnected short story initially set in 1963 presenting the character Jenny, who on the day before her thirteenth birthday experiences a magical encounter with seven magpies and whose first menarche consequently occurs. The only similarity between the story and the novella is the title and the fact that the magpie tells her "'You're going to Wall ... it's a secret...'"; also, the pub in *Stardust*'s Wall is called the *Seventh Magpie*. In the context of *Stardust* Wall is representative of Victorian reality and, by implication, puritanical and patriarchal values and ideologies. The significance and meaning of the short story seems to be contained in the last two paragraphs:

> Jenny Kerton never forgot that day. Although, as time went on, the time in the bathroom, and her mother's explanation, and the fitting of the sanitary pad, and the bitter taste of aspirin her mother dissolved in a glass of water for her, gradually took prominence over the event that preceded them. And after thirty years had passed, all that remained in her memory was the sheen of green and violet on a magpie's wings....

Gaiman suggests that growing up is unpleasant, associated with discomfort, loss of innocence, pain and bitterness, emphasizing the importance of the ability to fantasize. Jenny's pondering confirms this transformation: "It's the dividing line. I'm not a little girl any more." Without imagination and magic, reality seems starkly black and white; seen "up close," however, it reveals a magnificent world like the truly beautiful colours of the birds' feathers, a gloss of bluish-green.

The arrival of Jenny's menarche indicates sexual maturity and fertility which supplants the fantastical encounter with the birds: "[t]he magic was over," she now feels "sick" (Gaiman, "Wall"). The reference to the passage of time further hints at middle age and the approach of menopause. It poses the question: when the fertility cycle ends, what remains? The short story and novella suggest that physical fertility and sexuality (marriage or romantic unions) should not replace creative or imaginative productivity. This theme is prominent in many postmodernist fairy tales by female authors and most remarkably addressed in A.S. Byatt's *The Djinn in the Nightingale's Eye*.

The feminine agency of *Stardust* is confirmed by Gaiman in his claim that "[b]ooks have sexes; or to be more precise, books have genders. They do in my head, anyway," adding that "*Stardust* ... is a girl's book, even though it also has an everyman hero..." ("All Books"). But as McCabe observes, Gaiman's stories "refuse to adhere to any strict boundaries of genre or medium" (1). Gaiman illustrates this ability in his revision of "The Three Billy Goats Gruff." If *Star-*

dust has a predominantly feminine agency, then one could argue that by contrast, "Troll Bridge" is a story with a predominantly masculine agency which not only challenges the conventional concepts of masculinity but further explores and investigates social constructs of contemporary society.

Facing the "Other" in "Troll Bridge"

"Troll Bridge" draws on and alludes to the tale of "The Three Billy Goats Gruff."[6] In Kevin Smith's insightful text *The Postmodern Fairytale: Folkloric Intertexts in Contemporary Fiction*, he identifies eight types of intertextuality or categories "in which the fairytale can operate as an intertext within mass-produced fiction," namely:

1. Authorised: Explicit reference to a fairytale in the title
2. Writerly: Implicit reference to a fairytale in the title
3. Incorporation: Explicit reference to a fairytale within the text
4. Allusion: Implicit reference to a fairytale within the text
5. Re-vision: putting a new spin on an old tale
6. Fabulation: crafting an original fairytale
7. Metafictional: discussion of fairytales
8. Archtextual/Chronotopic: "Fairytale" setting/environment [10].

He further explains that one or more of these categories can be present in a tale. At least four of these elements apply to "Troll Bridge," yet in Gaiman's revision of the old tale, he breaks away from the traditional narrative by replacing the three goats with one man named Jack, poised at different stages and ages in his life. At each stage Jack confronts a troll who wants to "eat [his] life" (62). Original renditions of the tale are didactic in nature with a moral lesson which warns the reader or listener against the dangers of greed and gluttony. Gaiman's narrative maintains certain motifs, but is non-didactic and contains an ontological inquiry.

The initial setting is evoked in lush and descriptive imagery with recurring references to light or "daylight" (Gaiman, "Troll Bridge" 60), suggestive of the young boy's innocence and ability to fantasize and dream. Environmental deterioration and the protagonist's physical and emotional decline become evident as the story proceeds and variations on "darkness" (65) become more prominent. Despite the enchanting semi-pastoral descriptions at the story's onset, imagery such as the "weed-clogged ornamental pond" (60) hint at urbanization, technological development and commodification, further emphasised by the repetitive metaphoric references to trains, railway lines and stations. These images foreshadow the gradual erosion of the narrator's sense of identity and his increasing sense of dislocation and isolation in a world of displacement.

The first-person narrator, Jack, remembers how in his childhood the train that passed their Victorian house appeared to be a "panting ... iron dragon" (Gaiman, "Troll Bridge" 59), rushing through the surrounding open fields. By the age of seven the railway lines were quiet, the house was sold and new "small and square" (68) dwellings crammed the meadows and garden. Towards the end Jack, now married and a father, commutes to London where he keeps a "small" apartment (67). These references indicate the impact of urbanization and are symbolic denotations to Jack's gradually diminishing figurative and imaginary world.

The young Jack's adventurous journeys into the hills and forests contain descriptions of flourishing trees, filtered with golden sunlight (Gaiman, "Troll Bridge" 60), trees which later appear "skeletal black against the harsh grey winter sky" (67). The spatial constriction from a rural to urban setting and the transformation of the nature imagery coincide with Jack's moral and emotional decline and parallels the shift from utopian to dystopian space and place. Although he is married and his family live in the country, the flat in the city provides Jack with the opportunity to frequent venues where he can view and review bands that perform late at night and pursue his adulterous endeavours to "get laid" (67). As a result he loses everything that is dear, including his wife, Eleanora, whom he nonchalantly refers to as someone "I should have mentioned ... before" (67). Jack's behavior towards his wife, ironically, confirms Madame Semele's rather stereotypical assumption in *Stardust* that "all" men eventually break their partners' hearts. But Gaiman does not leave us to gloat long in the confirmation of suspected sexually promiscuous masculine behavior as Jack's feelings of loneliness gradually become more apparent and his subsequent identity crisis stirs the reader's compassion.

It is during one of his solitary wanderings after his separation that Jack rediscovers the train bridge under which he encountered the troll previously. He recalls how, as a child, he experienced this space as "*anywhere*" and "nowhere" (Gaiman, "Troll Bridge" 61), an imaginary world with endless possibilities. He now meets the troll for the third and final time, confirming his childhood notion that the troll is a metaphorical representation of "all [his] nightmares given flesh" (62). This fantastical manifestation of his life's destructive forces, desires and fears is Jack's "other," the dark and hidden side which threatened to devour the life he longed for.

The bridge is symbolic of the crossroads between reality and imagination, illusion and disillusion, expectation and resignation. As Byatt remarks, "The fairy-tale gives form and coherence to formless fears, dreads and desires. Recognising a fairy tale motif, or an ancient myth ... in the mess of a life lived or observed gives both pleasure and security and the sense, — or illusion — of wisdom" ("Fairy Stories"). The bridge becomes the space which ultimately reflects Jack's "polluted" existence, dirty and inscribed with sexual profanities and political slogans. The space like his personal life is soiled by the impact of commodification and sexual promiscuity, symbolically represented in the "single, sad, used condom..." (Gaiman, "Troll Bridge" 68).

Gaiman consistently juxtaposes reality (the empty house, the dirty depressing city and suburbs) and magic (the forest and reference to witches, ghosts and fairyland), reinforcing the child's innocent ability to fantasize and imagine in contrast to the adult narrator's defeated and disenchanted consciousness. There is no shock or fear evident when the boy meets the troll for the first time ("Troll Bridge" 62), but he becomes more fearful and anxious as the years elapse. During the final encounter Jack offers himself to the troll — or to his "nightmare"— to remain behind in the "shadows" and the "darkness" (70) under the bridge, isolated and alone. The troll who initially seemed threatening, grotesque and dangerous now stands before Jack "trembling," meekly allowing him to hold his "clawed paw" (69). Both seem frightened. The fear and loneliness evident in both the protagonist and the fantastical manifestation of his alter ego are not elements associated with the traditional, stereotypical and archetypal male, but rather are linked to femininity. Thus Gaiman succeeds in blurring the boundaries between conventional gender roles in fairy tales and instead commentates on the impact of capitalist culture, greed, and the general effects of a chaotic and dystopian world on the psyche of the contemporary male. The description of Jack's final resignation to the troll is paradoxically tender, yet sad and contains erotic and homosexual innuendoes when amongst the trash, debris and used prophylactic, the troll "lower[s] himself on top of [Jack]" (69) and "eats" his life. Jack surrenders himself willingly and unlike the previous two encounters, he offers no resistance and voices no objections or desires. He embraces and succumbs to his "other" despite the fact that he admits never to reveal his submission and never to come out again (70). They have exchanged appearances, the troll inhabits Jack's "life comfortably" (69) while the latter listens to "*you*" all out there ... trip-trapping over [his] bridge" (70). The use of the personal pronoun "you" suggests the universality of Jack's struggle for identity and survival and hints that the implied reader similarly treads softly, "trip-trapping" over his or her darker characteristics in fear of having their lives devoured by issues they dread to confront.

Whereas in the original story, the biggest goat butts the troll off the bridge, the adult Jack in Gaiman's rendition becomes prey and surrenders to his "nightmares." The shadow side of the psyche is not defeated but is realized and self-acknowledged (Jung qtd. in Walker 34–35). Jack's ontological inquiry is fuelled by the loneliness of a life "overwhelmed by psychological turbulence and social meaninglessness" (Boggs 363), a life which has become stagnant amongst the frivolous, harsh and dehumanized constructions of contemporary consumer society. Gaiman uses fantasy to scrutinize the futility of such an existence and seems to question the validity of superficial pursuits, the pressures that undermine the contemporary (male) individual's sense of self and the powerful and often disturbing insights that come with self-realization and self-awareness.

Gaiman further undermines the fairy tale motifs of heroism and bravery when Jack emasculates himself by offering first his sister and then his adolescent girlfriend as trades so as not to be eaten by the troll. This cowardice is further underscored when he literally offers up his wife and child in a similar immature manner in search for additional self-gratification. The gender implications are underscored by Jack's witty yet hedonistic excuses to remain alive: to whistle, to fly, to have sex and to travel.

The reader is initially lulled into a false expectation that the protagonist might outwit the threatening troll every time. When Jack eventually offers himself to the troll, his self-sacrifice becomes an act of self-acknowledgement; he recognizes his own failures, desires and vulnerabilities but vows never to reveal these to the world. With the final exchange Gaiman employs another fairytale motif in ambiguous manner, namely, disguise. Arguably, he seems to suggest that inside every Jack (swaggering, perhaps lonely, potentially self-aware male) there is a troll (threatening though gullible male) and within every troll there is a Jack. Nevertheless, the male protagonist in "Troll Bridge" emerges at the end of the story as anything but the conventional masculine Billy or bully goat. Gaiman continues this notion of revising old tales in a rather unsettling manner in his re-invention of *Snow White*.

Stepmothers and Daughters: Transforming Perspectives in "Snow, Glass, Apples"

In "Snow, Glass, Apples," Gaiman's retelling of the Grimm Brothers' *Snow White*, he takes a refreshing narrative approach by describing events from the stepmother's perspective. Other than in "Troll Bridge," Gaiman's intertextual reference is here explicit in the title and within the tale (Smith 10). The narrative provides a platform from which Gaiman explores and questions good and evil binaries and gender roles so clearly defined in the original tale. He transforms and inverts the dichotomy of good and evil in most of his work.[8]

The extradiegetic or implied reader becomes the intradiegetic narratee, and here I draw on Smith's revised discussion of Gerard Genette's interpretation of "embedded narration" (89–90). The intradiegetic narratee and implied reader remain anonymous, yet are identified as participating characters. At the outset, the queen uses the pronouns "I" and "us" in combination with the comparative "none" when she introduces the character of Snow White, "I do not know what manner of thing she is. None of us do" (Gaiman, "Snow" 371). This suggests that the reader might, by implication, be an accomplice to the action, a notion which becomes a source of discomfort as the queen proceeds with her tale. Furthermore, by presenting the reader with a narrator who acknowledges her shortcomings and claims to be neither wise (371) nor "innocent" (381) in her victimization, Gaiman allows the reader to accept her description of Snow

White as a cold, cruel and calculated character. Besides undermining the traditional view of Snow White as sweet, pure virgin, the narrative further destabilizes stereotypical and traditional biases towards the cruel stepmother, so prominent in many fairy tales. The princess becomes the wicked persona instrumental in the destruction of the royal couple's seemingly happy union and the overall moral and economic decline of not only the kingdom, but also the forest people and fairy folk that live outside the borders of the kingdom. In fact, none of the characters are represented as morally good or flawless; even the dwarfs are deformed (379) and corrupt and live off the income generated by Snow White's "depredations" (381).

Besides the stepmother and stepdaughter Gaiman retains much of the magic and many of the original motifs and elements present in the traditional story, such as the mirror, the apples, the glass coffin, the dwarfs and the prince, yet he inverts, changes and adds elements to traditional motifs to create an brutal world in the story. Most significantly, he steeps the story in violent and sexually perverted behavior to present a tale of great complexity which emphasizes the underlying violence and sexuality contained in the traditional tale.

The queen's tale reads very much like a confession or bearing witness before a court. She attempts to justify her seemingly involuntary involvement in the gruesome acts of vampirism, incest, murder, rape, necrophilia, bloody revenge and cannibalism by claiming that she would have committed suicide (Gaiman, "Snow" 371) had she seen her destiny in the magic mirror. The power invested in the mirror of the original tale is nullified by this lament, and I return to this point later. As further evidence of her abuse and inability to curb the princess' barbarous deeds, the queen claims she became fearful and powerless after Snow White's first vampire attack and that her retaliations hereafter were not successful in curbing the girl's cold-hearted, bloody deeds because the queen herself was not violent enough.

It is exactly this victimized attempt at portraying Snow White as the villain which undermines the queen's narrative authority. In her attempt to retell, she often invents. She admits her absence at certain events, her tendency to "imagine" (Gaiman, "Snow" 382) and her failure to know for certain what happened (383). These remarks illustrate her limited knowledge or insight into acts she did not witness (Lothe 26). Her personal involvement in the plot and her manner of imaginatively reconstructing events is clearly subjective and therefore renders her narration as unreliable despite her forceful and repeated claims to reliability. Her moral character is further undermined by her repeated egotistical references to herself as queen and coy remarks, such as "another monarch — myself, for instance" (Gaiman, "Snow" 381). She is clearly aware of her position of power, a position which Snow White as the sole offspring of the king and legal heir to the throne certainly threatens. Furthermore, her seemingly innocent descriptions of Snow White's cruel and sexually deviant nature often reveal something about her own sexual prowess and lustfulness. So, for example, when the young prince asks the queen to remove her clothes and simulate an act of necrophilia, she does not resist, but admits that she "match[ed] him, grind for grind, push for push" (382). Gaiman remodels both female characters into cunning sexual partners who shamelessly pursue their goals. As a result, both the king's and the prince's position of power and masculinity are undermined by the female characters' perverted sexual behavior.

The queen's lustful reaction to the prince's vulgar advances causes him to lose his erection (Gaiman, "Snow" 382). This physical act of rejection prompts the queen to embark on another imaginary re-invention, namely the first meeting between the prince and Snow White in "the glass-and-crystal cairn" (382). She imagines Snow White as the passive recipient of the prince's sexual advances and that it is this sexual passivity which gives her power over the queen and awards her the prince. This part of her vision renders the truth of her narrative the most questionable, for she does not witness events either in person or in the magic mirror and without evidence (as was the case with the scars on the king's body). Her own perverse thoughts are emphasized by her jealous range of questions: "Did he shake the apple from her throat? Or did her eyes slowly open as he pounded into her cold body; did her mouth open ... washing down ... my own, my poison?" (382–83). Her narrative suggests that she regrets her own sexual activity and the ambiguity contained in "my poison" confirms her jealousy. The sexual violence and perversity in her narrative reveals her own decadent nature.

Jealousy is a prominent motif in the original tale and Gaiman skilfully obscures the eminence of jealousy in his retelling. In a Grimm Brothers' rendition of the original tale, the queen's question: "'Looking-glass, looking-glass, on the wall, who in this land is the fairest of all?'" and the mirror's responses run like a refrain throughout the text and the stepmother is described as "a beautiful woman, but proud and haughty" ("Snow White"). Conversely, Gaiman's narrator never confirms or denies her own beauty or lack thereof. He omits the questions to the mirror and by so doing removes the deliberate narcissistic act. In underplaying the prominence of the mirror — the reflection of the self — in favor of "glass and quartz" (Gaiman, "Snow" 382) — transparency, Gaiman subverts the element of female objectification contained in the original story. His story instead emphasizes the same sex rivalry between the stepmother and daughter through the queen's repeated reference to age (the queen is only ten years older than Snow White) and her descriptions of the younger girl's features comply to the established iconography of Snow White: the hair black as coal, the lips as red as blood, the skin as white as snow. In the original text the queen refers to Snow White as "you paragon of beauty" (Grimm) but this mythification of Snow White in Gaiman's rendition is undermined when the queen describes her as a vampire with "sharp" fingernails ("Snow" 383) and teeth (372). This image is further enhanced by the "thin blackish liquid" (378) that dribbles down Snow White's legs when she fornicates vampirically with the monk, a symbol of her tarnished sexuality. Ironically, the queen omits any negative addendums to Snow White's appearance in the final sentence of the story and Gaiman hereby allows space for an individual interpretation by the implied reader. This technique confirms his remark in the interview at the end of the short story collection: "I'm going to show ["Snow White"] to you in a mirror so you've never seen it ... before. And you'll never be able to think of it in the same way ever again" (*Smoke and Mirrors*).

Gaiman skilfully employs the construct of implied reader in his representation of *Snow White*. Jakob Lothe explains that "the implied reader's activity is very much a structuring process in which we no least attempt to establish a connection between the text's 'blanks'" (19). Lothe clarifies the concept with reference to Wolfgang Iser's and Maclean's work:

> For Iser, the literary work arises through the interplay, the *interaction*, between text and reader. The implied reader, who enters into this interaction, is a "role" or "standpoint" which allows the (real) reader to assemble the meaning of the text (Maclean 131). The implied reader is thus both active and passive: active by making the text meaningful, passive since the premises of the text's production of meaning are given in its discourse and narration. The author has, according to Iser, a certain control of the way in which we read, but this form of control is indirect and based on shared conventions which have matured over time — repertoire of social, historical, and cultural norms regulating the manner in which fictional prose works and communicates. The meaning of a text arises in *productive tension* between the role or model reader the text presents and the historical reader's dispositions and interests [19].

This kind of productive tension is present from the onset of the story when we experience discomfort over why the stepmother is attempting to present us with a justification of her actions and involvement, emphasizing our struggle as historical reader with our knowledge of the original text. It is only towards the end of the story when we realize (with great horror) that the queen is actually recollecting events while she is being roasted alive in a kiln (covered in goose fat) that we are presented with a reason which further complicates our interaction with the current text.

The queen's ambiguous remark "They have told the people bad things about me ... mixed with many lies" (Gaiman, "Snow" 384), emphasizes the narrator's inability to distinguish between the truth and the lies and the reader's— who became one of "us" at the outset of the story — participation in constructing meaning through narrative interaction. Productive tension between text and reader is further heightened when the queen claims that her body might be destroyed, but her "soul" and "story" will "die" with her (384).

The brutality of roasting the queen alive is somewhat undermined when we recall the queen's confession at the beginning where she admits that she would have murdered and maimed Snow White in a similar fashion had she known the outcome (Gaiman, "Snow" 374). The admission establishes the stepmother's inferred capability of the exact same cruelty she is subjected to had the outcome been reversed. This realization is reinforced when we read that Snow White observes her stepmother's execution without expression and the queen admits she sees herself "reflected in [Snow White's] eyes" (384).

The cannibalistic intention suggested in the words "to add savour to the dish" (Gaiman, "Snow" 384) is another motif from the traditional story that Gaiman retains but transforms. The narrative hints at Snow White's and the prince's intention to roast and eat the queen, and as horrific as it might seem, the suggestion seems on par with the cruelty contained in the original story which ends along these lines: "But iron slippers had already been put upon the fire, and they were brought in with tongs, and set before her [the step mother]. Then she was forced to put on the red-hot shoes, and dance until she dropped down dead" (Grimm). In the original tale, the queen instructs the huntsman: "'Kill her, and bring me back her lung and liver as a token'" (Grimm). The huntsman deceives the queen by bringing her the organs of a young bear which "the wicked queen ate ... and she thought she had eaten the lung and liver of Snow White" (Grimm). Gaiman maintains the basic elements of the plot, but he changes the organs to a heart and the queen never admits to any form of cannibalism, but distinctly denies it: "Some say ... that I was given the heart, and that I ate it" but "I did not eat it" ("Snow" 375). Instead, she hangs it in her chamber to dry. The seasoning of the heart with garlic and apples (372), which she earlier admits is for winter when food is scarce (372), again forces one to question the reliability of her narration and her feigned morality as well as to contemplate the underlying violence contained in the original tale.

In addition, the violent and sexual nature of Gaiman's tale draws attention to the sexual undertones in the traditional story and thereby parodies the archetypal virginal behavior of the original Snow White. He undermines the traditional female objectification of Snow White and the heroic masculine behavior of the prince. As Gaiman says: "The prince comes along ... thinking, 'That girl in the coffin's really gorgeous—I'll take her back to my castle.' It's really kind of peculiar behaviour. And for that matter, what kind of a person gets to lie in a coffin for six months and get better? And have skin as white as snow, hair as black as coal and lips as red as roses?" (*Smoke and Mirrors*, interview). The reader is presented with a couple (Snow White and the prince) and a narrator whose sexually deviant behavior and brutalities are reminiscent of many similar couples and characters in postmodern cinematic productions.

"Snow, Glass, Apples" has a predominantly female agency with the male characters subjugated to lesser roles. They either succumb to the queen's or Snow White's desires for revenge and participate in the acts or they suffer as a result. For example, the young queen (sixteen years old) has pre-marital intercourse with the king at what she describes as "my cottage" (Gaiman 371)— note her independence — and although she describes him as an attractive man he never develops beyond the point of being her object with which she "take[s] pleasure" (372). Similarly, Snow White uses men such as her father, the monk, the dwarfs and the prince for the fulfilment of her own needs. This confirms Aytül Özüm's argument that "the representation of female evil in the reappropriation of the fairy tales saves the woman subject from being victimized in the traditionally acknowledged frameworks" (1). Instead of the prince carrying Snow White off on his horse, he stands by her side, watching the queen burn. The story illustrates the cultural shift in gender hierarchies evident in contemporary society and reflects on the notion that women are able to control men and can be sexually fierce in their pursuit of power.

Thus Gaiman holds a prominent position as postmodernist writer in the adult fairy tale genre not only because of his refreshing reinventions of "existing patterns" (Coelsch-Foisner, "A Body") but for the manner in which he addresses contemporary concerns and argues the significance of creativity and imagination as escapism through a blending of magic and realism. He incorporates transformed narrative perspectives, "the liberating power of fantasy" (Coelsch-Foisner, "A Body") and reshapes folklore motifs not only to challenge dominant ideologies surrounding society and gender, but to stimulate the reader's sense of the ontological. Gilmore writes that Gaiman's stories "hit home with a rare emotional force" and Gaiman himself explains that "'tales of myth and horror are probably the easiest and most effective way to talk about the real world. It's like they are the lies that tell the truth about our lives'" (*Black Orchid*, introduction). Gaiman's work confirms that postmodern literature continues to explore and to challenge the sense of self, cultural constructs and conventions, prominent ideologies and views about humanity. Paradoxically, his stories leave one with a sense of discomfort and pleasure, but always with a desire to read the next one.

Notes

1. I adhere to Heiner's definition that fairy tales, myths and legends are subgenres of folklore.

2. See my unpublished doctoral thesis, pp. 149–90.

3. The bonus material of *Stardust* contains an interview with Gaiman (pages unnumbered).

4. *Stardust* is now a feature film directed by Matthew Vaughn, starring Charlie Cox as Tristan and Claire Danes as Yvaine.

5. This short story is included in the bonus material of *Stardust* and its pages are unnumbered.

6. The original author of the tale is unknown, although variations containing the same motifs are present in Norwegian, Polish and German vernaculars. One German rendition of the folktale ("How the Goats Came to Hessen") contains a kid, a mother and a father goat, while the genders of the goats in the other tales are assumed to be male. The Norwegian folktale contains a troll and the other renditions contain a wolf (see Ashliman).

7. My italics.

8. In *Good Omens* Gaiman and Pratchett satirize Milton's *Paradise Lost* through the

humorous actions surrounding the supposedly evil angel, Crowley and the good angel, Aziraphale. Similarly, good and evil binaries are explored in Gaiman's other short stories from *Smoke and Mirrors*, such as "The End," which inverts the creation myth, and "Murder Mysteries," which is set in the Silver City before the creation of the universe.

Works Cited

Ashliman, D.L., trans. "How the Goats came to Hessen." *Folklore and Mythology Electronic Texts*. University of Pittsburgh. 14 June 2007 <*http://www.pitt.edu/~dash/type0122e.html*>.

_____. "The Three Billy Goats Gruff." *Folklore and Mythology Electronic Texts*. University of Pittsburgh. 14 June 2007 <*http://www.pitt.edu/~dash/type0122e.html*>.

_____. "The Three Goats." *Folklore and Mythology Electronic Texts*. University of Pittsburgh. 14 June 2007 <*http://www.pitt.edu/~dash/type0122e.html*>.

Boggs, Carl. "Postmodernism the Movie." *New Political Science* 23.3 (2001): 351–70.

Byatt, A.S. "Fairy Stories: The Djinn in the Nightingale's Eye." May 1995. 27 Aug. 2005 <*http://www.asbyatt.com/Onherself.aspx*>.

Coelsch-Foisner, Sabine. "A Body of Her Own: Cultural Constructions of the Female Body in A.S. Byatt's Strange Stories." *Reconstruction: Studies in Contemporary Culture* 3.4 (2003). 24 June 2006 <http://reconstruction.eserver.org/034/coelsch.htm>.

Gaiman, Neil. "All Books Have Genders." *Essays by Neil*. 23 Nov. 2008 <http://www.neil-gaiman.com/p/Cool_Stuff/Essays/Essays_By_Neil/All_Books_Have_Genders>.

_____. *Black Orchid*. New York: DC Comics, 1991.

_____. *Fragile Things*. London: Review, 2006.

_____. *Smoke and Mirrors*. London: Review, 2005.

_____. "Snow, Glass, Apples." *Smoke and Mirrors*. London: Review, 2005. 371–84.

_____. *Stardust*. London: Review, 1999.

_____. "Troll Bridge." *Smoke and Mirrors*. London: Review, 2005. 59–70.

Gilmore, Mikal. Introduction. *Black Orchid*. New York: DC Comics, 1991.

Grimm, Jacob, and Wilhelm Grimm. *Little Snow White*. Trans. Margaret Hunt. London: George Bell, 1884.

_____. *SurLaLune Fairy Tales*. Ed. Heidi Anne Heiner. 4 July 2007 <*http://www.surlalunefairytales.com/sevendwarfs/index.html*>.

Heiner, Heidi Anne. "What is a Fairy Tale?" 1999. *Sur La Lune Fairy Tales*. 26 July 2006 <*http://www.surlalunefairytales.com/introduction/ftdefinition.html*>.

Lothe, Jakob. *Narrative in Fiction and Film: An Introduction*. Oxford: Oxford University Press, 2000.

McCabe, Joseph. *Hanging Out with the Dream King*. Seattle: Fantagraphics Books, 2004.

Meletinsky, Eleazar M. *The Poetics of Myth*. Trans. by Guy Lanoue and Alexandre Sadetsky. London: Routledge, 2000.

Özüm, Aytül. "Deconstructed Masculine Evil in Angela Carter's *The Bloody Chamber* Stories." *Wickedness.Net*. 2006. 28 Aug. 2008 <*http://www.wickedness.net/Evil/Evil%208/ozum%20paper.pdf*>.

Propp, Vladimir. *The Morphology of the Folktale*. Austin: University of Texas Press, 1968.

Renk, Kathleen Williams. "A.S. Byatt, the Woman Artist, and Suttee." *Women's Studies* 33 (2004): 613–28.

Rubinson, Gregory J. *The Fiction of Rushdie, Barnes, Winterson and Carter: Breaking Cultural and Literary Boundaries in the Work of Four Postmodernists*. Jefferson, NC: McFarland, 2005.

Slabbert, Mathilda. "Inventions and Transformations: An Exploration of Mythification and Remythification in Four Contemporary Novels." Diss. University of South Africa, 2006. <http://etd.unisa.ac.za/ETD-db/theses/available/etd-09222006-104134/unrestricted/thesis.pdf>.

Smith, Kevin Paul. *The Postmodern Fairytale: Folkloric Intertexts in Contemporary Fiction*. New York: Palgrave Macmillan, 2007.

Walker, Steven F. *Jung and the Jungians on Myth*. New York: Routledge, 2002.

"And the Princess, Telling the Story"
A.S. Byatt's Self-Reflexive Fairy Stories

JEFFREY K. GIBSON

In an essay exploring the tradition of storytelling, A. S. Byatt writes, "I want to look at some of the ways in which these old tales and forms have had a continued, metamorphic life" (*On Histories* 124). While she focuses primarily upon classic literature such as Ovid's *Metamorphoses* and Boccaccio's *Decameron*, Byatt clearly includes fairy tales within this same tradition. Byatt herself actively participates in the perpetuation of these cultural forms, and not simply as a commentator on the history and tradition. Her critical ruminations on storytelling extend to her own short fiction, fairy stories that perhaps serve as even more significant examples of her recuperation of a tradition that has been marginalized for quite some time by prescriptive modernist aesthetics. As Kathleen Williams Renk observes, "In arguing on behalf of storytelling and her reinvigoration of it as it relates to fairy tales, Byatt renounces modernism's forms" (616), much in the same way that she can be said to refute the modernist conceptions of historical narrative in her new historical fiction, including *The Biographer's Tale* and, most notably, the Booker Prize–winning *Possession: A Romance*.

Byatt employs metafictional strategies similar to those she has honed in her new historical fictions to craft contemporary revisions of traditional Western European fairy tales, and, thus, these tales serve as theoretical commentary on the storytelling tradition and, more specifically, on the generic conventions of the fairy tale form. Just as Byatt can be placed among those "writers of historical fiction," as Martha Tuck Rozett puts it in her study of the genre, who "are inspired to construct and furnish past worlds by a desire to participate in the ongoing revision of what we call 'history'" (165), she may also be placed among those who heed Donald Haase's call to continually revise and reinvent the fairy tale for the current and subsequent generations (362–64). Additionally, the self-reflexive commentary of these metafictional tales does more than interrogate the formal constitution of the genre alone. Adding to the political force behind so many revisions and critical interpretations of traditional fairy tales, Byatt appropriates the fairy tale form in order to both challenge and, ultimately, rectify the very limiting and even injurious portrayal of female potential.

Though many of Byatt's contemporary tales would suffice as examples of her critical and creative practice, this study will focus specifically upon "The Story of the Eldest Princess" from her 1994 collection *The Djinn in the Nightingale's Eye*, because it deals so explicitly with the formulaic situations and structures of traditional fairy tales; this story also confronts the standard representation of women found in so many classic fairy tales. Moreover, this tale deserves particular attention because its self-reflexive commentary moves even beyond the general critique of the form and its feminist implications. As Mark Currie explains in *Postmodern Narrative Theory*, Byatt is one of those contemporary writer-critics who "personify the boundary between fiction and criticism," and whose work often "dramatizes that boundary or uses it as an energy source" (53). This is especially true for "The Story of the Eldest Princess," in which this boundary, this overlapping space between fairy tale and theoretical study, further includes the merging of Byatt's own personal history. In fact, the tale exists as a narrative self-portrait of Byatt — as storyteller, as critic, as reviser of grand narrative traditions.

Since the publication of *Possession* in 1990, Antonia Susan Byatt has often been associated with other highly-esteemed contemporary practitioners of what Mark Currie refers to as theoretical fiction, or what has most commonly been identified as metafiction.[1] He counts these writers among the "philosophers and historians who have forsaken theoretical discourse for the advantages of fiction, for its subtle mechanisms of persuasion, for its ability to explore ideas or historical forces as they are lived by individuals" (*Postmodern* 51). Fellow writer-critics of this distinction include John Barth, David Lodge, Toni Morrison, and Umberto Eco, whose innovative *The Name of the Rose* is frequently invoked in the same breath as Byatt's *Possession*.

Each of these writers, and others like them, employs narrative structures and/or embeds commentary within the narrative that compels readers to focus upon the text itself and the generic conventions at work in the construction of that text. In simple terms, this writing is fiction about fiction, stories about storytelling, or even more broadly, narrative about the narrative process; from a slightly different perspective, it is the kind of narrative that continually reminds readers that they are readers, and at times, it even implicates these readers in the development of the text at hand. Some have faulted metafiction for undermining the illusion of reality, yet others still tend to resist the notion that metafiction spoils the fun of reading, instead finding that, at its best, it playfully, though nonetheless seriously, celebrates the reality of the illusion, the very art of representing entire worlds, fictive or otherwise, in just so many words and phrases.

For Currie, theoretical fiction benefits as "a performative rather than a constative narratology, meaning that it does not try to state the truth about an object-narrative but rather enacts or performs what it says about narrative while itself being a narrative" (*Postmodern* 52). In this sense, the fiction maintains its integrity as fiction while still allowing for self-reflection upon its own compositional processes. The self-reflexive commentary occurs through the author's use of familiar elements of fiction. According to David Lodge, "Metafictional discourse most commonly occurs in the form of 'asides' in novels," which will frequently entail engaging the reader directly and remarking upon the narrative as such. As Lodge puts it, these comments

> acknowledge the artificiality of the conventions of realism even as they employ them; they disarm criticism by anticipating it; they flatter the reader by treating him or her as an intellectual equal, sophisticated enough not to be thrown by the admission that a work of fiction is a construction rather than a slice of life [207].

Other metafictional devices include the blending of disparate textual forms, the development of numerous narrative layers, the allusion to and intertextual sampling of other literary works, the exaggerated imitation of parody, and, as is quite common, the characterization of a protagonist as a writer, researcher, historian, or literary critic who serves as a surrogate reader within the text.

Possession contains nearly every one of these self-reflexive devices, and since it also deals heavily with the representation and recuperation of historical subject matter, it stands as a perfect example of what has come to be known as historiographic metafiction, a genre noted for the way in which it "helps construct a world by gradually and repetitively immersing the reader in conversational styles, thought patterns, landscapes, and that residue of miscellaneous details and allusions that constitute the culture of a particular time and place" (Rozett 168). Focusing on the formal complexity of Byatt's theoretical fiction, Simon Dentith notes that she "goes to extraordinary lengths to create a series of mock nineteenth-century poems, letters and fairy stories, as well as more recognizably parodic recreations of contemporary literary criticism, to establish multiple interactions between the cultural concerns of the late twentieth century and those of a century earlier" (165). Byatt performs this feat by fusing these disparate modes of historical writing, so the reader may experience these various documents as textual fragments pieced together to form the broader narrative. In a demonstration of the textual nature of history, the novel provides the reader with fictional samples of historical writing, including a journal dated "May 1ST May Day 1858" (*Possession* 49), portions of the Victorian correspondence between Randolph Henry Ash and Christabel LaMotte, as well as literature attributed to the novel's characters. These mock literary works, to Byatt's credit, have the feel of historical authenticity: as she herself has admitted, the poetry appropriates the voices and styles of Alfred, Lord Tennyson and Emily Dickinson, among others (Noakes and Reynolds 18); and Christabel LaMotte's fairy tales, especially "The Glass Coffin," have the flavor of the nineteenth century, evoking the classic stories of Ludwig Tieck and the Brothers Grimm. The reader, then, witnesses, and participates in, the construction of the historical project carried out by the novel's present-day scholars and the composition of the novel itself. Through her skillful shifting of style and voice, A. S. Byatt "ruminat[es] self-consciously on the fictional representation of history," thus "contribut[ing] to a new philosophy of historical representation in which the ideological function of story-telling is central" (Currie, *Metafiction* 14). But we need not rely solely on an analysis of these various formal elements to get a sense of how she employs metafictional commentary in her writing.

Byatt has described *Possession* as "a tremendously solid novel about the processes of reading and writing" (Noakes and Reynolds 19), and Jackie Buxton, in "'What's love got to do with it?': Postmodernism and *Possession*," confirms that there is no shortage "of such self-reflexive comments on the fictive nature of readerly — and writerly — constructs" (94). Byatt provides the most significant example of metafictional commentary indirectly through the ponderings of Roland Michell, who, along with Maud Bailey, is one of the two academic protagonists of the novel: He "thought ... that he and Maud were being driven by a plot or fate that seemed, at least possibly, to be not their plot or fate but that of those others"; and "Finding themselves in a plot, they might suppose it appropriate to behave as though it was that sort of plot" (456). Clearly, this commentary anticipates those readings that will find an easy symmetry between the hidden love affair of the novel's Victorian characters and the impending romantic coupling of its two late-twentieth-century scholars. One can thus understand "the element of superstitious dread" Roland experiences in this "self-reflexive, inturned postmodernist mirror-game or plot-coil" (456) as he confronts the notion that he and Maud may be characters themselves; even more disconcerting to Roland, they may simply be mere counterparts to their historical subject matter, whose plot threatens to overwhelm the young, present-day scholars, robbing them of their agency and status as self-actualized human beings.

Byatt has stated that questions of the kind at the heart of Roland's concern were the catalyst for the novel and one of the principle connotations of its title, *Possession*. Apparently, the title was inspired by an editor of Coleridge's notebooks who would obsessively patrol the collection in the British Museum Library. In Byatt's observation, Coleridge dominated the editor's thoughts and, it seemed, gave shape and purpose to her entire being, and Byatt wondered about the consequences of the infatuation displayed by this eminent scholar: "Does he possess her? Had this dead man taken over this living woman? or has she taken possession of him, because we read his thoughts as mediated by her?" (Noakes and Reynolds 12). Beyond its relationship to the predicament in which Roland finds himself, this anecdote has historiographic implications as well. To rephrase Byatt's questions in a broader context, are historians inert conduits through which their subjects reveal the past? Or, as writers— as progenitors and manipulators of text —, do they exert control over their historical subjects? While contemporary historiography would certainly lean toward viewing historians as plotters of the past, Byatt reveals that this control is tenuous, at best, and inevitably fraught with the kind of anxiety experienced by Roland. In terms that evoke the fairy tale tradition so often drawn upon in her fiction, she warns that "with scholarship, you think you will get to the end of the quest and find out what this person was really like, and what they really felt, and actually the chances are that the most important moment of their life, or most important moments, are forever hidden" (20).

Having confronted this troubling notion of possession and what it implies in his own case, Roland attempts to reassert control over his "plot or fate" (indeed, his very life) and avoids further introspection on the point. Of course, even as the author allows Roland to retreat back into the deliberate realist trappings of the novel, the sophisticated reader will have noticed that Byatt has simultaneously laid bare the fictional apparatus of the novel as a whole. Therefore, the reader cannot ignore that Roland's attempt to shrug off the postmodernist crisis of consciousness and reestablish individual identity is itself a fiction. And, whereas at first glance, Roland's commentary directs the reader toward *Possession's* inner narrative layer of the nineteenth century, the metafictional commentary ultimately points to the exterior narrative layer of the present and the fact that he and Maud (along with Ash and LaMotte, Wolff and Blackadder, and so many others) are subjects of, and subject to, Byatt's plot.

Byatt claims that she "was never, to be truthful, as interested in the modern plot, except as a detective story ... almost all *readers* know that the story is an occluded story about the Victorian lovers, and the other two [Roland and Maud] are there for finding it out" (qtd. in Noakes and Reynolds 13–14). So, in the end, it turns out just as Roland had feared.

In her book on Byatt's life and career, Kathleen Coyne Kelly concludes that "Byatt reveals a nostalgia for a past (however illusory) in which novels had the power to teach and delight" (115). This nostalgia, then, must extend to fairy stories, a genre of the past with equal capacity for didacticism and wonder. Otherwise, why would Byatt so often turn to this classic form to provide the model for many of her short stories and to augment the narrative complexity of her novels? Furthermore, Byatt's contemporary fairy tales, or "wonder-tales" (as Annegret Maack and Richard Todd refer to them in their critical analyses), contain metafictional commentary on a par with that found in her new historical novels. And, as theoretical fiction, her fairy stories strive to delight readers, but at the same time, they promise to teach readers about stories and storytelling; as with *Possession*, this entails "self-contemplation, or reflexivity," which "is fundamentally critical because it refers [readers] to other texts, to narrativity in general, not from some Olympian position of metalingual distance but from within the discourse on which it reflects" (Currie, *Postmodern*

69). More precisely, Byatt's fairy tales continue to deal with the specific metafictional motif that so preoccupied Roland Michell, one which conflates plot and fate.

Though it may be tempting to look first to the fairy tales developed in *Possession*, "The Glass Coffin," "The Threshold," "Gode's Story," etc., several critics have found isolating these tales from their novelistic context problematic, despite the fact that Byatt included word for word duplications of both "The Glass Coffin" and "Gode's Story" amongst the five fairy stories of *The Djinn in the Nightingale's Eye*. "The Glass Coffin" offers a fine example of this interpretive difficulty. In short, the story follows a well-mannered tailor, described as a "good and unremarkable man" (*Possession* 65), on an adventure in which he rescues a maiden from captivity in, as one would reasonably assume, a glass coffin. Before finding the coffin, the tailor had acquired the means of the damsel's freedom, a glass key, as a gift from an old man who dwells in the forest with his discerning canine companion, Otto.

In *Twice Upon a Time: Women Writers and the History of the Fairy Tale*, Elizabeth Wanning Harries concludes that Byatt's allegorical revision "resonates with meanings" within "its context in *Possession*"; as a stand-alone tale, however, "it seems simply an accomplished reworking of one of the Grimms' tales" (113). Yet, Harries does credit Byatt for her decision to remove this story from its original context because "She has given us an opportunity to see what happens when a tale is framed, and what is missing when the frame disappears" (110). Likewise, Richard Todd has asserted that these fairy tales "are absolutely transformed by their existence within the narrative matrix of *Possession*" (43), and noting the exegetical potential of "The Glass Coffin," he provides a reading that demonstrates the range of meanings lost to readers who are denied the frame narrative. For example, a number of the characters within the fairy tale have their own analogues in the Victorian setting of *Possession*: the lady in the glass coffin is Christabel LaMotte; the black artist (the villain) represents Randolph Henry Ash; and Otto stands in for Blanche Glover. The actions of these characters correspond figuratively, as well, to the troubled affairs of these Victorians. As it relates to the frame narrative, "The Glass Coffin," attributed in the novel to Christabel, functions as a "wish-fulfillment fantasy" to alleviate the emotional turmoil wrought by her relationship with Ash. From this reading, Todd concludes that the fairy tale "attains a resonance within *Possession* that it simply cannot have when excised from it" (44).

Since these particular examples of Byatt's fairy tale fiction are "the most deeply inset narratives" in *Possession*, their metafictional commentary seems limited to that suggested by the novel's textual mélange. In this case, as embedded narratives that can, nevertheless, be presented as self-contained stories, they do raise a structural question about whether or not the frame narrative *possesses* "The Glass Coffin" and "Gode's Story"; because these are, as Harries describes them, "tales that send out ripples through all the Chinese boxes" of the novel's narrative structure (114), the frame narrative appears equally dependent upon the fairy stories for the meaning they bear in the novel. Perhaps the novel's combination of various genres and writing styles serves as the formal parallel to the metafictional motif of plot/fate.

One of Byatt's fairy stories that more directly utilizes this metafictional motif is "The Djinn in the Nightingale's Eye," a lengthy tale independent of a broader narrative context. Though a self-contained story, it contains quite a few attributes familiar to readers from Byatt's other work. As with Byatt's most notable examples of metafiction, the story is, according to Annegret Maack,

> profoundly intertextual, alluding to the Arabian tales from *The Thousand and One Nights*, to Grimm's fairy tales, Coleridge's "Rime of the Ancient Mariner," the *Epic of Gilgamesh*, Euripedes's *Bacchae*, Shakespeare's *Winter's Tale*, Balzac's *Peau de Chagrin*, and Wilde's *Picture of Dorian Gray*, to mention only some of the more clearly marked sources. Explicit quotations are made from Chaucer's *Canterbury Tales*, Milton's *Paradise Lost*, and Shakespeare's *Hamlet* [123].

Also, like *Possession*, its protagonists are scholars of literature; surrounded by the "realm of academia," the characters' academic focus is primarily the interpretation of myth and fairy tales (123). Hence, Byatt has supplied yet another surrogate reader who will no doubt discourse at length on the pleasures and peculiarities of reading and writing.

"Djinn" tells the story of Gillian Perholt, a middle-aged divorcee who specializes in narrative theory. While at an academic conference on "The Stories of Women's Lives" in Turkey, she discovers a genie, or djinn, in an ancient artifact, and trades a life a dry abstractions for a passionate affair with a mystical demi-god. For Lisa M. Fiander, this tale exemplifies the way "straightforward storytelling blurs into narrative experiment and back again, and well-realized characters surprise the reader by wandering from time to time into the realms of myth, fantasy, fable and fairy tale" (15).

Maack focuses on Gillian's penchant for retelling tales, as well as the way "she accepts her own contingency and finitude" (132), and from this emerges the metafictional motif of plot/fate. As a scholar of the vast storytelling tradition, aptly demonstrated in her presentation on Chaucer's "Patient Griselda" and conversations with fellow academics, Gillian has extensive knowledge of conventions that structure, and therefore limit, the narrative possibilities of any given genre. As Maack points out, this knowledge allows her to recognize "the often-told fairy tales," which seem to be coalescing around her, so Gillian "is able to comprehend her situation and to act accordingly" (131). She witnesses the familiar plot developing in her life, and she understands her fate. This knowledge affords Gillian the opportunity to map out the boundaries of her plot, and the ability to re-tell tales provides provisional license to adjust course, if need be.

One of the most interesting of Byatt's metafictional fairy stories, "The Story of the Eldest Princess," deals somewhat more lightheartedly, though no less insightfully, with the issues touched upon in "Djinn." Perhaps this tale is more accessible to readers who may lose their way in Byatt's more erudite and densely allusive fiction. But as the sort of acute parody one might expect from Byatt, the story offers a broad range of customary fairy tale tropes and themes, familiar to both those who have poured over the classic texts as well as those whose experience with the fairy tale genre has been relegated to expressions transmitted through popular culture. As a work of fiction abounding in metafictional and social commentary, it deserves more critical attention.

As the title suggests, this fairy story pertains to the eldest of three princesses. Over time, the sky in her land gradually loses its blue hue, turning various shades of green. Once the new sky begins to adversely affect the crops and the people become restless, the king and queen gather together a cadre of political advisors, clergy, witches and wizards to come up with a solution. On the advice of the witches and wizards, they choose to send their eldest daughter, who could recall the sky as it once was, on a Quest to capture a silver bird and its nest of ash-branches. The ensuing Quest features a recognizable amalgam of fairy tale, chivalric romance, and fable formulae: a path through the forest, a mysterious old crone, a cottage in the woods, foreboding obstacles, a handsome woodsman, and loquacious wildlife companions (a rather brusque scorpion, a parched toad, and a stoic cockroach, to be precise).

Not long after she begins her journey, the Eldest Princess takes a break to ponder her state of affairs, displaying a narrative self-awareness that has emerged as a regular facet of Byatt's theoretical fiction. As in each of the examples that have come before, this metafictional capacity should be attributed to the Eldest Princess's fondness for texts. That is, she is identified, first and foremost, as a reader: "She was by nature a reading, not a traveling princess." Thus, as a *reading* princess, she knows of a "great many stories" about quests and is familiar with their customary plots: the elder prince or princesses "set out very confidently, failed in one way or another," and had to wait for a younger sibling, "who did everything well," to come to the rescue and complete the quest (47). We see in Byatt's description of the princess traces of the self-reflexivity illustrated by Roland Michell in *Possession* and Gillian Perholt in *Djinn*. While perhaps lacking the disciplinary sophistication and terminological finesse of Byatt's academic protagonists, the Eldest Princess proves to be, nonetheless, a perceptive reader, fully capable of recognizing the contingencies and conventions applicable to the story she inhabits. These patterns, which the Princess can identify from reading the stories about other quests, delimit the plot and set before her a restricted assortment of possible fates, each of them, to her mind, unsatisfactory.

Thus the metafictional motif of plot/fate is again attended by an anxiety over restricted agency, as it was with Roland. Once these self-reflexive characters begin to recognize that they may be consigned to a plot (which, of course, they are), an air of fatalism overtakes them. The Eldest Princess articulates this in decidedly constrictive terms and even resigns herself to prescriptive generic conventions: "She thought, I am in a pattern I know, and I suspect I have no power to break it, and I am going to meet a test and fail it, and spend seven years as a stone" (Byatt 48). This suggestion of powerlessness can be found in the tale's other metafictional commentary, as well.

The Princess's awareness is further revealed in her ability to ascertain the intertextual links to stock fables beyond the realm of quest narratives, and these references should anticipate the connections drawn by the reader. For instance, from the moment she frees him from being pinned under a stone, the Princess associates the wounded Scorpion with the tale of "The Frog and the Scorpion." With this new insight, and leery that she may have shifted into a hazardous new narrative, she reads this new character as a symbol of deception and mortal danger, and she affects an appropriate level of caution. She tells the Scorpion, "I know that story too" (51). She will carry the Scorpion, and, despite his promises, he will sting her. As they both suffer, she will inquire why, and he will blame it all on his nature. But it is this very example, so notable for perpetuating the maxim that one is a slave to his or her "nature," regardless of the consequences, that challenges the necessary adherence to an externally-imposed pattern or plot, and it challenges the notion of a predestined nature or fate.

The Scorpion responds to the Princess by reminding her that he has a disabled stinger, and, thus, he would be free from the obligations of that plot. His argument leads her to consider the possibility of taking charge of her own fate for the first time. She realizes quite suddenly, "I *could* just walk out of this inconvenient story and go my own way" (Byatt 52). Therefore, just as she releases the Scorpion, the Toad, and the Cockroach from their doomed fates— their various physical entanglements— they guide her away from the path in the woods and, finally, to a place where she can be at liberty to craft her own stories. Because the Eldest Princess wrested herself away from the dictates of the Quest plot, the Old Woman applauds her wisdom and daring; she praises the Princess both for recognizing she was caught within a common plot and for having "the sense" to "change it to another" (65). As a storyteller, the Princess is no longer subject to the plots of others. Storytelling, it seems, offers unprecedented freedom.

Finally, extending the self-reflexivity of this fairy tale will reveal the author caught in the story herself. "The Story of the Eldest Princess," in a liberal sense, is an abstract history of Byatt's life and career as a storyteller, refracted through the prism of the fairy tale form. She is herself a pseudo-eldest princess, one who seemed fated to be outpaced, professionally speaking, by her younger sibling, Margaret Drabble, a renowned novelist who achieved critical and popular success long before her elder sister. According to Kelly, "In interviews, Byatt is often asked about her relationship with Drabble. She says, 'I've suffered quite badly from being thought of Margaret Drabble's sister, and there expected to write books like hers, which I don't do'" (118n.). Byatt's own admission suggests a correlation to the initial defeatist attitude that the Eldest Princess displays early in the story. Resigned to her fate, the Princess tells the Scorpion that she has been crying because she is but a character doomed to failure (50). Fortunately, through persistence, and with a little guidance from her animal friends, she does find an escape, plotting a new course for herself as a storyteller. And, unsurprisingly, so too did Byatt. In an interview revealingly titled "Out from Sister's Shadow," Byatt states that the various awards and accolades she received following the publication of *Possession* eventually "freed her from the shadow of her younger sister's greater reputation" (qtd. in Foote).

It is, perhaps, within this same biographical context that the metafictional motif of plot/fate can be best understood as a marker of female empowerment, one that symbolizes a broader effort by Byatt to urge readers to question the plots and fates imposed upon women in a patriarchal society. That Byatt should utilize postmodernist strategies in her fairy tales to critique gender stereotypes is no surprise, for, as Cristina Bacchilega demonstrates throughout *Postmodern Fairy Tales: Gender and Narrative Strategies*, revision of the genre often "involves substantive though diverse questioning of narrative construction and assumptions about gender" (50). Byatt's focus on narrative and the storytelling tradition has often coincided with an interrogation of the way women have historically been represented within that tradition, especially with the way these female characters are given very few choices in their own lives. For example, the maiden in Christabel's reworking of Grimm's "Glass Coffin" assumes she must wed her rescuer according to convention, although even he questions this determination: "Though why you should have me, simply because I opened a glass case, is less clear to me altogether" (74). Also, Byatt dedicates a large portion of Djinn to Gillian's lecture on a phallogocentric Western literary tradition, which is presented to the reader as, in Susan Sellers' opinion, "an exposition of women's entrapment within stories that are not of their making" (38). And "The Story of the Eldest Princess," as has been argued, hinges on the heroine's abiding desire to redefine her status within the narrative, and this takes on its more precisely gendered dimension when considered alongside Byatt's own experience.

It only seems appropriate that Byatt, as a reviser of traditions, modify this bit of her story, allowing the fairy tale heroine to avoid circumstances that threatened Byatt early in her own career as a writer and critic. In the introduction to a reissue of her first novel, *The Shadow of the Sun*, Byatt writes:

> Men could have both work and love, but it seemed that women couldn't. No woman of my generation would have expected any putative husband to consider her work prospects when making his own decisions. I myself went on to do academic research, and had my grant taken away when I married. Men in my position had their grants increased, to provide for their households [viii].

In this statement, Byatt expresses a palpable frustration with the double-standard and the loss of autonomy she and other women have suffered in a patriarchal society that so often forces them to choose between their personal ambitions and marriage. Thus, Byatt spares the Princess this "closed future" (viii), but the threat of it remains in the form of the bare-chested Woodsman, to whom the Princess is drawn by a song promising love, sex, and other sensual delights. In this tale, finding a man and falling in love, an ending so commonly associated with the fairy tale promise of *happily ever after*, is revealed as ominous a fate as the inevitable captivity the Princess evaded when she chose to abandon her Quest. The Woodsman divulges as much in the final verse of his song:

> And you may scour and sweep and scrub
> With bleeding hands and arms like lead
> And I will beat your back, and drive
> My knotty fists against your head
> And sing again to other girls
> To take your place, when you are dead ["Eldest Princess" 59].

Indeed, this domestic fate, itself a form of captivity, seems a crueler destiny than, for instance, being placed under a sleeping spell; it guarantees the drudgery of menial labor, the pain of routine violence, and, unavoidably, death. But death comes not from the physical hardships: of the Woodcutter's former wives, the Cockroach tells the Princess, "He doesn't kill them, he weeps drunken tears for them, but they lose their will to live" (59). So these women suffer a death of body and spirit, brought on by a life of drudgery and confinement. In the Last House, the Old Woman praises the Princess for avoiding romantic entanglement and continuing on to, as she puts it, a place where "we are free," a place where "we collect stories and spin stories" — a life much like the one Byatt herself now leads.

The Princess's self-awareness presents her with the choice of whether to follow the proscribed plot to its inevitable fate or to take control of her plot, guiding herself toward a different fate — a less certain fate, to be sure, but one freely chosen and constructed by the character herself. The irony that must be acknowledged, in this case as in that of *Possession*, is that this agency — this independence, this freedom of choice — is an element of fiction; the Princess's fate is, nevertheless, always already plotted by A. S. Byatt. However, this metafictional conundrum need not fatally undermine the message of empowerment inherent in the story. In "The Story of the Eldest Princess," Byatt provides the most enthusiastic and optimistic treatment of the metafictional motif of plot/fate, and optimism, according to Lisa M. Fiander, "resides at the heart of fairy tales" and "is one dimension of those narratives about which scholars taking very different approaches to fairy tale would seem to be in agreement." Accordingly, that Byatt takes fairy tales "seriously as offering ways of thinking about modern life signals an essential optimism in [her] work" (15). Therefore, while at once probing and highlighting the narrative conventions of the form, the metafictional commentary in Byatt's fairy stories may also be viewed as a means to ultimately affirm narrative's ability to affect positive change, especially as it applies to the roles of women in society. If, as Byatt has stated, her works of fiction "all think about the problem of female vision, female art and thought" (*Shadow* xiii), then "The Story of the Eldest Princess" offers an inspiring resolution by providing readers with a model heroine who consciously and competently resists the stereotypical trappings of this storytelling tradition.

Note

1. Currie acknowledges that both labels refer to "narrative self-contemplation," but he prefers his terminology because "metafiction implies a difference between normal fiction and its metalanguage, even when that language is fiction itself" (*Postmodern* 52–53). Since my analysis does not depend on this fine distinction, I will use the terms interchangeably.

Works Cited

Alfer, Alexa, and Michael J. Noble, eds. *Essays on the Fiction of A.S. Byatt: Imagining the Real.* Westport, CT: Greenwood Press, 2001.

Bacchilega, Cristina. *Postmodern Fairy Tales: Gender and Narrative Strategies.* Philadelphia: University of Pennsylvania, 1997.

Buxton, Jackie. "'What's love got to do with it?': Postmodernism and *Possession.*" Alfer and Noble 89–104.

Byatt, A.S. *The Djinn in the Nightingale's Eye: Five Fairy Stories.* 1994. New York: Vintage International, 1998.

_____. *On Histories & Stories.* Cambridge, MA: Harvard University Press, 2000.

_____. *Possession: A Romance.* 1990. New York: Vintage International, 1991.

_____. *The Shadow of the Sun.* 1964. San Diego: Harcourt Brace, 1992.

Currie, Mark, ed. *Metafiction.* London: Longman, 1995.

_____. *Postmodern Narrative Theory.* New York: Palgrave, 1998.

Dentith, Simon. *Parody.* London: Routledge, 2000.

Fiander, Lisa M. *Fairy Tales and the Fiction of Iris Murdoch, Margaret Drabble, and A. S. Byatt.* New York: Peter Lang, 2004.

Foote, Jennifer. "Interview: Out from Sister's Shadow." *Newsweek* 21 Jan. 1991: 12. June 2008 <http://newsweek.com/id/121233/page/2>.

Haase, Donald. "Yours, Mine, or Ours? Perrault, the Brothers Grimm, and the Ownership of Fairy Tales." *The Classic Fairy Tales: Texts, Criticism.* Ed. Maria Tatar. New York: Norton, 1999. 353–64.

Harries, Elizabeth Wanning. *Twice Upon a Time: Women Writers and the History of the Fairy Tale.* Princeton, NJ: Princeton University Press, 2001.

Kelly, Kathleen Coyne. *A. S. Byatt.* New York: Twayne, 1996.

Lodge, David. *The Art of Fiction.* London: Penguin, 1992.

Maack, Annegret. "Wonder-Tales Hiding a Truth: Retelling Tales in 'The Djinn in the Nightingale's Eye.'" Alfer and Noble 123–134.

Noakes, Jonathan, and Margaret Reynolds. *A. S. Byatt.* London: Vintage, 2004.

Renk, Kathleen Williams. "A. S. Byatt, the Woman Artist, and Suttee." *Women's Studies* 33 (2004): 613–28.

Rozett, Martha Tuck. *Constructing a World: Shakespeare's England and the New Historical Fiction.* Albany: State University of New York Press, 2003.
Sellers, Susan. *Myth and Fairy Tale in Contemporary Women's Fiction.* New York: Palgrave, 2001.
Todd, Richard. *A. S. Byatt.* Plymouth, UK: Northcote House, 1997.

Between Wake and Sleep
Robert Coover's *Briar Rose*, A Playful Reawakening of *The Sleeping Beauty*

Marie C. Bouchet

In his novel *Briar Rose*, published in 1996, Robert Coover plays with the reader's expectations and knowledge of the popular Brothers Grimm tale to compose his narrative. Like many metafictional and postmodernist works, *Briar Rose* is intertextual, offering a playful parody to be decoded by the reader, but it is not an idle nor purely speculative game. As the present study will illustrate, the game-like dimension of the novel is the means chosen by Coover to "awaken" the reader: "Playfulness, then, becomes a deliberate strategy used to provoke readers to critically examine all cultural codes and established patterns of thought" (McCaffery 14).

Summarizing the "plot" of Coover's *Briar Rose* is deceptively easy, as nothing really happens. What does not happen, then? The story begins *in media res*, precisely when the princess has been asleep for about 100 years, and the prince has just entered the thorny brambles encircling the castle, with the intention of freeing her from the curse. This beginning illustrates the way Coover resorts to the reader's knowledge of the tale, but instead of being the starting point of the narrative, it proves to be the only and inescapable time and space of the story: the "narrative" begins at that moment and never leaves it. There is no satisfactory happy ending for the reader, because there is no progression of the action on a purely diegetic level. The prince never reaches the castle; the princess never wakes up.

Instead of the well-known course of events, the reader is offered 42 sections in which are alternatively given the thoughts and dreams of three protagonists: the prince, the princess, and the fairy who has taken care of Briar Rose during her sleep — a peculiar narrative stance that will be further analyzed.

This essay focuses on two main points. The first postulates that the overall and intrinsic structure of Coover's work corresponds to a repetition with variation. The second point deals with the ambiguous nature of the work due to the blurring of textual limits, suggesting a possible interpretation of Coover's intention in writing this stunning piece of fiction.

"Back for more of the same?" (44)[1]— Repetition with Variations

Coover's *Briar Rose* constitutes one more repetition with variation of a palimpsest myth dating back to the thirteenth century A.C.[2] The best known variations on the myth are Charles Perrault's 1696 *Sleeping Beauty* (translated into English in 1729) and the Brothers Grimm's 1812 *Briar Rose*, deriving from the former. Coover's work playfully uses those earlier versions, thus providing further variations on the variations. Moreover, his 1996 version also integrates the tale on which Perrault based his own variation, a 1636 Italian story by Giambattista Basile, entitled *Sun, Moon, and Talia*. This tale is the most sexually explicit and violent of all. While she is in her enchanted sleep, Talia (also Beauty or Briar Rose) is raped by a married king and gives birth to twins. The king's wife finds out and, in jealous rage, attempts to eat Talia's children, Sun and Moon. This cannibalistic element is also present in Perrault's *Sleeping Beauty*, though it is usually little known, as most published versions of the fairy tale end the story once the prince awakens the princess. Indeed, in Perrault's tale, Beauty marries the Prince, gives birth to a girl (Dawn), and to a boy (Day). Later on, the Prince takes his wife and children to his court. There, while he is away hunting, his ogress mother wishes to eat Beauty and her children, who are saved by the cook (he substitutes animals for them, as in Basile's story).

It is important to have in mind those earlier versions of the myth, because Coover borrows many elements from them in his own version. Moreover, *inside* Coover's *Briar Rose*, the repetition-with-variation principle also rules: the fairy in charge of the princess during her sleep keeps on telling her tales of Sleeping Beauties, thus multiplying the possible awakenings and endings that could arise from the moment in which narration is stuck. Furthermore, she also inspires Briar Rose's many dreams that offer even more possible scenarios. In fact, as Redies points out, this "structure follows the well-known fairy-tale technique of repetition and variation, albeit in different context" (14).

Thus at the macrocosmic level of the work, *Briar Rose* is a repetition with variation of the Sleeping Beauty myth, but at the microcosmic level, the plot, structure and narration also follow this principle. Here is an example:

> Her ghostly princes have come to her severally with bites and squeezes, probing fingers, slaps and tickles, have pricked her with their swords and switched her thighs with briar stems, have licked her throat and ears, sucked her toes, spilled wine on her or holy water, and with their curious lips have kissed her top to bot-

tom, inside and out, but they have not in these false wakings relieved her ever of her spindled pain [10].

Repetition with variations governs this description: the various ways in which the princes touch Briar Rose are humorously detailed, very often grouped in pairs, thus creating a binary rhythm that is expanded through the use of alliteration, a stylistic device also relying on repetition with variation. In fact, throughout the pages, the variations on the initial myth seem endless, playfully debunking the classical narrative. For instance, in her dreams, the princess is repeatedly awakened: by a monkey rummaging between her legs, with the royal family and court watching and hooting (46–49); by a prince who wakes and undresses her in front of everyone before turning away (43–44); and by a vampire-prince who awakens her by biting her throat (57). The myriad of variations on the awakening scene enhances the fact that it is the key-moment, the end of the curse — which in fact never comes. Notably, *Briar Rose* follows the same rule as another work of Coover's, the 1969 short story entitled "The Gingerbread House," in which "rather than simply altering the pattern, [Coover] allows parts of the original story to engage other possibilities openly" (McCaffery 79).

Coover also plays with the earlier versions of the myth, believing, as Marc Chénetier points out, that "the only way to struggle against myth is on myth's own ground" ("Robert Coover's" 80): hence, since "Tale is the servant of Myth," and since even though the writer can be taken in "Myth's iron clutches, Tale lets you go,"[3] Coover chose to rework the tale itself to struggle with myth. The purpose of this struggle will be explored in the second part of the present analysis, as one must first describe the way Robert Coover battles with the Sleeping Beauty myth itself.

Briar Rose presents a mix of the older tales, persistently insisting upon the least "polished" and proper elements that the Grimm Brothers (and Disney) evicted from their versions (Beauty's rape during her sleep, the ensuing babies, the jealous murdering wife, the ogress). Significantly, those elements resurface in the princess's *dreams*, in a playful return of the repressed, which weaves those elements in different variations, making the stories fork and re-fork, producing hyperbolic exaggerations. For example in section XI, Beauty is visited by several princes, has several children in her sleep, and then has her children taken and cooked (for good) by the jealous wives, multiplied according to the same logic (19).

The fairy (also called the old crone) constantly debunks the princess's expectations through a question that becomes a leitmotiv of the novel: "Of course, what did you expect, my child?" This question is at the core of the writing process, as Coover similarly thwarts the reader's expectations and destroys the assumed pattern of the fairy tale. In that regard, the reader finds in Briar Rose a double, since she also seems to be acquainted only with the Grimms' version of the story. Quite often, Briar Rose receives those "new" stories with incredulity. When the fairy explains that the princess awoke with two babies suckling at her breasts, she expresses her hatred for this tale in which the princess does not know whether she was kissed or not, and then she states that it does not "sound right" (40).

Not only does the old crone weave elements from previous Sleeping Beauty tales into her own narratives, but she also resorts to other myths to produce the numerous variations offered to her goddaughter. This provides further ground to fragment the initial tale announced in the title, and to underline the common patterns of suffering among myths, in comprehensive summaries in which she links the fates of various figures (31). The fairy even modifies the myth of Andromeda (note that her Greek name means "to think of a man," making her an apt double for Briar Rose) so as to relate the prince-figure of her own tale to other stories in which he is due to perform a feat:

> She tells her the story of the princess chained to a rock ... and guarded by a fire-breathing sea monster.... And they lived happily ever after?... Oh, who can say? The prince had other tasks and maidens to attend to, making a name for himself as he was, for all I know, my dear, that one's chained there still [37–38].

Through the manipulation of those myths and tales, the old crone often insists on the sexual aspects of the story, thus breaking the propriety rules of traditional fairy tales. This can be seen in her distorted version of Beauty and the Beast, with undertones of Goldilocks and the Three Bears (34–35), in which the poor princess is married to a stinky old bear who brutally mates with her, as she is concomitantly fiercely bitten by the she-bear (a variation on the jealous-wife motif). In this version of Beauty and the Beast, the elements of animality safely contained in the original tale are violently exposed.

Coover subverts many a convention of the fairy tale, both appropriating the genre and distancing his fiction from it. Marc Chénetier identifies Coover's technique as "the re-subjectivization of an institutionally objectified set of mythical references, [which] leads to destabilization" ("Robert Coover's" 80). For example, Coover provides very graphic, "realistic" details about the princess's long sleep, such as the recurrence of her menstrual blood, which the fairy godmother must clean up for Briar Rose to be ready for her prince, and which she calls the "curse of the bad fairy" (6). This is taken from the first section in which the fairy's voice is directly perceived by the reader, and the first element she mentions is this realistic detail, itself related to the notion of curse, in a reference to the curse of Eve, since the menstrual period is often referred to as "the curse." Actually, this mention of the princess's menses is not so destabilizing, as it echoes one of the psychoanalytic interpretations of the tale developed by Bruno Bettelheim. According to him, the blood running from the princess's finger after being pricked by the spindle can be seen as a symbol of the maiden's first menstruation (225–35). The other reading Bettelheim proposes is that her shed blood can also be paralleled to the loss of virginity — a sexual element explicitly and largely referred to throughout *Briar Rose*. The novel seems to disenchant the fairy tale by laying bare the sexual symbolism encoded in it: in almost every dream of awakening of the princess, her virginity is taken, or her body is bared for that purpose.

Yet considering the playful and ironic stance of the novel, it seems more appropriate to consider those elements which could be read as an apparent confirmation of Bettelheim's analyses as intertextual references using Bettelheim's analyses as a foil. Indeed, the novel offers extremely ironic scenes in which Freudian interpretations are literalized, and thus appear to be just as fictitious as all the other variations mentioned above. In section VII, the princess dreams of her own father with whom she has sexual intercourse. The many humorous details in the passage tell the reader that this oedipal dream allowing repressed desire to be expressed should not be taken too seriously.[4] Similarly, from the very start, the novel clearly indicates that all sexual connotations are to be noticed (no Freudian slip here), as the briar branches "part like thighs, the silky petals caress[ing] his cheeks" (Coover 1). As a prelude to the awakening of Briar Rose, the prince sensually experiences her double — the blossoming briar hedge, whose soft touch is reproduced in the alliteration of the letter s. As a parallel to the obvious images that recurrently relate the prince's quest to his sexual desire, the interpretation that assimilates the spindle to a penis is recalled in the very first section dealing with the princess: "she is being stabbed again and again by the treacherous spindle, impregnated with ... despair" (3). The simplistic symbolization is even further ridiculed. Throughout her dreams, the princess always returns to the spinning room, and even searches to be pricked again, in a particularly comic dream scene from chapter XL, in which the spindle, repeatedly hammered "at the center of her pain" (80–81), transforms itself into a green frog sliding away from her grip, croaking. On the one hand, this scene could epitomize the maniacal and almost masochistic desire of the princess for the penis (even though the "center of her pain" is playfully not clarified), but the hyperbolic repetition and the comic deflation through the introduction of another fairy tale motif (the frog) debunks this reading. Hence this episode could be seen as a mirror held to the ever-repeated use throughout academia of Bettelheim's reducing interpretation.

On the other hand, from a structural point of view, this scene shows how sterile and ridiculous pure repetition is, indicating that it is variation (the frog in lieu of the spindle) that creates not only humor, but also renews meaning and opens signification. The systemized use of repetition with variation should not be seen as a mere structuring device, but ought to be viewed as a celebration of polysemy, as a way to recall that the relation between signifier and signified is not univocal. Hence the numerous puns and *double entendres* that are scattered throughout the pages, or the bits of tale re-used in Coover's narrative, but placed in such different contexts that they create jokes primarily of a sexual nature. For instance, during one of the fake awakening scenes, Briar Rose asks her prince what sort of thing the element "that jumps about so funnily" (67) is. Here, in a subverted quote referring to the spindle in the Grimm brothers' tale, penis and spindle are paired again, laying bare the repressed sexual elements.

The playful distortion and fragmentation of the fairy tale in the dilatated moment of the princess's near awakening is also brought about through a dazzling set of embedded structures: dream within the dream, tale within the tale, enchantment within enchantment — all these elements awaken the reader to a renewed vision of the age-old tale.

Indeed, as has been shown, the eponymous sleeping heroine is taken in delusional dreams within her own century-long dream. To those dreams within her dream she "awakens" (Coover 67), but the eye-opening process is itself dreamed: typically, when she "wakes up" from her embedded dreams, she finds herself in another room of the castle (kitchen, servery, or spinning room) where she sees the old crone, who then tells her a story in order to calm her down after her dream. In fact, those dreams frequently turn out to be nightmarish awakening scenarios instead of the expected love kiss. Hence, the text smoothly moves from the dream within a dream to the tale within the tale. This can be exemplified by the end of section XXV and the beginning of section XXVI (49), which aptly opens with the set formula "once upon a time." The tale inside the tale is thus introduced through a *cliché* and is followed by a summary of the story, which is precisely similar to the point at which the action is now for Coover's Briar Rose. As she notices the similarities between her fate and that of the girl in the crone's story, the narration is interrupted by the princess's questions and the crone's answers (50). Thus, inside the tale within the tale (here Basile's version of the myth), the reader finds an embedded dialogue that comments upon the story. This high degree of self-reflexiveness is part of the metafictional features of the novel. Linda Hutcheon defines the metafictional novel as "self-referring or autorepresentational: it provides, within itself, a commentary on its own status as fiction and as language, and also on its own processes of production and reception" (xii). *Briar Rose*, like many works by Coover and his contemporaries, thus follows the "view that literature is a free, consciously false construction" (McCaffery 12): indeed the novel provides many instances of *mises en abyme* of the writing process, or of the structure of the tale, such as in the following excerpt: "so often have her dreams revisited fragments and images of dreams dreamt before, a sort of recognizable architecture has grown up around them, such that, though each dream is, must be, intrinsically unique, there is an ambient familiarity about them ..." (Coover 5). The structure of the princess's dreams, as described here, precisely mirrors the overall structure of the novel: it presents fragments of dreams and tales that are themselves repetitions with variations of the Sleeping Beauty myth. In fact, the fragmented nature of *Briar Rose* as a narrative is itself echoed in Princess Briar Rose's craving for unity. Just like the reader who is anchoring his comprehension of the "narrative" on the recognizable elements of the well-known tale, the heroine feels everything is scattered and out of place (she feels all the stories offered by the fairy are not "right" nor "real").

In the first "princess section" of the book, Briar Rose complains about her persistent feeling of being fragmented, and she longs for being "whole again" (Coover 2–3); this can be viewed as an announcement of the way the story bearing the name of the princess will be constructed, or, to be more precise, deconstructed. Similarly, in one of the last sections of the novel, an episode encapsulates the book that the reader is about to finish. It collides the image of the fairy spinning thread and her weaving stories like fabric, imagining for her charge an "assortment of beauties and princes, obstacles, awakenings, and what-happened-nexts, *weaving* in a diverse collection of monsters, dragons, ogres, jests, rapes, ... and babies" (56–57, my emphasis). The fairy's long reflection on her own tales is a very thorough *mise en abyme* of the entire novel: the parallel between spinning thread and telling stories provides a unifying metaphor for the overall structure, a leading thread that echoes the founding episode of the tale, namely the curse of the spinning room. In fact, the dazzling set of embedded tales, mirroring each other and the novel as a whole, entails an overall destabilization of the textual boundaries. The indistinction of limits is a prominent feature of *Briar Rose* in terms of narration, characterization and thematic structure.

"The Illusion of Boundaries" (57) or Blurring Textual Limits

In Coover's novel, the reworking of mimetic traditional fiction entails a constant blurring of limits, especially in terms of narration. Indeed *Briar Rose* is not a typical third-person omniscient narration, but is, instead, polyphonic. "One of the ways Coover attempts to create new perspectives on familiar material is simply by telling the familiar story from an unfamiliar point of view" (McCaffery 62). It is precisely what the narration illustrates, thanks to the three focalizers who alternatively offer their points of view (expressed in direct or indirect style), to whom can be added various voices cropping up — the bones of previous princes whispering in the wind, the king, the queen, and the various princes talking to Beauty in her dreams.

At some points, the voices of the protagonists seem to dialogue from one section to the other (see sections IV and V), but once the reader has become familiar with the peculiar narrative mode and knows how to identify whose voice it is, Coover subverts the system he himself had created, blurring those referents:

> He labors on, slashing determinedly at the hedge with his sword, ... and musing the while upon this beautiful maiden, fast asleep, called Briar Rose. *Does she ever dream of her disenchantment? Does she ever dream of him?* [26, my emphasis].
> Certainly, she dreamt of her sweetlipped prince all the time, *says the fairy*, in reply to *Rose's question* [26–27, my emphasis].

For the reader it is like being plunged into a dream in which logic is elusive: whose voice was it in the last lines of section XIV? The prince's? The princess's asking questions about the tale? The fairy's, in one of her tales? In that case as in many other instances, the source of narration is unclear. Similarly, when reading section XXXII (61–62), the reader first gathers the impression that it is a "prince section," but it turns out to be one of the old crone's tales within the tale.

The blurring of referents is also achieved through the circular nature of the novel. Redies states that "the fairy-tale world is circular, without a real ending" (24). As described earlier, in Coover's *Briar Rose* action is but repetitive: the prince keeps on slashing brambles, the princess keeps on dreaming she is awakened, the old crone keeps on telling her stories. This is reflected in the recurrence of the famous starting formula "once upon a time" at various points in the novel, and in various places in each section (beginning, end, or even in the middle of a section), thus subverting the traditional role and place of the fairy tale *incipit*. Many episodes seem to be endlessly coming back through the embedded dreams and tales (awakenings, rapes, babies, beasts, jealous wives, ogresses) and also contribute to the circular structure.

The feeling of being stuck at one point in space and time is reinforced by the absence of temporal markers and the use of the present tense throughout, which creates a sensation of timelessness or of an eternal present without any possibility of going forward. The past tenses are only used in the fairy's tales, thus contrasting with the never-progressing present of the action. The feeling of temporal dilatation is also rendered through the many verbs ending in –ing (especially to start new sections) that create the feeling of action in the making.

Circularity is conveyed in the many leitmotivs that are woven into the fabric of the text, but contrary to a traditional fairy tale, they do not bring the reassuring feeling of a well-known structure. In Coover's novel, those leitmotivs have two purposes. They often point to the absurdity of repetition without variation: such is the case for the "I am he who will awaken Beauty!" leitmotiv, which is repeated over and over, turning into an empty set of signifiers, as the modal "will" is contradicted by the non-progressing action. Coover lays bare the forceful nature of the formulaic sentence and undermines its legitimacy by ridiculing the very concept of "making one's name" at many points in the novel (sections I, IX, XXXII, XXXIII, XLII). During one of these scenes, the prince ends drying up like a dogturd in the desert, never making "his—" (63–64). The disappearance of the word "name" in a dash reflects the failure of the prince to conform to the pattern. Moreover, to this unhappy ending, Briar Rose objects that it is "not how stories are," a phrase supplied at the end of this section which constitutes another leitmotiv in the novel. This leitmotiv belongs to the second category of leitmotivs: those that have a double meaning and that are repeated throughout the pages in order to make the reader aware of the narrative conventions. Indeed, the princess keeps on telling the old crone that her stories are not "real" nor "right," because they do not correspond to the story of Sleeping Beauty. The recurrence of those adjectives is there to lead the reader into questioning what a "right" story would be: in what way are the traditional and pre-established patterns of narration more legitimate than others? Coover seems to remind us that they are just patterns.

At this point, it is important to focus upon the fairy-character. Just like many elements in the novel, she is extremely ambiguous; she is "the bad fairy, who is also the good fairy" (Coover 80). By merging two opposite, "flat" characters from the original fairy tale, Coover creates a "round," unique protagonist who reflects on her role and tries to provide Rose with other options for her destiny. The fairy is a key-figure from many points of view. During an informal talk at a conference in Paris, Robert Coover explained that he had been stuck (somewhat like the characters of his novel!) with the first two sections for years (one prince-section and one princess-section) and it was only thanks to the introduction of the third party that he finally managed to write his novel. Indeed, with the creation of this character, Coover could fill his mock fairy tale with many witty, humorous, satirical and brilliant "fairy's tales" that explore some of the infinite possibilities of narration. Being the only "active" character not bound in a predetermined role, the fairy is the only creative protagonist. Consequently, she is also the source of all the astounding variations on the Sleeping Beauty myth. Being *the* story-teller of the book, she can naturally be seen as the double of the writer, and her virtuosity in arranging new variations, playing with myths and mocking tradition, is indeed Coover's. Hence her ever-recurring "cackle" can be read as the writer's laugh gently mocking the characters he borrowed from others.

Circularity and repetition have an obvious comic purpose, but the subversion of those traditional fairy-tale devices is also there to reflect upon the endless repetition of the same narrative formulae across the centuries, with the example of the Sleeping Beauty myth. McCaffery explains this principle: "In these stories [i.e., *Pricksongs and Descants*], as with the best fictions of Borges and Nabokov, the structure itself is used to serve his central thesis about the dangers involved in dogmatic perspectives on our fictional systems" (71). With his own version(s) that counters the "right" and "real" story, Coover condemns the idea of a sterile, unique pattern possible, showing how non-creative and alienating it is. Through the myriad of alternative routes he offers, he opens space for freedom, making the reader aware of the imprisonment of his own reading reflexes within set narratives:

> Like other contemporary manipulators of myth..., Coover relies on this sort of material precisely because our responses to it are pre-set; since the material is familiar and our responses predictable, Coover can manipulate these expectations by rearranging familiar patterns into unfamiliar–but frequently wondrous or liberating shapes. Coover hopes that his strategies will create in their formal manipulations a sort of freedom from mythic imperatives which Robbe-Grillet has recently described: "As his imagination manipulates the mythological material, *the novelist establishes his freedom which exists only in language*" [McCaffery 61, my emphasis].

Indeed, Coover wishes to liberate the reader from the arbitrariness of pre-set narratives, but also from the arbitrariness of fixed links between signifier and signified: this is achieved through his work on words themselves (constant puns, neologisms, unusual metaphors) and through the deconstruction of myth (which, as Barthes stated is itself a form of language).[5]

Just as he wishes to free his readers, Coover also attempts to free the fairy tale characters. At first sight, Briar Rose seems reluctant to accept divergent versions. For instance, in section XXXII (61–62) she doubts the horse's ability to talk and wonders if her prince will come on a talking horse. To this statement, the fairy reproaches her with being self-absorbed, because she always assumes the stories are about her. Indeed, the fairy multiplies efforts to take her charge away from her self-centered, planned destiny by offering her other options. These options seem to work their way through the sleeping princess's mind: even if she senses there is a "right" story, she ceaselessly questions her identity and the reason for her being there (12; 10; 44).

As Redies points out, it appears that "the old crone often refuses to give her stories traditional, happy, and fulfilling structures and outcomes" (22). To her, this gives "complexity" to the novel, but in fact, what is at stake here is not only the subversion of the notion of happy ending within the overall deconstruction of the fairy tale's features, nor the revelation of the potential violence and cruelty of the genre: if the fairy's versions of the story are so dreadful it is also to awaken the princess and the reader to the arbitrary "fairy-tale" nature of the traditional narrative. Why do endings "have to" be happy and fairy-tale like? Section XV (Coover 27–28) provides a *mise en abyme* of the subversion of happy endings, as the fairy claims she provides, for once, a happy ending: this time, Beauty is woken up by ruffians who rape her, but "fortunately" they also wake up the knights of the castle who castrate and hang the rapists. This variation also illustrates how efficient the fairy's strategy is, as it results in having Briar Rose wanting to wake up and ask why she is the one. It is interesting to note that the heroine's desire to wake up is paired with her refusal of her fate: the fairy has told so many terrible stories that she no longer wishes to conform to the pattern:

> [Coover's fairy tale characters] mouth their respective desires and expectations, memories, repressed unorthodox motivations, give voice to longings one had not expected from figures that have regained autonomy.... Deconstruction is not brought about by the analytic scholarly interferences of a Bettelheim, himself debunked, with herds of academic colleagues, as the source of further stultification, but by the personalized scrapings and subversive doubt of the folk hero, focusing on familiar surroundings [Chénetier, "Robert Coover's" 80].

The recurrent motif of "being the one" is used by Coover to represent the autonomization of his characters from their set roles. This fairy-tale notion is questioned in two ways in the novel: first, by the Princess, who keeps on asking why she is the one ("Why me?" appears often on pages 28 and 44), and second, by the Prince, who repeatedly wonders if he really is the one (22). If "'to be the one' is the state to which all actions and experiences point, [which means that] real action, or choice, is not an option" (Redies 25), then doubting one's fate is in fact the door to freedom. As was seen earlier, Coover debunks the omnipotence of the fairy-tale structure by many structural devices, but he even undermines the fairy tale's age-old authority from within, from inside the characters themselves. The prince especially permits such subversion of the fairy-tale pattern. Section XXXVI, for example, introduces a cogitative prince, who is not too sure if he is at the right place. The prince's doubts break the pattern, and Briar Rose screams, "You are not the one!" (72). In addition, his doubt metatextually points to the inner ambiguity of any narrative, and especially Coover's *Briar Rose*: "It's so hard to know what's real and not in such a place" (72). Moreover, not only do the characters doubt about their fate, but also about the story itself: the prince "doubts there is really anyone in the castle, or that there is even a castle" (29).

Throughout the pages the very concept of "happily ever-after" is also systematically mocked and even turned into a mere action verb: the prince wishes to make his name "not by single feat but by *forever-aftering*" (Coover 9). What lies behind "forever after" is envisaged and realistically debunked in the dreams of both the princess and the prince, who envision the pains of matrimony, their boring royal obligations, the doubts and betrayals. Reusing a cliché, they even foresee the paradoxical "exhaustion of the 'inexhaustible fountain of their passion'" (55) and wonder once more whether they were the ones. Again, Coover confronts a mythical ideal to down-to-earth elements (here the fate of a married couple): once more the lie of fiction is exposed, the naive belief in eternal bliss ridiculed. The paradox here is that the fairy tale turns out to be a nightmare. The realistic face of "happily ever-after" is revealed in a powerful alliterative formula closing the paragraph: "the death of dreams" (55). This phrase echoes not only the major theme of the tale and the novel, but also figures the position of the writer regarding the myths that shape our perception of the world and our relation to it and to others, as McCaffery points out:

> Coover reveals that his concern with fiction-making extends far beyond the categories of narrative or literary art to the fundamental systems through which we perceive and organize our knowledge of the universe.... When such systems lose their utility and become stale, they need to be overhauled or discarded completely. Unfortunately, our desire for permanency and order often tempts us to ignore the fictional nature of our systems, and as the works of Coover, Gass, and Barthelme often dramatically demonstrate, without this understanding, we tend to become trapped within our fictional systems, victims of our own decayed or obsessive creations [8–9].

Conclusion

In one of his essays, Robert Coover describes Gabriel Marquez's "fascination with the twilight zone between sleeping and waking" ("The Master's Voice" 364), and in *Briar Rose* he seems to have echoed this fascination. The heroine of his tale is indeed in an ambiguous state between wake and sleep, always dreaming she is awakened by someone, and paradoxically waking up to those dreams within the dream, only to realize she is "in her moldy bed once more, waiting for she knows not what in the name of waiting for her prince to come" (85). In many respects, the situation of the readers mirrors that of Briar Rose: just like her, they are expecting the prince to come. Yet just like the old crone tries to make the princess aware of the fiction by which she is taken, the writer uses his skills to awaken the readers to the fiction in which they are entangled.

Coover, as a metafictionist, first multiplies devices to raise awareness of the fiction-making process at play in his own novel. Then, as an artist, he "shares with the cubists the relativistic view that the role of the artist is not to render reality unambiguously but to create realities whose ambiguities suggest something of our own relationship to the world" (McCaffery 73). In *Briar Rose*, Robert Coover tries to wake the readers up to their pre-set expectations, and, more importantly, to their dependence upon narrative and blind belief in the fictions that shape their behavior.

One day the prince will not come, but readers will wake up!

Notes

1. References to quotes from Coover's text cite page numbers, although a hypertextual version organized by section numbers is also available at: http://www.brown.edu/Departments/MCM/people/scholes/BriarRose/texts/BRhome.htm.

2. In her study of Coover's *Briar Rose* Sünje Redies dates the tradition back to Arthurian legends (14th-century Legend of Perceforest) (10), but it seems that a Nordic tale from the 13th-century, the Volsunga Saga, already contained the basic elements of the plot.

3. From the lecture given by Robert Coover at the conference "Passages of American Fiction: Transmissions, Transitions, Translations," held at the University of Paris 7-Denis Diderot, March 22–24, 2007 (to be published).

4. This is not the only Freudian aspect to be debunked: "In his novel *Briar Rose*, Coover reconsiders and parodies not only the Freudian idea of a dream as a representation of wish fulfillment, but also other important aspects of Freud's theory, especially the ones of the libido, incest, the pleasure principle, death, Oedipus and the castration complex" (Kusnir 45).

5. In his analysis of myth, Barthes equates it to speech — "*Le mythe est une parole*" (181) — and he develops a semiotic analysis of the mythic concept: "A signified can have various signifiers: it is the case of the linguistic signified and the psychoanalytical signified. It is also the case for the mythic concept: it has an unlimited amount of signifiers at its disposal" (192, my translation).

Works Cited

Barthes, Roland. *Mythologies.* 1957. Paris: Seuil, 1970.
Bettelheim, Bruno. *The Uses of Enchantment: The Meaning and Importance of Fairy Tales.* 1975. New York: Vintage, 1989.

Chénetier, Marc. "Robert Coover's Wondershow." *Amerikastudien* 1 (1984): 75–85.
Coover, Robert. *Briar Rose.* New York: Grove Press, 1996.
_____. "The Master's Voice." *American Review* 26 (1977): 361–88.
_____. *Pricksongs and Descants.* New York: Dutton, 1969.
Hutcheon, Linda. *Narcissistic Narrative: The Metafictional Paradox.* New York: Methuen, 1984.
Kusnir, Jaroslav. "Subversion of Myths: High and Low Cultures in Donald Barthelme's Snow White and Robert Coover's *Briar Rose.*" *European Journal of American Culture* 23. 1 (2004): 31–49.
McCaffery, Larry. *The Metafictional Muse: The Works of Robert Coover, Donald Barthelme, and William H. Gass.* Pittsburgh: University of Pittsburgh Press, 1982.
Redies, Sünje. "Return with New Complexities: Robert Coover's *Briar Rose.*" *Marvels & Tales* 18.1 (2004): 9–27.

Winterson's Wonderland
The PowerBook as a Postmodern Re-Vision of Lewis Carroll's Alice Books

MAUREEN TORPEY

> "Who are *you*?" said the Caterpillar. Alice replied, rather shyly, "I–
> I hardly know sir, just at present- at least I knew who I was when I
> got up this morning, but I think I must have been changed several
> times since then."
> —*Alice's Adventures in Wonderland* 40–1

> What is it you want? Freedom for a night, you say. Just for one night
> the freedom to be somebody else.
> —*The PowerBook* 3–4

In her article "When We Dead Awaken: Writing as Re-Vision," Adrienne
Rich defines re-vision as "the act of looking back, of entering a text from a new
critical direction" and claims that "it is an act of survival" (18). Jeanette Winterson, adhering to this idea of "looking back," believes "a writer needs to be
soaked in books. A writer can't ever read too much or know too much about
the literature of the past. Those writers are your teachers and private ances-
tors. Their work informs your work ... [and you should] try to honour their
experiments with some of your own" ("Books"). Winterson demonstrates this
belief in all of her books, including the postmodern novel *The PowerBook*.
Though *The PowerBook* includes many obvious cover versions and re-visions
from stories of Lancelot and Guinevere, to Paolo and Francesca, to George Mal-
lory, it also honors the experimentation of one of Britain's most celebrated children's authors by re-visioning his most famous works.

As Lewis Carroll, Charles Lutwidge Dodgson started a revolution and Alice
was his leader. Carroll is attributed with writing the "first English children's
classic" (Wullschläger 3) with *Alice's Adventures in Wonderland*, a book that
forever changed the course of children's literature. Prior to Lewis Carroll's writ-

ing, and that of his contemporaries, especially in the Victorian Age, as Jack Zipes reports, "Fairy tales and children's literature were written with the purpose of socializing children to meet definitive normative expectations at home and in the public sphere" (9). Beginning with Carroll, however, British children's writers' stories served "as a radical mirror to reflect what was wrong with the general discourse on manners, mores, and norms in society" (99). Wullschläger explains two primary changes adopted by these writers in her book *Inventing Wonderland*: "First, by establishing fantasy as a key element in children's writing, they determined the nature of all subsequent children's literature. Second, in discarding morality and teaching, and in making humour and satire essential ingredients, they set the tone of that literature in comedy and anarchy" (103). The world of children's literature became a fantasy land where the writers and readers alike could play out their deepest desires, push the boundaries of societal repression, and remake their present lives to carve out new futures.

Charles Dodgson once wrote to his sister Mary, "If you limit your actions in life to things that *nobody* can possibly find fault with, you will not do much" (qtd. in Stoffel 121). Throughout his life, though much more so post-humously and after the discoveries of Sigmund Freud, Dodgson's lifestyle, specifically his seemingly inappropriate friendships with young girls, was questioned. No misconduct was ever proved, however, and out of these friendships, his greatest stories were born. The Alice books were written for the most treasured of these girls, Alice Liddell, the daughter of the dean of Christ Church College at Oxford where Dodgson taught. Dodgson spent a great deal of time with Alice and her sisters and was greatly loved by them for his storytelling skills. *Alice's Adventures in Wonderland* was conceived on a boat trip with the three Liddell sisters and recorded at the request of Alice Liddell. Thus, the story and the children's literature revolution began with Alice's desire to have her account written down by her great friend, Charles Dodgson, who was soon to be much better known as Lewis Carroll. The resulting books are still making an impact on readers, both in their original form and in other writers' re-visions of the originals.

Jeanette Winterson has demonstrated her familiarity with Carroll and his Alice books in many of her novels. In the semi-fictional autobiography *Oranges Are Not the Only Fruit*, she begins the Judges chapter with a quote from the Queen of Hearts to the Duchess: "'Now I give you fair warning' shouted the Queen, stamping her foot on the ground as she spoke; 'Either you or your head must be off'" (127). In *Written on the Body*, the narrator declares in the first chapter, "I shall call myself Alice and play croquet with the flamingoes. In Wonderland everyone cheats and love is Wonderland isn't it? Love makes the world go round" (10). The entire declaration is a reference Alice's game of croquet with the Queen of Hearts, and the final sentence is clearly an echo of one of the Duchess' morals, "Oh, 'tis love, 'tis love, that makes the world go round!" (Carroll 79). These early references simply show Winterson's knowledge of

Carroll's Alice books and her ability to draw on them to create obvious and straightforward intertexts.

In her later book, *The Passion*, Winterson references the Alice books less directly, but perhaps more significantly, and develops a more complex intertextual relationship with Carroll. Adrienne Rich asserts of re-vision,

> If the imagination is to transcend and transform experience it has to question, to challenge, to conceive of alternatives, perhaps to the very life you are living at the moment.... [N]othing can be too sacred for the imagination to turn into its opposite or to call experimentally by another name. For writing is re-naming [23].

In her opening section of *The Passion*, Winterson illustrates her talent for the "play" that Rich encourages. The section is called "The Queen of Spades," and the title character embodies some of the same character traits of the Queen of Hearts, especially the tendency for unprovoked violence in the midst of games. The Queen of Spades is the mirror image, the Looking-Glass House version of her predecessor. The character is much the same, but she has been re-named as Winterson plays with the original text and adds her own re-vision to the existing story line. Similarly, *The PowerBook* uses the Alice books as an intertext much more subtly than *Oranges are not the Only Fruit* or *Written on the Body*. In this novel, Winterson broadens the idea of more playful re-vision that she begins in *The Passion*.

Winterson, of course, is not the only author to see the merits of re-vising Carroll's masterpieces of children's literature. Since *Alice's Adventures in Wonderland* was published in 1865 and its sequel, *Through the Looking-Glass*, in 1871, hundreds of authors and journalists have imitated and parodied the story. Carroll himself rewrote his story in a picture book for small children called *The Nursery Alice*, published in 1889 (Stoffel 115). In the introduction to her anthology, *Alternative Alices: Visions and Revisions of Lewis Carroll's Alice Books*, Carolyn Sigler argues that the imitations between 1869 and 1930, works such as Christina Rossetti's *Speaking Likenesses*, Frances Hodgson Burnett's *Behind the White Brick*, John Rae's *New Adventures of "Alice,"* and John Kendrick Bangs' *Alice in Blunderland, An Iridescent Dream*, are truer to Carroll's text than more recent imitations. Sigler claims that "recent works use the *Alice* books as starting points from which to comment on questions unrelated to the books themselves and the issues they raise" (xvii). Sigler attributes the shift to changes in literature, society and culture, and believes that contemporary authors use recognizable references loosely and to their own advantages while the earlier imitators addressed issues in the original books. However, three years after the publication of Sigler's anthology, 135 years after the first publication of *Alice's Adventures in Wonderland*, Jeanette Winterson published *The PowerBook*, a book that challenges Sigler's claim. This heavily intertextual novel, unlike Winterson's own earlier novels, as well as the "false imitators" to which Sigler is referring, not only alludes to events in the Alice books, but it also amplifies the ideas of fulfilling desire and challenging boundaries through the use of fantasy present in the Alice books and utilizes many of the themes and techniques of Carroll's originals.

At first glance, this novel might seem, as Sigler accuses, to merely use the Alice books as a "starting point," moving quickly onto other issues unrelated to Carroll's stories. Winterson is often quickly dismissed as a lesbian writer because she herself is a lesbian and her love stories often involve homosexual or bisexual women, or ambiguously gendered characters. Thus, *The Power-Book*, with its numerous references to *Alice's Adventures in Wonderland* and *Through the Looking-Glass* and an obvious social and cultural agenda of challenging readers' normative assumptions, could easily be relegated to the realm of literature pertaining only to the gay and lesbian movement. Though of course this reading is one of Winterson's intentions, it is not the only possible reading and such pigeonholing would be a mistake. Winterson has often addressed the idea of being categorized as a "lesbian writer," or even a "postmodern writer," in interviews, essays, and even her own novels. She continually refutes the categorizations, saying, "I don't write for any group — male, female, straight, gay. I write to bring about a change in consciousness" (qtd. in Jaggi). In an interview with Laura Miller of *Salon*, Winterson stated,

> There has to be ... a point where whatever has had meaning, whatever is powerful to you, can be translated into something which will matter to somebody that you will never know, whose life is entirely different from yours. Otherwise you will always fall into the trap of talking to a peer or interest group and you can't reach people whose experience is quite different to yours.

Though many critics and readers have tried to label them, Jeanette Winterson's books defy simplistic classification. They have a much more universal appeal and message, and it so happens that the message in *The PowerBook* is quite similar to that of Carroll's Alice books. Both concern changing personas and involve a quest to discover identity. Through their playful but subtly powerful attitude toward challenging conventions, both push the boundaries between the real world and fantasy worlds and encourage readers to question themselves and their world extensively.

In *Alternative Alices*, Sigler sets a list of criteria that true imitations must share with Lewis Carroll's originals, including

> an Alice-like protagonist or protagonists, male or female; ...a clear transition from the "real" waking world to a fantasy dream world; ...rapid shifts in identity, appearance, and location; an episodic structure; ...an awakening or return to the "real" world; ...and usually, a clear acknowledgement of indebtedness to Carroll through ... textual or extratextual reference[s] [xvii].

By meeting each of these criteria and even moving beyond them, *The Power-Book* proves that it uses Carroll's books as more than a mere starting point to pursue other goals, and rather is a true and effective re-vision of the Alice books.

Because of her continual return to fellow Oxford graduate Lewis Carroll in almost all of her books, we can easily recognize Winterson's "clear acknowledgement of indebtedness" to him. Thus, we can begin our examination of her imitation by exploring how she mimics the basic structure of the Alice books. Like many postmodern novelists, she relies upon the "classical tale-within-a-tale" (Onega 184) narration of *1001 Arabian Nights*, using a frame story and embedded texts. *Alice's Adventures in Wonderland* both begins and ends with Alice "sitting by her sister on the bank" (Carroll 9), and her adventures are a dream that occurs from that spot. Similarly, *Through the Looking-Glass* begins and ends with Alice in a room in her house playing with Kitty, one of Dinah's kittens. Wonderland and the Looking-Glass House are made out to be dreams into which Alice falls and from which she reawakens. Carefully following this framing technique, *The PowerBook* opens in the narrator Ali's shop, where "the sign on the shop says VERDE, nothing more, but everyone know something strange goes on inside" (Winterson 3), and concludes with Ali telling us, "I live above the shop. The sign on the shop just says VERDE and no one can see inside" (235). The emails exchanged between Ali and the character known as "you" become the driving force of the narrative, the stories told in those emails, the dream world where "you can be free for just one night" (4). Winterson gives us the word "Night" (*PowerBook* 3, 25, 63, 83, 119, 13, 161, 209, 235, 243) as a clear signal that the characters have exited their story and are once again sitting at their computer screens; instead of one embedded story, Winterson offers a series of embedded stories. While Alice dozes off to find her dream world, Ali is the active creator of *The PowerBook's* Wonderland, always playing the central role in the stories told opposite "you," thus creating the metanarratological line of the novel. This frame of creator and creation sets up the contrast between the real world and the dream world and allows for a clear exit from that dream world at the end of the novel.

The name of the narrator of *The PowerBook*, Ali, or Alix in one story, can be seen as an obvious derivative of Alice, as well as other names of course. Ironically, as Sigler says the protagonist can be male or female, Ali is both male and female, depending on the story being told at the moment. As Carroll describes, Alice is a "curious child ... very fond of pretending to be two people" (14). Ali can also be two people, both the male and female versions of him/herself. Winterson takes this two-person aspect of Alice one step further, and includes a second protagonist-like character, who the reader simply knows by her screen name, "Tulip," but who is most often referred to only as "you," adding a postmodern twist to Sigler's criteria. Abiding by Roland Barthes' idea that the text "become a device to undo the reader's passivity and actively engage him in the creative process of literature by letting him discover his own solutions to the story" (Markey 117), Winterson demands that both the character "you" and the reader of the novel participate in the creation of *The PowerBook*. In the book, Tulip enlists Ali to write her into a story to give her "freedom for just one night." Throughout the story, the character "you" must not only read the story, but also begins to participate in the creation of the stories as her relationship with Ali develops. Similarly, just through the use of pronouns, Winterson demands active participation on behalf of the reader of *The PowerBook* both to turn the pages of the novel and keep the story going, and also to use previous knowledge to disentangle the intertextual threads of the story and follow the multiple levels of meaning. By updating the narrator with clearly postmodern techniques, Winterson gives us a 21st century Alice in the characters of Ali and "you."

Carroll used actual events from the life of his muse, Alice Liddell, to create the Alice books for her. Ali uses what little he/she knows of "you" to create stories. For instance, the screen name "Tulip" becomes the basis for the first story which Ali begins by writing, "I want to start with a tulip" (*PowerBook* 9). Just to ensure that readers of *The PowerBook* immediately recognize the allusions to the Alice books, the Princess, the character played by "you" in the first story, tells Ali, "You will be gentle. You will be slow. If I do not like you I shall behead you" (20), sounding not unlike a less openly aggressive version of the Queen of Hearts of Carroll's Wonderland.

Because the stories told by Ali are based on fulfilling the desire of "you" to be transformed, he/she allows "you" to choose details rather than basing the details on the physical "you." Ali lets "you" decide on hair color ("Red. I've always wanted red hair" [22]), wardrobe ("'Combat or Prada?' 'How much can I spend on clothes?' 'How about $1000?'" [27], and location of stories ("'You tell me. Where are we?' 'Paris. We're in Paris. There's the Eiffel Tower'" [28]). Carroll knew Alice Liddell and thus could incorporate aspects of her appearance and personality into his stories, but he also took suggestions from Alice and her sisters for events that occurred. Similarly, Ali needs a little help from "you" to get started, then takes off at a breakneck speed, incorporating answers and building on them in subsequent stories. Throughout the book, a single detail from the conversations between Ali and Tulip in the virtual world of the internet — which, ironically, is the "real" world of this novel — is often the starting point for the next story which simultaneously seems to be completely disconnected from and to build upon the previous stories. Though the stories appear to be sitting in separate geographical, historical and narrative locations, threads from the stories spin out, intertwining in that liminal space that exists between them, weaving a single multi-layered web.

When Alice enters her dream, the episodic structure to which Sigler refers begins. Throughout these episodes, Alice shifts locations and moves through time in strange and unexpected ways. One way Carroll allows for all the shifts in location in his stories is by manipulating time. In Wonderland, time does not work the same way that it does in the real world, something Alice discovers in her *Adventures in Wonderland* by looking at the March Hare's watch. She observes, "It tells the day of the month, and doesn't tell what o'clock it is!" (62).

In *Through the Looking-Glass,* Carroll alters not only time, but distances as well. When the Queen makes Alice run as fast as she can, Alice realizes that they do not move from where they started under the tree. When Alice comments that in her world, all of that running would certainly have gotten them someplace, the Queen replies that this is "a slow sort of country.... Now, *here,* you see, it takes all the running *you* can do, to keep in the same place. If you want to get somewhere else, you must run at least twice as fast as that!" (143). In Wonderland, time and place are not fixed entities.

Winterson uses this same episodic structure and manipulation of time and place in *The PowerBook.* Ali and "you" become different characters from history, literature, and imagination, while traveling all over the world and all through time. Just as "you" requests, in the second story they are in Paris. After that, Ali and "you" travel to Mt. Everest, and to Italy and London, both in the present and Middle Ages. In one chapter, Ali and "you" travel from the Capri of the Middle Ages, to the Capri of the 19th century, to the Capri of present day in just a few pages. Time in the world of imaginative internet writing is just as malleable as time in Wonderland. The nonlinear narration of *The PowerBook,* the accumulation of stories, puts the reader in mind of Carroll's narrative where at any moment a rabbit hole might open, a mirror might serve as a doorway, and Alice can slip down or through to another level of Carroll's world. In *The PowerBook,* the stories run alongside each other. Sometimes the narrative lines intersect and the reader slips from one time and place to another right with the characters.

In both of these Wonderlands, physical appearance is as unfixed as time and distance. Alice changes appearance several times and meets all kinds of different creatures often based on nursery rhymes or other children's literature. While Alice can change shape depending on what she eats, sometimes shrinking to 10 inches high, sometimes growing to the size of a house (an episode that is mimicked as an emotional stand-off in *The PowerBook*), Ali and "you" change shape and character which each new story, each new location, putting on new identities they same way they would put on a new outfit. As Ali commands in the opening chapter, "Undress. Take off your clothes. Take off your body. Hang them up behind the door. Tonight we can go deeper than disguise" (*PowerBook* 4). In *The PowerBook,* bodies are in excess and can be inhabited at will throughout the journey. Ali and "you" become Lancelot and Guinevere, Francesca and Paolo. Ali relives Winterson's personal literary history in the story of the Muck House, a clear re-vision of *Oranges are Not the Only Fruit.* Instead of parodying popular nursery rhymes like Carroll, Winterson, postmodernist that she is, parodies classical and popular literature from the works of Dante and Boccaccio, to the King Arthur stories, to her own earlier books. Carroll uses the fantasy setting of Wonderland to create new rules of existence while alluding to past influences; Winterson relies on the technological age, on the idea that nothing is permanent in the internet world, yet she still recognizes and honors her literary forebears.

In *The PowerBook*, Winterson, along with meeting the criteria for a true Alice imitator, accomplishes a feat that did not make Sigler's list but perhaps belongs there: Winterson maintains the main theme of the Alice books. Like Carroll's books, *The PowerBook* is a quest story. After entering another world, Alice is driven forward in search of more than just her way home; she is in search of herself, of her personal identity. Falling into the rabbit hole in the beginning of *Alice's Adventures in Wonderland*, Alice loses her sense of self and the objective of both Alice books is to help her relocate her identity, if it can be found. To trace some of the most significant points on this quest, the reader first sees Alice doubting herself in the second chapter. Once she has stopped crying after her unexpected growth spurt, Alice asks, "I wonder if I've changed in the night? Let me think: *was* I the same when I got up this morning? I almost think I can remember feeling a little different. But if I'm not the same, the next question is 'Who in the world am I?' Ah, *that's* the great puzzle!" (Carroll 18). Indeed, this is the puzzle that Alice spends the rest of her journey trying to solve. The White Rabbit mistakes her for his housemaid Mary Ann, the pigeon mistakes her for a serpent, and the Cheshire Cat simply tells her she is mad. Once she gets into the garden, she manages to introduce herself as Alice, but she is still not quite sure who Alice is anymore. She tells the Mock Turtle it is no use explaining her adventures starting from yesterday, because, as she says, "I was a different person then" (91). Her conversation with the Caterpillar reinforces the uncertain nature of her identity when she cannot answer the seemingly simple question, "Who are *you*?" (40).

Though Alice wakes up from the dream in her *Adventures in Wonderland*, she has not yet found the answer to the Caterpillar's question, and her quest continues in *Through the Looking-Glass*. She enters the wood where things have no name and expresses a desire not to forget her name. Despite this desire, she does forget her name and cannot remember it again until she leaves the wood. Soon after remembering her name, however, Alice encounters Tweedledee and Tweedledum who tell her she is merely a part of the Red King's dream. Tweedledum says to Alice, "You know very well you're not real" (Carroll 165). Alice is horrified and begins to cry and protest. She is eventually made a Queen and she wakes from this dream as well. At the conclusion of *Through the Looking-Glass*, though all seems to end happily, Carroll leaves his readers with a great deal of ambiguity. Alice discusses the issue of dreams with her cat, saying, "Let's consider who it was that dreamed it all. This is a serious question, my dear.... You see Kitty, it *must* have been either me or the Red King. He was part of my dream, of course — but then, I was part of his dream too!" (240). Similarly, the final line of Carroll's concluding poem is "Life, what is it but a dream?" (241). Though Alice is home again, in the place where she should be most certain of her sense of self, Lewis Carroll abandons his heroine and his readers to the uncertainty of the difference between dreams and reality, an issue Winterson continues to debate in her novels.

Winterson preserves Carroll's theme, the quest story, and his ambiguity in *The PowerBook.* Her protagonists are often looking to complete themselves, to find another to supplement and shape their identities. Living in a recognizably modern world where self-help and self-fulfillment are an industry, they *know* how difficult it is to answer the question, "Who are *you*?" The quest for self has a dual nature. The character "you" tries to abandon her real world identity, searching for the freedom to try on as many identities and personalities as possible in one night on the internet. To fulfill this desire, "you" enlists Ali, the owner of the shop where, Winterson writes, "People arrive as themselves and leave as someone else" (3). While it's clear that "you" is on the quest for her identity, Ali is in search of his/her identity as well. Ali admits outright

> I'm looking for something, it's true.
> I'm looking for the meaning inside the data.
> That's why I trawl my screen like a beachcomber — looking for you, looking for me, trying to see through the disguise. I guess I've been looking for us both my whole life [*PowerBook* 64].

Ali is definitely looking for another to help complete his/her identity. The added complication of having two Alice-like protagonists in the quest is no longer for one identity, but for two, or perhaps for an identity as a couple. Ali, to discover, his/her identity, must also discover the identity of "you." Ali is not hopeful in this quest, saying, "My search for you, your search for me, is a search after something that cannot be found. Only the impossible is worth the effort" (78); therefore, "the journey must be made" (79). Ali asks "you" why she disappeared after the night in Paris and "you" replies, "To save my sense of self. You make me wonder who I am." "Who are you?" (104) Ali counters, echoing Alice's caterpillar. The identities of you and Ali coincide with each other, one depending on the other, thus making the quest more complicated.

As Ali changes the stories for "you," Ali changes as well. He/she loses control of the stories, and his/her sense of self mutates along with the stories. Ali, Winterson writes, "puts himself in the stories. Once there, he cannot easily get out again..." (*PowerBook* 216). As Ali spins the story, he/she is no longer certain whether he/she is writing the story, or the story is writing him/her. Finally, Ali withdraws from the story, the dream, the internet Wonderland at the end of the novel. Once out of the story, however, Ali discovers him/herself suffering a problem Charles E. Winquist describes in his essay "The Act of Storytelling and the Self's Homecoming": "To live without a story is to be disconnected from our past and our future. Without a story, we are bound to the immediacy of the moment, and we are forever losing our grip on the reality of our own identity with the passage of discrete moments" (108). In the last lines of *The PowerBook*, in an ending as frustratingly ambiguous as Carroll's, Ali walks along the banks of the Thames River, takes off his/her watch, drops it into the water, and thinks,

> Time take it.
> Your face, your hands, the movement of your body...
> Your body is my Book of Hours.
> Open it. Read it.
> This is the true history of the world [243].

Just like the conclusion of *Through the Looking-Glass*, the conclusion of *The PowerBook* abandons the reader in a world where, as Winterson describes, "The partition between the real and invented is as thin as a wall in a cheap hotel room" (93–4). Dreams and reality bleed together, each one trading position for which is more tangible and more significant, vying for the position of "true history." Identity becomes relative, depending on who is asking and where one happens to be. Invented stories are more realistic and hold more weight in shaping identity than any aspect of "real" life. Alice cannot be certain whether she or the Red King dreamed up Wonderland, or whether she is real or still part of his dream. Ali cannot be certain that the story has ended or if he/she is trapped in it, waiting for "you" to return. Both quests for identity end in ambivalence.

In an interview with Margaret Reynolds, Jeanette Winterson says, "All texts work off other texts. It's a continual re-writing and re-reading of what has gone before, and you hope that you can add something new. There's interpretation as well as creation in everything that happens with books" (qtd. in Noakes and Reynolds 18–19). Winterson fully recognizes the long line of storytellers who have come before her. Her body of work both honors that lineage and extends the line by incorporating her own views and perspectives on the history of storytelling and its place in the contemporary world. In *The PowerBook*, itself, Winterson even gives us her re-vision of Rich's original definition of re-vision:

> Break the narrative. Refuse all stories that have been told so far (because that is what the momentum really is), and try to tell the story differently — in a different style, with different weights — and allow some air to those elements choked with centuries of use, and give some substance to the floating world [53].

Winterson parodies, refers to, and imitates other texts to add texture and depth or her own material, acknowledging the past but writing for the present and future. Carroll's Alice books are certainly not the only influence on *The Power-Book*, but understanding Winterson's re-vision of them gives us one more level of meaning in the text. Winterson is fascinated by storytelling in all of her novels, and with the idea that stories mean something different to every person who reads them. She encourages readers, in her books of essays *Art Objects*, to eschew their passivity and "to engage with a text as you would with another human being.... To find its relationship with you that is not its relationship to anyone else" (111). Clearly, she has read *Alice's Adventures in Wonderland* and *Through the Looking-Glass* and has formed her own relationship with them. In *The*

PowerBook, she further develops that relationship by adding something new, by allowing some air in, by telling the stories her own way. Carroll used fantasy in children's literature to push at the boundaries of societal repression. Winterson continues this tradition in *The PowerBook,* by addressing some of Carroll's themes in a contemporary setting and demanding that her readers challenge established ideas of norms and limitations, thus drawing the idea of fantastical subversion into the 21st century.

Works Cited

Carroll, Lewis. *Alice's Adventures in Wonderland and Through the Looking-Glass.* London: Penguin, 1998.
Jaggi, Maya. "Profiles and Interviews: Jeanette Winterson." *The Guardian* 29 May 2004. 1 March 2007 <http://www.jeanettewinterson.com/pages/content/index.asp?PageID=272>.
Markey, Constance. *Italo Calvino: A Journey Toward Postmodernism.* Gainesville: University of Florida Press, 1999.
Miller, Laura. "Jeanette Winterson: England's Literary Outlaw." *Salon.* Apr. 1997. 22 Nov. 2003 <http://archive.salon.com/april97/winterson970428.html>.
Noakes, Jonathan, and Margaret Reynolds, eds. *Jeanette Winterson: Vintage Living Texts.* London: Vintage, 2003.
Onega, Susana. *Jeanette Winterson.* Contemporary British Novelists Series. Manchester: Manchester University Press, 2006.
Rich, Adrienne. "When We Dead Awaken: Writing as Re-Vision." *College English* 34.1 (Oct. 1972): 18–30. Women, Writing and Teaching.
Sigler, Carolyn, ed. *Alternative Alices: Visions and Revisions of Lewis Carroll's Alice Books.* Lexington: University of Kentucky Press, 1997.
Stoffel, Stephanie Lovett. *Lewis Carroll in Wonderland: The Life and Times of Alice and Her Creator.* New York: Wonderland Press, 1997.
Winquist, Charles E. "The Act of Storytelling and the Self's Homecoming." *Journal of the American Academy of Religion* 42.1 (Mar. 1974): 101–13.
Winterson, Jeanette. *Art Objects: Essays on Ecstasy and Effrontery.* New York: Knopf, 1996.
_____. "Books: The PowerBook." *Jeanette Winterson Website.* 25 Feb. 2007 <http://www.jeanettewinterson.com/pages/content/index.asp?PageID=10>.
_____. *Oranges Are Not the Only Fruit.* New York: Grove, 1985.
_____. *The Passion.* New York: Grove, 1987.
_____. *The PowerBook.* London: Vintage, 2001.
_____. *Written on the Body.* New York: Vintage International, 1994.
Wullschläger, Jackie. *Inventing Wonderland.* New York: The Free Press, 1995.
Zipes, Jack. *Fairy Tales and the Art of Subversion.* New York: Wildman Press, 1983.

"I Think You Are Not Telling Me All of This Story"

Storytelling, Fate, and Self-Determination in Robin McKinley's Folktale Revisions

Amie A. Doughty

Robin McKinley's first novel *Beauty: A Retelling of the Story of Beauty & the Beast*, published in 1978, opens with Beauty, the narrator of the novel, telling the story of how she acquired her nickname Beauty when she was five and desired a name that she could understand better than her given name, Honour. Her narrative is peppered with smaller stories like this renaming tale as she recounts her role in McKinley's "Beauty and the Beast" revision, and each story acts to flesh out the details of the traditional tale more fully than the first person narrative alone. Much more detailed than most traditional versions of the folktale, McKinley's *Beauty* nevertheless follows quite closely the traditional elements of the folktale, the main exception being the three daughters' relationship with each other, which is very close and supportive in McKinley's text compared to the traditional unpleasant relationship based on jealousy.

In 1997, McKinley published *Rose Daughter*, her second revision of "Beauty and the Beast." This revision, presented in third person primarily from Beauty's point of view, while following closely along with many of the traditional versions of "Beauty and the Beast" through most of the novel — again with the noticeable exception of the positive relationship between Beauty and her sisters — diverges significantly from the traditional folktale as it reaches its climax. After Beauty has declared her love for the Beast, a storm erupts over their head, and she learns that victory over the enchantment is not as simple as she expected. At this point she is forced to choose how she wants the enchantment and her story to end: she can choose for the Beast to be transformed to what he was before the spell was cast on him and for them to live a life of "wealth and influence"; or she can choose for the Beast to remain in his present form and for them to live their lives ordinarily as residents of Longchance, the town to which she and her family moved after her father's financial collapse (274–5). Her choice to return to Longchance with the Beast represents a refusal of the traditional "Beauty and the Beast" ending in which Beauty is rewarded for her love with a handsome prince and untold wealth, though it does retain the happy ending for the main characters.

This choice of ending, Beauty's control of her own future, is a significant change from both the traditional folktale and McKinley's first revision *Beauty*, and it reflects the evolution in McKinley's presentation of her characters in her folktale revisions. Rather than relying on fate to control their lives, McKinley's characters choose their own endings just as McKinley herself chooses to reshape the traditional folktales and their resolutions rather than be constrained by the folktale tradition as she is to a great extent in *Beauty*. Her most recent novels challenge the conventions of the folktale tradition, conventions she challenges in smaller ways with her earlier novels, most notably with the strong female characters and positive relationships among women.

Paralleling the way in which McKinley's characters control their futures and their stories is a change in the way storytelling is presented in the novels. Though all of McKinley's work contains references to storytelling, it is only in her later works that the characters become aware of their place in stories and of their ability to shape their stories as they see fit. Though all of McKinley's work is intertextual, it is only her later works that have a significant metatextual element that challenges the authority of the texts upon which they are based. The intertext of the novels lays out the readers' expectations of the novels while the metatext allows for the breaking of these expectations. At the same time, McKinley maintains one of the primary expectations of folktales and fantasy fiction — the happy ending — even though her means of reaching that conclusion may diverge from the traditional stories.

McKinley's earliest folktale revision, *Beauty: A Retelling of the Story of Beauty & the Beast* (1978), contains a main character whose choices are limited and whose story is shaped by her connections to other stories and by the dreams and visions within the novel. *Beauty*, as the novel's full title indicates, is tied to the folktale "Beauty and the Beast" and follows the pattern of that story faithfully. Though Beauty is strong in her ability to survive and even thrive in the events fate has in store for her, she remains limited in her achievements because she lacks choices.

In *Beauty*, Beauty's primary choice is to go to the Beast in her father's place so that she can save his life, though even this choice is questionable since the alternative is to sacrifice her father. She tells her family, "I'm turned eighteen. I'm ready for an adventure" (78). Yet the night before she is to leave, Beauty thinks, "A sense of responsibility, if that was what it was, did not explain the intensity of my determination" to go to the Beast (81). Something, it seems, is pressing her toward the Beast and whatever he has in store for her — and she half fears he means to go back on his promise to her father and eat her. On her arrival at the Beast's castle, however, she discovers that it is a wondrous place in many ways, and she is given the chance to do her two favorite things: work with her horse Greatheart and study all the classic Greek and Latin works her heart desires, as well as read a variety of other works as yet unpublished but still available in the Beast's vast library. Indeed, Beauty is so fascinated with classical works that she compares the Beast to several mythological characters: Yggdrasil (116), Aeolus (141), Cerberus (146), and Nemesis (151). Events that happen at the castle are similarly compared, and she even allies herself to "King Cophetua's beggar maid" (106) when she first arrives at the castle, only to decide that it is a false comparison. Mythology, particularly Greek, has a strong influence on Beauty's life, and these intertextual elements of the novel dominate McKinley's revision of "Beauty and the Beast," for Beauty, uncomfortable with herself and feeling that she fits neither her given name, Honour, nor her self-chosen name, Beauty, is searching for a story of her own. It should not be surprising then that she fits so tightly within the parameters of the folktale on which her story is based — like the characters she reads about and compares her world to, she is bound by the conventions of her story.

The end of the novel — Beauty's return to her family, her overstay at home and subsequent frantic search for the Beast, followed by her declaration of love and acceptance of his proposal, and the Beast's transformation to his original form — follow the traditional story quite closely. Prior to her flight home, she had begun to adapt to the magic of the palace sufficiently to hear and understand what her magical servants, Bessie and Lydia, have been saying, that she will "figure it out in the end" (173). Yet Beauty does not "figure it out." Rather, she acts instinctively rather than with foreknowledge, and it is only after the transformation of the Beast that she comes to understand what they meant — that her promise to marry the Beast would free him from the spell cast upon him. For someone who is highly intelligent and who loves to read, Beauty is oblivious to her place in the creation of her story; she reflects on creating story only when her family asks her to tell them about her time with the Beast, when she reveals that "I found there was quite a lot I skipped over because I didn't feel that I could explain it" (207). In particular, she has difficulty discussing the Beast, though "I didn't leave him out of my narrative, yet I had tremendous trouble bringing him into it" (207). This metatextual aspect of the novel is very limited, and Beauty never makes reference to creating her story as it is unfolding, something that would be easy for her to do as narrator of the novel. Instead, she lets the events of the story carry her along until she reaches her happy ending. She accepts her fate to go to the Beast in the first place and then again when he is transformed and repeats his desire to marry her. Though Ellen R. Sackelman claims in "More Than Skin Deep: Robin McKinley's *Beauty: A Retelling of the Story of Beauty and the Beast* (1978)" when the transformed Beast asks Beauty to name him, "the privilege of giving a human name to the

Beast makes final and more significant Beauty's sense of control over her world" (34), this control is questionable. As Michael Cadden points out in "The Illusion of Control: Narrative Authority in Robin McKinley's *Beauty* and *The Blue Sword*," "There is nothing she can name him that will come before his title. He is already named 'King' and she 'Queen'" (19). The apparent control of naming the Beast, then, is an illusion — as with all other aspects of her life, Beauty lives at the whim of others. There is little significant difference between the Beauty of the folktale and the Beauty of McKinley's first novel.

This first folktale revision by McKinley is separated from her next revision of folk material, Robin Hood rather than a folktale, by two original fantasy novels, *The Blue Sword* and *The Hero and the Crown*, both of which also show the tendencies of *Beauty* of presenting seemingly-strong, self-determined main characters who are really at the mercy of fate. Each of McKinley's early novels presents characters limited in their choices on the few occasion they are offered choices.[1] With fate and destiny primary motivators of characters, and intertextual limitations in the case of *Beauty*, none of the characters moves beyond conventional strengths. McKinley's middle novels, *The Outlaws of Sherwood* (1988) and *Deerskin* (1993), however, reveal a slight shift away from characters whose fates are mapped out for them to characters more in control of their own stories. Though they approach storytelling and the characters' place in storytelling differently, both *The Outlaws of Sherwood* and *Deerskin* contain characters breaking away from the intertextual constraints of their traditional stories, usually with a nudge, if not a push, from helping characters.

The Outlaws of Sherwood, McKinley's reworking of the Robin Hood legend, is arguably a novel about storytelling and how it shapes and is shaped by real events. One of the first differences McKinley makes to most versions of the Robin Hood legend is with the Maid Marian character. In *The Outlaws of Sherwood*, Marian is a far better archer than Robin, while Robin is a mediocre archer at best, something he regrets because his father was a great archer. Robin's skill lies in the making of arrows, rather than in shooting them, and with his knowledge of the forest. When he is forced into hiding after accidentally killing a man who had been trying to kill him, Robin becomes the reluctant leader of a group resisting the Normans ruling Britain. As Geoffrey Gates in "'Always the Outlaw': The Potential for Subversion of the Metanarrative in Retellings of Robin Hood" comments, "The narrative stresses that Robin is a poor shot ... and hence it is by fate that Robin ends up outside the law" (71). His leadership is spurred on primarily by Marian, who, as Lorinda B. Cohoon indicates in "Transgressive Transformations: Representations if Maid Marian in Robin Hood Retellings," "uses the power of story to invent Robin Hood; she carefully crafts the leader/outlaw she believes the people of England need" (224). Robin himself has little to do with the creation of his legend — aside from agreeing to its creation. As the group hiding in the forest grows, he realizes "whether he wished to acknowledge it or not, the price on his head gave him an aura; however accidentally he had gained it, and however greatly he wished he could be rid of it, in their eyes because of it he was the real thing, and thus they would follow his lead" (McKinley, *Outlaws* 29). As with Beauty, Robin seems tied to his fate, though he does choose to accept his role, just as Beauty chooses to accept hers. As the group grows, so too does their reputation as outlaws, and the reputation passed along in various tales brings many people hoping to join Robin's group to the forest and leads to further tales about the group. One of the prevalent tales, that the group robs from the rich and gives to the poor, evolves from Robin's kindness to those people who come to join the group but do not stay. When these people leave, Robin makes sure they have enough food and money to relocate to a safer place, and their tales of his generosity, as with all other tales of Robin Hood and his outlaws, alter with each telling until Robin has become legendary, something Marian planned when she started the legend. Yet the tales of stealing from the rich and giving to the poor also eventually come true when the outlaws rob the person carrying the taxes to the sheriff. Much of that stolen money is given to the Saxon farmers to pay their rents, which have been raised (62–3). Here Robin Hood's stories become self-fulfilling, though he remains pessimistic about what they're doing, feeling it will become more difficult for them to steal in the future.

The importance of storytelling in relationship to the Robin Hood legend continues to develop as the novel progresses, and Robin has no control of the tales, something he knows only too well. The discussion of how his story is being told is constant. Following the biggest battle of the novel — when the outlaws fight the hired assassin, Guy of Gisbourne, and his men — Robin comments, "It was not so noble a fight as one might wish for the minstrel's version," to which Will Scarlet replied, "That depends on your point of view" (McKinley, *Outlaws* 237). All in the group are aware of the minstrels' interest in the outlaws and in the minstrels' poetic license, which will allow them to shape the story to their contentment. McKinley herself is a type of modern minstrel who reshapes the legend to her specifications, making Robin a young leader uncomfortable with the task of leading his group and casting the outlaws as a wide variety of outcasts and runaways. The outlaws include several very strong female characters, notably Marian, who is injured severely when she disguises herself as Robin for the sheriff's archery contest, and Cecily, Will Scarlet's sister, who pretends to be a boy and joins the outlaws. The point of view of the novel also shifts often from Robin to the outlaws, and even occasionally to some of the antagonists. For most of the characters, joining Robin in the forest is a choice, though Robin himself is forced into hiding by events out of his control, and he continues to lack control of events outside the forest. Even the initial creation of his story is not self-generated, aligning Robin more closely with Beauty than with characters in McKinley's later novels, though the fact that his story is created (and that he agrees to its creation) makes this novel different from *Beauty*.

The end of the novel, not fully satisfying, opens up new possibilities for Robin Hood and his surviving outlaws. King Richard, while seeming to impose his will, actually allows the characters to debate with him when he tries to separate them, asking some to remain in England while planning to take others, including Robin, to Palestine to fight the Saracens. Though Robin Hood is not offered the option of remaining in England, Much and Marian, along with several others, are, and all choose to accompany the king so that they may remain together. When Marian chooses Palestine, the king asks, "And Robin will let you?" to which Robin replies, "If this is my choice, then my choice is that I will no longer try to say her nay" (273). His choice, then, is to accept Marian's decisions, something with which he struggled through the events in the novel, despite agreeing to let her start the legend. Though limited in their choices, the characters have choices, unlike Beauty. McKinley herself has stretched a little further with her adaptation of the Robin Hood legend than she did with "Beauty and the Beast" in *Beauty*.

Deerskin presents a similar uneasy balance between the traditional text and McKinley's alterations. This novel, based on "Donkeyskin" and similar tales, also focuses on storytelling and its impact on characters. Main character Lissla Lissar's "first memories were of her nursemaid telling her stories, stories about her mother and father in the years before she was born; her second memories were of asking for these stories to be retold" (24). She does not have a close relationship with her parents, so these stories connect her to them, though she stops believing in the stories after her mother's death. Unlike traditional versions of the folktale, in which the main character escapes from her father before he can force himself on her, in McKinley's revision, Lissar's father rapes her three times when she refuses him and he nearly kills her dog Ash, who had tried to protect her. Following the rape, Lissar flees from the castle and ends up at a cabin to which Ash leads her. At this cabin, her body can heal, though she represses all memory of her former life, keeping only the name Lissar. The suppression of Lissar's memory — of her own story — is a major element of the novel. She does not want to acknowledge her story during most of the novel because of the trauma it contains.

After she has retreated to the cabin, she realizes that she is pregnant, a knowledge that brings her memory back to her before she is able to cope with it. Bleeding, she runs into the snow and collapses, only to be saved by a mysterious Lady who forces her back to life — something Lissar would not have chosen. The Lady gives Lissar "several gifts": "the gift of time, first; but I have given you other gifts, one that you must discover and one that you must seek" (118–9). Part of the element of time the Lady offers includes the ability to stave off her memories for a little longer, for Lissar is still not ready to confront the memory of her father raping her. The time also includes a physical transformation for both Lissar and Ash, which allows them to return to the world without being recognized. When they finally do travel back to civilization, Lissar and Ash do not plan the direction of their travel. Instead, there is some unknown force pressing them toward an unknown destination: "It was like following the direction of the wind beating in her face.... [S]he needed some direction to set her feet and this was at least as good as any other" (126).[2] Lissar allows this mysterious director to send her where it likes, for she is not yet ready to make her own decisions, just as she is still not ready to remember her past. Part of the denial of her past includes the adoption of a new name, Deerskin, which she takes from the snow white deerskin dress she finds herself wearing when the Lady forces her to return to life.

As with *The Outlaws of Sherwood*, *Deerskin* shows the importance of storytelling and how actions can influence stories and stories can influence actions. Lissar soon earns the nickname Moonwoman after a legendary character from the country, a name she associates with the Lady who brought her back to life. Part of the reason the citizens of the city where she has found work tending Prince Ossin's dogs call her Moonwoman is that they know nothing of her history, for she is still repressing her memory. Lissar does not know any of the legend of Moonwoman until a woman seeks her aid, saying, "We know you, the White Lady, the Black Lady, Moonwoman, who sees everything, and finds that which is lost or hidden" (202). This woman's son has gone missing, and she believes Lissar/Moonwoman "would not have missed him" (202). Though Lissar agrees to help find the boy, she denies the name and asks not to be called it. However, her success at finding the boy only increases her legend, much as Robin Hood's actions with the tax money increased his legend. Yet Lissar is led by the same "windless wind on her cheek" that had led her out of the mountains and to the city earlier (210). She chose to find the boy, but she is guided on her quest. On her return to the city, Prince Ossin tells her more about the Moonwoman legend, a story with strong parallels to her own story. Ossin also admits to his childhood fascination with Moonwoman, and his hope that she would descend to earth to marry him.

McKinley's incorporation of Moonwoman and Lissar's memory repression are alterations to the folktale, as is the way Lissar eventually confronts her father — though the confrontation itself is a part of the original tale. As she and Ossin become closer, Lissar gradually regains her memory, most of it returning when Ossin shows her the portraits of the princesses he's supposed to consider for marriage. Among those portraits is one of Lissar, painted when she was seventeen, and Ossin recounts what he knows of her story to Lissar, not knowing they are the same person. Not much later in the novel, Ossin proposes to Lissar, but, afraid of her emotions and unable to trust anyone, she flees Ossin and the city to return to the cabin where she lived before traveling to the city, only to return after a winter away with the knowledge that she has missed him. Though her flight from Ossin is a byproduct of the trauma she suffered at her father's hands, the decision to return to Ossin is a genuine choice, unlike her first emergence from the woods. During the second time she lives at the cabin —

this time with Ash and seven puppies given to her by Ossin — the real Moon-woman returns to Lissar, but rather than imposing her will, this time she merely asks, "can you not give yourself leave to run through the meadows too?" as Ash does (271). While the question encourages Lissar to free herself of the trauma caused by her father's rape, it does not force her hand.

Lissar's return to the city comes on the day Ossin's sister is to marry. When Lissar learns that the bridegroom is her father, she rushes to the wedding to confront him. He does not recognize her, and the point of view shifts briefly to him and to the story he has created about her: Lissar had been dead for five years, and he had "ordered dresses for his daughter lovelier even than those her mother had worn: one the color of the sky, one brighter than the sun, one more radiant than the Moon" (296). These thoughts mark an awkward return to an element of the traditional folktale, in which the daughter asks her father to make her different dresses in an effort to delay the wedding ceremony he has ordered. This story, one of many variations told after Lissar's disappearance, is refuted when Lissar, having regained her natural appearance, tells the real story to the entire city, for all the citizens are able to hear her voice when she speaks in front of the wedding party, including Ossin. At the end of the story, she tells her father that she returns "to you now all that you did give me: all the rage and the terror, the pain and the hatred that should have been love. The nightmares, and the waking dreams that are worse than nightmares because they are memories. These I return to you, for I want them no more, and I will bear them not one whit of my time on this earth more" (298). This declaration more than anything else in the novel shows Lissar making clear choices for her life, though her ability to maintain this stance comes into question almost immediately when Ossin proposes for a second time. Once again, Lissar runs from him, but this time he chases her, forcing a confrontation and an ending to the novel that is more realistic than the traditional folktale ending, for while Lissar chooses to marry Ossin in the end, she refuses to promise to stay forever because "I do not know how strong I am" (308). As Amelia A. Rutledge indicates in "Robin McKinley's *Deerskin*: Challenging Narcissisms," "Lissar's agency can be said to begin at the narrative's end" (179). Here the happy ending of the folktales is tempered by reality — Lissair's past has cast a shadow over her from which she is just beginning to emerge.[3] Tamara Paxton, in "McKinley's *Deerskin*: From Passive Princess to Independent Heroine," comments, "McKinley shows her heroine at the end not in a happily ever after of someone else's invention but living a future of her own choice, a life with unlimited possibilities that is hers alone to craft" (156). Though McKinley doesn't present this agency through metatext as she will in later novels, she has made a larger break from the intertextual ties than she has in previous novels. *Deerskin* is the precursor to her more recent novels in which the main characters not only take responsibility for their stories but are conscious that that is what they are doing.

Unlike her earlier work, two of McKinley's more recent novels—*Rose Daughter* (1997) and *Spindle's End* (2000)—contain characters who actively shape their own stories.[4] Though *Rose Daughter* and *Spindle's End*, like *Beauty* and *Deerskin*, rework traditional folktales, unlike the earlier novels, these more recent folktale revisions offer the characters a choice of ending and in the process radically alter the folktales from which they stem. As with most of McKinley's other works, storytelling plays a major role in *Rose Daughter* and *Spindle's End*, but in these novels, the stories told revolve around the main characters differently. Whereas storytelling in *Beauty* is primarily related to the character's history or is intertextual, and in the middle works focuses on how stories spread and change, shape and are shaped, in these later novels, the storytelling lays out possibilities and expectations of characters and makes them wonder about their future once they realize they are part of the stories being told. But while these stories are powerful elements in the novels, they do not control the characters, who possess strengths not evident in McKinley's earlier works—strengths that allow them to shape their own endings and break their intertextual ties.

Rose Daughter, McKinley's second revision of "Beauty and the Beast," like *Beauty*, has some close ties to the traditional tale—the loss of wealth, relocation to the country, the father's meeting with the Beast and theft of the rose, and Beauty's stay at the Beast's castle's in her father's place. Also like *Beauty*, McKinley has created a loving, supportive family that contrasts with the traditional tale. Yet the differences between the two revisions are significant. While dreams in *Beauty* show what is happening or will happen and are infrequent, in *Rose Daughter* Beauty is haunted by a dream almost from infancy. This dream, though it alters some as she matures, remains a major part of her life, and while readers familiar with "Beauty and the Beast" may expect the dream to prophesize Beauty's future, this is not quite the case. Further, Beauty learns that the Beast has had a dream similar to hers. Other dreams once she is in the Beast's castle show her what is happening to her family, though she doesn't realize the events are real at the time.

Storytelling also plays an important role in the novel. Once Beauty's family moves to Rose Cottage, a small house left to the three sisters, each sister learns about a curse that is associated with the house should three sisters ever live there. The people from Longchance, the closest town, are not worried about the curse because they believe one of the sisters, Lionheart, is a boy since she has disguised herself to gain employment. However, each sister is anxious about the unspecified curse, afraid to ask more details about it, and afraid to discuss it. They don't let the curse affect their daily lives, but once Beauty goes to live with the Beast, they wonder whether the curse is real and if their fates have been sealed by moving to Rose Cottage. The worry becomes acute on the night Beauty returns to Longchance, when Mrs. Oldhouse and Jack Trueword each tell a version of the story of why there is no magic in Longchance (from the point of view of different characters in the story) and the curse is finally revealed. Unfortunately, it is a cryptic rhyme that does not reveal the fate of the sisters, though Jeweltongue, Beauty's second sister, wonders if the curse involves the Beast whom she believes still holds Beauty captive.

Beauty's strength of character and shaping of her story are most evident at the end of the novel. She has already reflected on her role in returning creatures to the Beast's castle the night she encounters a unicorn, wondering if "this is a story like any nursery tale of magic? Where any maiden will do, any—any—monster, any hero, so long as they meet the right mysterious old women and discover the right enchanted doors during the right haunted midnights" (192). The thought that she is "any maiden" chills her, and she quickly dismisses the idea, thinking, "Well, I cannot know, can I? I can only do what I can do—what I can guess to try—because I am the one who is here. *I* am the one who is here. Perhaps it will make a good nursery tale someday" (192, McKinley's emphasis). By considering her place in the story that she perceives she is part of, Beauty takes possession of that story and takes responsibility for her part in the events, even speculating that the story will last. Her emphasis on the "I" is critical. She is the agent of her own story, unlike the characters in McKinley's earlier novels.

This agency becomes clearer when Beauty returns to the Beast's castle after a very brief visit home.[5] Upon her return to the castle, Beauty finds herself in the corridor that has haunted her dreams, and the memory of the dreams leads her to walk down the corridor searching for the Beast. But after walking until she is exhausted without success, she decides, "This will not do" (265). Thinking, "You will not have me so easily, nor will you have him" (265), she breaks the cycle of her dream by walking in the opposite direction, ignoring the pressure of the palace to go the other way, a great contrast to Lissar in *Deerskin*, who allows the directional forces to guide her on her way. The decision to break free of the dream's (and palace's) hold allows Beauty to escape the castle eventually and to find the Beast in a field. And here is where McKinley's revision really diverges from the traditional tale, for when Beauty tells the Beast, "I love you, and I want to marry you" (273), she feels sure that "we have won" and that they will be safe (274). However, the resolution is not the instantaneous one of *Beauty*. Instead, it's the start of a battle between the wild wood's evil magic and the gentler, earthy magic Beauty doesn't realize she possesses.

This part of the novel is also where both the curse and the enchantment are explained by a first-hand witness—the old woman who supplies milk and cheese to the castle and who has left Rose Cottage to Beauty and her sisters. Before she reveals that story, however, she offers Beauty two choices: "You may return the Beast to what he was before, if you wish. He was a good and wise man then.... He had great wealth and influence, you know, and you will have that wealth and influence again, and you will be able to do great good with it" (274). She also remarks that the Beast was a very attractive man before the change. The second option is to "take him back to Longchance" as he is now without any of the wealth and influence (275). When Beauty tells the woman, "I think you are not telling me all of this story" (275), the old woman allows her to ask questions and reveals her version of the story told earlier by Mrs. Oldhouse and Jack Trueword, filling in the gaps between their historical information and how the story extends to the present and Beauty's life. She also explains that the curse the sisters are so worried about is no curse but a "skipping-rhyme" used by children (280), freeing Beauty from the fear that her life is being manipulated by external forces.

At this point, Beauty asks the most important question: "How will our [the Beast's and her] names be spoken?" if she chooses to return him to his original form (280). When she learns "in fear and dread," she chooses "Longchance, and the little goodnesses among the people we know" (281). This choice, made with full knowledge of what each option entails, allows Beauty to shape her (and the Beast's) stories consciously. She knows she is writing the end of their story, and she is doing so on her terms. In the following battle with the wild wood's evil forces, Beauty must again muster her strength. She has no one controlling her actions in this battle, as many of McKinley's earlier characters do; instead, as her fear of the baying forces turns to anger, she faces them down, vanquishing them with her cry, "Go away! Can you not see that you have already lost? *There is nothing for you here!*" (284, McKinley's emphasis). This cry calls forth the creatures that she had returned to the enchanted castle — insects, small mammals, and amphibians— as well as the one creature that had yet to reappear, birds, and all of the creatures replace the wild enchanted forces and end the battle. Unlike McKinley's previous novels, *Rose Daughter* presents a main character who actively chooses her happily ever after and fights challengers to ensure that she gets that ending. In the process, she also breaks with the traditional end of the folktale, for the Beast remains a Beast, and they live in Rose Cottage without great wealth or position, a fact that does not detract from the happiness of the ending. The metatext, the character's shaping of her own story, subsumes the intertext.

McKinley's *Spindle's End*, like *Rose Daughter*, allows the main character choices that characters from earlier works do not have. This novel, a revision of "Sleeping Beauty," follows an initial plotline more similar to the Disney version of the story than the traditional version, especially in terms of the main character Rosie's separation from her parents (she is raised by two fairies) and her affinity with animals (gained when she is given the "baby magic" of being able to communicate with animals by Katriona, one of the fairies raising her). As with *Rose Daughter*, storytelling plays a major role in *Spindle's End*. Following the chaos of the princess's naming day, in which she receives twenty fairy gifts before being cursed by Pernicia, the evil fairy who has a vendetta against the royal family, stories not only spread about what happened at the naming day, but are also planted to protect the princess from the curse that, unlike in traditional versions, calls for the princess's death at any time before her twenty-first birthday. Though many tales are spread about the princess's whereabouts, only Katriona and her aunt, who are raising the princess as Rosie, a relation, know the truth about the princess. Rosie, not knowing that she is the princess, grows up hearing tales about the princess and feeling bad for her, though she has no interest in being a princess herself; instead, when she and Katriona pretend to be royalty, she tells Katriona, "You be the princess. *I'm* going to be the king" (98, McKinley's emphasis). She is also less than pleased with her appearance, which has been determined largely by the fairy gifts she received; in fact, when she is young, she cuts off her long golden curls and trims her eyelashes in an act of rebellion against her cuteness, which gets more attention than her intelligence (84). Rosie's stubbornness, reflected by her square jaw, is a trait that both infuriates Katriona and Aunt and that serves Rosie well as she matures.

As Rosie's twenty-first birthday approaches, her true identity is revealed and she is forced to accept that what she thought she knew about her life was a construct. Though she is not happy about the revelation, after some confusing moments, she steps forward to meet what she thinks is her fate, asking, "What is it we must do?" (235). And as with *Rose Daughter*, Rosie appears to be heading for a fairly conventional fate proscribed by the folktale from which the story is derived: she will prick her finger, fall into an enchanted sleep, and be woken by her prince. But the measures put into place to help her postpone, if not avoid, her fate change matters. Rosie's best friend Peony, a character far more suited to being a princess, agrees to pose as the princess while Rosie acts as her lady in waiting, a job also not well-suited to Rosie, who has spent most of her life working with animals and helping the local blacksmith. The bond of friendship between Rosie and Peony is enhanced by a spell created by Katriona, Aunt, Ikor, who was supposed to be the twenty-first fairy godparent, and Sigil, the queen's fairy who originally sent Rosie home with Katriona. The two girls spend the three months prior to the ball to introduce Rosie to the world together, adopting each other's mannerisms, their separate identities blurring and creating a type of doppelganger. Though Rosie has seemingly accepted that she's the princess, she has difficulty fully accepting it, for she frequently refers to the princess as a separate person before shifting to the first person pronoun. The fact that Peony is playing the role of the princess—and doing it very well—exacerbates the problem for Rosie, who has trouble believing horse Gorse's comment that "we are what we are" (250). Rosie is willing to do what she needs to do, but she never feels as if she's the princess.

The night of the ball marks McKinley's biggest shift from the traditional tale. Aunt, Katriona, Ikor, and Sigil had planned the resolution of Rosie's story, including the defeat of Pernicia and Rosie's ascension to the throne, when they wove the spell binding Rosie and Peony, but the resolution fails when Pernicia arrives at the ball and immediately recognizes the true princess. When Pernicia tempts Rosie to spin, Peony sacrifices herself according to the plan, pricking her own finger and sending everyone into an enchanted sleep, including Rosie and Katriona who was supposed to take Rosie to confront Pernicia in a final battle. The planned story shatters and Rosie must improvise with the help of Narl, the fairy blacksmith with whom Rosie has fallen in love, who revives her — using mouth to mouth resuscitation rather than a traditional kiss (he had escaped the enchanted sleep by carrying a piece of cold iron). Narl succeeds in waking Rosie only, however, and when she learns Pernicia has stolen Peony from the castle, a quest to recover her and to wake the castle ensues, joined by the animals who have also awoken. The character who should have been the victim of the evil fairy becomes the hero. Not only does she, with the help of Narl and her animal friends, rescue Peony, but she fights Pernicia bare-handed — her anger like Beauty's in *Rose Daughter* gives her power even though the fight must ultimately be finished by one of her animal friends — and succeeds in waking everyone at the castle except Peony, who seems fated to die in Rosie's place. But, desperate to save her friend, with Narl and Katriona's power aiding her, Rosie "leaned forward ... and kissed her on the lips" (409), thus breaking the spell but also passing on what makes her a princess to Peony. The result of the kiss, Peony becoming the princess while Rosie remains a horse-leech in the country town Foggy Bottom, pleases Rosie, who thinks, "She, Rosie, had been born a princess; and she had chosen to forsake her heritage forever" (417). The choice suits both her and Peony, who has fallen in love with the prince who'd vowed to find the princess and save her. Rosie's only regret is that she will never know her mother, father, and three brothers now that she has made her choice. The traditional folktale ending is in some ways maintained, though the Sleeping Beauty character is switched. Rosie's own story can evolve as she chooses, as the wife of the fairy blacksmith Narl, while "Sleeping Beauty" can take her place in line for the throne and her story can spread throughout the land.

Both *Rose Daughter* and *Spindle's End* mark a major change in Robin McKinley's approach to folktale revisions, indicating as they do her willingness to step away from the constraints of the traditional tales and reshape the stories more radically, just as her characters reshape their own stories. The results are fuller texts bursting with strong characters who control their own destiny in a way that McKinley's first Beauty could only wish for, and that Robin Hood and Lissar never quite achieve. *Rose Daughter's* Beauty and *Spindle's End's* Rosie break their intertextual bonds and forge their own paths in a more satisfactory happily ever after.

Notes

1. In both *The Blue Sword* and *The Hero and the Crown*, the primary artifact of the novels, The Blue Sword Gonturan, seizes control of the actions of the main characters Harry and Aerin.

2. A similar force guides Aerin in *The Hero and the Crown*.

3. In *Spindle's End*, there is an oblique reference to Lissar and Ossin's successful marriage that adds more closure to *Deerskin*.

4. McKinley has published two novels since the release of *Spindle's End*: *Sunshine* (2003) and *Dragonhaven* (2007); however, they are not folktale revisions and will not be considered here.

5. Each day in the Beast's world is equivalent to a month in Longchance, so though Beauty believes she has been away for seven days, for her family it has been seven months. The time difference also expedites the fading of the rose the Beast gives her, and it has lost all of its petals within a couple hours of her return to Rose Cottage.

Works Cited

Cadden, Michael. "The Illusion of Control: Narrative Authority in Robin McKinley's *Beauty* and *The Blue Sword*." *Mythlore* 20.2 (1994): 16+.

Cohoon, Lorinda B. "Transgressive Transformation: Representations of Maid Marian in Robin Hood Retellings." *The Lion and the Unicorn* 31 (2007): 209–31.

Gates, Geoffrey. "'Always the Outlaw': The Potential for Subversion of the Metanarrative in Retellings of Robin Hood." *Children's Literature in Education* 37.1 (2006): 69–79.

McKinley, Robin. *Beauty: A Retelling of the Story of Beauty & the Beast*. New York: Harper, 1978.

_____. *Deerskin*. New York: Ace, 1993.

_____. *Dragonhaven*. New York: Putnam, 2007.

_____. *The Outlaws of Sherwood*. New York: Ace, 1989.

_____. *Rose Daughter*. New York: Ace, 1997.

_____. *Spindle's End*. New York: Putnam, 2000.

_____. *Sunshine*. New York: Berkley, 2003.

Paxton, Tamara. "McKinley's *Deerskin*: From Passive Princess to Independent Heroine." *The Image of the Hero: Selected Papers of the Society for the Interdisciplinary Study of Social Imagery, March 2004, Colorado Springs, Colorado*. Pueblo: The Society-Colorado State University-Pueblo, 2004. 150–56.

Rutledge, Amelia A. "Robin McKinley's *Deerskin*: Challenging Narcissisms." *Marvels & Tales* 15 (2001): 168–82.

Sackelman, Ellen R. "More Than Skin Deep: Robin McKinley's *Beauty: A Retelling of the Story of Beauty and the Beast* (1978)." *Women in Literature: Reading Through the Lens of Gender*. Ed. by Jerilyn Fisher and Ellen S. Silber. Westport, CT: Greenwood, 2003. 32–4.

The Complete Tales *of* Kate Bernheimer
Postmodern Fairytales in a Dystopian World

HELEN PILINOVSKY

Kate Bernheimer tossed a stone into the waters of Fairy when she published *The Complete Tales of Ketzia Gold* ... but it wasn't until the arrival of its companion piece, *The Complete Tales of Merry Gold*, that we began to feel the ripples. *The Complete Tales of Ketzia Gold* told of the disjointed travails of suburban Ketzia, interspersing her suffering at the hands of her sister, her husband, parents, music instructor, and a majority of the casual passers-by in her life with lyrical retellings of traditional Eastern European fairy tales, oscillating back and forth between chronologically accurate presentations and postmodern revisions incorporating modern details. The tale of "The Star Talers," for example, became the tale of "The Star Pennies," wherein a desolate Ketzia found herself metaphorically all the richer for having given the last of her meager possessions away to those in need. However, in *The Complete Tales of Merry Gold*, Bernheimer further complicates the narrative, retelling her own retellings of the tales, presenting an additional perspective on the nature of their shared story. Their story is shared both between them communally — as siblings do, Ketzia and Merry share many experiences — and between them *individually*: though, for example, Merry is not there to witness Ketzia's abasement in the events of the chapter titled "The Star Pennies," she undergoes her own version in the tale of "The Star Nickles," wherein she, too, divests herself of the last of her possessions, only to reach completely different conclusions. As Cristina Bacchilega has put it, "Most narratives seek to resolve their contradictions. Even those literary narratives which celebrate paradox in the name of the avant-garde still rely on some norms and reproduce some minimal consensus simply to be intelligible" (8). Bernheimer goes a step beyond that, using the contradictions inherent in her narratives to strengthen their function *via* their form: she uses the conceits of post-modernism and post-structuralism to illuminate the fundamental nature of the fairy tale and its application in *our* time.

Fundamentally, the fairy tale is a utopian genre. However, the genre of the modern retelling, be its iterations the versions made known to us by Angela Carter, Emma Donoghue, or Kate Bernheimer, is predicated on the belief that the vernacular understanding of fairytale — the simplistic utopianism of the "happily ever after" — is false through and through, a thin veneer for a world which not only resembles our own in terms of the potential for misery, but tops it, using the metaphor of magic to illuminate its inadequacies. Contemporary authors of fairy tales use their knowledge of Story against itself: the expectations engendered by the imprinted belief of the "happy ending" work against themselves to guarantee the opposite, the *un*happy ending, the disappointment of the dystopia predicated upon the fatal flaw of unrealistic expectation.

Today, in the here-and-now, we call them "fairy tales." It's a loaded term. We may derive our usage from the 17th century literary movement that was known as the *conte des fées*, but we most certainly do not mean what they meant. Proto-feminist, politically subversive, and baroque in tone and content, the original *conte des fées*, the tales of the fairies, have been translated as referencing either those stories which literally concern the fairies, or, alternately, those tales which might fall beneath their aegis — that is to say, tales which the fairies themselves might have cared to tell. The latter translation is most certainly in keeping with the theory that the godmothers of those tales acted as authorial substitutes for their aristocratic, autocratic, mostly female authors ... but it does not begin to cover the way(s) in which we employ the term today. Nor do words such as *cunti*, from the Italian, *skazki*, from the Russian, or *Märchen*, from the German, all of which translate colloquially as "tale," or "story," but which carry with them a wholly different set of connotations, even when they include the prefixes which make them specific to the wonder-tale: as Marina Warner has said, "On a par with trifles, 'mere old wives' tales' carry connotations of error, of false counsel, ignorance, prejudice, and fallacious nostrums ... similarly, 'fairy tale,' as a derogatory term, implies fantasy, escapism, invention, the unreliable consolations of romance" (19). Warner does not specify, but it is safe to assume that her use of "consolation" is derived from, if not directly linked to, J.R.R. Tolkien's definition of Consolation as one of the primary purposes of the fairy tale: in "On Fairy Stories," Tolkien wrote,

> The consolation of fairy-stories, the joy of the happy ending: or more correctly of the good catastrophe, the sudden joyous "turn" (for there is no true end to any fairy-tale): this joy, which is one of the things which fairy-stories can produce supremely well, is not essentially "escapist," nor "fugitive." In its fairy-tale — or otherworld — setting, it is a sudden and miraculous grace: never to be counted on to recur [87].

Tolkien made an excellent point in 1938, but 71 years later, the problem with the consolatory aspect of the fairy tale is that it *is* expected to recur, and that

that expectation is applied outwards from the fairy tale into reality, creating a kind of a utopian entitlement that results in dystopian disappointment.

The modern English fairy tale is a unique conglomerate of expectations and applications (generally, of other people's content retrofitted to comply with Victorian value systems) employed according to a very specific formula: they illuminate an existing condition of woe, and they provide a solution, the ubiquitous "happily ever after" of the fairy tale as we have known it since the 19th century. How did the fairy tale move from the gendered, political, and social commentary of the *contes des fées* to the more strictly regimented form that we know today? And furthermore, where is it heading?

Children's literature became a booming business with Edgar Taylor's 1823 translation of the *Children's and Household Fairy Tales* of the Brothers Grimm. Publishers quickly came to the realization that there was an enormous untapped market of potential consumers—the children who might not necessarily see the appeal of the homilies and treatises on morals and manners which had previously been their lot. By the middle of the 19th century, fairy tales had become a trend, and a trend which did not necessarily discriminate between its potential audiences of adults and children. However, within a fairly short span, the two trends of fantasy and didacticism had merged: fairy tales (for the most part of foreign origin, as England had a rich store of nursery rhymes, but not, so much, a backstock of full-fledged tales of the fantastic) were translated, and, in being translated, heavily edited. Suddenly, those marvelous, subversive, appealing stories were being used for the same ends and means as their predecessors ... to indoctrinate children into the dominant ideology of their culture, frequently in a heavy-handed fashion. Andrew Lang's *Colored Fairy Books* are an excellent example of this: tales from all around the world were edited and subjected to the kind of cultural translation which would make them fit to impart the values of middle-class Victorian morality.

The process of cultural translation necessitated an abrupt divorce from their original messages. The frame fell away from Basile's carefully contextualized construction, the godmothers and transgressive heroines of the *contes* were, respectively, diminished[1] and denied autonomy, and the process of desexualization and desecration which had been begun by the Brothers Grimm in their efforts to make their 7th edition of the *Kinder-und Hausmärchen* more palatable to maternal buyers than their first had been was brought to full fruition first, in Victorian England, and then again in America with the rise of Disney in the early 20th century. The cultural imperialism of the Victorians translated the tales, quite literally, out of their myriad traditional values into a culturally monolithic representation of the "fairy tale." The fairy tale came to be understood as a genre whose central trope was that of the happily-ever-after, and the less said about what message(s) the specifics of that happily-ever-after sent, the better. Cristina Bacchilega points out that "the workings of this magic, however benevolent, rely on privilege and repression ... in modern times, the fairy tale has more often than not been instrumentalized to support bourgeois and/or conservative interests" (6–7). But as Jack Zipes has observed, there is a general resistance among common readers to treat the fairy tale as sacred, for "by dissecting the fairy tale, one might destroy its magic, and it appears that this magic has something to do with the blessed realm of childhood and innocence" (xv). Thus, its application can become a vicious cycle of sorts, with the messages of the fairy tale being mistaken for holy writ, with that writ being reproduced and further diluted and simplified with each passing generation, *ad infinitum*. The frequent responses to fairy tale criticism which accuse the critic of despoiling the innocent genre demonstrate that quite clearly: however, postmodern fairy tale retellings perform the same function, implicitly rather than explicitly.

Tales in other nations, and specifically tales from Eastern Europe, deviated from this pattern of tipping the fairy tale entirely onto one side: while many of these stories are inherently utopian, the scrupulously accurate styles of collection employed by folklorists such as Alexander Afanasyev reveal a consistent cultural application of darker representations and images of the world. The tales which Bernheimer incorporates into *The Complete Tales* are deliberately jarring: these women, products of the culture that glorifies the utopian elements of the bowdlerized fairy tale, are shown to have more resonance with folk anecdotes of miserable home lives (as in the application of stories such as "The Stubborn Wife" and "The Bad Wife" to Ketzia's situation) and nonsensical tales of misery paid forward (as in the incorporation of stories such as "The Bladder, the Straw, and the Shoe" into Merry's story). It is no coincidence that Bernheimer's selections hail from those regions, and there is an interesting argument to be made about old heritages in modern culture: but this is not the place for that discussion; we look at time, rather than place.

In her introduction to *Mirror, Mirror on the Wall: Women Writers Explore their Favorite Fairy Tales* (1998), Bernheimer wrote, "Clearly, fairy tales themselves are obsessed with 'the end'—and *they lived happily ever after*–and the contrived drama of the end of the century appears to lend itself well to the artifice and excess of enchantment literature" (xviii). She believes that our present age accelerates "the kind of drama that fairy tales present: the never-ending kind, the kind that always already is ending ... there is something beautiful about how the fairy tale is both 'now'and 'then,' like a mirror image of the self" (xxii-xxiii). Bernheimer continues onwards to consider the periodic, phoenix-like resurgence of fascination with fantasy as a product of end-of-days mentalities, comparing it to the Pre-Raphaelite movement, but that interest has taken a different term in *this* era: it is not just fantasy that fascinates, but its deliberate rescripting, conforming now to an iteration that is grimmer, darker, and more self-conscious than its predecessor(s).

Cristina Bacchilega has addressed this phenomenon at length in the important *Postmodern Fairy Tales: Gender and Narrative Strategies*, theorizing that postmodern transformations "are doubling and double: both affirmative and questioning, without necessarily being recuperative or politically subversive ... [they] reactivate the wonder tale's 'magic' or mythopoeiac qualities by providing new readings of it, thereby generating unexploited or forgotten possibilities from its repetition" (22). Bernheimer's incorporation of these strategies enacts a repetitive doubling that evokes the image of, not *a* mirror, but a *hall* of mirrors: each novel in itself references back to the older, darker stories of our fantastic past to evoke discomfort in our sanitized present, but, equally importantly, her second novel echoes her first in a fashion that is uncanny in the Freudian sense.

Selective representation on Bernheimer's part presents us with an image of the fairy tale that is considerably un-utopian ... which is, in fact, wholly dystopian, with the flaw in the perfect universe being, itself, the pressure and expectation of the fairy tale happily-ever-after. Postmodern retellings of traditional fairy tales differ greatly from their most recent predecessors, although they may be seen to have a great deal in common with their earlier predecessors, the *cunti*, the *contes*, the *Märchen*. Modern authors are reinserting the societal criticisms, and, yes, most certainly the sex and the violence, with one additional, crucial element: an awareness of Story. As much, and sometimes more so than tyrannical rulers, abusive parents, or problematic circumstances, Story and its expectations are the enemy of the postmodern hero(ine), sometimes implicitly, as in the work of Carter and Donoghue, and sometimes explicitly, as in the work of more humorous writers such as Patricia C. Wrede,[2] Terry Pratchett,[3] or Mercedes Lackey,[4] to name only a few. Generally, those who acknowledge Story as an enemy to be fought tend more towards the optimistic/utopian conceptualization of the enemy which can be vanquished, whereas those who take it as an implicit factor to be worked around tend to be bleaker. Bernheimer draws upon all of these and more in the messages which she sends with the *Complete Tales*, where the notorious Gold sisters imagine one another to be their greatest enemies, never imagining that in each case, it is themselves.

Bernheimer's first tale begins with a strong, meta-narrative voice: She transforms "The Ditmarsh Tale of Lies" into "The Saltmarsh Tale of Lies," the narration assuming a modern tone with the injunction, "I want to tell you something, so *listen*" (*Ketzia*, 11, emphasis added). Informed readers are aware, and new readers will discover halfway through the novel, that "Saltmarsh" concerns four men, one blind, one deaf, one dumb, one lame, who work together to catch a hare in the midst of nonsensical wonders. So, too, "Ditmarsh," where four girls—one sad, one afraid, one insecure, and one plain mean—try, and fail, to catch a rabbit. The key difference, as we discover at the tales' end, is that these four girls are in all likelihood all part of the same girl—Ketzia, shattered, fragmented, and torn, just like her story. It is a kind of a foreshadowing of the greater message of Bernheimer's work: that all of these characters are part of the same character, part of the same story, but lacking the self-awareness necessary to work together to overcome their false expectations to work towards a true resolution. However, the initial critical suggestion of narrative unreliability is strong, here: as readers, we wonder, is Ketzia's tale, too, a lie? The suggestions lie dormant in the subconscious of the reader, but sprout enthusiastically with the arrival of Merry's tale, when we discover that all is not as it seems, and the "unreliable" is an understatement when it comes to *these* narrators.

The Complete Tales of Ketzia Gold interpolates the many levels that fairy tales influence in contemporary culture. Bernheimer references various tales — "The Star Talers," "Bluebeard," "Little Red Riding Hood," and "The Armless Maiden," to name only a few — from a number of perspectives that, with each recurrence, grant deeper insight into the character of the narrator, the titular Ketzia Gold. As Bacchilega notes, "Postmodern fairy tales exhibit an awareness of how the folktale, which modern humans relegate to the nursery, almost vindictively patterns our unconscious" (22). Such is definitely the case here, both micro- and macroscopically, as Ketzia's immersion in the archetypes of the tales requires no explanation, but can be taken for granted by the reader when considering the symbolism of "common" tales: it is in her application of lesser-known images and their darker meanings that the true significance of use of the fairy tale format, and its subversion of modern standards, becomes clear.

In the manner of other postmodern fairy tales, Ketzia possesses a knowledge of the structure and format of traditional lore that informs her views, a knowledge that reveals itself as the source of her difficulties in many instances. In the introduction to her collection of essays on fairy tales by women writers, *Mirror Mirror*, Bernheimer notes that "subversive, lovely, and frequently perverse, fairy tales — and particularly those popular tales that foreground women — can dramatically influence women's perceptions of themselves" (xvii). Just so. Ketzia, in particular, has internalized the problematic passivity demonstrated by the heroines of so many bowdlerized fairy tales, but given that she operates in a putatively "realistic" world — a world of suburban expectations, contemporary obsession concerning weight gain from the age of 12 onwards, sexual revolution and, commensurately, entitlement from the men in her life — the stage is set, not for a happy ending, but for a dystopian disappointment of gargantuan proportions. As Sylvia Plath put it,

> Why the hell are we conditioned into the smooth strawberry-and-cream Mother-Goose-world, Alice-in-Wonderland fable, only to be broken on the wheel as we grow older and become aware of ourselves as individuals with a dull responsibility in life? To learn snide and smutty meanings of words you once loved, like "fairy" [Kukil 35].

Sentence fragment, or succinct analysis? Choosing to believe the latter, Plath's musing becomes a koan on the purpose of the fairy tale in its pseudo–Utopian guise: we are conditioned to that lovely fable *precisely so* that we can better learn the snide and smutty side of life, understanding it all the more for having something pure and perfect to compare it to.

Ketzia is the middle child of the Gold family, possessing a disagreeable older sister, Merry, and a charming younger sister, Lucy. As in A. S. Byatt's poststructuralist tale, "The Story of the Eldest Princess,"[5] Ketzia seems fully cognizant of what would be her "place" in a traditional tale by dint of birth order. She says, "As the story goes, there were three of us—I was in the middle" (*Ketzia* 123). Ketzia is well aware that the role of the middle daughter is rarely a blessed one: why, then, does Bernheimer begin her chronicle with Ketzia's tale? Even that is a deliberate inversion of the traditional expectation of the tale. She continues on, saying, "We are all, I am told, as beautiful as the others.... Our heads are all the exact same shape and size, but one of us has loose amber curls that lift and fall in delicate waves, one a blonde head—full thick and straight, and I, fine brown strands that bend strangely this way and that" (*Ketzia* 123). The individualization that Ketzia grants herself and the lack of self-esteem implied in her choice of self-descriptive adjectives are symptomatic of the attitudes she displays throughout the novel, of isolation and self-denigration.

Many of Ketzia's insecurities, founded in her youth, carry through into her life as an adult and are projected onto her husband, Adam, as can be seen through the roles that he plays in the versions of the fairy tales that Ketzia superimposes over her own life. In the original version of "The Star Talers," for example, the main character's destitute condition is due to her orphaned state; in the retelling, Ketzia is poverty stricken as a result of her separation from her husband. A chapter entitled "The Tiny Closet" reminds readers of "Bluebeard"; Adam bestows the key to a closet containing his secret things upon Ketzia. Curious, she explores it to find mementos of his life with other women—his sister, strangers. Her transgression goes undiscovered, but it affects her marriage with Adam nevertheless. They both survive, but the marriage does not. In one very disturbing scene that brings to mind the story "Little Red Riding Hood," Ketzia drowns her marital sorrows in a combination of alcohol and narcotics, dressing cheerfully in a red, fuzzy coat with a hood before she collapses into a stupor. Her husband later confesses to molesting her as she lies there, defenseless, an act which is witnessed by a mutual friend who fails to protect her and, in fact, plays the voyeur. Here, we find no woodsmen; only wolves.

Two of the chapters, respectively entitled "Ketzia Without Hands" and "Armless Abbelina," are clearly connected to one another and to "The Armless Maiden." The structure of the main tale is bifurcated, remade to more closely fit the specifics of Ketzia's situation. In the first of the chapters, Ketzia describes her feelings of helplessness when she is faced with drudgery at the hands of an aunt unsympathetic to her adolescent rebellion, and her only escape lies in her dreams of Adam; here, we see the scenario of abuse at the hands of the substitute mother. However, though the aunt does interfere with Ketzia's attempts to contact Adam, this is not an overt attempt at sabotage as is the letter intercepted by the mother-in-law in the original tale. As an adult, Ketzia's relation to the story grows more complex; in "Armless Abbelina," we see a structure that is reminiscent of the tale's original opening. However, the reflection is distorted. In many of the original versions, the armless maiden is persecuted by her male kin and set upon by an envious mother/sister-in-law. Here, she is the bride, yet, she is also the one to feel excluded, as the result of the overly close relationship between her husband and his sister. The order of relations is precisely inverted, in an intriguing revision of the Russian variant of the tale, where the heroine's sister-in-law is the villain: as readers, we ask ourselves, *which* sister plays that role here? Ketzia chooses to leave of her own volition, and is welcomed at the home of her parents; unbeknownst to any but herself, she is pregnant. We read:

> Of course, soon the baby left me too.
>   I wrote to Adam. "Your wife has given birth to a child. His arms were golden to the elbows, his bones were studded with stars, there was a radiant moon on his forehead and another near his heart." I tore the letter into pieces. "Your wife," I wrote, "has given birth to a half dog and half bear that she conceived with beasts in the woods." I mailed it that evening [*Ketzia* 95].

Here, we see the ambivalence of a woman who is unable to admit that her husband is complicit in villainy, unable to blame others for her misfortune, and who, accordingly, is left with no one to blame but herself for the failure of her marriage. In *Mirror, Mirror*, Bernheimer remarked that "in many instances, fairy tales invite — and incite — a certain kind of female self-encodement" (xix). For Ketzia, that encoding is quite nearly a Turing machine: the internalized passivity of the generic fairy tale format has occupied her to the extent that she is unable even to envision, not autonomy, but justice. She needs no ogress to stand as intermediary — the only person from whom she seeks rescue is herself, and that is something that neither Adam nor she can provide.

The updated fairy tales are all recounted in relation to her tempestuous relationships with others; when Ketzia speaks of herself, in a period that appears to postdate her relationship with Adam, her accounts are purely straightforward, concerning her career as a transcriptionist for the Triple D company (standing for Depraved, Dishonest, and Debauched) in a manner that is more similar to *Bartleby the Scrivener* than to any folk tradition. This stenographic habit arises from Ketzia's dissatisfaction with her marriage, as an attempt to lessen the pain of her husband's infidelities. After it becomes a part of her life, it succeeds, apparently, all too well; her contact with the outside world diminishes. Her stories cease to concern others, either in reality or in imagination. Whereas before, Ketzia had placed too much value upon the opinions of others, now they are discounted completely, to the point that fairy tales, with their intimations of heritage and tradition, are discarded along with all other interactions. The use of typing as a distancing technique, as opposed to other forms of communication, is a mechanical distinction that would surely be appreciated by Walter Benjamin. The division between the two states of being — imagination and transmission, interaction and isolation — which are discussed in chapters throughout the novel set cheek-by-jowl, appears to be as artificial as that between the conscious and the unconscious; the two are inextricably linked. One is left with the impression that only through their integration will Ketzia's tale finally be complete.

Integration is precisely what *The Complete Tales of Merry Gold* provides, although possibly, not the kind that one would have expected. A tale of two sisters such as this (as the two must most definitely be considered as a whole greater than the sum of its parts) is inextricably linked in our imagination — as Bacchilega says, vindictively patterned upon our unconscious— to the myriad tales of feuding sisters, which inevitably seem to present an oppositional scenario wherein each sister defines herself as much by what she is not as by what she is. It is the pattern of "Diamonds and Toads," or "The Kind and Unkind Girls," repeated across cultures and times: most certainly, it is our insistent response to Ketzia's tales of woe, wherein her sister despises her very existence, and manifests that dislike in ways that range from the relatively innocuous (complaining about the sound of her breath), to the genuinely sadistic (a game reminiscent of those to be found in the fiction of Margaret Atwood, called The Punish, in which Ketzia — unsurprisingly — plays the role of the submissive).

Throughout Ketzia's tale, traditional oppositional construction has contributed to the demonization of Merry: if Ketzia is a victim, then, by nature, Merry must be a villain: however, *The Complete Tale of Merry Gold* indicates that reflexive subjectivity can be a false mistress. *Mirror, Mirror*— perhaps the *Complete Tales* as well?— emerged "from an impulse to explore the desire for stories— and for telling stories— as a way to think about that awful, awfully-alluring Princess-within" (*Mirror, Mirror* xx). Acting in dichotomy to *Ketzia*, Merry's tale does just that, by exploring the aspects dual aspect of femininity: when Ketzia is good, she is very, very good, but when Merry is bad, she is *horrid*. And yet, the joint reading of the tales reveals that neither character can be quite as two-dimensional as her sister imagines.

Even more so than the older stories, fairy tale retellings tend to be *women*'s stories, in the same way that the *contes des fées* were translated as stories by/of the fairies. They are a medium whereby to address the disjuncture between where women have been, and where they are going. They do so in numerous ways, through numerous relationships: mother-daughter, lover-lover, but at their core, they are sister-sister, Other-Other. In modern retellings, it can create an interesting tension when a character who we assume to be benevolent is revealed to malevolent, and vice versa: writers such as Tanith Lee and Neil Gaiman have provided fascinating examples in perspective-shifting tales such as "When the Clock Strikes" and "Snow, Glass, Apples." However, only more recently have writers been exploring the possibilities of dual complexity, humanizing the characters of the fairy tale within the context of their world: I would suggest that it is only *because* of the earlier work that such shifts are possible today.[6] Readers have been primed to consider alternative perspectives in tales where both the kind girl and the unkind girl are kind and unkind simultaneously. These tales are not, however, to be categorized as realistic fiction, focusing upon and explicating the motivations and decisions of the characters: rather, they depend on the framework provided by the genre to fill in the interpretive spaces left by the author. As A.S. Byatt says, "Traditional realism works with probabilities, correcting the melodramatic or fairy-tale expectations of romance. Later magical realists use the conventions of older genres to explore unconscious fantasy of psychic truth" (*Passions of the Mind* 113). Bernheimer's work does both at once.

Freud's theory of the *unheimlich* is well known: his definition of the uncanny seems apropos here. He says,

> The word "*heimlich*" exhibits [a meaning] which is identical with its opposite "*unheimlich*." What is *heimlich* thus comes to be *unheimlich*. In general we are reminded that the word "*heimlich*" is not unambiguous, but belongs to two sets of ideas, which, without being contradictory, are yet very different: on the one hand it means what is familiar and agreeable, and, on the other, what is concealed and kept out of sight [224–25].

This is an apt metaphor for the purpose and application of the retelling, and most particularly for that which is undertaken in Bernheimer's *Complete Tales* when considered in conjunction. Merry's story has been part of Ketzia's story, from the perspective of the reader, and now that pattern is inverted, as Ketzia's tale becomes a part of Merry's, and both become part of a greater whole. Freud acknowledges that "the factor of the repetitions of the same thing will perhaps not appeal to everyone as a source of uncanny feeling," but in this case, the magnitude of the revelations which Merry provides concerning Ketzia and her shared youth are significant enough to make that unlikely (236). Freud's observation that "the quality of uncanniness can only come from the fact of the 'double' being a creation dating back to a very early mental stage ... the 'double' become[s] a thing of terror" describes, quite accurately, the degree to which each sister fears and loathes the possibility of resembling her sibling, becoming her own untimely-constructed Other: it explains a good many of the choices which each makes in error (236).

There are significant disparities between the accounts of the two sisters. Ketzia believes that Merry is the favored child, while Merry quite clearly ascribes that position to young Lucy, whose story is still to come. Ketzia believes herself to be downtrodden, identifying as a victim while thinking Merry indestructible, whereas Merry sees power in Ketzia, and vulnerability within herself. For example, in remembering the game called The Punish, the sadistic game derived from their grandfather's reading material of choice where "punishments varied: getting bound to a chair and forced to witness the violent death of a doll; getting polio or requiring amputation, followed by 'rape' by a suitor," Ketzia recalls a specific encounter with excitement (*Ketzia* 71). She remembers how Merry forces her to eat a spider that's wandered upon the site of a bruise resulting from a previous "game." We read, "Merry grabbed at the thing and shoved it in Ketzia's mouth before Ketzia could protest. 'Chew, my pretty,'" Merry said. "'Yes, sir,' Ketzia said, muffled, feeling the tiny legs break in her mouth" (*Ketzia* 72). In contrast, in Merry's recollection, "She picked a spider off Ketzia's leg and held it up in front of her sister's mouth, just to see what would happen. Imagine Merry's surprise when Ketzia opened her mouth and defiantly ate it!" (*Merry* 74). It would appear that each sister imagines the other to exceed her own autonomy: when the second accounting of the early Gold(en) life reveals that "Merry could not remember who had first invented the marvelous game of The Punish, but she suspected it was her sister," we're forced to remember the question concerning dominance/submission and who *really* holds the power (*Merry* 147). Students of BSDM relationships have occasionally theorized that the balance of power shifts, counter-intuitively, in the direction of the submissive partner: certainly, this appears to be the case in the relationship between Ketzia and Merry.

There is a strong implication within the text that Ketzia's victim-status is, from Merry's perspective, somehow self-selected: Merry remarks with apparent envy that, when they play in the forbidden woods, a local pervert exposes himself to Ketzia more frequently than to herself: there is an intimation that Ketzia's apparent vulnerability possesses a certain allure. And yet, cyclically, the same quality that attracts men to her allows them to abuse her: as Merry puts it, "Poor Ketzia, always abandoned by men. I have no such problem for all that I need is air" (*Merry* 122). Her claims of frequent lovers (who appear, with equal frequency, as abusers) puts the lie to this: but the attitude behind the phrasing is intriguing. Once again, Merry is determined to beat potential detractors to the punch: like Ketzia, she may be alone, but she will differentiate herself by *choosing* to be so.

Of Ketzia, Merry says: "Such insecurity!... Merry knew, as Ketzia did not, that what was missing from her was neither strength nor confidence; rather it was acceptance of being sad, no more depth than that" (*Merry* 119). Merry, on the other hand, has named and claimed her sorrow, and transmuted it, first into anger, and then into acceptance: acceptance which is curiously similar to that which is eventually earned by Ketzia. Like Ketzia, Merry is a product of middle-class suburbia, facing many of the same issues: there is a strong implication within both texts that their grandfather is a pedophile, and quite possibly likewise their father. However, whereas Ketzia has responded to this situation by seeking a "protector" of sorts in the form of her likewise abusive spouse Adam, Merry reacts, first, by recreating that cycle in miniature with Ketzia as her victim, and second, by embracing the dangerous possibilities of the world in a traditional self-harming fashion. Alcoholic,[7] casually promiscuous, and low-achieving, Merry is determined to hurt herself before anybody else can claim the privilege (*Merry* 19).

Attending a School of Design, Merry attains professional heights unexplored by Ketzia, winning awards for her avant-garde designs ("skirts made of rose branches, pants sewn of apple-peel," and laminated frogs garbed in sweaters of human hair), and acquiring two kindred spirits, Semyon and Tibor, to share in her revelries (*Merry* 79–80). It is at this point that she begins to take solace in drink. It is a part of her story, a key accessory to her image of herself as a Bad Girl — the modern variant of the Unkind Girl, in some ways. We read, "Our lives were laden with wine. We had wine so often we lived in it. We each had our favorite kind: Semyon liked red, deep as what lived in your veins; Tibor liked golden, with bubbles, need I explain? And I was happiest with wine that was faded between: an imperfect almost-pink" (*Merry* 131). Finally, Merry has found a "family" unit where she belongs, with two "brothers" to offset the sisters with whom she never connected: friends, after all, are the family one chooses. Alas, her illusions are shattered, first when Semyon and Tibor discover that their love for one another is decidedly un-fraternal, second when Semyon overdoses on drugs, despite Tibor's love for him, and despite Merry's (which has extended to her placating his dealer with her body). Merry is left with only alcohol for comfort....

Bernheimer writes, "Once there was a girl who had talent, but she became a beggar and dropped out of school ... nothing could enter my mind except for the cold flow of liquor. Without it I would perish. So every day for vodka I searched" (*Merry* 123). Merry's substance abuse acquires a quest-like function which is interrupted only by the application of true archetype to her life when Merry enacts her own version of "The Star Talers." Where Ketzia fell into destitution after her self-inflicted separation from her husband, Merry's situation seems more the result of external events: where Ketzia interprets the world around her as providing kindness, Merry's expectations shape a different reality. While Ketzia is too proud to ask her husband for money, saying, "Money should not pass hands that way, though one must give it to strangers," her parents fall into a different category: of them, she says, "My parents had lent me so much over the years I was finally too embarrassed to ask them for more" (*Ketzia* 15–16). Merry, on the other hand, *begins* from the position that she cannot approach her parents, and specifies that "I was so bad that I had no friends to rely on": she is a living embodiment of the adage that if you keep your expectations low, you will never be disappointed (*Merry* 19). Where Ketzia calls her husband every day from the squalor of her motel, imagining "an erotic scene that might save me," accepting the charity of the kindly manager with his beautiful hair, Merry calls their father and keeps company with a mournful urban psychopomp, a pigeon, while making "other arrangements" with the lascivious proprietor of her rented room (*Ketzia* 17). Whereas the Star Pennies resulting from Ketzia's selfless charity bring luck and the first good night's sleep she's had since beginning on her journey, the Star Nickels which follow Merry's sacrifices bring only nightmares of birds in glass coffins and children within birds in some ghastly *matroshka*. The additional deathlike imagery is borne out by their respective conclusions concerning their separate experiences. Where Ketzia, garbed in the armor of her kindly manager's cast-off band tee-shirt and tough leather pants experiences an epiphany of commonality — "The pants were so heavy on my legs that I understood how we are all animals" (*Ketzia* 20) — which allows her to forgive Adam, Merry's darker revelation upon receiving her lecherous keeper's fur coat — "With the seal so heavy upon me, I understood that all animals die" (*Merry* 23) — only forces her to surrender her pride and to contact her parents, who take her in. And yet, despite these disparities, both sisters end up in similar situations....

Merry feels that she has "disappointed her parents so much that their disappointment inhabited me like a second body," but nevertheless, "of course they still took me in for a while, just as they'd taken in Ketzia during her barren season" which implies that hers, too, will come to an end (*Merry* 132). Merry takes up residence in a suburban landscape that replicates her vanished youth: having ventured outwards, and failed, she muses, "Yes. Reproduction is what I want" (*Merry* 61). She refers to the repetitive patterns of suburbia, tract house after tract house receding into infinity, but the implications here are deeper. When, ensconced in her middle-class cocoon, she reads books of fairy tales (which she utilizes as ledgers inside their front covers — a very Merry detail), to herself and to the neighboring children whom she adores, crafting small fairy tale outfits for them, she says that "it feels to me that I am living in a fairy tale or book of paper dolls" (*Merry* 91). This description is quite telling in regards to the overarching message of Bernheimer's work.

Like Ketzia, Merry takes up a symbolically significant position: where Ketzia is a transcriptionist, Merry is a pattern-maker. The fact that both sisters doom themselves to repetitive actions speaks to the level at which they are denied any other action. In opposition to Ketzia's position at Triple D — Depraved, Dishonest, and Debauched — Merry is employed by the Children's Clothing Company — Triple C, representing the virtues of Correctness, Comfort, and Charm (ironic, given their representative natures as the Kind and Unkind Girls). Approaching their lives from diametrically opposed positions, Ketzia and Merry end up in the same place. It's not a happy place: they are cogs in the machine, transcriptionists rather than actors, participants in a pattern not of their own devising. The message here appears to be that so, too, are we all, no matter what the generic happily-ever-after may aver. Bacchilega's observation that from a semiotic perspective, the "anti-tale is implicit in the tale, since this well-made artifice produces the receiver's desire to repeat the tale anew: repetition functions as reassurance within the tale, but this very same compulsion to repeat the tale explodes its coherence as well-made artifice" radiates outwards from the set-up that Bernheimer provides, here: her characters have consumed and reproduced the messages of society, first upon one another, then in the larger world of the fiction, and finally, upon us, as readers (22–23). As children innocently mimicking the images they find in their perverted grandfather's magazines, they enact plays which are "fairy tales with no happy ending": as adults, they reenact that scenario in life, influenced by the messages of the pornography and the traditional fairy tale in equal measure, having internalized their passivity, their objectification, and their disappointment; and finally, they project them outwards to us (*Merry* 99).

The *Complete Tales* of Kate Bernheimer are, as yet, *in*complete: we retain The Question of Lucy (which differs, certainly, from the traditional Narnian Problem of Susan, though perhaps not as much as one might imagine). In "The Tale of the Three Sisters," Merry recounts how Lucy, Ketzia, and she competed for their mother's love through a competition to sleep, wake, and see who would reach her bedroom first: Ketzia is first, but she loses her nerve and begins to weep; Lucy moves slowly, and steadily, but is overtaken by the forceful Merry; but Merry, uncharacteristically (both as she has been presented to us by Ketzia, and in terms of how she sees herself) takes pity on them and carries them along with her when they beg, saying, "What can I say? ... I wasn't always so awful...." (*Merry* 117). Ketzia's need to be rescued and Merry's heedless recklessness hold true throughout their adult lives: what so of Lucy's steady determination? In Ketzia's tale, she is a cipher: in Merry's, a traditionally successful Youngest Daughter. Will Bernheimer take us into a traditional structure where the youngest daughter succeeds against the odds of her abusive, destructive, troubled family? Or will she be another rendition of the dystopian pattern? Lucy is described as following the rules without fear ... and only time will tell if that is enough for her to break the pattern, or if her fate is to demonstrate the ways in which a win in a dystopian structure is still, at best, a loss of self, if nothing else.

As Bernheimer tells us in her essay from *Mirror, Mirror,* fairy tales tell us a lot about how society sees women, and vice versa: what do the *Complete Tales* tell us? For one thing, they demonstrate how the imagery has expanded. Kate Bernheimer is no fairy godmother, in the sense cast down to us by the *contes des fées*: nor is she a *wicked* fairy, despoiling our pleasure in the old tales. Bernheimer is a latter-day Rumplestiltskin, turning the straw of a two-dimensional modern sterotype of the fairytale into the gold of complex subversion, an ambiguous helper-figure dragging her audience towards betterment. It may require us to consider sacrificing our infant(alism), but the wisdom and self-knowledge that we gain in the process is worth it. She is the new, blended, composite figure: the postmodern author whose substitutes are not singular, but legion. In a time when the Princess Industrial Culture is beginning to sound more threatening than observant, carrying with it both a deepening misunderstanding of the nature of the fairy tale and a commensurate set of unrealistic personal expectations, tales such as Bernheimer's function as anodyne to that sweet nepenthe: they preemptively inoculate us against disappointment, not by preempting it, but by replacing it with something better; if the unexamined life is not worth living, then the micro-considered life proffered beneath *this* lens, *is*.

Notes

1. All too literally, as Carol G. Silver's brilliant discussion of the flower-fairies of the 19th century in *Strange and Secret Peoples: Fairies and Victorian Culture* demonstrates.
2. See Wrede, *Dealing With Dragons*.
3. See Pratchett, *Witches Abroad*.
4. See Lackey, *The Fairy Godmother*.
5. See Byatt, *The Djinn in the Nightingale's Eye: Five Fairy Stories*.
6. Examples of such tales can be found in stories such as "Among the Leaves so Green" (see Lee in *The Green Man: Tales from the Forest*).
7. Merry's voice hearkens back to those of the *skoromokhs* or bards of Russian tradition when she opens her tales by saying, "Long ago I reached the end of my luck. Then I began to drink vodka," a ritual epithet intended, in the context of the original culture, to indicate the worth of the story to be told as it must be paid for in kind (*Merry* 19).

Works Cited

Aarne, Antti Amatus. *The Types of the Folktale*. Trans. Stith Thompson. Bloomington: Indiana University Press, 1964.

Bacchilega, Cristina. *Postmodern Fairy Tales: Gender and Narrative Strategies*. Philadelphia: University of Pennsylvania, 1997.

Bernheimer, Kate. *The Complete Tales of Ketzia Gold*. Tallahassee: FC2, 2001.

_____. *The Complete Tales of Merry Gold*. Tuscaloosa: FC2, 2006.

_____, ed. *Mirror, Mirror on the Wall: Women Writers Explore their Favorite Fairy Tales*. New York: Anchor, 1998.

Byatt, A.S. *The Djinn in the Nightingale's Eye: Five Fairy Stories*. New York: Vintage International, 1998.

_____. "The Omnipotence of Thought: Frazer, Freud, and Post-Modernist Fiction." *Passions of the Mind*. New York: Vintage International, 1991.

Freud, Sigmund. "The 'Uncanny.'" *The Complete Standard Edition of the Complete Psychological Works of Sigmund Freud. Vol XVII (1917–1919)*. 1953. Ed. James Strachey. London: Hogarth Press, 1971.

Kukil, Karen V., ed. *The Journals of Sylvia Plath, 1950–1962*. London: Faber and Faber, 2000.

Lackey, Mercedes. *The Fairy Godmother*. New York: Luna, 2004.

Lee, Tanith. *The Green Man: Tales from the Forest*. Ed. Ellen Datlow and Terri Windling. New York: Firebird, 2002.

Pratchett, Terry. *Witches Abroad*. London: Victor Gollancz, 1991.

Silver, Carol G. *Strange and Secret Peoples: Fairies and Victorian Culture*. Oxford: Oxford University Press, 1999.

Tolkien, J.R.R. "On Fairy Stories." *Tree and Leaf.* New York: HarperCollins, 1965.

Warner, Marina. *From the Beast to the Blonde: On Fairy Tales and their Tellers.* New York: Farrar, Straus, and Giroux, 1994.

Wrede, Patricia C. *Dealing With Dragons.* New York: Harcourt, 1990.

Zipes, Jack. "Towards a Definition of the Literary Fairy Tale." *The Oxford Companion to Fairy Tales: The Western Fairy Tale Tradition from Medieval to Modern.* Oxford: Oxford University Press, 2000. xv-xxxii.

The Fairy Tale as Allegory for the Holocaust
Representing the Unrepresentable in Yolen's *Briar Rose* and Murphy's *Hansel and Gretel*

MARGARETE J. LANDWEHR

Jane Yolen's *Briar Rose* and Louise Murphy's *The True Story of Hansel and Gretel: A Novel of War and Survival* appropriate fairy tales as allegories for the Holocaust. *Briar Rose* depicts Gemma's survival from the Kulmhof (Polish: Chelmno) camp, where inmates from the Lodz ghetto were kept in a ruined manor house, the "Schloss" (castle), and where 320,000 people died, gassed in vans, from January 1942 until January 1945. Only four men, but no women escaped or survived (Yolen 240). Becca, Gemma's grandchild, believes "Briar Rose," Gemma's favorite story, serves as a coded narrative of her wartime experiences and tracks down her history in Poland. This assumption is confirmed when Gemma reveals on her deathbed that she is Briar Rose (17).

The novel's suspense plays with the story's literal and metaphorical aspects. Yolen foregrounds the tension between the two levels of meaning early in the novel when Becca claims that the fairy tale constitutes a metaphor (13). Indeed, Gemma describes the bad fairy who puts the curse on Sleeping Beauty as "the angel of death" and "the one in black with big black boots and silver eagles" (19), a reference to either the guards or the camp commandant. Both Gemma's nickname Dawna or Dawn (29) and the official name on her immigration record Gitl Rose Mandelstein (62) refer to Sleeping Beauty's names — Princess Aurora (dawn) and Briar Rose — and suggest the link between her cursed sleep and awakening, death and rebirth, and Gemma's own miraculous survival from a near-death experience. Moreover, another name on her record, Ksiezniczka, means "princess" in Polish (65). Indeed the details of Gemma's "resurrection" from almost certain death closely parallel the fairy tale character's mock death and rebirth. Gassed inside a van and thrown into an open mass grave, Gemma is discovered in the woods by some Jewish partisans and revived. Joseph Potocki, whom Becca later meets on her trip to Poland, resuscitates Gemma by breathing into her mouth (207), a scene evocative of the prince's kiss that awakens Sleeping Beauty from her deep sleep, a metaphor for death in the novel.

Murphy's retelling of Hansel and Gretel describes the survival of two Jewish children in occupied Poland during World War II, primarily through the quick-thinking of their stepmother, who saves Gretel's life by shooting her rapists, and the care of an elderly, eccentric woman, Magda, who lives on the edge of the woods and is perceived as a witch (thus, this modern version of the Grimms' fairy tale subverts the stereotypes of the evil stepmother and witch). Believing that their chances of survival would be higher if they separated, their father and stepmother abandon the children in the woods to save them from Nazis who are chasing them on the road. Because their real names would reveal their Jewish identity, the stepmother renames the children Hansel and Gretel. Murphy borrows, reworks, and often inverts various plot twists of the Grimms' fairy tale. For example, in a chapter entitled "The Cage," Magda puts an ill Gretel into a chicken coop placed onto the "platform" where she is sleeping to protect rather than harm her. Placing the sick child inside the "cage" prevents her from falling off the "platform" during her feverish hallucinations. Similarly, in a chapter called "The Oven," Magda dies in the ovens of a concentration camp. Murphy, who claims that as a child, she found this fairy tale the most frightening, admits that her reworking of the tale "mirrors my worst adult fears about what the abandonment and blind violence of war does to children all over the world" (appendix 4).

Authenticity vs. Empathy

Why do fairy tales serve as particularly appropriate allegories for the Holocaust? First, they resolve one central dilemma in Holocaust narratives—the tension between *historical knowledge* and *emotional understanding*, between facts and the representation of those facts that is not only accurate, but which also allows the reader to grasp their significance and empathize with the characters. Before I discuss how fairy tales provide a framework for depicting the Holocaust, I will briefly outline this fundamental dilemma in Holocaust narrative between authenticity and empathy.

If the reality of the Holocaust was anti-reason ("Hier ist kein warum!"/ "There is no why here!"),[1] then any narrativization of Auschwitz that includes an attempt to arrive at a rational understanding of events that defy ordinary comprehension is regarded by many Holocaust survivors as a falsification. In particular, any narrative with a sequence of occurrences that can be traced back to comprehensible causes appears insufficient in portraying events that defy all logic and reason. Primo Levi warns us against thinking we can understand the Holocaust and Georg Steiner refers to it as the "unspeakable" (Parry 111).[2] Reflecting upon his deportation in *Mauthausen: Hermetic City*, Aldo Bizzarri observes: "What sense is there to this story?... The reply is *no sense, no reason*. That goes for everything at Mauthausen, it is absurd to search for a thread of connection, for a logic.... The only fixed point in the landscape, behind the constantly changing absurdities of each day, is death" (qtd. in Gordon 41).[3] Similarly, the French philosopher Lyotard views Auschwitz as the symbol of the failure of reason "that ... cannot be represented" and compares the problematic of portraying the Holocaust to that of the Kantian sublime which "overflows the framing power of the imagination to 'invest, fix and represent.'"[4] Leon Yudkin states the dilemma of creating an "authentic" Holocaust narrative best:

> One of the effects of the Holocaust on literature has been that it has brought about a situation which transcends the possibility of any sort of adequate representation. Any mimetic effort true to its subject would cease to be aesthetic production, literary material, and become gruesome chronicle. The literature that takes in the Holocaust has to go beyond representation of the facts [146].

Thus, the dilemma for any Holocaust narrative is the following: how can apparently senseless events be represented in narrative form? Since authors who portray the Holocaust have unique ethical concerns of truthfulness and authenticity, this is a particularly urgent question. If historical narratives and diaries offer an authentic depiction of specific events, then fictional narratives of the Holocaust seek to balance the tension between authenticity and understanding.

How is this balance accomplished by employing the fairy tale genre? On the one hand, the Holocaust narratives discussed in this paper are anchored in a specific, historical time and place, the characters are three-dimensional, their behavior is convincingly motivated, and the broad outlines of the plot are credible with some details drawn from actual events. On the other hand, the fairy tale trappings of the narrative with its overpowering evil serve as an appropriate vehicle for portraying unimaginable villains. As the folklorist Jack Zipes has observed, the oral and literary forms of the fairy tale derive from the effort to civilize that which has "terrorized" us, both individually and collectively (370). Similarly, Max Lüthi notes that although the fairy tale hero is part of a community, he may find himself "confronted with an uncanny world which he finds hard to comprehend and which threatens him with death" (301). Thus, the fairy tale portrays a basic human condition: "...man feels abandoned, cast into a threatening world which he can neither understand nor view as a whole" (302). Consequently, fairy tales are particularly suited as Holocaust narratives as they put the horrific, the unimaginable, into a comprehensible form.

Moreover, the fairy tale plot with its existential struggle to survive in a threatening environment offers an appropriate template for a Holocaust tale, particularly for children and adolescents. Bruno Bettelheim, the eminent child psychiatrist and concentration camp survivor whose Viennese mother read him Grimms' fairy tales, notes that the fairy tale expresses the child's existential anxieties such as the fear of death (10).

Furthermore, both folk and literary fairy tales, unlike myths or legends, do not portray protagonists as intrepid, larger-than-life heroes/heroines, but rather as ordinary human beings with fears and weaknesses; consequently, the reader can identify and empathize with them. In particular, fairy tale protagonists are frequently depicted as helpless, as homeless, and as outcasts, a similar condition to that of the Jewish Europeans during the Nazi era and reminiscent of their marginalized and diasporic identity, which makes them particularly appropriate protagonists for Holocaust narratives. As Lüthi observes: "The folk fairy tale, too, has a partiality for a negative hero: the insignificant, the neglected, the helpless" (304). Similarly, Zipes notes that the more the literary fairy tale (the *Kunstmaerchen*) became developed, "the more it became individualized and varied by intellectuals and artists, who often sympathized with those society marginalized or were marginalized themselves" (375).

To sum up, fairy tales with their universal themes of the existential struggle to survive and their commonplace protagonists can evoke both understanding for the events and empathy for the characters. As the philosopher Martha Nussbaum observes, fiction is ethical when it allows us to identify with the characters, when it "places us in a moral position that is favorable for perception and it shows us what it would be like to take up that position in life."[5] I believe that successful Holocaust fiction should be able to evoke the reader's empathy for the characters even if their experiences are extraordinary and verge on the incomprehensible.

Both Yolen and Murphy maintain this balance between accuracy and empathy by setting their stories in a specific time and locale (in Nazi-occupied Poland) and by creating believable characters, but also by using the fairy tale as a bridge between the horrific world of the Holocaust and the commonplace world of the reader. Yolen underscores this link between the horrific past and the present by interspersing Gemma's version of "Sleeping Beauty" in between chapters. This repetitive portrayal of the grandmother's retelling of "Briar Rose" to her grandchildren foregrounds the fairy tale's bridging of the unimaginable, unrepresentable horrors of the camps and present everyday life. Thus, on the one hand, Gemma's obsessive reciting of "Briar Rose" reveals how the tale powerfully portrays her own horrific experiences in a coded narrative. On the other hand, it appeals to her grandchildren, because it depicts universal themes such as the fear of and triumph over death and the redeeming quality of love (the Prince's kiss) that resonates with them. Similarly, "Hansel and Gretel" portrays children's fear of abandonment by their parents as well as fear of death. In short, the fairy tale's universal plot presents commonplace dilemmas happening to characters with whom most readers can emotionally identify. If history, with its facts— names, numbers, dates—"misses the pain" as Robert Eaglestone

(102) has noted, then, art, the alternative narrative, offers an opportunity to acquire an understanding, however inadequate, of suffering.

Many Holocaust writers and scholars privilege the evocation of understanding over authenticity in their narratives. In particular, many prefer the experiential mode of personal memory, even if it entails sacrificing some accuracy, to the conventional (detached and unemotional) way of portraying history. For example, the autobiographical fiction of Patrick Modiano, *La Place de l'etoile* and *Dora Bruder*, which take place in occupied France, privileges aesthetic effect over historical factuality. Modiano claims that he attempts to capture the Zeitgeist of the Occupation; consequently, he evokes a certain understanding in the reader. For Modiano, emotional power is more important than authenticity: "Of course, the Occupation I deal with is a mythical one. I didn't want to paint a realistic picture of the Occupation but instead to evoke a certain moral climate of cowardice and confusion. Nothing at all to do with the real Occupation. No historical accuracy, but instead, an atmosphere, a dream, a fantasy."[6]

Fairy-Tale Metaphors in Holocaust Narratives

Secondly, fairy tales consist of powerful and evocative metaphors that portray unspeakable horrors, a role that everyday language cannot fulfill as successfully. Many Holocaust writers agree that ordinary language serves as an inadequate vehicle to convey the unbearable and the incomprehensible. In *A Man and Three Numbers*, Enea Fergnani explains the inadequacy of words in depicting the torments of the camps: "Work, hunger, cold, illness, death. They aren't the same words for us as they were before coming to Germany. Here work, hunger, cold, illness, death mean torture, massacre, torment; or worse, hatred, cruelty, violence."[7] The poetic metaphors of fairy tales, on the other hand, provide images both mysterious and recognizable to readers that can depict both the threatening and familiar aspects of evil. For example, both the dark, ominous and seemingly endless forest with its hidden dangers, employed skillfully by Murphy to evoke the constant and omnipresent threat of death, and stock figures such as the witch suggest the anxiety of confronting overwhelming and destructive natural forces or evil agents. These metaphorical locales and figures depict an evil that is simultaneously frightening and strangely familiar, the "uncanny" that Freud spoke of in his famous essay. Consequently, these metaphors bridge the gap between the foreign and the common and insinuate that evil constitutes simultaneously both an alien, exterior force, as well as one that exists, at least as a potential, in each one of us.

Furthermore, fairy-tale metaphors indirectly portray that which may be too monstrous to comprehend both emotionally and cognitively, and, thus, serve as a protective buffer between the horrors and the reader's experience of those horrors. In particular, if a fictional scene is too horrific or graphic, then the emotional reaction that it may evoke may be too overwhelming and would repulse the reader rather than elicit empathy. As Aharon Appelfield has commented on depictions of the Holocaust: "One does not look directly into the sun."[8] Consequently, an indirect depiction of the Holocaust such as Modiano's "fantasy" or fairy tales serves as an appropriate allegory that both reveals and conceals the horror and the suffering of Holocaust victims.

The well-regarded fairy-tale scholar and experienced oral storyteller Jane Yolen expertly uses fairy-tale motifs from "Sleeping Beauty" as metaphors for the Holocaust and cites Jack Zipes' familiar description of fairy-tales as an introduction and a description of her own novel *Briar Rose*:

> (B)oth the oral and the literary forms of the fairy tale are grounded in history: they emanate from specific struggles *to humanize bestial and barbaric forces*, which have terrorized our minds and communities in concrete ways, threatening to destroy free will and human compassion. The fairy tale sets out to conquer this concrete terror through *metaphors* [italics, my emphasis].

Yolen exploits the multivalent meanings of fairy tale motifs to indicate various aspects of the horrors of the Holocaust. For example, the motif of sleep from Gemma's version of "Sleeping Beauty" cited on the initial page of the novel serves as a powerful symbol of forgetfulness, even indifference, as well as death and deserves to be cited in full:

> A mist. A great mist. It covered the entire kingdom. And everyone in it — the good people and the not-so-good, the young people and the not-so-young, and even Briar Rose's mother and father fell asleep. Everyone slept: lords and ladies, teachers and tumblers, dogs and doves, rabbits and rabbitzen and all kinds of citizens. So fast asleep they were, they were not able to wake up for a hundred years.

Thus, the "sleep" that overcame a nation could be understood either as an unawareness, an indifference to the plight of fellow citizens (the sleeping of the conscience) or to the atmosphere of paralysis and death that encompassed inhabitants of the German Reich. The image of mist and, alternatively, fog, both alludes to this same forgetfulness, perhaps an inability or an unwillingness to see (such as the "fog of war") as well as to vehicle "exhaust" (Yolen 43), which refers to the exhaust fumes of vans that killed its occupants. Thus, sleep and its related terms mist and fog refer to the realm of death. On her deathbed, Gemma tells Becca: "I was the princess in the castle in the sleeping woods. And there came a great dark mist and we all fell asleep" (16). Similarly, the manor house of Kulmhof/Chelmno with its prisoners is referred to as a "Schloss" or castle (146) and the forest, a common fairy tale locale that designates danger, even possible death, constitutes the site into which the vans drive to kill the occupants and the site of their burial. Furthermore, the thorns in Gemma's narration of "Briar Rose" serve as metaphors for the barbed wire surrounding both the concentration camps as well as the internment camp for war refugees in Oswego, New York (80) whereas the rose garden functions as a euphemism for the gas chamber (128). Thus, Yolen skillfully employs fairy tale motifs to both describe the horrors and to disguise them albeit for aesthetic purposes.

In a similar fashion, Murphy expertly employs the central metaphor of the oven in the Grimms' "Hansel and Gretel" to depict Magda's death in a concentration camp. Not only does the oven both reveal and conceal the horrific nature of her death, but it also inverts the oven's original function in the fairy tale. Whereas in the Grimms' story the oven serves as an appropriate means of death for the witch, who wanted to "cook" the children there to eat, in Murphy's story it alludes to the "ovens" of the camps in which innocent people died. If the oven in the Grimms' tale "punishes" the witch for her evil, then Magda is "punished" for her good deeds, namely harboring and saving Jewish children. Moreover, by inverting the moral message of the fairy tale that the good are rewarded and the evil are punished, I believe that Murphy is also suggesting that the unimaginable and incomprehensible events of the Holocaust subvert all our notions of good and evil and justice and world order.

In sum, Yolen's and Murphy's use of familiar fairy tale motifs not only adds a universal dimension to their Holocaust narratives, which transcends the specific circumstances of their stories, but also creates a tolerable distance between the reader and the event through an indirect, symbolic depiction of horrific events. Thus, instead of a graphic portrayal of torture or murder that could repulse readers and inadvertently dissuade them from seeking more information on the Holocaust, or worse still, cause them to deny that such horrors could happen, metaphors present scenes in a disguised, more tolerable manner in much the same way that Freud's dream symbols depict the dreamer's disguised, taboo wishes. This method of depicting the Holocaust serves as a particularly appropriate and useful style in literature for adolescents in that the author is caught between an obligation to depict the Holocaust accurately, but also to enable the reader to grasp it at an emotionally bearable level. Consequently, readers are able to identify with the protagonist's dilemma and empathize with his/her situation even though they have never had any direct experiential knowledge of the Holocaust.

Relevant to this discussion of fairy tales' beneficial role as allegories, extended metaphors of horrific events, are psychologists' findings on the therapeutic use of metaphor in trauma narratives. The benefits of using metaphor in psychotherapy in treating patients of posttraumatic stress disorder are well known. In "Metaphor and the Psychoanalytic Situation," Jacob Arlow observes that the metaphor serves as a favorite means of communication because it "enables the patient to maintain the necessary, the safe distance from content" (370). Furthermore, he states: "Because of the element of displacement of meaning, metaphor readily lends itself as a means of warding off anxiety" (371). Some analysts even actively stimulate the patient's associations by using specific metaphoric expressions such as those borrowed from myths, folklore, and fairy tales. Narration of the traumatic event in the past offers the survivor of the trauma a double distancing from the trauma: First, the event is narrated in symbolic form; secondly, the traumatic event is viewed as past: "The event is experienced as no longer present, or having a direct affective connection with the present.... As now past, sealed off from the present, it no longer overwhelms the subject in emotional pain" (Mishara 189). Consequently, the act of narrating enables the narrating subject to detach him/herself from the self who experienced the trauma (187) while still dealing with it, albeit indirectly.

Caruth and Ekstein succinctly describe the dual role of metaphors as both a distancing tool as well as an indirect method of gaining insight and creating a closer bond between patient and therapist:

> The metaphor simultaneously maintains discontinuity by not forcing the conflict into direct consciousness, and yet, paradoxically, creates greater continuity by permitting insights that can be tolerated from the increased psychic distance which the metaphor facilitates. The use of the metaphor serves the defensive function of allowing the patient to maintain the necessary distance from conscious awareness of the content of the conflict, while at the same time it serves the adaptive function of facilitating a reduction in distance between the therapist and patient [36-37].

These findings are particularly relevant for my interpretation of *Briar Rose*, in which Yolen draws attention to the act of narrating the fairy tale itself, in particular, its revelation of Gemma's fictional interpretation of her past, which involves the loss and recovery of her identity. Retelling the fairy tale allows Gemma to work through her traumatic experiences by creating an alternative self, Sleeping Beauty, who lives in a fantasy world. The fairy-tale figure enables Gemma to distance herself from the actual traumatic events, while also allowing her to create a self, an alter-ego, that undergoes these ordeals, in which sleep serves as a metaphor for death, and to survive them.

In her landmark study *Trauma and Recovery*, Judith Hermann discusses the therapeutic role of testimony in the construction of a new identity. Hermann observes that traumatized patients often speak of the loss of one's past self: "Long after the event, traumatized people feel that a part of themselves has died. The most profoundly afflicted wish that they were dead" (49). If trauma fragments the sense of self, then narrative helps to reconstruct it. One stage of recovery includes the ability to reconstruct the memories of the traumatic event into a coherent narrative linked to feeling (213). Thus, the restorative power of truth-telling, of the reconstruction of one's past and one's self through narrative, constitutes "a ritual of healing" (181).

In "Embodied Memory, Transcendence, and Telling: Recounting Trauma, Re-establishing the Self," Roberta Culbertson presents a more detailed account of the fragmentation of the self caused by trauma and the restorative power of narration in reconstructing a whole self. After a traumatic event, the victim frequently remembers the trauma in fleeting images and often the accompanying feelings are forgotten, yet they do not disappear. Instead, one learns to separate trauma, placing it into other parts of the mind and body where it lies hidden. Culbertson explains that "such memories—of abject fear, pain, anguish—are left apart from the story of the self because if included in it they would destroy it, being so counter to the self's conception of itself as a whole as to be inimical and threatening to it" (174). Abused as a child, Culbertson describes how the act of narrating the traumatic events not only reestablished a sense of self, but also offers a renewed connection to the community from which the victim feels cut off as a result of the trauma:

> But how to reconstitute the self taken away by the violator?... To return fully to the self as socially defined, to establish a relationship again with the world, the survivor must tell what happened. This is the function of narrative. The task then is to render body memories tellable, which means to order and arrange them in the form of a story, linking emotion with event... [179].

How can this trauma narrative be told without overwhelming the fragile sense of self that has been violated? Culbertson acknowledges that "the truth recalled is finally subordinate to the truth that can be heard, the truth which responds to certain expectations of genre and structure" (183). Culbertson concludes that to become "true," the trauma must be transformed to narrative (183). In her case, Culbertson transforms her traumatic experiences into fantasy, a genre which enables her to distance herself from the trauma and "conquer" her attackers:

> Fairy tales ... became my truth, my experience, and the places in which I won. Titanic battles, monsters, became as much my memory as any grunting or any crying, as simple and graphic in their own way as any other. Now, these are as much my memories as any objective accounting of events that I might do in the present, assembling facts. In fact, they are more truly my memories, because they are descriptive of an internal state, of a child's internal state. They are of the events as I experienced them [189].

Like Culbertson, Gemma has experienced life-threatening trauma, albeit as a young woman. Clearly, "Briar Rose" enables her to relive her wartime experiences from a safe, metaphorical distance while also focusing on her survival. Most importantly, the familiar genre of the fairy tale enables her to share her experiences and traumatized self with her grandchildren and, thus, reintegrate this past self into her present. It is significant that this narration constitutes the only means that Gemma uses to share her past with her family.

It is well known since Freud that the presence of an empathetic witness, whether a therapist, family member, or friend, of the trauma narrative can facilitate the healing process. Employing common cultural metaphors such as those from fairy tales in trauma narratives strengthens the relationship between patient and therapist (or narrator and listener/reader) who share this cultural legacy. As Beres and Arlow observe, whether in therapy or poetry, certain aesthetic devices such as symbolism and metaphor transmit both meaning and feeling to the therapist (or reader) and make empathy possible (45). Fairy tales offer familiar plotlines, stock characters, and motifs that both narrators and listeners share and which bridge the gap between the traumatic past and the listeners' lack of understanding. Thus, Gemma's grandchildren serve as sympathetic listeners although they are unaware of the true "meaning" of Gemma's version of Briar Rose. It is only after her death that Becca, an investigative journalist, discovers the details of Gemma's past, reinterprets the fairy tale as Gemma's aesthetic reworking of her own life story, and continues Gemma's narration in a sense by reframing her "fairy tale" as an allegory of horrific events to which Gemma merely alluded.

Fairy Tales as Narratives of Redemption and Subversion

Thirdly, fairy tales serve as effective Holocaust narratives, particularly for adolescents, as their protagonists not only survive, but thrive. With their plots of self-transformation and redemption, fairy tales give meaning to suffering, hope to those in despair. As Tolkien has remarked, fairy tales do not deny that sorrow and failure exist, but they deny universal defeat and offer a glimpse of an underlying reality, the possibility of a "sudden and miraculous grace" and "of the joy of deliverance" (285). In particular, fairy tales offer redemption in two possible ways, which are not mutually exclusive: either the protagonist reaches external goals and is integrated into society, for example, through marriage, wealth or a rise in social status, usually with the assistance of helpers, or one undergoes an inner redemption, a transformation, for example, from weak, helpless, and often naïve or foolish to strong, resourceful, resilient, and wise.

The protagonist usually reaches his or her goal through the advice or assistance of helpers, who miraculously appear when the hero/heroine needs help the most. Thus, Lüthi describes the positive *Weltanschauung* of fairy tales in which the protagonist survives and lives in a world that has a spiritual dimension:

> The fairy tale ... presents its hero as one who, though not comprehending ultimate relationships, is led safely through the dangerous unfamiliar world.... Supernatural beings lavish their gifts on him and help him through battles and perils.... Even though man may feel outcast and abandoned in the world, like one groping in the dark, is he not in the course of his life led from step to step and guided safely by a thousand aids? The fairy tale is the poetic expression of the confidence that we are secure in a world not destitute of sense, that we adapt ourselves to it and act and live even if we cannot view or comprehend the world as a whole [301–04].

In a similar vein Vladimir Propp and other folklorists have observed that the fairy tale plot frequently consists of the triumph of the humble and lowly but virtuous characters, such as Cinderella, over strong but evil ones through the assistance of helpers. In his analysis of the functions of the fairy tale in *Morphology of the Folktale*, Propp notes that the fairy tale hero/heroine, who must undergo certain ordeals, riddle-guessing, or tests of strength, endurances, or adroitness (60–61), is assisted by donors or helpers, who are either natural or supernatural agents. Usually these heroes/heroines are of lowly origins and conquer or triumph over adversaries, who are either of higher social status such as aristocratic rivals or are more powerful such as giants or evil fairies.

Similarly, in Murphy's and Yolen's plots the young and the helpless survive with the help of humans appearing at the moments of greatest need. Thus, the Jewish partisans are present to discover Gemma in the pit, revive her, enable her to survive in the forest, and to reach the United States. Potocki both resuscitates her from near death and furnishes her with the necessary documents to escape Poland. Similarly, helpers who appear at critical moments assist Hansel and Gretel when their need is greatest. Magda offers them food, shelter and a false Christian identity. Gretel's stepmother appears just at the moment that she is being raped and shoots her rapists. Hansel has near brushes with death and is always "rescued" or escapes. In an interesting plot twist of the Grimms' tale, Murphy enables the children to find their father in a soup kitchen by following the breadcrumbs back to the kitchen in the former Jewish ghetto. Murphy herself admits that she allowed all the children in her story to survive although it wasn't a realistic portrayal of conditions in Poland: "When I finished the writing, I realized that I had not killed a single child in the novel. You hear of children dying, but do not see it. This was ... quite unrealistic since Poland lost over twenty percent of its children" (appendix 7).

Moreover, Yolen's and Murphy's protagonists, like their fairy tale counterparts, undergo a transformation that endows their suffering with meaning. Lüthi concludes that fairy tales offer meaning to the protagonist's trials and tribulations by depicting "how suffering can purify and strengthen" (303) and how the protagonist discovers an "unrecognized spiritual strength" (299). In a similar vein, Zipes claims that oral fairy tales "fostered a sense of belonging and the hope that miracles involving some kind of magical transformation were possible to bring about a better world" (370). Claiming that metamorphosis constitutes the central theme of most fairy tales, Zipes observes that this power of metamorphosis was a "mysterious power of compassion" (380). Viewing fairy tales as projections of the child's process of maturation, Bettelheim, a concentration camp survivor, claims that the fairy tale offers the vision of a world in which good ultimately triumphs over evil: "Consolation is the greatest service the fairy tale can offer the child: the confidence that despite all tribulations he has to suffer (such as the threat of desertion by his parents in 'Hansel and Gretel' ... the nastiness of evil powers in 'The Sleeping Beauty,') not only will he succeed, but the evil forces will be done away with and never again threaten his peace of mind" (147).

Both Yolen's and Murphy's characters survive not only through help from others, but also through their courage and wits. Their various trials transform them from helpless and powerless victims to resilient, strong, and wise agents of their own destiny. Gemma manages to adapt to her changing circumstances by adjusting to life in different mileaus — the camp, the forest, the DP camp in New York — as well as adopting different identities and names. Similarly, Hansel and Gretel adopt new names and Christian identities and learn how to survive in the wilderness. In true fairy-tale fashion, Hansel even "captures" the arch enemy of the novel, the Oberfuehrer, in a David vs. Goliath scene. In an ironic plot twist, Hansel's declaration of his true identity ("I am a Jew!") in the former Bialystok Jewish ghetto draws attention to the Nazi pursuing him and brings liberating Soviet soldiers to his rescue.

Thus, the underlying message of the fairy tale — that one can discover meaning in suffering and that the ultimate reality consists of goodness — serves as a particularly apt and encouraging message in Holocaust narratives for adolescents. For example, although neither Yolen nor Murphy shies away from depicting the horrors of the Holocaust, triumph over death and creating meaning through narrative are the messages in both stories. In *Briar Rose* Gemma reconstructs her past as a meaningful narrative of survival and redemption through love by employing the Sleeping Beauty plot. Thus, narrating a coded fairy tale of her past enables Gemma to transcend her trauma by transforming herself from passive victim to a creator both as (grand) mother and storyteller. As a result, her fictionalized life story endows her suffering with meaning. In the final chapter (and telling of the story) Gemma concludes the last version with the usual optimistic ending: "'Happily ever after,' Gemma said firmly, 'means exactly what it says.' And one child in her arms, the other at her heels, she went directly up the stairs" (Yolen 239). The traditional happy ending refers, of course, not only to the fate of Briar Rose, Gemma's alter-ego, but also to Gemma herself. The presence of grandchildren underscores this redemptive ending as it refers to the restorative power of love and new life, the baby that Gemma bore from her union with Aron Mandlstein, a resistance fighter whose love enabled her to survive the harsh existence in the woods. Moreover, her life will continue not only through her grandchildren, but also through Becca's amplification of her story. Thus, narrating "Briar Rose" enables Gemma to find meaning in her suffering both as a survivor who not only has risen above her circumstances, but who also has found redemption, and as a storyteller whose narrative resonates with future generations.

Furthermore, Becca's reworking of Gemma's "fairy tale" depicts not only the well-known tradition of female oral storytellers passing the fairy tales from one generation to the next, but also the role of storytelling as a creative, life-affirming counter-force to the destructive forces of evil. For example, at least eighty percent of Grimms' collection of folktales, the *Kinder-und Hausmaerchen* (1812–15), were collected from female informants (Maclean 37). Moreover, the victory of the lowly protagonist over the more powerful and evil rival or enemy through helpers offers a "feminine" worldview of cooperation and compassion triumphing over evil and destruction. As Carol Gilligan explains in *In a Different Voice: Psychological Theory and Women's Development*, women find their

sense of identity in the context of relationships and their need for interdepend-
ence, whereas violence sometime results from the absence of close bonds: "Yet
in the different voice of women lies the truth of an ethic of care, the tie between
relationship and responsibility, and the origins of aggression in the failure of
connection" (173). Thus, the story of redemptive love between Gemma and
Aron and their child serves as a counter-narrative of survival and hope that
counteracts the violence and death of war.

Similarly, Murphy allows Magda's narrative to continue beyond the grave,
thus portraying the triumph of creativity over destruction. The novel begins
and ends with Magda's words and suggests the defeat of death and evil.
Although Magda herself dies in a camp, her story as well as the children she
has protected survive. Therefore, Magda's personal story depicts the power of
narration to transcend suffering and meaninglessness. She risked death to save
others and succeeded in her endeavors although she herself perished in the
process. The novel itself concludes with her encouraging words:

> There is much to love and that love is what we are left with. When the bombs stop
> dropping, and the camps fall back to the earth and decay, and we are done killing
> each other, that is what we must hold. We can never let the world take our memo-
> ries of love away, and if there are no memories, we must invent love all over again.
> The wheel turns. Blue above, green below, we wander a long way, but love is the
> cup of what our soul contains when we leave the world and the flesh. This we will
> drink forever. I know I am Magda. I am the witch [297].

The essential message of these final words of Murphy's novel embodies the
underlying assumptions of fairy tales—the ultimate triumph of goodness and
love over evil and death and the creative magic of words as a life-affirming
force.

Finally, Magda's role both as storyteller and the "witch," the outcast
shunned by the villagers, who has the rarely found courage to defy the author-
ities and harbor other outcasts, calls to mind not only the fairy tale's message
of compassion, but also its potentially subversive aspects. As discussed above,
fairy tales often depict protagonists who are marginalized or outcast from society. More contemporary folklorists such as Marie Maclean interpret folk tales
not merely as containing a message of compassion, but as potentially subversive texts. In "Oppositional Practices of Women's Traditional Narratives,"
Maclean observes that narrating folk tales originally was a woman's task until
it became appropriated by Monsieur Perrault, the Brothers Grimm, and other
men and claims that this appropriation constituted the "reterritorialization of
popular culture and especially of women's culture by the ideologically dominant" (41). Drawing from Michel de Certeau's study "On the Oppositional Practices of Everyday Life," Maclean distinguishes between strategy, "the force of
the dominant and the tool of ideological repression," and tactics, "an art of the
weak," of those who lack power and "an art of adaptability, of survival, and of
maneuver" (40), which de Certeau linked to popular culture, but Maclean links

to women's art. Maclean points to the tales of Scheherazade of *The Thousand and One Nights* who beguiles the king with her stories night after night in order to survive as a paradigm of women's tactics both in narrative and gender. Maclean outlines three categories of fairy tales that demonstrate female oppositional tactics (40). The third category depicts women's stratagems against violence and illustrates Magda's use of oppositional tactics both as renegade and storyteller. Not only does Magda illegally harbor Jewish children and, thus, defy those in power, the Nazis, but her tale of hope which bookends Murphy's narrative "survives" her death in a camp and demonstrates Magda's power and authority as narrator which supercede her power as a character. Thus, like the folk tales, both Yolen's and Murphy's novels demonstrate the power of storytelling to triumph over death as well as to survive the temporary rule of evil, offering the hope and consolation that are particularly needed in Holocaust narratives.

Notes

1. Cited from the Introduction of Leak and Paizis 8. Future references to this work will be indicated in the text as Leak.
2. See also Levi 32 and 396 and Steiner 348.
3. Originally cited in Bizzarri 87–8, 110.
4. Cited in Parry 111. Parry takes the Lyotard quote from *Heidigger and the Jews* , trans. Andreas Michel and Mark S. Roberts (Minneapolis: University of Minnesota, 1990) 15.
5. Cited in Eaglestone 101. Cited originally in Nussbaum 162.
6. Cited in Khalifa 161. Originally cited in "Patrick Modiano: un homme sur du sable mouvant," *Les Nouvelles Literaires*, 30 Oct. 1972, 2.
7. Cited in Gordon 40. Originally cited in Fergnani 188.
8. Cited in Lang 21.

Works Cited

Arlow, Jacob A. "Metaphor and the Psychoanalytic Situation." *The Psychoanalytic Quarterly* 48 (1979): 363–85.
Beres, D., and Jacob A. Arlow. "Fantasy and Identification in Empathy." *The Psychoanalytic Quarterly* 43 (1974): 26–50.
Bettelheim, Bruno. *The Uses of Enchantment: The Meaning and Importance of Fairy Tales.* New York: Vintage, 1977.
Bizzarri, Aldo. *Mauthausen: Citta Ermetica (Mauthausen: Hermetic City).* Rome: OET/Edizioni Polilibraria, 1946.
Caruth, Elaine, and Rudolf Eckstein. "Interpretation within the Metaphor: Further Considerations." *Journal of the American Academy of Child Psychiatry* 5 (1966): 33–45.
Culbertson, Roberta. "Embodied Memory, Transcendence, and Telling: Recounting Trauma, Re-establishing the Self." *New Literary History* 26 (1995): 169–95.
De Certeau, Michel. "On the Oppositional Practices of Everyday Life." Trans. Frederic Jameson and Carol Lovitt. *Social Text* 3 (1980): 3–43.

Eaglestone, Robert. "From behind the Bars of Quotation Marks: Emmanuel Levinas's (Non)-Representation of the Holocaust." Leak and Paizis 97–108.

Fergnani, Enea. *Un uomo e tre numeri (A Man and Three Numbers)*. 1945. Milan/Rome: Avanti, 1955.

Gilligan, Carol. *In a Different Voice: Psychological Theory and Women's Development.* 1982. Cambridge, MA: Harvard University Press, 1993.

Gordon, Robert S. "Holocaust Writing in Context: Italy 1945–47." Leak and Paizis 32–50.

Hallett, Martin, and Barbara Karsek, eds. *Folk and Fairy Tales*. 2d ed. Peterborough, Ontario: Broadview Press, 1996.

Herman, Judith. *Trauma and Recovery: The Aftermath of Violence — from Domestic Abuse to Political Terror*. New York: Basic, 1997.

Khalifa, Samuel. "The Mirror of Memory: Patrick Modiano's *La Place de l'etoile* and *Dora Bruder.*" *The Holocaust and the Text: Speaking the Unspeakable.* Leak and Paizis 159–73.

Lang, Berel. "Holocaust Genres and the Turn to History." Leak and Paizis 17–31.

Leak, Andrew, and George Paizis, eds. *The Holocaust and the Text: Speaking the Unspeakable*. New York: St. Martin's Press, 2000.

Levi, Primo. *If this is a Man*. London: Abacus, 1987.

Lüthi, Max. "The Fairy Tale Hero: The Image of Man in the Fairy Tale." Hallett and Karsek 295–305.

Lyotard, J.F. *Heidegger and "the jews."* Trans. Andreas Michel and Mark S. Roberts. Minneapolis: University of Minnesota Press, 1990.

Maclean, Marie. "Oppositional Practices of Women in Traditional Narrative." *New Literary History* 19 (1987): 37–50.

Mishara, Aaron L. "Narrative and Psychotherapy: The Phenomenology of Healing." *American Journal of Psychotherapy* 49 (1995): 180–95.

Murphy, Louise. *The True Story of Hansel and Gretel: A Novel of War and Survival*. New York: Penguin, 2003.

Nussbaum, Martha. *Love's Knowledge: Essays on Philosophy and Literature*. Oxford: Oxford University Press, 1990.

Parry, Ann. "Idioms for the Unrepresentable: Postwar Fiction and the Shoah." Leak and Paizis 109–24.

Propp, Vladimir. *Morphology of the Folk Tale*. 2d ed. Trans. Laurence Scott. Austin: University of Texas Press, 1968.

Steiner, George. "The Hollow Miracle." *Literature and the Modern World: Critical Essays*. Ed. D. Walder. Oxford: Oxford University Press, 1990.

Tolkien, J.R.R. "On Fairy Stories." Hallett and Karsek 263–94.

Yolen, Jane. *Briar Rose*. New York: Tor, 2002.

Yudkin, Leon. "Is Aaron Appelfeld a Holocaust Writer?" Leak and Paizis 142–58.

Zipes, Jack. "Spells of Enchantment." Hallett and Karsek 370–92.

"This Gospel of My Hell"
The Narration of Violence in Gaétan Soucy's *The Little Girl Who Was Too Fond of Matches*

Lauren Choplin

Ever since fairy tales began to be marketed to children in the early nineteenth century, assumptions about the delineations of childhood have informed not only the content of the stories but also critical debates about their literary value. Beliefs about what constitutes normative child development have resulted in various editorial, authorial, and critical responses to what are considered problematic aspects of the genre, violence and sexuality in particular. Jacob and Wilhelm Grimm, for example, revised their collections of folk and fairy tales to reflect what they thought was the proper behavior of children, while the authors of many contemporary fairy tales make their own revisions to the genre as a response to plots they view as outdated or politically incorrect. Meanwhile, in critical discourse, theorists such as Bruno Bettelheim and Jack Zipes have worked to revise our understanding of what it means to read fairy tales by emphasizing their potential liberating value: not despite the genre's preoccupations with violence and sex, but because of it.

Gaétan Soucy's 1998 young-adult novel *La petite fille qui aimait trop les allumettes*, published in English in 2001 as *The Little Girl Who Was Too Fond of Matches*, sits at the intersection of these anxieties about fairy tales, children, and violence. A trauma narrative about an adolescent girl whose abusive father has isolated her and her brother on the estate where they were born, the novel concerns itself with what happens when a child brought up in a profoundly limited and brutal environment is suddenly forced to contend with a world outside her narrow "fairy-tale" conception of reality after her father's death.

Insofar as the English translation of the novel has courted any critical response at all, critics and reviewers have interpreted Alice's struggle very narrowly as an effort to adapt to the so-called real world as she attempts to deal with painful memories from her past. While this certainly represents one aspect of her crisis, the novel is also situated firmly in the fairy-tale genre, which, as I will argue, complicates the way that we should understand how it functions as a trauma narrative.

Fairy tales, as Max Lüthi reminds us, narrate violence without mention of pain; the trauma narrative, however, depends upon the recuperation of pain through the narration of painful memories. Both genres posit some kind of happy ending, a particular vision of liberation for their victims-turned-heroes, but these happy endings come about by vastly different means. If we think about the novel as both fairy tale and trauma narrative, the operating logic behind these two kinds of storytelling — both of which are intended to liberate their protagonists in some way — begin to contradict each other. How can you narrate pain and not narrate pain at the same time? If a happy ending can emerge from such a scenario, what might it look like?

One way to resolve this paradox is to look at how Soucy puts these two genres into dialogue with each other, superimposing the fairy tale over the trauma narrative to deepen and revise our understanding of what it means to narrate violence and pain. As I will show, Soucy imprisons his heroine inside a fairy tale to illustrate that the crisis of the novel, more than just an attempt to deal with the onslaught of traumatic memories, is a struggle against the dictates of genre. Instead of coming to terms with pain through memory, and achieving liberation from her past in that way, Alice must reclaim and redefine her role in the fairy tale into which she has been permanently written by her tyrannical father.

Because of the radically isolated manner in which she was raised, Alice occupies a flat, depthless, highly stylized world in which violence produces no expression of suffering. She has internalized not only the character tropes of the fairy-tale heroine but also stylistic conventions of the genre that have to do with what it means to be human and to narrate humanness. Her adherence to the generic rules of fairy tales complicates her ability to acknowledge pain — not only the pain of other characters, but her own psychological pain — which in turn complicates the way that we think about the novel as a trauma narrative.

Soucy emphasizes in multiple ways that Alice cannot escape from this fairy tale, with the result that we must reconsider the means by which she "comes to terms" with her suffering. As I will argue, this occurs only in the most literal sense: through an obsessive fondness for the stylized arrangement of words, without recourse to the narration of pain, which is unavailable to her as the narrator of a fairy tale. To achieve anything resembling liberation from her father's influence, she must continue telling the story he has written, a revision of genre that must occur from within. Considered in this way, the novel becomes a profound meditation on what it means to experience, read about, and narrate cruelty and pain, not only in fairy tales, which offer an important alternative to realistic descriptions of violence, but as human beings forced to depend upon language for knowledge of the self and the world.

Alice and her brother live in a world created by their father, a former priest from a wealthy, powerful family who has so circumscribed their experience of reality that their way of being in the world has been drastically altered. Following the death of his wife, who was killed when Alice's twin sister was playing with matches, he has raised them alone on a decrepit, sprawling estate, preventing them from interacting with others and maintaining a system of rules, routines, and punishments that ranges from the arbitrary to the cruel. He has also locked up their sister, who was badly burned in the fire, in the woodshed next to the glass-encased corpse of his wife — which, he later tells Alice, was a "fair punishment" for her crime, hence the title of the novel and the name that Alice affectionately bestows upon the creature whom she fails to recognize as her sister nor even acknowledge as a human being.

Alice's father is simultaneously author, parent, and villain. Because he commits suicide before the novel begins, we never encounter their father alive. We quickly realize, though, that he is a shockingly authoritarian figure — abusive, and likely insane. As a figure who punishes his children because of his own guilt and a desire to appease the forces that he considers responsible for their ruined lives, he operates according to the same perverse logic as many fairy-tale fathers, especially the widowers. Except for her corpse rotting in the glass coffin (a grotesque send-up of Snow White), the mother-figure is notably absent, which as Ruth Bottigheimer writes, always "has disastrous results for her beautiful daughter," helping to facilitate the abuse that the father subsequently inflicts on his children (95). After their mother's death, the family's idealistic existence is shattered, setting in motion the trauma of the story from which Alice emerges as heroine. As in the Grimm Brothers' "The Girl Without Hands," the mother's absence creates a problematic relationship between daughter and father, who subsequently demands radical sacrifices of his children to meet his own emotional needs.

Positioning his children as characters in a tightly controlled narrative of which he is sole author, he has raised them alone in a radically enclosed world that has a language of its own. Alice is aware that she exists only insofar as she is a character in his story. Because of the powerful influence he has had over their lives, they are only his "dolls of ash," or mere words in a narrative that he has created, all their thoughts and actions no more than a collection of sentences that express his will (126). Instead of complex individuals with independent interiorities, they are controlled figures forced to move through a narrowly defined world, even after his death: "We've done nothing but continue to obey him, ... unable to do otherwise, the two of us swept away by an inevitable movement that emanated from him and continued to drag us in its wake..." (126). They exist only inside of language, his language, compelled to obey invisible rules that, like the rules of genre, determine the parameters of their identities and the plots in which they can participate.

Their father's suicide, which represents the sudden death of the author of their story, is Alice's impetus for writing: her attempt to assume responsibility as narrator, or "secretarious" (Soucy 3). In the course of this narration, Alice is forced to reconcile her distorted and often magical expectations about the world with the more mundane and bewildering reality that she encounters in her father's absence. Her crisis is ontological in nature, a rupture in terms of how she exists in the world compared to the people she encounters, such as the villagers. By setting the novel up in this way, Soucy raises issues of authority and authorship, which, besides being linked etymologically, have a lot to do with the ontological influence a parent has over a child, the power a person has to determine how that child conceives of reality. The novel asks us to consider what happens when a child is so entrenched in a narrative perpetuated by a domineering parent that she cannot escape from the version of reality that it presents to her. If Alice remains caught up in her father's narrative, forced to speak to his language and obey his rules, how can she recover her own story and liberate herself from his control?

The novel is concerned primarily with how Alice's experience of reality has been composed, in a very literal sense, by her tyrannical father. If she is to resolve this crisis, or "take the universe in hand" (Soucy 3), as she says in the novel's opening line, she must recreate the terms by which she continues the narrative that he has begun. This will first involve contending with her problematic role as heroine of a fairy tale, which is how Soucy positions her. She must accept that in the bewilderingly alien reality that she encounters after her father's death, many of the narrative rules to which she has been accustomed no longer suffice. Specifically, Alice must move past the idea that her ontological crisis will be resolved simply by the logic of the fairy-tale genre, which grants happy endings to characters who, as Maria Tatar has noted, exhibit certain traits and emerge from particular plots (*The Hard Facts* 88–94). Alice clings to this model of narrative resolution for most of the novel. As if to declare her fulfillment of the generic criteria necessary to ensure a happy ending, she frequently emphasizes her possession of the traits that are common to fairy-tale heroines: beauty, compassion, obedience, a privileged intimacy with nature, and a matter-of-fact faith in magic. These traits, which separate her from other, less virtuous characters, such as her father and brother, help to position Alice as heroine of the story she is narrating and according to fairy-tale logic, they should be enough to guarantee that her crisis will easily resolve itself. However, Soucy consistently undermines our generic expectations about what will constitute the novel's happy ending to illustrate the radical nature of Alice's imprisonment, escape from which will require more than simply the fulfillment of generic criteria, as Alice discovers.

In declaring again and again her close relationship to the natural world, for example, Alice suggests to her audience that she is one of the genre's "children of nature," to use Tatar's phrase, "aided by nature and protected by it from the highly unnatural villains of [her] home life" (*The Hard Facts* 80). She narrates as if she is conscious of her role as heroine in a fairy tale and the rewards that should result from this position because this is the only way she can conceive of an end to her suffering. Like any good heroine, she tells us that she turns to nature for aid and consolation, saying, for example, that she prefers to sleep outside away from her family, "with my hair spread all around me in the chilly beads of dew, to say nothing of the emerald mosquito, ... or all the small creatures that avoided me, scurrying quietly away so as not to disturb my bad dreams" (90). Further aligning herself with the limited possibilities for happiness offered by the genre, she insists upon the sympathy that animals have for her and the sympathy she has for animals, who are particularly attuned to her emotional state: "all birds waltz with me, that's my secret" (60). Most importantly, she expresses pity for the pain of animals: the partridges her brother set on fire, the goat her family sacrifices each Christmas, and even their horse the moment after she "put a whack on him in memory of father" (8). The frequency with which she emphasizes her intimate connection with nature and compassion for living creatures suggests that she realizes that the demonstration of traits particular to fairy-tale heroines will help bring about a happy ending, which she cannot imagine in any other terms.

However, at the same time as nature offers Alice a certain kind of relief, it fails to offer aid that is sufficient enough to deal with the ontological crisis precipitated by her father's death. After Alice flees to the pine grove because the mine inspector has rejected her rather bizarre advances, she discusses her spiritual affinity with nature but then admits that some elusive factor has compromised her ability to enter fully into a relationship with it: "I've often dreamed of being able to dance on the summits of pine trees the way elves do, ... sheaves of powdered gold would tumble from my hands to spangle the countryside with stars, I was born for that, but I can't" (64). Because of her father's oppressive influence, she is unable to completely fulfill her role as heroine, restricted in some strange way from functioning completely as a character. In the end, Soucy suggests, it doesn't matter if she is close to nature, if she meets the demands that genre makes of her, because that kind of happy ending — emerging directly from the possession of certain ideal traits — is not possible here.

Soucy continually subverts genre by complicating and sometimes eliminating altogether elements of the narrative that would, according to the conventions of classic fairy tales, result in a happy ending. Because Alice's father has held her captive ontologically as much as literally, fairy-tale tropes having to do with the heroine's liberation, such as nature coming to the heroine's aid, or the heroine's willingness to sacrifice her happiness for the sake of her father's, or the timely arrival of the good prince, will not work here; the prospects for rescue and emancipation offered by genre will not be enough to resolve her crisis. The doomed relationship between Alice and the mine inspector, or "the prince" as she quickly begins referring to him, represents one of the more startling subversions of the genre's idea of a happy ending, in this case related to her experiences of gender and sexuality. Because her father has raised her to believe that she is male, one of his "thin, daydreamy sons," Alice is isolated not only on the estate but also inside her body. As she admits late in the novel, after the mine inspector has tried to persuade her that she is female, this gender confusion has caused her to feel estranged from her physical self, unable to inhabit it fully; she experiences her body as another form of ontological confinement, contributing to her belief in a kind of mind-body dualism which, as we shall see, also affects her experience of pain: "My father had treated me as his son, and that had put a rod between my legs, figuratively speaking.... I was forbidden to move freely within myself, I was all boxed in, stifled, unable to proceed calmly toward my own simple truth" (128). Because of the power her father has had to determine the way that she exists in the world, Alice doesn't understand the feelings and changes associated with puberty nor realize that her brother has raped her repeatedly. She is trapped in such a way that the modes of rescue typically offered by genre are no longer viable. Unlike in "Rapunzel" or "Sleeping Beauty," the mine inspector cannot rescue her from this sleep, this tower, because conveniently Alice's brother kills the hero as they attempt to flee together on his motorcycle. Just as Soucy refuses to let nature come to Alice's aid, he prevents the mine inspector from fulfilling his fairy-tale role as liberator. By subverting the genre's usual routes to a happy ending, Soucy emphasizes the radical nature of her imprisonment and even more importantly, the difficulties involved in her liberation.

Alice's father has confined her both literally and figuratively in a world of his own making, insulating her from outside realities to such an extent that she is able to experience life only in his terms, understanding "terms" here in the most literal sense. She understands herself and her world only through his language, and she must, in turn, narrate in his language. As a parent, he is the real author of her story, an invisible but omnipotent presence who determines not only her thoughts and actions as a character but also, even more disturbingly, the kinds of sentences she can use. If, as Wittgenstein says, that one's world is bound by the confines of one's language (*Tractatus Logico* 149), then the fact that Alice's father has mandated her use of language will directly affect how she conceives of reality.

We realize from the outset of the novel that Alice uses language in a distinctly strange way. From the irregularity of her prose we begin to suspect that her world is not like ours, making us witnesses to a different, more profound kind of confinement that goes beyond how she functions as a character and extends into how she uses words. Because of the highly restricted manner in which she acquired language, Alice's stunningly ornate and oddly beautiful narrative relies upon bizarre terms created by her father and culled from books, such as secretarious and inflations; it also employs what we would consider incorrect grammar, especially comma splices and run-ons. The style of her prose — which she claims to have picked up from her father and the memoirs of the duc de Saint-Simon, the seventeenth-century memoirist famous for his striking and inventive vocabulary — reveals the ontologically different world that she occupies, and is discomforting insofar as it offers even more extreme evidence of how deeply her father has influenced her. Through language, we are estranged from a familiar reality, as we would be while reading a fairy tale, while Alice, as a narrator, remains oblivious that there is any separation at all between her and her audience. Just as she is trapped as a character in the role of a fairy-tale heroine, she is also trapped as a narrator by the gulf between how she uses words and our ability to understand them.

Soucy structures the novel so that we discover the radical extent of our estrangement from her world only gradually, through Alice's maddeningly (but unintentionally) oblique disclosures, which are further mystified by the obscurity of her language. At the same time, the series of revelations she makes about her life on the estate — for example, her relatively carefree and jubilant exposure of the Fair Punishment to the horrified mine inspector — are neither horrifying not revelatory to Alice. Soucy creates a troubling divide between Alice's seeming naivete and our slowly increasing awareness of how drastically violence has influenced her life to indicate that the lasting effects of her father's abuse have been primarily ontological, so bound up in the way that she experiences reality that she doesn't know that any abuse has occurred. Together with the grammatical anomalies and linguistic rifts that punctuate her narrative, the fact that she doesn't seem to recognize the brutality that she and her siblings have suffered suggests the existence of an alternate ontology, evident in her use of language, another way of participating in and comprehending the world that would account for her discordant tone as narrator.

If isolation and abuse have affected the way that Alice uses words, then her problematic use of language can be considered a sustained enactment of the trauma she has experienced, an unconscious performance of how violence has determined her ontology. The narrative itself depicts Alice's lived experience of abuse without her having to recognize it as abuse, as she would in a conventional trauma narrative. One way in which the effects of abuse are discernible in her use of language is in her conception of interiority, which in turn contributes to the way that she experiences pain. When she describes her own self and the selves of others, Alice maintains strict distinctions between interiority and exteriority, mind and body, subscribing to a kind of Cartesian dualism which, if we consider how she functions as a narrator, brings to mind the description of fairy-tale aesthetics offered by Max Lüthi. In his view, characters in fairy tales possess no internal reality and are narrated with what he calls *depthlessness:* a one-dimensional description of surfaces (events, actions, and behaviors) in contrast to psychological realism, for example, which focuses on penetration into the mind. "Its characters are figures without substance, without inner life, without an environment; they lack any relation to past and future, to time altogether" (*The European Folktale* 11). Although Alice does not deny the existence of inner lives, her method of narration operates similarly to fairy tales insofar as it privileges exterior realities over speculations about motive and internal action. When she describes her interactions with the mine inspector, her brother, and the villagers, for example, we receive accounts only of their actions, leaving us to speculate about what's happening inside their heads, the effect of which is at once piercingly comical and excruciatingly tragic. Our emotional reaction as we imagine with horror what the mine inspector must be thinking as she shows off her sister's writhing form depends upon the cognitive work that we must do as a response to Alice's refusal to narrate interiority. As the narrator of a fairy tale, Alice doesn't attempt to speculate about the thoughts of other characters but merely reports, in a very matter-of-fact way, their words and behavior.

Part of this narrative unconcern for interiority has to do with how she defines humanness. Alice conceives of people very narrowly as spirits contained "in" bodies or "dressed in [their] future remains," as she cheerfully puts it (15). In her view, the self is not directly identifiable with the body and in fact remains distinct from it. Her picture of internality invokes the false analogy described by Wittgenstein in which, as Stanley Cavell writes, the body is thought of "as a veil [that] expresses our sense that there is something we cannot see, not merely something that we cannot know" (368). Alice thinks of the mind as being enclosed in the body, trapped inside "a bonnet" with the eyes offering the only indication that there is someone — or something — alive in the container. When the officer and the priest inquire about her father's death, for example, Alice implies that he continues to exist somewhere without his body; death is the unproblematic discarding of the body, which waits to be abandoned like a set of clothes. She also interprets pregnancy as a way of easing the loneliness she experiences by being trapped "inside" her restricting mortal container: "I was no longer all alone inside myself, I had someone to caress" (132). Because Alice conceives of herself and other people as minds trapped inside bodies, with the contents of other characters' "bonnets" considered hidden and unreachable, she has no reason, and no real ability, to narrate their inner lives.

The strict distinctions Alice makes between interiority and exteriority and her disinterest in narrating interiority aligns with Lüthi's idea of depthlessness in the sense that she does not go "inside" the minds of her characters but instead presents them as flat, one-dimensional figures whose behavior, in contrast to their psychologies, is of primary importance. This method of narration informs Alice's problematic sense of her own body and her conception of death; it also affects how she relates to the Fair Punishment, whom she refers to for most of the novel as "it" and seems to consider a thing, not a human being. Alice narrates the Fair Punishment with the same depthlessness as she does other characters, preferring to dwell on their behavior instead of their psychologies; but at the same time she remains skeptical about whether or not she has any interiority at all. Alice doubts her personhood on these grounds, considering her more like homemade dolls, or "halves," than she does "neighbors," or figures with psychological depth: "We called them halves because they had only a body, made of wax and wood. They lacked the portion of their insides that allows one to suffer and so to call oneself a full-fledged neighbor...." (99) For the duration of the novel, Alice can't decide whether or not the Fair Punishment has any "insides," which she views as necessary for the acknowledgment of pain.

This becomes a problem, however, a disturbing indication of how deeply Alice is imbedded in this world, when she narrates the violence inflicted upon the Fair Punishment without seeming to realize that a person is experiencing pain: "She was beside herself, ... swinging her heavy head very very slowly to the right and left while emitting a long, dreary uninterrupted aaaaaaaaah that just barely emerged from her throat" (124). As with other characters, Alice narrates this pain in terms of exteriorities only, limiting her narration to what she observes of bodily action; but the impression Soucy creates here is that Alice somehow doesn't recognize that this pain is happening to a particular person. The result is uncanny, throwing into stark relief the extent to which Alice's experience of other people has been compromised by her immersion in a fairy-tale world. We acknowledge pain because we realize that the Fair Punishment is a human being, but Alice does not.

Because she believes that there is a deficit in her certifiable knowledge about whether or not the Fair Punishment possesses interiority (her criteria for personhood), Alice evades a description of pain, which is disturbing precisely because we recognize its presence. As a narrator, then, Alice subscribes to fairy-tale conventions concerning the depiction of violence "without" the acknowledgement of pain. In his discussion of the relationship between the style of the genre and the way that it depicts violence, Lüthi writes that characters in fairy tales are "play figures, not living persons. No blood flows; one hears nothing about whether the eyeball protrudes or its liquid flows out — nor does one imagine the situation in these terms" (*The European Folktale* 153). Alice narrates the Fair Punishment's pain as if she were a "play figure," as if the violence she (or it) experiences has no effect on an actual person. Her skepticism regarding the interiority of the Fair Punishment impels her to narrate only her "pain-behavior," to use Wittgenstein's phrase (*Philosophical Investigations* 89) — what is seen on the "surface" — without being able to attribute that pain to a three-dimensional human being. As a result, she does not react with horror, as we (and the mine inspector) do, to the Fair Punishment's grotesque writhing and unintelligible, anguished cries, which we, in contrast to Alice, are able to understand as pain that "belongs" to someone.

As a fairy-tale narrator, Alice isn't able to process the pain-behavior she witnesses except by externalizing it, making it into only surface, playing out the Wittgensteinian fantasy invoked in the epigraph of pain without an owner:

Perhaps all the silence that fills the life of the Fair allows my brother and me to be on first-name terms with speech ... it's as if the Fair had taken all the silence on herself to free us from it and enable us to speak, and what would I be without words, I ask you. Hurray for the Fair, that was a fine piece of work. Can you see? You could say this is suffering in the purest state, all wrapped up in a single package. She's like pain that doesn't belong to anyone. We don't know if there's even a hint of understanding in her bonnet. I myself would be inclined to think yes, there is, a little bit, at least [Soucy 116].

Because she remains skeptical of the Fair's interiority, Alice makes an interior experience of pain, which she can't verify, into an independent object. She aligns with the rules of fairy-tale narration by refusing to grant her character complete interiority or an internal experience of pain, but she also momentarily acknowledges something "called" "pain." This would seem to be the closest Alice comes to subverting genre in an ontological sense: she does not go so far as to ascribe pain to the Fair Punishment, which might imply that she had overcome the fairy-tale dictate to not describe an interior experience of pain, but she at least acknowledges that pain exists in her story. Still, she neither fully understands the Fair Punishment's suffering nor recognizes, as we do, that she is a human being. Soucy suggests that Alice remains in this other world, and that even this opportunity for liberation — redefining her role to the Fair Punishment — will not work out.

Although we see from this passage that the non-narration of pain prevents Alice from comprehending what has happened to her twin sister, the connection she makes here between the Fair Punishment's suffering and her own ability to use language is important to understanding how the novel functions simultaneously as fairy tale and trauma narrative. Alice suggests that the Fair Punishment's pain — and accompanying silence — are what allow her to use words. She equates her ability to narrate with her own non-narration of pain. Not only does this statement align with what Lüthi says is the fairy tale's "tendency to make feelings and relationships congeal into objects, so to speak, and thus become outwardly visible," but it also represents an important subversion of the logic of the trauma narrative (*Once Upon a Time* 51). Throughout the novel, Alice disavows the narration of psychological pain just as she disavows the utility of memory. Alice does not think of herself as recuperating pain through memory because "my imaginings have never brought me anything good, any more than my memories..., and now I have less desire than ever to go mad...." (138). Alice says repeatedly that the process of discovering and exposing painful memories has not helped her. But if, amid all the chaos and violence that occurs at the end of the novel, we still cling to the idea that a happy ending has occurred, that trauma has somehow been overcome, what kind of happy ending is it? In what manner has this trauma been overcome?

As it becomes clear that she might be irreversibly trapped as both character and narrator in the strange world her father has created, Alice decides to deal with trauma through the act of writing. "All my friends are words," she says, ushering in a series of comments privileging the creation of text over the kinds of happiness she is not able to find in memory, nature, or love (64). Like the silverware that Alice obsessively cleans and organizes, the organization of her thoughts into words and sentences helps to soothe her mounting anxieties about her role in the unfamiliar narrative with which she is suddenly and devastatingly confronted. Especially when Soucy begins to undermine the fairy tale's usual paths to the happy ending, such as in the mine inspector's murder, Alice realizes that continued narration represents the only possible respite from misery:

> I sensed that my only chance ... was to bear witness, and I took my courage in both hands, ... my book of spells and my pencil, and I traced this first sentence with tears stinging my eyes: We had to take the universe in hand, my brother and I, for one morning just before dawn ... or something close to that, because I was short of time, I was short of everything — that I could read myself over again [96].

As the only way of coping with what she ultimately realizes is her inescapable captivity inside her father's story, Alice begins writing her narrative; all other modes of liberation, she implies, are insufficient. As her reality becomes increasingly horrifying and unstable, culminating in her brother's surrender and the villagers' descent upon the estate, Alice flees to the ballroom and looks to language as her only solace. Even when she's suffering through labor — the only instance in the novel where we observe Alice in sustained pain — she continues writing. Because the Fair Punishment has given Alice "the gift of words," she has effectively taken all the pain of the story onto herself so that Alice may speak (Soucy 130). She therefore does not have to narrate pain, which implies that her recovery can — and must — take place through other means. If the only way for Alice to come to terms with her suffering is to use her father's "terms," then she is, in a certain sense, trapped in his story. To be able to survive without him, she must continue narrating, even if that means she continues obeying fairy-tale rules about not narrating pain. The alternative, she suggests, is devastating silence.

As her world collapses around her, Alice takes solace in text, in the idea that she and her child will read "till we fall to the ground ecstatic because after all, what does it matter if stories tell lies as long as they spangle with stars the bonnets of children who've tumbled from the moon and lie together side by side, two by two, she and I?" (136). Considering a statement like this, do we take the happy ending to really be "happy" as Alice's ecstatic tone suggests? We can perhaps reflect this statement back upon her own narrative and on fairy tales generally: stories that tell lies insofar as they do not acknowledge pain, but they remain beautiful, which might be liberating in a different way.

Even if we can call the ending "happy" on these grounds, Soucy has one last move to make, subverting and playing with the way we think about genre. What we first take to be a conventional narrative, a story told with a narrator who is perhaps unusually conscious of audience, successively becomes a "last will and testament;" a lover's appeal addressed to the mine inspector, and something resembling a diary. In the end, though, Alice tells us that she has simply been writing the same letter in cursive over and over again, which means that it is theoretically impossible for us to be reading the text before us. With the realization that what we're reading is a written document that should be incomprehensible, we shift from what we think is an experience of Alice's interiority to what ultimately is an experience of only text. Conceptually we move from depth to surface, inside to outside, which forces us to reconsider what kind of access we have to *Alice's* interiority and what that means in terms of her relationship to her own pain. We can no longer feel comfortable presuming that she has thoughts we cannot "see." We cannot still insist upon the idea that there is pain hidden "inside" our narration: dissociated, suppressed, or denied. In the end, she too, becomes only surface, without recourse to memory, claiming that she will burn the manuscript, "this gospel of my hell," which, regardless, she is not able to reread. By suddenly barring us from Alice's interiority, Soucy forces us to see her once again as a character in a fairy tale, a character in a story, a story on a page—only words, which is what she was, and what she will remain. Soucy also reiterates the idea that we cannot evade the acknowledgement of pain on the grounds that we do not have access to a person's interiority, because we leave the novel with a powerful experience of another person's pain, the narration of which did not depend—as it likely would in a realist novel—upon memory or interiority.

Alice's narrative brings grammatical order to the violence she has experienced, aestheticizing it to the point where it is no longer painful. This offers a powerful commentary on what it means to write and read fairy tales. Rather than expect the genre to be liberating through the symbolic rendering of violence—which seems to be the only way most contemporary critics have come to terms with it—the novel suggests that it is adequate, it is powerful, it is beneficial, to experience *literal* violence, even if that violence takes no real account of pain.

Works Cited

Bottigheimer, Ruth. *Grimms' Bad Girls and Bold Boys: The Moral and Social Vision of the Tales.* New Haven: Yale University Press, 1987.

Cavell, Stanley. *The Claim of Reason: Wittgenstein, Skepticism, Morality, and Tragedy.* Oxford: Oxford University Press, 1979.

Lüthi, Max. *The European Folktale: Form and Nature.* Trans. John D. Niles. Philadelphia: Institute for the Study of Human Issues, 1982.

_____. *Once Upon a Time: On The Nature of Fairy Tales.* Trans. Lee Chadeayne and Paul Gottwald. Bloomington: Indiana University Press, 1976.

Soucy, Gaétan. *The Little Girl Who Was Too Fond of Matches.* Trans. Sheila Fischman. New York: Arcade Publishing, 2001.

Tatar, Maria. *The Hard Facts of the Grimms' Fairy Tales*. Princeton: Princeton University Press, 2003.

Wittgenstein, Ludwig. *Philosophical Investigations*. Trans. G.E.M. Anscombe. New York: MacMillan, 1953.

_____. *Tractatus Logico-Philosophicus*. Trans. C.K. Ogden. New York: Harcourt, 1922.

Negotiating Wartime Masculinity in Bill Willingham's Fables

MARK C. HILL

In 2002, Vertigo Press, a subsidiary of DC Comics known for its adult audiences and mature themes, began releasing a new monthly serialized comic book, *Fables*, that follows an ensemble cast of immortal European fairy tales that have fled an invasion of their homelands into the "real world." Written by Bill Willingham, *Fables* quickly earned a great deal of praise within the industry, and to date has won seven Eisner awards, including Best New Series in 2003 and Best Serialized Story in 2003, 2005, and 2006. A majority of the comic is set in Fabletown, a secretive community founded during the initial colonization of what would become the United States. Hiding within New York City, the fables have constructed a government whose sole purpose is to keep humanity, to whom they refer as the mundys, unaware of their existence. Living within Fabletown, or in its sister community the Farm (a place where fables unable to pass among human society are forced to live), are dozens of familiar characters, including Cinderella, Beauty and the Beast, Jack Horner, the Three Little Pigs, and Pinocchio. Willingham, like Angela Carter, Anne Sexton, and countless others before him, has reshaped these iconic figures with his own reinterpretations that interrogate and complicate their traditional representations, many of whom reflect political and social issues of the present era. Willingham's Goldilocks, for example, is a firebrand who spews socialist rhetoric while arming for a confrontation with a Fabletown government she sees as having forced its non-human constituents into an oppressive commune.

The character who stands in opposition to Goldilocks, or any who would attempt to oppose Fabletown's lawful government, is its Sheriff — Bigby Wolf. Part hard-nosed detective, part soldier, part anti-hero (to name only a few of the myths that inform his character), he is the embodiment of the villainous wolves of European fairy tale and the closest *Fables* has to a protagonist. After receiving a pardon for past deeds, along with every other fable that successfully fled the Adversary, Bigby was convinced to serve as the strong arm of the new

181

community, a position he has held continually for nearly 400 years. With a cigarette perpetually in hand, Bigby works as "a pretty eclectic mix of small town sheriff and clandestine spy-master," complete with the bedraggled uniform of the Hollywood police detective (*Mean Seasons* 104). His dress shirt is rolled to the sleeves, his tie is loosened, his face is covered in a constant five o'clock shadow; with the inclusion of the habitual beige trench coat, his appearance is distinctly reminiscent of Clint Eastwood à la *Dirty Harry*, only with more muscle mass. The stereotypic cop, however, is only one aspect of the myriad narratives that create Bigby Wolf; there are centuries of cultural ideologies that contribute to his makeup. His personal history strongly reverberates with Campbellian mythical heroes, who are marked as outsiders from birth with powers beyond mere humanity. Also a werewolf, a monstrous creature with its own mythology, Bigby is linked to creatures like Grendel as much as he is connected to heroes like Beowulf. He is also twice cast directly into the mold of a soldier, one set on the German front during World War II, and the other a "modern day" counterinsurgency story that is strongly attuned to the mythology of the Vietnam War era.

Because of the plethora of mythical facets that contribute to Bigby's persona, I argue that he serves as what Homi Bhabha calls a "liminal margin," where pedagogical, nationalistic and resistant narrative discourses construct, maneuver, and negotiate identity (208–09).[1] Since *Fables* has only been published in a post 9/11 America during a time of war, its narratives are influenced by the politics of the war that surrounds its creation. While Bigby's character provides numerous inroads from which to understand the current cultural production of a country at war, it is the ties between his heroic portrayal and the complex discourses of masculine identity, specifically for men at war, that I find particularly illuminating. Bigby's masculinity is in constant negotiation with a hybridity of older engendering narratives, from the mythical hero soldier of World War II to the cowboy/outlaw hero at war with a capitalist oppressor, to name only a few. As a lover of *Fables*, I am disturbed by the stiflingly rigid masculinity that is privileged within the text, but I am not surprised that such a nostalgic, hypermasculine ideal as found in the propaganda narratives of World War II is evidenced during a time of growing national conservatism.

This should, perhaps, not be surprising; the comic medium has long had a reputation for "its apparently hegemonic and sometimes overtly authoritarian texts," which is remarkably cogent considering the role they play in shaping American youth (Reynolds 7; Wright 86–105). As a genre, comic books are often the first introduction that American boys have to literature. With emblematic figures and stories that transcend singular mediums of popular culture (*Superman*, *Sin City*, *V for Vendetta*), the comic industry is an excellent place to investigate how Americans are currently addressing any form of cultural production, including the mythologizing of a wartime masculinity. Famed historian Richard Slotkin, in his discussion of the cowboy myth in American culture, states,

While the play of continuity and revision in the grand structure of a myth/ideological system cannot be described in its totality, indications of the balance of change and continuity in the system can nevertheless be followed by examining developments within particular forms or genres of expression....Within the structured marketplace of myths, the continuity and persistence of particular genres may be seen as keys to identifying the culture's deepest and most persistent concerns. Likewise, major breaks in the development of important genres may signal the presence of a significant crisis of cultural values and organization [*Gunfighter* 7–8].

In this vein, *Fables* serves as an important crossroads of genres, which only begin with revisionist fairy tales and comic books, that map the incorporation, resistance, or continuation of hegemonic processes in American masculinity.

Slotkin also argues that the actions of the protagonist define a code of behavior for the audience, not only within the realm of the story, but in the "real world" which the story represents (*Regeneration* 8–9). This process is first achieved through the celebration of Bigby as a mythical hero, which inscribes the Sheriff as an emblematic figure to revere. In *Legends in Exile*, the first story arc which earned *Fables* two of its seven Eisner Awards, Bigby investigates the apparent murder of Rose Red, while beginning to woo his boss, Deputy Mayor Snow White and sister to the murder victim. Throughout this episode, he demonstrates a character built upon strength, perception, and intelligence. More importantly, he exerts his authority in his relationships with other fables; he bests a muscled Jack Horner, intimidates the noble and authoritarian Bluebeard into humiliated tears, and asserts dominance continually over Snow White. The action of the first collection of *Fables* is entirely controlled by Bigby, and the narrative literally becomes his show when he stages a "big reveal," ala serial detective fiction, where he calls all involved together to "reveal *who* did *what*, *how* they did it — and most *important* — how *I* figured it all out" (*Legends* 99).[2] While later episodes do not place Bigby at the center of every individual issue, he is still portrayed as Fabletown's central heroic figure whose presence (or absence) dominates the comic.[3]

As the central hero of Fabletown, Bigby more closely resembles the outlaw cultural heroes (ala Jesse James or Robin Hood) more than the traditional ones, especially more fairy-tale oriented heroes like Prince Charming. In fact, Prince Charming in *Fables* is a manipulative, womanizing cad whose wives (who include Snow White, Sleeping Beauty, and Cinderella) leave him soon after discovering his weaknesses. Bigby, unlike his love interest's ex-husband, takes direct action, sidestepping certain legalities that would hamstring him in protecting the citizens of the community.[4] As part of his duties as Sheriff, he recruits private fables to spy for him amongst the larger fable community, stashing away hidden resources (like the goose that lays golden eggs) to finance these semi-legal activities. After Baba Yaga is defeated by Frau Totenkinder, the embodiment of the witches of European folktale, the Russian sorceress is imprisoned by Bigby beneath the earth for interrogation, while publicly burying someone else in her place to assuage the fears of the populace. When dealing with bureaucrats or those like Bluebeard who control capitalist modes of production (similar to the cattle barons of 40s era westerns), he refuses to obey civil rules, knowing that a forceful confrontation will gain him the knowledge that diplomacy cannot.

Bigby's past, occasionally hinted at during the main narrative, helps to underscore his cultural hero status. Born the runt of a litter off of a she-wolf by the North Wind, Bigby endures punishments and ridicule by his older siblings, until he vows to devour something larger every day than he had the day before. Because of the power of this oath, Bigby grows into a monstrous beast, whose first human meal is Little Red Riding Hood and her grandmother. His destruction of the populace of the fairytale landscape continues until he is turned into a tool of civilization after falling in love with the princess Snow White, who casts a spell allowing him to shift between wolf and human at will. Bigby's lycanthrope nature only aids in evoking terrifying imagery for an American audience (Oakley 1).[5] That the line between hero and monster can be tenuous, however, is not only a trait of *Fables*; Victor Brombert argues that "[heroes] live by a fierce personal code, they are unyielding in the face of adversity; moderation is not their forte, but rather boldness and even overboldness. Heroes are definitely committed to honor and pride. Though capable of killing the monster, they themselves are often dreadful, even monstrous" (3). Bigby's connection with a horrific past, as well as his current honorable conduct, only strengthens his connection to an American heroic imagination fueled by stories of redemption and second chances found within the mythology of Jesse James.[6]

These heroic narrative roles are only elements of the heteroglossia of Bigby's portrayal, though their presence strengthens the power of disseminating (or mirroring) constructions of American masculine identity. One of these heteroglossic threads that most predominantly structures wartime masculinity takes place in two issues of *The Mean Seasons*, where a mundy gives a diary-like account of a secretive mission where he infiltrates the German front in 1944 with a hand-picked team (straight out of John Sturges's *Magnificent Seven*) that included Bigby.[7] Like many glamorized stories of Americans at war, this war narrative is fueled with ideology-driven marketing. The gritty realism of war is absent in these historical productions, and in their place are poster tales found in recruitment advertisements and propaganda films of the 1940s that create an ideology of soldiers as heroic champions serving their country (Grandstaff 8). In a reaction to this idealization, Paul Fussell wrote *Wartime* to detail vividly the physical and psychological brutality of war, as well as the frequent incompetence of a military system that encourages doubt in its soldiers (ix).[8] This historically accurate structure of feeling for an American military has been ignored, however, during our most recent time of war, as demonstrated in the political rhetoric of our national leaders invoking the fictional cultural memory of World War II (Noon 338–40).

Fables issues #28 and #29, entitled "Dog Company: War Stories," also invoke this cultural memory, creating a narrative filled with artificial and restrictive notions of a masculinity that encourages emotional reserve, the ability to endure pain, a refusal to admit fear in the face of death, and an ability to connect with other men only in the womanless space of war. The front cover of issue #28 seems straight out of 1940s pulp adventure fiction displaying Bigby, cigarette clenched between his teeth, and "his" men wearing a curiously vague American uniform storming over barbed wire guns in hand (ironically, not only is stealth, rather than heroic action, the focus of the two-issue story, Bigby is never seen wearing an American uniform). The truth of the story, however, is not as important as the ideology it enforces, which concentrates on honor, stoic acceptance, and bravery (Phillips 177).[9] The framing story accounts Bigby's relationship with the only surviving member of Dog Company, Duffy. After reservedly accepting the news of his impending death by cancer, Duffy reveals to Bigby that he had recorded the fantastic events that occurred that summer in 1944. When Bigby expresses concern that Duffy broke his promise never to tell a soul, the old soldier's response demonstrates his continual concern for his fellow soldier and his own principles: "But I never promised I wouldn't write it down—*strictly* for myself. And since you've still got *your* secrets to keep, I can't pass this on to anyone but you and still check out with any honor" (*Mean Seasons* 32). During the soldier's ordeal, which eventually leads them to Frankenstein Castle deep in German occupied territory, the men encounter heavy resistance which decimates their numbers. In the words of the narrator Duffy:

> And then the shooting started, and just like that we were all back in the war again. We had good positions. But they had us outgunned and outmanned. Basically, we knew we were screwed. We had no idea where Sergeant Harp or that Bigby fellow had disappeared to. Inevitably it turned out bad for us. But we held on. And then, all of a sudden, Harp *appeared* again — a vengeful god of war. But ultimately still mortal. And finally a small ray of hope — the order to retreat [*Mean Seasons* 59–65].

Dispersed amongst this prose (that underscores their refusal to quit until given permission by authority) are visuals of the American soldiers fighting overwhelming odds, shouting out encouragement like "one shot, one kill, Zilmer," and "fish in a barrel, Sarge."[10] It is not out of their own pain that they cry out for their medic, but when one of their own is felled. Multiple soldiers sacrifice their lives in order to protect others, Sergeant Harp dies attempting to save Bigby and Sergeant Supinski gives the rest of the men time to flee by "staying behind" to stall the German forces. Bigby also participates in this camaraderie by entrusting the remaining men with his secret, in violation of the Fabletown Charter, in order to save the lives of his fellow soldiers.

It is not the admirable behavior under fire, or the companionship that the men develop that are of concern, but the hegemonic ideology that is connected to this mythical archetype. I am disquieted that during this current war, when superhero comics are experiencing a rupture in their pro-authoritarian structures,[11] *Fables* invokes the cultural memory of the masculine hero-soldier in a war worth fighting (Kading 221). In a discussion over masculine portrayals of wartime identity, Christina S. Jarvis argues:

> Until we recognize both war's true impact on the body and the countless abject masculinities that existed alongside the hypermasculinized hegemonic models offered during World War II, we will continue to perpetuate narratives of the "good war" passed down by the victory culture. Without a more complicated and embodied account of the war, the cultural memory of World War II will no doubt be wrongly invoked time and again to engender and legitimize other armed conflicts [191].

Fables continues the perpetuation through its connection to older, idealized masculine tropes. The strength of a large, muscular male body is consistently on display, as blatantly demonstrated in the physical battle between Bigby-as-werewolf and Frankenstein's monster, both ripping through clothes and flesh. Neither courage nor duty are questioned; both the possibility of cowardly behavior and the potential to disobey direct orders is entirely removed from the narrative. Never does Bigby or his "Dog Company," question the righteousness of the American cause or the treatment they receive at the hands of the military. When discussing Bigby's leave of absence during both World Wars, Snow White casts doubt on their connection to the mundy plight. Bigby responds by stating that she had a "short-sighted way to look at things. A wolf grows up knowing he needs to *protect* his territory or risk losing it. We've each been part of this country *far* longer than any mundy. Some might reasonably argue that that only *increases* our duty to fight for it" (*March of* 92). The reality of military blunders is absent, as are the ingrained behaviors, faulty communication, and poor decisions that make military life worse than necessary — what Paul Fussell refers to as "chickenshit" (79–95).

Intriguingly, this pro-government attitude carries over into the counterinsurgency tale "Happily Ever After," removing the powerful social critique that is a hallmark of the Vietnam era story genre on which it is based. *Fables* issue #50 is a nine part-narrative, eight chapters and an epilogue, which ends in Bigby's marriage to his estranged lover Snow White. In the interim volumes, Bigby impregnates Snow White while they are both ensorcelled, and because she bears seven partially-human children, she is forced by law to take the children to the Farm — where Bigby is not allowed to live. Separated from his family, he escapes into the wilds of Alaska, until he is recalled by an operative of the Fabletown government to infiltrate the Adversary's stronghold in order to make a strategic strike on an important military resource. "Happily Ever After" depicts this mission, covering his insertion into enemy territory, his skills as a counterinsurgency warrior, his confrontation with the Adversary — Gepetto, the father of Pinocchio, the return to the community, and his rewarded marriage to Snow White.

With the sole exception of Bigby's welcome return, this narrative is highly reminiscent of the counterinsurgency tales that originated after the Korean War and remained influential up through the Reagan era. Richard Slotkin details the origination of the Special Forces, contemporary counterinsurgency warriors, whose methods returned to a style of warfare developed in America during the confrontations with the Native Americans.[12] The American fascination with counter-guerilla soldiers, whose knowledge of the enemy allowed them to skillfully and purposefully conduct violence, began to cross into Hollywood with the 1956 classic *The Searchers* where John Wayne portrays Ethan Edwards, "the man who knows Indians."[13] There is a decided shift, however, in the portrayal of these counterinsurgency warriors, especially as the nation becomes increasingly more doubtful of their presence in countries, like Korea and Vietnam, which require them. Movies like *Missing in Action* and *Rambo: First Blood, Part II* seriously question the nature of the government that attempts to use the hypermasculine skills of their heroes. In these films, the hero is recruited by a feminized government, responsible for the alienation of the hero from his society, and the government ultimately proves to be a greater threat to soliders than any outside force (Jeffords 168–69).[14]

These negative connotations are absent in "Happily Ever After," though the other elements of these tales remain. Mowgli of *The Jungle Book*, "the boy raised by wolves," has been asked by Prince Charming[15] to locate Bigby, the "only man who *can*" penetrate the enemy home base (*Homelands* 142). With his masculine body on display in a sleeveless, tight t-shirt and cargo shorts, Bigby infiltrates the enemy after climbing a beanstalk into the clouds and parachuting behind enemy lines. After quietly massacring dozens of guards through stealth and skill, he rigs explosives to Gepetto's magical wood that allow him access to the automatons that had invaded Fabletown in *March of the Wooden Soldiers*. Once he has determined that he is unable to further damage Gepetto's resources, he confronts the Adversary to deliver an ultimatum: stop attacking Fabletown or suffer exponentially greater damage in return, which he then demonstrates by detonating the explosives and destroying the wood and Gepetto's home.[16] Retreating to his exit point, he climbs another beanstalk, before escaping into the cloud realms and eventually back to Fabletown.

His specialized skills, hypermasculine body image, and competency in infiltration uncover the narrative of the counterinsurgency warrior within Bigby's heteroglossia; however, the anti-government stance is missing. The new mayor of Fabletown does nothing to impede Bigby's progress, providing all materials necessary to his success. When Bigby returns triumphant, it is not to an uncaring institution, but to a collection of friends who embrace his return to the community. Beast, who had taken his position of Sheriff in the interim, even attempts to give Bigby his former position — one he declines. Instead, Bigby accepts a large swath of land that neighbors the Farm where he and his family are allowed access, ending the story in the arms of his new wife. In the end, this particular narrative, with its pro-government "hero wins the day" resolution, is significant because it is demonstrative of Slotkin's "major breaks in the development of important genres" that underline a growing conservatism in American culture (*Gunfighter* 8).

The anti-government stance is not the only traditional aspect of cultural war narratives that are missing in Bigby's war stories. Within "Dog Company" and "Happily Ever After," there are no *overt* attempts to construct manhood in blatant opposition of the feminine, a significant aspect of what Robert Connell terms hegemonic masculinity (183–86).[17] The casual insults of "sissy" or "lady," so familiar in our war narratives to encode an anti-emotional masculinity, are absent. In fact, teasing of any kind is gone; it is only outside of war that this form of hegemony occurs within *Fables*. It is not among the soldiers, but in connection to (or truly, opposition against) the other main male characters that Bigby's masculinity is constructed. Instead of building manhood in opposition to a femininity seen as weak, the men of *Fables* return to 19th century models of masculine identity that are formed in opposition to boyhood, which is intriguing considering the medium's cultural connection to children. Childishness, impulsiveness, and cowardliness are the hallmarks of the "boys" — Jack, the Frog Prince, and Bluebeard — and Bigby is the first to openly scorn those characters for their failings. Throughout *Fables*, Bigby constantly teases Jack, calling him "sonny boy" or "poor baby" (*Legends* 41).[18] When Boy Blue and the Frog Prince (whom they refer to as Flycatcher) complain about the work Bigby has given them, he mocks them for their weakness, then demonstrates his own exhaustion privately, covering his face with one hand while alone in his bedroom. Other characters participate in this teasing, especially Bluebeard, who calls Jack a "pathetic, bleating child" or insinuates that Bigby has become a tamed, domesticated animal.

Even when Bigby pulls together Boy Blue, Flycatcher, Prince Charming, and Bluebeard as a special team to confront a reporter fully aware of their immortal nature, their masculinities are each questioned in turn. Boy Blue, eyes and smile wide, cheerfully and innocently asks if the others feel like they are in a caper flick while in mid-mission and is later called "sonny boy" by Jack, establishing a hierarchy of masculinity. When Bluebeard confronts Bigby about his unwillingness to carry through on his threats, Bigby intimidates the noble in the most humiliating scene in the comic to date, leaving Bluebeard in silent tears:

> I haven't *needed* to act, because you've always backed down and always *will*. Sure, you're a terror when gutting unarmed *brides* on their wedding night, or gunning down an unconscious man on a *toilet*. You're a *coward* bluebeard, hiding behind a lifetime of wealth and privilege. Now, unless you're prepared to throw down ... I *thought* so, tough guy. When you get done pissing yourself with fear, tuck tail and do what I *told* you to do. *Obey me* [*Storybook Love* 56–57].

Even Beast, Bigby's replacement as Sheriff, is described in comparison to Bigby as "an overgrown kid having fun playing secret agent," while Bigby is authentic (*Homelands* 139). It would be a mistake, however, to assume that physical age (or appearance, as these characters are centuries old) has a direct bearing on "boyishness" or masculinity. Mowgli, for instance, is "the boy raised by wolves," but is depicted in the same terms of masculinity that inform Bigby, perhaps because of his connection to Bigby's natural form. As well, Boy Blue is at his most "masculine" when he single-handedly assaults the Homelands in order to assassinate the Adversary.[19] The idea of "boy" in these stories is reserved for behavior, as nearly everyone remarks that Jack is an immature child when he physically appears to be in his twenties, and Flycatcher was a father when the invasion of his kingdom began. These constructions of a manly behavior in opposition to boyhood are inherently problematic; they reserve "true" feelings of bravery and strength for those who have demonstrated dominance, while systematically deteriorating respect for boys and youth culture.

This is not to say that the creation of masculinity within *Fables* escapes the sexism inherent in earlier versions, where men are trained to identify "womanly" traits as objectionable. It is true that the male-oriented hegemonic negotiations in *Fables* are not built upon men teasing men about being women, feminine empowerment, or at least a lack of feminine demonizing, questioned by the portrayal of Bigby's counterpart, coworker, and co-star, Snow White. When the portrayal of women is closely examined, specifically in the relationship between Bigby Wolf and Snow White, masculinity in *Fables* can be seen continuing to encourage masculinity in opposition to femininity that is perceived as emotional and submissive. I argue that lack of insults like "sissy" and "little girl" in Bigby's war narratives are examples of what Fredric Jameson terms manifest content that is censored by the underlying feminine "weakness" that underscores Bigby and Snow White's portrayals (15).

Despite the portrayal of overly-emotional females as "weak," *Fables* does not necessarily imply that vulnerability to emotions is inherently weak, only that Bigby does not participate in them, even when forcibly separated from his family. During this five year span, he experiences his grief stoically in forms that meet masculine approval. When finally united with Snow White, he admits to having an affair, explaining that: "Sarah's *one* of the ways I tried to forget you. I also tried booze and solitude. Nothing worked. How could it?" (*Wolves* 91). Snow White, however, is frequently portrayed with tearful expressions, or in crying "fits." While Bigby does not mock Snow White for her perceived femininity, he frequently reminds her of her inherent emotionalism. During the questioning of Jack for her sister's murder, Snow White breaks down, demanding answers from him with her eyes visibly tearful. Afterwards, Snow White apologizes for her moment of "weakness":

SNOW WHITE: I apologize for the *waterworks* in there. That wasn't very *professional* of me.

BIGBY: Nothing to apologize for. I *expected* it to happen sooner....
Why don't you let *me* handle things from now on?

SNOW WHITE: Not a chance. I had my *one* loss of composure. You won't have to worry about further *emotional* fits from me.

BIGBY: Don't beat upon yourself so much, Snow. Sometimes pitching a *fit* is just the right way to interrogate a suspect [*Legends* 42–43].

When Bigby "pitches a fit" in the next scene where they question Bluebeard, however, it is not with tears in his eyes; his emotional outbursts are full of curses, insults, and accusations, his body violently thrust in Bluebeard's personal space. Even as a child, Bigby channeled his emotional responses into avenues of revenge and hatred, rather than vulnerability. After his mother's death, he was the only one of his litter to remain behind to guard her corpse from the carrion eaters, until he was chased off by the large buzzards, causing him to swear the oath that would result in his becoming monstrous. Witnessing pain only causes Bigby to grow angry, rather than frightful. After forty-four hours of labor, when he "can hear Snow. She's in a *lot* of pain. And at the absolute end of her endurance," Bigby is seen with sweat covering his forehead, his face twisted into a grim frown, his hands transformed into claws actively tearing at the couch on which he sits (*Mean Seasons* 83). Snow White, on the other hand, sees the severed head of her friend, one of the Three Little Pigs, and is pictured with one hand covering her throat, as if to protect it, while the other covers her chest, as if in fear.

At the comic beginnings, Snow White is cast as a highly competent administrator with a powerful and determined personality. This persona, however, is absent in her relationship with Bigby. When first investigating Rose Red's murder scene, Snow White attempts to take charge of the investigation prompting Bigby to order her to shut up, going further to tell Jack that "if she opens her mouth *again*, pick her up and carry her back *home*. If she screams or resists, you have my permission to knock her *senseless*" (*Legends* 23). After this affront, she promptly relents, but not until threatening Jack to leave her alone — not Bigby. She has no trouble demonstrating her authority against other men, as she easily controls Prince Charming and Beast. She does not, however, exert power over Bigby until they have become intimate, but even then her power remains within the domestic sphere. Eventually, all of her power is transferred into the domestic, as she voluntarily gives up her public position when she becomes a mother. While a desire to place family over profession is not a sign of weakness, she does make a near fatal mistake directly before being forced to move to the Farm to raise her children. During the campaign against the wooden soldiers, Snow White leads the Fabletown troops in the battle, but makes a damaging decision to set the enemy on fire, not realizing that the enemy is able to continue to fight while aflame. Forced to watch the battle turn against her troops, Snow White becomes despondent until the arrival of Bigby on the battlefield. Single-handedly reversing the tide, Bigby takes control from Snow White and organizes a successful engagement. When she sees Bigby, Snow White screams his name triumphantly, running down several flights of stairs while nine months pregnant, to throw her arms around the giant wolf, stating: "I knew it ... I *knew* you'd come in time to save us! You always do! You *always* save me" (*March of* 216–17).

Perhaps the most damning evidence of Snow White's submission to Bigby's authority, thus continuing the masculine identification as one in opposition to a passive woman in need of protection, is the progression of the cover art. On the cover of *Legends in Exile*, Snow White is the only recognizable fable in motion. Attempting to catch up with a subway train, her arms and legs are posed actively running. Her hands clutch a pair of high heels, while she wears a pair of running shoes, evoking the image of the 9-to-5 working woman. Bigby's arm is trapped in the closing doors while trying to help, but her head is tilted towards the audience and away from the man failing to truly offer assistance. This vigorous portrayal reverses in later covers; as Bigby becomes more active, Snow White is shown as less so. *Storybook Love* features a wide-eyed Snow White staring emotionlessly off into the distance. Behind her, nearly three times her size, is Bigby as a wolf, growling in anger at whatever the two of them see. It is not surprising that in this episode, Bigby protects Snow White from a second assassination attempt by Goldilocks, using his "native" knowledge of the natural landscape to outwit the assassin. The next collection, *March of the Wooden Soldiers* features a pregnant Snow White, one hand on her belly, the other on the small her back, with a human Bigby behind and turned away from her, exhaling from his ubiquitous cigarette. This is followed by *The Mean Seasons*, which has Snow White in the foreground, drawn only in black and white, her hands covered by a muff, while six strings fly off into the sky attached to her flying infants. In muted yellows and reds, behind Snow White stands an enormous wolf, pinning a much smaller Frankenstein to the ground, while surrounded by the bleeding corpses of American soldiers. The final episode with the couple on the cover is *Wolves*, which has the classic romance portrait, Snow White with her head tilted back, hand in the hair of her lover, passively receiving a kiss from a descending, dominant Bigby.

I am not attempting to argue that femininity in *Fables* is constructed only through passive acceptance of male authority. Just as there is a heteroglossia of masculine identities, there are also numerous femininities revealed within the text, as demonstrated by the witch Frau Totenkinder, the special operative and spy Cinderella, the anarchist murderer Goldilocks, and the adventurous Rose Red. Instead, I see Snow White as a specific foil to Bigby that assists in the representation of a masculine identity in opposition to a femininity perceived as weak. This is merely one aspect of Bigby's mythic masculinity that remains connected to a wartime ideology that privileges a politically slanted history. As a man, Bigby symbolizes a hypermasculine ideal that limits alternative modes of masculine behavior while systematically questioning the power of women. Moreover, this system supports a "sentimental idealism" where "war [ceases] to be regarded as an inevitable calamity and [becomes] thought of as a kind of rainbow of promise" (Burns 239). It was brought to my attention that this is a collection of fables, and as such it may be playing with American mythology as much as it is European folklore. In this, I agree, but the ideology that *Fables* invokes is not wholly satiric. While there are moments of political slander, which include a joking comparison of the Young Republicans to the Nazi Party, the comic is not a political satire, but is instead subtly informed by the politics of the day (*March of* 185). In an interview with *The Comics Journal*, the author addresses the inherent politics of *Fables*:

> Someone much smarter than me said, "The purpose of art is not to tell your readers what to do, but to show your readers who they are." And so, as much as politics are going to intrude in *Fables*, that's as far as I think I'm willing to go. It's impossible to keep that out entirely. We're all political creatures whether we cop to it or not.... And every once in a while, something does get in ... it's not going to be a political tract ... but at the same time, it's not going to shy away from the fact that there are characters who have real moral and ethical centers, and we're not going to apologize for it.... There's never going to be my substitute story for the war in Iraq and what I think about it. But my opinion will get in there on just the defining qualities for why we do stuff like that [qtd. in Deppey 29].

In this, the author believes he is revealing the readers for "who they are," and his construction of an ideal, heroic man is inherently problematic in his connections to a rigid, conservative hegemonic masculinity. The intentions of the author are impossible to determine, yet if *Fables* is a magic mirror held to American society, then it displays a country that glorifies war and the soldiers who fight them.

This is especially cogent considering the newest target of the Adversary's forces, the Arabian Homelands. With the current tension between America and Iraq, the portrayal of Baghdad and its citizens are ripe for critical attention. In *Arabian Nights (and Days)*, the European fables encounter the Arabian fables seeking sanctuary within the "real world." While a full examination lies outside the boundaries of this essay, it is necessary to address the dichotomous presentation of the Arabs within the text. Sinbad, the Arabic hero, is positively portrayed, they are encouraged to free their slaves, to allow women to unveil themselves, and to adopt the laws of the European Fabletown Charter — the laws of the white fable world. In opposition, the vizier (a political advisor to a Muslim monarch) attempts to assault the Europeans with a genie, literally described as more powerful than a nuclear device, and ends up destroying himself and his cohort through his own machinations. This inclusion of the Middle Eastern mythic community, especially in a comic that has focused strongly on heroics and war, cannot help but imitate contemporary tensions and underscore the important negotiations of American ideology that are reflected within the *Fables* world.

Notes

1. For further discussion of this concept, see Bhabha 208–209.
2. In the comic medium, it is traditional to use bolded words for emphasis in most

of the dialogue. The words that the author chose to highlight will become increasingly more important in the construction of Bigby's masculine identity.

3. For clarity, I will use episode to indicate a graphic novel collection like *The Mean Seasons* or *Legends in Exile*, while the word issue refers to the monthly serials that make up those collections (i.e., the episode *Legends in Exile* collects *Fables* issues #1–5).

4. In a discussion of the heroic portrayal of Jesse James in Hollywood westerns in *Gunfighter Nation*, Slotkin notes: "He is first of all the incarnation of the principle of direct and pragmatic action.... He solves problems without resort to litigation or abstract theory, confronting each question on its own terms and resolving it in the handiest, most efficient way" (298).

5. In discussing the werewolf myth in American culture, Oakley states that "wolves prowl through our subconscious: ... [and] may have little in common with the wolves that live and die, largely unseen, in the northern forests and tundra. But centuries of legends, myths, stories, art and belief in a wolf that is the physical embodiment of evil are not easily dispelled" (1).

6. This is especially relevant considering Bigby's refusal to murder, even though it provides a useful solution for the problems of an inclusive community that desires privacy and secrecy above all else.

7. Braudy contends, "Just as epic formulas focus on the hero with his undying fame, war focuses attention on certain ways of being a man and ignores or arouses suspicions about others" (xvi). This is doubly true for Bigby, as the epic hero is as part of his characterization as his warrior nature.

8. In his preface, Fussell states that "for the past fifty years the Allied war has been sanitized and romanticized almost beyond recognition by the sentimental, the loony patriotic, the ignorant, and the bloodthirsty. I have tried to balance the scales" (ix).

9. Phillips states, "Western gender discourse has further associated masculinity with bravery, and then defined bravery in terms of stoically bearing physical pain ... rather than the emotional courage of opening oneself to caring or the moral courage of standing with a minority against a push of war. Courage may also be erroneously defined as fearlessness, assumed of 'real men' but not of women" (177).

10. Note that the names chosen for the soldiers, Zilmer, Schmactenberg, Levine, Supinski, Tice, Harp, and Duffy, resonate with the inclusionary myth of the World War II military.

11. In a review of the works released by DC Comics and Marvel Comics, Kading finds that "perhaps noteworthy by their absence, is that there are no declarations affirming faith or trust in political leaders or government institutions, even though our superheroes failed us. Rather, the superheroes admonish contemporary political powers to act as superheroes would" (221).

12. In *Gunfighter Nation*, Slotkin argues that "their missions, which were usually coordinated with conventional operations, involved the infiltration of enemy positions prior to an assault, the seizure (by speed and stealth) of objectives too strong to be taken by conventional assault, and various type of raids designed to divert enemy forces or damage vital facilities" (453–58).

13. Another possible avenue of investigation is the racial production within *Fables*. Bigby is more than a native, a "man that knows Indians"; he is a nature deity and a god among wolves. That he has chosen to appear as a white man, and actively desires a woman named Snow White, complicates this relationship.

14. Jeffords accounts how Vietnam veterans in the mass media increasingly became seen as "victimized by [their] own government ... [and] the final step of this process was to transfer the accumulated negative features of the feminine to the government itself" (168–69).

15. As I will address later in the essay, Prince Charming is aligned with the feminized, childish masculinity that defines Bigby through its opposition to his pragmatic, direct heroism.

16. This chapter is entitled "The Israel Analogy," in which Fabletown has decided to mimic Israel, who when surrounded by enemies that desire their extinction, cause greater damage to anyone who assaults them. In an interview with Dick Deppey, Willingham comments on his political sympathies for Israel's battle against the Arab nations.

17. Connell defines hegemonic masculinity as "embedded in religious doctrine and practice, mass media content, wage structures, the design of housing, welfare/taxation policies, and so forth" (184). As men are encoded through these methods to become masculine, they internalize their own dominance over women and other marginalized and subordinate masculinities. These other masculinities are vaguely defined, thus preventing alternatives from gaining any recognition in the public sphere.

18. Further eliminating Bigby from "alternative masculinities," Bigby's past with Little Red Riding Hood removes his connections to cross-dressing. Jack challenges Bigby by asking "Or does that *protection* only apply to granny-gobbling *wolves* who don shepherd's clothing to become low-rent *cops* during the exile" (41). Jack mixes his metaphors, beginning with the well known legend, but ending with the adage about a wolf in sheep's clothing.

19. Unlike Mowgli and Bigby, however, Boy Blue requires the aid of two powerful magical items to make this attempt, which ultimately fails in its stated purpose, though he is able to escape with desperately needed information.

Works Cited

Bhabha, Homi K. *The Location of Culture*. 1994. New York: Routledge, 2006.

Braudy, Leo. *From Chivalry to Terrorism: War and the Changing Nature of Masculinity*. New York: Knopf, 2003.

Brombert, Victor. *In Praise of Antiheroes*. Chicago: University of Chicago Press, 1999.

Burns, Edward McNall. *The American Idea of Mission: Concepts of National Purpose and Destiny*. Westport, CT: Greenwood Press, 1973.

Connell, Robert W. *Gender and Power: Society, the Person and Sexual Politics*. Stanford: Stanford University Press, 1987.

Deppey, Dick. Interview with Bill Willingham. *The Comics Journal*. 18 Sept. 2006. 15 Apr. 2007 <http://www.tcj.com/index.php?option=com_content&task=view&id= 410&Itemid=48>.

Fussell, Paul. *Wartime: Understanding and Behavior in the Second World War*. New York: Oxford University Press, 1989.

Grandstaff, Mark R. "Visions of New Men: The Heroic Soldier Narrative in American Advertisements During World War II." *Advertising and Society Review* 5.2 (2004). Project Muse. 1 May 2007 <http://muse.jhu.edu.spot.lib.auburn.edu/journals/ advertising_and_society_review/v005/5.2grandstaff.html>.

Jameson, Fredric. "Metacommentary." *PMLA* 86 (1971): 9–18.

Jarvis, Christina S. *The Male Body at War: American Masculinity during World War II*. DeKalb: Northern Illinois University Press, 2004.

Jeffords, Susan. *The Remasculinization of America: Gender and the Vietnam War*. Bloomington: Indiana University Press, 1989.

Kading, Terry. "Drawn into 9/11, But Where Have All the Superheroes Gone?" *Comics as Philosophy.* Ed. Jeff McLaughlin. Jackson: University of Mississippi Press, 2005. 207–27.

Noon, David Hoogland. "Operation Enduring Analogy: World War II, the War on Terror, and the Uses of Historical Memory." *Rhetoric & Public Affairs* 7.3 (2004): 339–64.

Oakley, Glenn. "Historical Overview." In *Wolf!* Ed. Wolves in American Culture Committee. Ashland: NorthWord, 1986. 1–7.

Phillips, Kathy J. *Manipulating Masculinity: War and Gender in Modern British and American Literature.* New York: Palgrave Macmillan, 2006.

Reynolds, Richard. *Superheroes: A Modern Mythology.* Jackson: University of Mississippi Press, 1994.

Slotkin, Richard. *Gunfighter Nation: The Myth of the Frontier in Twentieth-Century America.* New York: Atheneum, 1992.

_____. *Regeneration through Violence: The Mythology of the American Frontier, 1600–1860.* Middletown: Wesleyan University Press, 1973.

Willingham, Bill. *Homelands.* New York: DC Comics, 2005.

_____. *Legends in Exile.* New York: DC Comics, 2002.

_____. *March of the Wooden Soldiers.* New York: DC Comics, 2004.

_____. *The Mean Seasons.* New York: DC Comics, 2005.

_____. *1001 Nights of Snowfall.* New York: DC Comics, 2006.

_____. *Storybook Love.* New York: DC Comics, 2004.

_____. *Wolves.* New York: DC Comics, 2006.

Wright, Bradford W. *Comic Book Nation: The Transformation of Youth Culture in America.* Baltimore: Johns Hopkins University Press, 2001.

Philip Pullman's I Was a Rat! and the Fairy-Tale Retelling as Instrument of Social Criticism

VANESSA JOOSEN

The fairy-tale renaissance is an international phenomenon that has been identified in several Western countries since the late 1960s, and one of its manifestations is a spectacular increase in the production of fairy-tale retellings. As the fairy tales by Charles Perrault, the Brothers Grimm, and Hans Christian Andersen are recycled in the late twentieth and early twenty-first centuries, their content and meaning are transformed and combined with contemporary issues and ideologies. In some retellings the fairy-tale plots, conventions and discourse are adapted in such a way that they merge as harmoniously as possible with the new setting. Adèle Geras' *Pictures in the Night*, which relocates the tale of "Snow White" to the early 1960s, can be named as an example: this retelling makes a smooth transition from magic to realism, several aspects of the fairy tale appear as universal (most notably the difficult relationship with stepparents, the importance of beauty, and female jealousy), and the traditional happy ending is retained.

More frequently, especially in the ideology-critical revisions of the 1970s and 1980s, but also in more recent examples, retellings produce a vehement clash between the traditional fairy tale and the new, contemporary context — a clash from which neither recovers completely unharmed. *Roodlapje* (Little Red Rag) by the Belgian author and artist Pieter Gaudesaboos (2003) can be considered an example here. This provocative picture book about a neglected, lonely child relocates the story of "Little Red Riding Hood" to a bleak late twentieth-century urban environment. Gaudesaboos deprives the traditional Grimm version from most of its plot, as well as from its optimistic conclusion. Both the traditional fairy tale and the new setting are affected by the critique implied in this mismatch: the fairy tale for providing illusionary happiness and false sentimentality, the grim reality depicted for not being able to give children a sense of security and a hopeful perspective for the future (Joosen, "Scene 9" 68–69).

Philip Pullman's *I Was a Rat!* (1999) is a retelling that, like *Pictures of the Night* and *Roodlapje*, negotiates between the fairy tale's traditional generic features on the one hand and a late-twentieth-century setting and thematics on the other hand. Whereas in some aspects it produces a confrontation between the two frames of reference, in several others it smoothes out the tensions. In this article I will focus on the following specific and in many ways related aspects: the fairy tale's one-dimensional chronotope, its narratological characteristics and implied reader, the image of childhood presented in the fairy tale, and the fairy tale's optimism. That Pullman's harmonization covers a number of contradictions will be addressed in the final part of the article.

A Sequel to "Cinderella"

I Was a Rat! is a sequel to Charles Perrault's "Cinderella," the best-known version of the tale. The title of the retelling refers to a sentence uttered by its protagonist, Roger, when he knocks one evening at the door of Bob and Joan, an elderly, childless couple. Roger is one of the rats that Cinderella's godmother had transformed into a page boy—by accident, he did not change back to his animal shape at the stroke of midnight. At the beginning of the book, he is a three-week-old rat stuck in the body of a nine-year-old boy. What follows is a series of events that is highly reminiscent of the adventures in *Pinocchio*. Just like Carlo Collodi's wooden doll, Roger is a non-human being who has to learn how to behave in order to be accepted in society. But he has knocked on the right door and is lucky to have landed in a warm family: Bob and Joan almost immediately find a place for him in their hearts. Their love for him is unconditional and they want to offer him all possible chances, even if they cannot really understand him. But just as Collodi's Gepetto cannot follow his wooden son everywhere he goes, Roger too is soon exposed to figures who do not mean well. After a traumatic first day at school, Roger is consecutively abducted, locked up, exposed in a cage, involuntarily involved in a burglary and, in a court case that is reminiscent of the finale to *Alice in Wonderland*, sentenced to death.

A New Chronotope

One of the central defining features of the traditional fairy tale is its location in an unspecified time and location, as becomes clear in the opening formula "once upon a time in a place far far away." The chronotope of the fairy tale is marked by the fact that both time and place are beyond our reach. It is one-dimensional (Lüthi 9; Nikolajeva 122): in contrast to fantasy stories, characters do not travel between times or worlds. This does not mean that the fairy tale's content is completely isolated from any more specific time and place, however. Like all stories, fairy tales carry the traces of the historical context and geographic area in which they originated, even if their intended relationship to this reality is not mimetic. Comparative overviews of tales that appear in various periods and locations, such as Jack Zipes' *The Trials and Tribulations of Little Red Riding Hood* or Maria Tatar's *Secrets Beyond the Door: The Story of Bluebeard and His Wives* have addressed this topic extensively, showing how a specific fairy tale differs and evolves according to the context in which it is told.

It is a popular strategy in fairy-tale retellings to update the time of the fairy tale to a twentieth-century reality and to make the location more easily recognizable. Examples that are now classic in this respect are Gillian Cross' *Wolf* and Fiona French's *Snow White in New York*, and updated retellings of "Cinderella" include Babette Cole's *Prince Cinders*, Ellen Jackson and Kevin O'Malley's *Cinder Edna* and, most recently, Melissa Kantor's *If I Have a Wicked Stepmother, Where's My Prince?*

Trying to determine the time and setting of Pullman's *I Was a Rat!* is a more difficult task than may appear at first: this retelling places itself in between the unspecified but clearly pre-industrialized society that is the usual setting to the traditional fairy tale on the one hand and, on the other hand, the late twentieth-century United Kingdom in which Pullman's book itself was written. The realm of "once upon a time" is evoked by a combination of several features in the book. Although the typical opening formula of the fairy tale is not included, the first descriptions of Bob and Joan place them in a society marked by stability and tradition:

> Old Bob and his wife, Joan, lived by the market in the house where his father and grandfather and great-grandfather had lived before him, cobblers all of them, and cobbling was Bob's trade too. Joan was a washerwoman, like her mother and her grandmother and her great-grandmother, back as far as anyone could remember. And if they'd had a son, he would have become a cobbler in his turn, and if they'd had a daughter, she would have learned the laundry trade, and so the world would have gone on [Pullman 3].

Cobblers and washerwomen could only thrive in the age when shoes were still hand-made and washing machines had not yet been invented. The complete absence of technology from Bob and Joan's home — they still tell time by a cuckoo clock (3) and heat milk by the fire (4) — confirms that this story takes place in the pre-industrialized traditional environment that is also typical of the fairy tales by Grimm and Perrault.

With the inclusion of pages from the newspaper *The Daily Scourge*, however, a clear allusion to twentieth-century British society emerges. Not only does this mark a disruption with the typical fairy-tale chronotope, in which news is still proclaimed by trumpet (Perrault 453), it also contrasts with the genre's conventional homogenous use of discourse and straightforward narratological organization. From the beginning it is clear that *The Daily Scourge* is a twentieth-century newspaper: both the themes addressed and the style in which the articles of *The Daily Scourge* are written would clash severely with the conventions of newspapers from the nineteenth century or earlier. The discourse of *The Daily Scourge* is strongly reminiscent of British tabloids such as *The Sun* or *The Daily Mirror*. The first page of *I Was a Rat!* features the front page of an issue of *The Daily Scourge*, announcing the engagement of Prince Richard with Lady Aurelia Ashington, as Cinderella has called herself in this book since the Royal Ball. It features a short section written by a "romance correspondent" and announces articles on "the playboy Prince's previous girlfriends" (Pullman 1). The "playboy Prince" is an epithet that the popular press associates with Prince Edward of Britain or Prince Albert of Monaco; it is not what we imagine the contemporaries of Perrault or the Grimms to be labeled, nor such fictional characters in the traditional fairy tale as Cinderella's or Sleeping Beauty's princes.

The inclusion of pages from a tabloid newspaper also marks a disruption in the typical narratological organization of Perrault's and Grimm's fairy tales, the plot of which is narrated in a simple and linear manner by an omniscient, third-person narrator. Although the fairy tale can be argued to be, through its origin in oral discourse, a polyphonic genre by definition, the traditional versions of "Cinderella" do not make this network of voices and discourses explicit. Whereas the main plot of *I Was a Rat!* follows the conventional third-person narration, the newsflashes from the tabloid constantly interrupt these to provide (unsolicited) comment and judgment. Together with these disruptions, the implied reader of the story shifts: the book requires an active reader who does not only link the story about Roger to "Cinderella,"[1] but also confronts the report of the course of events through the supposedly objective lens of the narrator with the blatantly prejudiced and sensationalist discourse of *The Daily Scourge*.

Disenchantments

With regard to the chronotope, a further distinctive characteristic of the traditional fairy tale lies in the role that magic has to play. It is one of the characteristic features of the so-called "Zaubermärchen" (fairy tale of magic), to which "Cinderella" belongs, that the supernatural is an evident part of the fairy-tale realm and that magic is not felt to intrude in human life (Lüthi 9). This aspect of the fairy tale can be linked to its one-dimensionality, to which magic naturally belongs, and stands again in contrast to fantasy stories and other related fantastical genres such as sagas. Perrault's Cinderella does not act surprised in the least when her fairy godmother appears and begins her enchantments. When Cinderella is asked by her fairy godmother to bring "the finest pumpkin she could find" (451), she is "unable to guess" how it will play a part in taking her to the ball. She watches as her godmother transforms the hollowed-out pumpkin into "a beautiful coach gilded all over"; then, her god-mother finds six mice in a trap, each of which she "tap[s] with her wand ... producing a fine-looking team of six handsome, dappled mouse-gray horses" (451). Lacking a suitable coachman, Cinderella offers her assistance, saying, "'I'll go and see if there's a rat in the rattrap. We could make a coachman out of him'", to which her godmother replies, "'You're right ... go and see'" (451). Although Cinderella cannot imagine how a pumpkin can take her to the ball, there is no mention of any surprise to the rest of the fairy's enchantments. Nor does anybody raise an eyebrow when the prince decides to track his future wife by means of a shoe, and the reader too is invited to accept this as a logical strat-egy within the fairy-tale realm. The fairy tale as a non-mimetic genre relies on our "suspension of disbelief" (Samuel Taylor Coleridge) towards events which are unlikely to occur in reality (Joosen, "Disenchanting" 228–39).

In Pullman's sequel, the enchantments have taken place outside the scope of the book: it is the presupposition of Roger's condition that indeed he once was a rat and that some magical transformation has taken place. Nevertheless, within the book itself, the supernatural does not intervene in the story, not even when Roger is most desperate. In Perrault's "Cinderella," the protagonist's tears sufficed to summon the fairy godmother; in *I Was a Rat!* she does not even appear when Roger and Aurelia wish with all their hearts for her to come back (159). Throughout the book, nearly all references to magic are met with incredulity by characters who are not willing to "suspend their disbelief." Most people react similarly to Roger as the lady at the City Hall where Bob and Joan initially take him, and who refuses to listen to what she calls their nonsense (18). Other characters try to rationalize the fact that Roger was a rat, referring it simply to his imagination (50). The concluding remark that the Philosopher Royal makes about Roger can be read as a humorous meta-comment with regard to the fairy tale: "*Cannot distinguish truth from fantasy*" (49). Nevertheless, the story makes a strong appeal to the reader to give Roger at least the benefit of the doubt. The fact that Roger's former being as a rat is never denied by the third-person narrator and that all the characters who believe in magic (Bob and Joan, Aurelia) are the ones that the retelling presents as the most kind-hearted (110) demonstrates the story's favorable attitude towards the fairy tale as a genre and the enjoyment that comes from suspending one's disbelief. In this context it should be noted that the greatest harm caused in this book is excused in the name of rationality and science.

A Little Boy Called Bulger

Philip Pullman does not feel restricted to limit himself to simple stories: he is convinced that children have the capacity to grasp even complex scientific or philosophical concepts and moral dilemmas, as long as these are incorporated in a good story: "Children's books ... are capable of expressing just about any idea, and illuminating just about any subject" (Pullman, "Republic of Heaven" 655). What Pullman deems essential, though, is that authors deal with difficult or controversial subject matter in a responsible way, and that they teach children to think critically and independently.

The informed active reader of *I Was a Rat!* is invited, moreover, to link Roger's story and the discussions in *The Daily Scourge* to a controversial event that was high on the agenda of the British press and politics in the 1990s. *I Was a Rat!* first appeared in Britain in 1999 and an important cultural frame of reference is the public outcry that followed the murder of the two-year-old toddler James Bulger. Jamie, as he came to be known with the general public, was abducted on 12 February 1993 from the Bootle Strand Shopping Centre in Merseyside, Liverpool. It was soon established that two ten-year-old boys, Robert Thompson and Jon Venables, had led James a few miles further to a railway, where they tortured him with stones and an iron bar and eventually killed him (Wolff & Smith 133). His cruel death and the young age of the perpetrators shocked the United Kingdom and the rest of the world. The event initiated a long-lasting debate on juvenile crime and the rights and responsibilities of young criminals, a debate that continues up to this date.[2]

During a lecture given at the 9th British IBBY Conference "Children's Literature and Childhood in Performance" in 2002, Peter Hollindale convincingly showed that the public discourse surrounding the court case against the two young killers reflects the ambiguity with which our society thinks about children: "it polarises our confusions" (16). On the one hand stands Jamie, the small, innocent, almost angelic child, who needed adult protection and whose innocence led him into death. This image of the child is informed by romantic and enlightened discourses and functions as "a reservoir for desperately held grown-up beliefs" (16).

On the other hand stand the two killers, also children, who embody the adult fear of the evil child, the child as an uncontrollable force as it has also been portrayed, Hollindale shows, in such novels as William Golding's *Lord of the Flies*[3] and in such documentaries as Channel 4's *Boys Alone*.[4] This image of childhood can be traced back to a pre-romantic discourse, argues Roni Natov: "Previous to Rousseau, children were seen as potentially sinister, their sinful nature contained and socialized. But long after their innocence was recognized, they continued to be viewed as threatening in their sensuousness, envied for the youth that our culture distorts and fetishes" (3). Natov sees this fear of the evil child and envy of youth expressed in nursery rhymes such as "Rock-a-bye-Baby," "Three Blind Mice," as well as in various children's stories and some fairy tales, which she states "suggest a hidden hostility and secret fear about childhood, not just about the protection of children from the world, but about our denial of the inner darkness of which we suspect them" (133).

The fear of the child that Natov and Hollindale describe is linked to the fact that the child is and remains ultimately unknown. The adult needs to devise strategies to grasp or confine this child as constitutive "other." In her doctoral dissertation *Het kind zonder gezicht* (*The Child Without a Face*, 2005), Katrien Vloeberghs underlines that every image of childhood is a construct:

> The attribution of a limited number of essential characteristics to the child, as well as the spatial and temporal localisation and limitation of the sphere of childhood are strategies to curb the unknowable foreignness and to neutralize the possible alienation and dislocation in confrontation with the child [Vloeberghs 19, my translation].[5]

Both the unilateral image of the child as angelic (James Bulger) and the representation of Thompson and Venables in the press as unpardonable and incurable evil monsters can be seen as strategies through which adults try to limit the endless array of meanings that can be attached to the signifier "child." An important discourse in the construction of such images is children's literature, Jacqueline Rose argues in *The Case of Peter Pan* (1984): "If children's literature builds an image of the child inside the book, it does so in order to secure the child who is outside the book, the one who does not come so easily within its grasp" (2). Pullman's *I Was a Rat!* can be read as a fictional exploration of several images of childhood and as a reflection on how the construction of these images takes place.

The image of childhood that Pullman presents in *I Was a Rat!* confronts the characteristics attributed to the young in the traditional fairy tale with the public image of Venables and Thompson. The protagonist of "Cinderella" in Perrault and Grimm exemplified an idealized image of the child with a typical mixture of romantic and enlightened aspects: kindness, piety, innocence, victimhood, closeness to the spiritual and to nature (her relationship with the birds), hope for a better future and social progression. Roger, the protagonist of *I Was a Rat!* shares with Cinderella many of these idealized features of youth. In the third-person narrative that dominates the story, he appears rather as the equivalent of the innocent James Bulger than as the monstrous children that his killers were accused of being. The reader sees him for the first time through the eyes of Bob, who has a fondness of children (5). Roger appears as a boy in need. On countless repeated occasions his small size is stressed: he is a "little boy" (5, 9) and a "poor little soul" (5), with "little hands" (6), "thin little shoulders" (12), and "a thin little body" (11). His smallness is evoked visually as a sign of harmlessness and cuteness, for instance when his foster parents give him one of Bob's nightshirts, "and very small he looked in it" (9). Several references are made to his ignorance and bewilderment, and Bob and Joan believe he is an orphan in need of care. Their attitude is summarized in Joan's exclamation: "He doesn't know anything, poor little thing" (6) and in Bob's remark: "You can't look after yourself, you're too little" (14). Roger rewards their efforts to teach him "proper manners" by doing his utter best, being cheerful, polite (48,

76), helpful (46) and by learning fast (76). In one scene in particular, Roger comes close to the visual image of Jamie Bulger that was stamped on the British public's collective memory. When Roger is led away by the evil Mr. Tapscrew, the narrator visualizes them from behind, as the shopping center's CCTV footage showed the last images of James Bulger: "Roger took Mr. Tapscrew's hand and walked away with him because he thought he ought to be a good boy" (59). Like James Bulger, Roger is pictured as the innocent child victim, led along by the hand by those who want to do him harm.

The Child as Monster

The image of Roger presented through the lens of the narrator and Bob and Joan differs strongly from the way he is perceived by other characters in the book. Most people do not take the effort to get to know Roger and try to fit him into a pre-established image of what a child is or should be. Like Thompson and Venables, the rat-boy Roger does not correspond to the ideal image of childhood shared by most characters in *I Was a Rat!* That Roger alienates adults is described by a royal servant: "Said he *used* to be a rat, sir.... My cousin said it give him a creepy feeling all up his spine" (44). Bob and Joan's neighbor too feels uncomfortable: "There's something uncanny about it, mark my words" (57). At the beginning of the story, even Bob fears a wild nature underneath the harmless surface of the little child that Roger is presented to be (10). Jack Zipes points at the resemblances between Roger and Kaspar Hauser, a nineteenth-century German feral child who had lived in isolation until he was an adult. He was killed in well-meant attempts to civilize him as a grown-up (*Why Fairy Tales Stick* 122). An important difference with such feral children is that Roger does speak, a fact which is explained by his magic transformation and which guarantees that unlike most feral children he is still able to integrate in society.

The uncanny feeling that Roger raises is caused by the facts that adults realize their inability to understand what a child is. Particularly frightening is that monstrous children are usually believed to lie hidden under the exterior appearance of the innocent child, an illusion that many horror stories and movies exploit. As a scientist who deals with Roger thinks: "The monster didn't look very monstrous, but the Chief Scientist didn't go by surface appearances. It was what lay underneath that mattered. This little shivering naked thing might have had the form of an ape, or even (to be more accurate) a human boy, but that only made it more horrible and unnatural" (119). The British popular press made a similar point with regard to Robert Thompson and Jon Venables: "Freaks of nature" was the main title on the front page of *The Daily Mirror* of 25 November 1993. Under the pictures of Thompson and Venables could be read: "The faces of normal boys but they had hearts of unparalleled evil. Killing James gave them a buzz." If monsters can hide under the surface of innocent-looking children, then no child is to be trusted, and in *I Was a Rat!* this becomes the excuse for serious child abuse.[6]

The first time that Roger experiences physical violence is in school. But the most serious abuse takes place when he is arrested after having involuntarily assisted in a burglary and seeking refuge in the sewers. Roger is no longer regarded as a child, not even as a human being. Again a parallel with the Bulger trial arises. Robert Thompson and Jon Venables deviated so strongly from the ideal of childhood that there was a public outcry for the boys to be trialed as adults, even though they were only ten years old at the moment the crime was committed. The home secretary, Michael Howard, gave in to the pressure and raised the sentence to fifteen years. It was later reduced again by the House of Lords, "which ruled that it is unlawful to apply a tariff system without regard to the progress and development of a child; and that, when exercising the judicial power of sentencing, the Home Secretary must remain detached from the pressure of public opinion" (Wolff & Smith 133).

In his retelling, Pullman criticizes most notably the unilateral, prejudiced way in which the British tabloids tried to influence the court's decisions by portraying the children as monsters. In December of the same year that *I Was a Rat!* was published, 1999, the European Court of Human Rights came to a similar conclusion, claiming that the boys Jon Venables and Robert Thompson had not had a fair trial (133) and that their human rights had thus been violated. The Court also considered that the children had been subjected to a higher level of suffering than necessary, among others by their exposure to the hostile press and public in and outside of the court.

The British popular press indeed had an important and influential voice in the public debate surrounding the Bulger trial and they were held responsible by many for exploiting and invigorating the public outrage. Several petitions were organized to raise the sentence from ten years, as recommended by the Lord Chief Justice, to fifteen or even twenty-five years. *The Sun* collected 20,000 signatures to send the children to prison for life (Wolff & Smith 133). Although Roger has not committed any major crime in *I Was a Rat!*, the press depicts him as a monster, tuning in on urban legends and public fear. *The Daily Scourge* organizes a petition highly reminiscent of *The Sun*'s in order to have Roger put to death. The box with "yes" is remarkably bigger than the one with "no," signaling the newspaper's biased position. Reproaches for prejudiced, sensationalist discourse were also held against the British popular press during the Bulger trial. "In a tabloid frenzy the two [killers] were compared to Myra Hindley and Saddam Hussein, and the people who saw the boys take James away but failed to act were dubbed the 'Liverpool' 38" ("The Bulger Case").[7]

The popular press, both in the Bulger case as in the fictional frame of Pullman's book, uses the advice that the evil Mr. Tapscrew gives when he puts Roger on show: "Good shivers were good business" (56). In order to raise money, the fictional tabloid is happy to publish anything that will make people curious, and the "best kind of story was one that went on and on, with a new twist every day" (111). The Bulger case, in which details of the killing and trial were gradually released, proved to be such a goldmine for the British tabloids, and so is Roger's for *The Daily Scourge*, which sells 250,000 extra copies (116). Pullman shows, moreover, that it served the British tabloids well to deny the boys their protected status as children; by degrading them to freaks, thus denying them not even their rights as children but also as humans, they justified their own exploitation of them. Mr. and Mrs. Tapscrew in *I Was a Rat!* do the same by labeling Roger as a freak and exposing him to a curious but unsympathetic crowd on a fancy fair (92). Like Thompson and Venables,' Roger's exposure may be deemed inhuman, but certainly it makes some people very rich.

Innocent as a Rat

Pullman also seems to take the opposite stand as *The Daily Scourge* with regard to the young Thompson and Venables' responsibility in Bulger's death. He shows that Roger is a boy involved in a learning process. Whenever he does something wrong, it is stressed, he does so out of ignorance, not malice. The reader, whose surplus knowledge creates an ironic distance, is invited to sympathize with him. This is for instance the case when he enthusiastically puts his face in the hot yolk of a fried egg (14), or when he gets whipped with the cane at school and faces his punishment unprepared because he thinks the head of school asked him to bend over in order to play leapfrog (41). Comparing him to an animal — which in the logic of the story, he is indeed — the narrator pardons his behavior by explaining that he merely follows his instincts, acting not as an immoral but as an amoral being. As Bob says: "They weren't really bad things anyway, only the kind of things a poor innocent beast would do" (110). A similar apology is made by the narrator when Roger takes a pencil to eat it: "He couldn't help it any more than a dog can help tiptoeing round the corner to eat the cat's food" (Pullman 17). In the Bulger case, a lot of stress was put on the fact that Thompson and Venables knew right from wrong, and that they had attempted to cover up the murder. The major difference between *I Was a Rat!* and the Bulger case is that Roger is only the perpetrator of relatively small mistakes, whereas he is always the victim of more serious abuse. Pullman thus conflates both the roles of James Bulger and those of his killers in the figure of Roger: James, because Roger is an innocent and loving boy who is abducted (not only by Mr. Tapscrew but also by another gang of slightly older boys) and whose (foster) parents are desperately looking for him; Thompson and Venables because Roger is perceived as they were, as inhuman, as a freak, as someone who deserves the worst punishment possible. Thanks to this conflation of roles, Pullman is able to retain an idealistic image of the child and to achieve a happy ending but fails to get to the heart of the matter of what was at stake at the Bulger trial: how do we treat children who have committed a serious crime? When do we deem people responsible for their deeds? How should juvenile criminals be treated and punished in a way that does justice both to the seriousness of their deeds as to their young age? In this respect it should be noted that the reader never finds out what happens to the gang of children who had led Roger astray and used him to assist in their burglary.

Happily Ever After?

The red thread that runs through *I Was a Rat!* is a plea for the rights of the child that should be protected at all times. The only methods to raise children are love, patience and care, the message spells, and Pullman criticizes all the violent and repressive didactic methods that are promoted by the dubious medium of *The Daily Scourge* and practiced in schools. The attitudes of the adults towards Roger are symptomatic of different ways in which children are regarded: some wish to protect him, some wish to educate and socialize him, several try to commodificate and exploit him, some think that he is a threat to society and should be removed from it. The adult characters' moral stand is directly linked to their attitude towards Roger and the static, flat characterization that results from this brings the retelling back to the conventions of the traditional fairy tale. The critical reader may note that this didactic strategy stands diametrical to the message that Pullman gives with regard to Roger: there are always several sides to a story and people deserve more than one chance. Whereas Pullman implicitly criticizes the black-and-white characterization around the Bulger case in the popular press, such dramatic contrasts also form the cornerstone of the didactic impulse in his own narrative.

With regard to the bestselling trilogy *His Dark Materials*, Pullman's own image of childhood has been scrutinized by several critics. It was already mentioned above that Pullman believes that child readers should not be protected from challenging subjects if they are offered with consideration of their age, and this is certainly the case in the trilogy. In *I Was a Rat!* Pullman too appears as an enlightened thinker who believes in the good nature of the child and in the importance of education to raise children into responsible and critical adults. His attitude stands in contrast to the British tabloids, who strove for Thompson and Venables to be locked up for life and denied them the chance to rehabilitate themselves, and to the fictional Mr. Tapscrew. The latter stresses that Roger, who he believes is a monstrous giant rat, cannot be educated: "Just let it get big enough and nothing'll stop it from tearing your throat out and chewing it up before your very eyes" (140). Roger, Bob, and Joan, in contrast, strongly believe in the power of education, if it is carried out with respect for the child as a human being with needs and rights of its own. Roger explains that being a human being is not so difficult if other people treat you as such

(165). His reasoning seems equally valid with regard to being a child, which again puts emphasis on love and education.

When at the end of *I Was a Rat!*, Roger is pictured back in Bob and Joan's house, ready to learn his trade as a cobbler, the happy end seems to be a fact: "The world outside was a difficult place, but toasted cheese and love and craftsmanship would do to keep them safe" (164). At the beginning of this essay, it was argued that Pullman's retelling oscillates between the traditional fairy-tale realm and a late twentieth-century context. It is clear that Roger's happy ending mainly exists within the fairy-tale scope. As Jack Zipes wonders: "Safe from whom, one must ask? Safe from society? Safe from the media? Safe from the forces of 'civilization'?" (*Why Fairy Tales Stick* 122). A reference to twentieth-century society had already disrupted the happy ending of the traditional fairy tale to which *I Was a Rat!* is a sequel. Princess Aurelia, Pullman's counterpart to Cinderella, is an ordinary girl who is raised to the status of fairy-tale princess—from the tabloid reports, the link with Princess Diana is easy to infer. History has shown, however, that the "fairy-tale wedding" of Diana and Charles did not lead them into a happy future together, and at the end of this book Princess Aurelia's marriage too displays its first cracks. She admits to Roger that most of all, she would like to be a normal girl again. In conclusion, one may thus say that although Pullman points at the illusionary nature of the fairy tale's optimism, he still invites his readers to suspend their disbelief and step back into the conventions of this genre at the end of his own book. It is within the fairy-tale realm that the innocent child survives, and that happy endings can still last ever after.

Notes

1. Nicholas Tucker notes that readers often do not make the connection with "Cinderella" until the final pages of the book (73).

2. As recently as 8 May 2007, I received the following email, with 465 signatures included. All factual and linguistic mistakes were taken literally from the email: "Remember February 1993 when a young 3 yr old boy was taken from Liverpool ,United Kingdom , by two 10-year-old boys? Jamie Bulger walked away from his mother for only a second and Jon Venables took his hand and led him out of the mall with his friend Robert Thompson. They took Jamie on a walk for over 2 and a half miles, along the way stopping every now and again to torture the poor little boy who was crying constantly for his mother. Finally they stopped at a railway track where they brutally kicked him, threw stones at him, rubbed paint in his eyes and pushed batteries up his anus. It was actually worse than this. What these two boys did was so horrendous that Jamie's mother was forbidden to view his body. They then left his beaten small body on the tracks so a train could run him over to hide the mess they had created. These two boys, even being boys, understood what they did was wrong, hence trying to make it look like an accident. This week Lady Justice Butler-Sloss has awarded the two boys anonymity for the rest of their lives when they leave custody with new identities. They will also leave early this year only serving just over half of their sentence. They are being relocated to Australia to live out the rest of their lives (didn't think it was a convict settlement anymore).

They disgustingly and violently took Jamie's life away — in return they each get a new life. Please ... if you feel as strongly as we do, that this is a grave miscarriage of justice copy entire email and paste into new email ... then add your name at the end, and send it to everyone you can! If you are the 500th person to sign, please forward this e-mail to:cust.ser.cs@gtnet.gov.uk < and attention it to Lady Justice Butler-Sloss. Then start the list over again and send to your friends and family. The Love-Bug virus took less than 72 hours to reach the world. I hope this one does as well."

3. Hollindale draws convincing parallels between James Bulger's killers and the fictional character of Roger in *Lord of the Flies*. Note that the protagonist of *I Was a Rat!* is also called Roger. It is unclear whether this is an intentional intertextual reference or not. The name Roger also bears phonetic resemblances to Robert, as one of Bulger's killers was called.

4. *Boys Alone* is a television documentary in which ten boys needed only five days to wreck a house, displaying disturbing and violent behavior that was reminiscent of several scenes in *Lord of the Flies* (Hollindale 24).

5. Original text: "Het toekennen van een beperkt aantal wezenlijke eigenschappen aan het kind evenals de ruimtelijke en temporele lokalisering en begrenzing van de sfeer van de kindertijd zijn strategieën om de onkenbare vreemdheid in te tomen en de mogelijke verontrusting en ontwrichting in confrontatie met het kind te neutraliseren" (Vloeberghs 19).

6. An analogy can be drawn here to woman as a constitutive other. See the depiction of woman as discussed in Gilbert and Gubar's *The Madwoman in the Attic*.

7. In the mid-1960s, Myra Hindley and her partner Ian Brady killed five teenagers after having abducted most of them to the Saddleworth moors.

Works Cited

"The Bulger Case: Chronology." *The Guardian* 6 Dec. 1999. 16 June 2008 <*http://www.guardian.co.uk/bulger/article/0,,195274,00.html*>.

Carroll, Lewis. *The Annotated Alice*. Ed. Martin Gardner. Rev. ed. London: Penguin, 1970.

Cole, Babette. 1987. *Prince Cinders*. London: Puffin, 1997.

Collodi, Carlo. *The Adventures of Pinocchio*. London: Roydon, 1975.

Cross, Gillian. *Wolf*. London: Puffin, 1990.

French, Fiona. *Snow White in New York*. Oxford: Oxford University Press, 1986.

Gaudesaboos, Pieter. *Roodlapje*. Tielt: Lannoo, 2003.

Geras, Adèle. *Pictures of the Night*. 1992. London: Red Fox, 2002.

Gilbert, Sandra M., and Susan Gubar. *The Madwoman in the Attic: The Woman Writer and the Nineteenth-Century Literary Imagination*. New Haven: Yale University Press, 1979.

Hollindale, Peter. "The Professional Child: Performing *Lord of the Flies*." *Children's Literature and Childhood in Performance*. Ed. Kimberley Reynolds. Lichfield: Pied Piper Publishing, 2003. 13–25.

Joosen, Vanessa. "Disenchanting the Fairy Tale: Retellings of 'Snow White' Between Magic and Realism." *Marvels and Tales* 21.2 (2007): 228–39.

_____. "Scene 9, Take 45: Collage and the Postmodern Fairy Tale." *The Journal of Children's Literature Studies* 4.2 (2007): 54–76.

Kantor, Melissa. *If I Have a Wicked Stepmother, Where's My Prince?* New York: Hyperion, 2005.

Lüthi, Max. *Das europäische Volksmärchen: Form und Wesen.* 8. Auflage. Tübingen: Francke Verlag, 1985.

Natov, Roni. *The Poetics of Childhood.* New York, London: Routledge, 2003.

Nikolajeva, Maria. *Children's Literature Comes of Age.* New York: Garland, 1996.

Perrault, Charles. "Cinderella; or, The Glass Slipper." *The Great Fairy Tale Tradition: From Straparola and Basile to the Brothers Grimm.* Ed. Jack Zipes. New York: Norton, 2001. 449–54.

Pullman, Philip. *I Was a Rat!* Ill. Kevin Hawkes. New York: Dell Yearling, 2000.

_____. "The Republic of Heaven." *The Horn Book Magazine* (2001): 655–67.

Rose, Jacqueline. *The Case of Peter Pan or The Impossibility of Children's Fiction.* 1984. Philadelphia: University of Pennsylvania Press, 1992.

Tatar, Maria. *Secrets beyond the Door: The Story of Bluebeard and His Wives.* Princeton, NJ: Princeton University Press, 2004.

Tucker, Nicholas. *Darkness Visible: Inside the World of Philip Pullman.* Cambridge: Wizard Books, 2003.

Vloeberghs, Katrien. "Het kind zonder gezicht: Figuraties van het kind in interferenties tussen het literaire modernisme, de filosofische theorie van Lyotard, Kristeva en Agamben, en de hedendaagse kinder- en jeugdliteratuur." Diss. University of Antwerp (Belgium), 2005.

Wolff, Sula, and R.A.A. McCall Smith. "Child Homocide and the Law: Implications of the European Court of Human Rights in the Case of the Children Who Killed James Bulger." *Child Psychology & Psychiatry Review* 5.3 (2000): 133–38.

Zipes, Jack. *The Trials and Tribulations of Little Red Riding Hood.* New York: Routledge, 1993.

_____. *Why Fairy Tales Stick: The Evolution and Relevance of a Genre.* London: Routledge, 2006.

The Wicked Witch of the West
Terrorist? Rewriting Evil in Gregory Maguire's *Wicked*

Christopher Roman

Gregory Maguire's *Wicked: The Life and Times of the Wicked Witch of the West* uses the rhetorical ambiguity of the term "terrorism" to question the nature of the Witch's wickedness. Are there factors in the Wicked Witch's life that would explain exactly why she is labeled "wicked"? Maguire's novel situates the back story of the Wicked Witch in a politically tumultuous Oz, so that wickedness, rather than something innately defined in a theological sense, becomes something bandied about to provoke political leverage. Whoever can name what is evil or wicked proves to be the one with the power as rhetoric proves to be the ultimate political tool.

In examining Maguire's retelling of the stories of Oz as a political critique, there is a sense that he may be creating an alternate world which diminishes or distorts the original. Michiko Kakutani, for example, writes, incredulously, in a book review for the *New York Times,* "The Wicked Witch of the West revealed as an idealistic victim? The green-skinned harridan ... unmasked as the dermatologically challenged product of a dysfunctional family? The scourge of Oz depicted as a dissident, a brave fighter against a totalitarian regime?" (C17). Kakutani's review indicates the problem of emphasizing the political underbelly in a reworking of an original work. Even though Kakutani is in disbelief over Maguire's transformations to this character, Elphaba is indeed all of these things. Further, Kakutani writes that "[Maguire's] insistence on politicizing Oz and injecting it with heavy doses of moral relativism turns a wonderfully spontaneous world of fantasy into a lugubrious allegorical realm, in which everything and everyone is labeled with a topical name tag" (C17). In this review, Kakutani seems to be confusing the movie with the book, for what she misses is that Maguire is simply updating the political allegory of Baum's original work. He features the evident authoritarianism from *The Wonderful Wizard of*

Oz and turns his interpretation to the present age. The first author to suggest a political allegory for *The Wizard of Oz,* Henry Littlefield, writes:

> Those who enter the Emerald City must wear green glasses. Dorothy later discovers that the greenness of dresses and ribbons disappears on leaving, and everything becomes a bland white. Perhaps the magic of any city is thus self imposed. But the Wizard dwells here and so the Emerald City represents the national Capitol. The Wizard, a little bumbling old man, hiding behind a facade of paper mache and noise, might be any president from Grant to McKinley. He comes straight from the fairgrounds on Omaha, Nebraska, and he symbolizes the American criterion for leadership — he is able to be everything to everybody [6].

The movie version of *The Wizard of Oz* of course does not reveal this detail; instead, it presents an Oz that is truly green and magical complete with chameleon-like horses. However, the film does represent Oz the Terrible as a phony, although his political acumen is not nearly as totalitarian as in Baum's or Maguire's books. Although Littlefield's allegoricization of Baum's work did not occur until 1964, and Littlefield himself indicated that his observations were not meant to suggest that Baum had written a political satire, other writers have taken the idea of Oz's political allegory further.[1] The politicizing of Oz from Littlefield to the present day indicates the genealogy of Maguire's work. Whereas Kakutani feels that Maguire is ruining a children's book, examining Oz for its political allegory has been going on for over five decades.[2]

Maguire's book is not as concerned with creating allegory as much as examining the problem of political dissent in an autocratic state. Although his work was published in 1995, our post-9/11 world is fraught with questions about the identity of terrorists and their motivations. Maguire questions the rhetoric of terrorism by offering us a character whom we are pre-disposed to believe is evil (from her representation in Baum's book and the movie adaptation) and by showing us the very ambivalence at the heart of the term "terrorism."

The Wicked Witch of the West in movie form is nasty, threatening, plotting, and clearly the villain. As soon as we meet her döppleganger, Miss Almira Gulch, who dislikes Toto so deeply, the audience recoils. Filmic power creates a palpable sense of evil and wickedness. However, in the original text, wickedness is something much more intangible. The Wicked Witch of the West is not the witch of the fairy tale who will eat the children or give the princess the poisoned apple. In fact, the Wicked Witch of the West appears in L. Frank Baum's *The Wonderful Wizard of Oz* for exactly one chapter. Additionally, she is given no real back story. She is referred to, but she only *acts* in one chapter. As readers, we must ask, why is this bit player wicked? In Baum's text, she is wicked simply because Oz the terrible says so (it is true that she defends herself against Dorothy and her friends using bees and flying monkeys, but she is under attack for no real reason that Dorothy can fathom, other than the Wizard has said she is bad). Later, when Dorothy reveals Oz for who he is and asks him about why he feared the Witches so much, he says, "One of my greatest fears was the

Witches, for while I had no magical powers at all I soon found out that the Witches were really able to do wonderful things.... The Witches of the East and West were terribly Wicked, and had they not thought I was more powerful than they themselves, they would surely have destroyed me" (153–54). Thus even in this quote the source of their evil is never explained. Dorothy and the reader are meant to take Oz's remarks at face value as hearsay.

By contrast, the nature of evil figures prominently in Maguire's book. If we think of wickedness and evil in terms of religion, we get a sense of sinfulness, of something turning against God. Theologian Hans Schwarz describes evil using Augustine: "when evil exists, and Augustine never entertained the slightest doubt as to its reality, then it exists only to the extent that a part of God's good creation has risen up against its creator and entered into conflict with him" (107). Although Maguire's work is not necessarily Christian in a C.S. Lewis sense, the meditation on evil in *Wicked* concerns itself with a number of Oz's competing faith traditions. There is the faith of Elphaba's father, Frex, who is a Unionist minister, and there is the new "pleasure" faith, a kind of small-scale witchcraft, which Frex abhors because of its falseness and showiness. There is also a pagan-like religion devoted to Lurline who created Oz from her body to which Elphaba's Nanny is partial. None of these denominations, however, have an answer for Elphaba and her question regarding the nature of evil. Elphaba complains the Unionists are "obsessed with locating [evil] somewhere. I mean, an evil spring in the mountains, an evil smoke, evil blood in the veins going from parents to child" (80). However, Elphaba comes to the conclusion that the Unionists had no clear idea where evil resides; rather, "every evil thing is a sign of the absence of the deity" (80). However, for Oz, it is unclear from what deity evil is absent. Although religion does not offer a clear answer to the nature of evil, Maguire's book suggests political structures may have more to do with declaring what and who is evil than religion does. As Schwarz mentions, "Although evil is perpetrated by individual persons, it must always be seen within the context of the society as a whole, in which it manifests itself. Evil actions always have a social aspect" (10). Maguire creates a world in which the reader finds the government of Oz autocratic and malevolent, yet evil is situated within those who turn against the government of Oz. For this reason, Maguire breaks new ground by invoking the reader's sympathy for the unsuccessful terrorist.

In what has been called a meditation on evil, Maguire's text encourages readers to identify with Elphaba, the Wicked Witch of the West, because she is on a quest to define evil and understand herself. She is also motivated to overthrow a corrupt government which oppresses the various "minorities" of Oz. As the novel progresses, Elphaba becomes, in turns, a student, a terrorist, a nun, and, finally, a recluse. If the reader sees Elphaba as evil, this occurs only in her one moment as part of an underground organization that plans to liberate the Animals. In involving Elphaba in a possible terrorist threat to the government, Maguire frames the problem of evil in terms of political power. If a citizen is a member of an authoritarian government which is oppressing, and in some cases killing, its citizens, is it a terrorist act to fight against the oppressor? As Oatsie Manglehand says, as she is transporting Elphaba to the Vinkus: "To the grim poor there need be no *pour quoi* tale about where evil arises; it just arises; it always is. One never learns how the witch became wicked, or whether that was the right choice for her — is it ever the right choice? Does the devil ever struggle to be good again, or if so is he not a devil? It is at the very least a question of definitions" (231). Therein lies the heart of this analysis: it would seem the question of definitions can only be solved by truly pulling back the curtain on the power of the definer. Manglehand's statement occurs in the middle of the novel. By this time the reader has seen how Elphaba has been raised, and yet, with the knowledge of Baum's text and her labeling as wicked by the Wizard, readers do not see Elphaba actually become wicked. Instead, Maguire questions the common meta-explantions of the dysfunctional family as the catalyst for later terrorist activity.

Terrorism is at the heart of *Wicked.* Late in the novel, when Elphaba speaks with her father, Frex, about taking over as ruler of Munchkinland, he says that Elphaba's sister "'hides behind her devotion the way a terrorist hides behind his ideals—' He saw her flinch at this and paused. 'I have known terrorists capable of love,' she said evenly" (319). Elphaba's flinch, possibly born of her own attempts at terrorism, partly born of her guilt over her lover, Fiyero's, death because of her terrorist activities, indicates how sensitive she is to the very word. Earlier, when Fiyero asks her about the purpose of her activities, Elphaba replies, "[to] Kill the Wizard" (206). This single-minded purpose, to which she returns at the end of the novel, indicates the source of her Wickedness. But, what is the context of this terrorist activity? Why is Elphaba involved with a splinter cell that is attempting to overthrow Oz the Terrible? Before answering these questions, I would like first to turn to definitions and causes of terrorism as a background to understanding more fully the meditation on evil as presented in *Wicked.* Although the literature and analysis I will be dealing with comes from scholars who deal with real world terrorism in terms of sociology, political science, and psychology, their work provides a background in looking at *Wicked* and the society that produces a sympathetic terrorist like Elphaba, the Wicked Witch of the West.

The exact meaning of terrorism is elusive, though many scholars have focused on a definition that expresses both acts and causes. David Whittaker suggests that the characterization resides in perception:

> In the eyes of a responsible authority, nationally or locally, a workable definition ... might run like this: "terrorism is the premeditated threat or use of violence by subnational groups or clandestine individuals intended to intimidate and coerce governments, to promote political, religious, or ideological outcomes, and to inculcate fear among the public at large." ... Terrorism is rated as a criminal offense, wholly disproportionate to any expression of grievance or any attempt to work for change [10].

Whittaker acknowledges that the word "terrorism" may be "a misnomer" for the terrorist himself, for "the actions of those who dedicated to a cause may be seen by others as destructive and perverse but for those who believe in what they are trying to achieve the end justifies the means" (12). Thus, Whittaker raises the issue of the very ambivalence of the definition. For the British government, the Boston Tea party could be seen as an act of terrorism. Furthermore, Thomas Mockaitis writes that "most current definitions classify an act of terrorism based on three broad criteria: target, weapon, and perpetrator. Virtually all experts agree that indiscriminate attacks on civilians constitute terrorism"(1). Mockaitis also points out that the use of weapons deemed illegal by the international community is another factor that should be considered in deciding if an act should be labeled terrorism. Finally, he indicates that most experts "assess the legitimacy, goals, and objectives of the perpetrators in deciding where or not to declare their actions 'terrorism'" (1). However, for Mockaitis, these definitions and methods blur. He points out that strategic bombing occurs in wars, and that although it is easily labeled terrorism when the act is perpetrated against civilians, the bombing of the U.S.S. *Cole*, a military target, was labeled terrorism (1). Rather than becoming distracted by academic definitions, Mockaitis rallies for a functional explanation of terrorism that focuses on actors who use terrorism to achieve political goals: "terrorist attacks are never completely arbitrary. Those who use terror select targets less for their military value than for their symbolic significance" (3–4). Mockaitis and Whittaker both suggest that an exact definition of terrorism is difficult and dependent upon context. Terrorism is most clearly understood when looking at political goals of the organization, for, in understanding those goals, the motives of terrorism are more thoroughly understood and a counter-terrorist solution more easily found.

However, what motivates someone to move from lawful protest to terrorist activity? In her book *What Terrorists Want,* Louise Richardson writes that there is no simple explanation for the motivations of terrorism. Richardson explains that "the two most common explanations of terrorism are that it is the work of either crazy individuals or of warmongering states..." (69). Mixed with these kinds of simple root explanations are reasons found from pop psychology. Recent works of fiction, such as John Updike's *Terrorist,* attempt to point to nurture gone wrong as a source of terrorism. Because one is brought up in a "dysfunctional" family, then the terrorist is explained as missing something of her childhood that she is trying to recover through political action. Updike's main character, for example, comes from a single parent who barely pays attention to her son. Sometimes the explanations of terrorist activity are more nuanced. In the film *Syriana,* the men become members of a terrorist cell because of a mixture of unemployment, disenfranchisement (they are immigrants from another country and the host country refuses to find them more work or provide them with any social services), religious fundamentalism, and the seduction of a charismatic friend. However, as Louise Richardson writes, "One of the most obvious difficulties in identifying a cause or causes of terrorism is that terrorism is a microphenomenon. Metaexplanations cannot be used successfully to explain microphenomenon" (*The Roots of Terrorism* 2). So although *Syriana* claims nuance, its message comes off as a metaexplanation rather than examining a microphenomenon (which, to be fair, may be something beyond the range of a film of this scope). Common metaexplanations include dysfunctional family life, alienation, or nationalism. However, in places where it would seem that nationalist fervor, for example, should cause terrorism to erupt, as Richardson writes, "Why have other ethnic and nationalist groups—who do not occupy a territory consistent with their sense of identity—not also resort [...] to terrorism?" (2). Richardson summarizes the cause of terrorism thusly:

> Terrorism needs a sense of alienation from the status quo and a desire to change it. Terrorism needs conditions in which people feel unfairly treated and leaders to make sense of these conditions, to organize a group and make it effective. Terrorism needs an all-encompassing philosophy—a religion or secular ideology—to legitimize violence [sic] action, to win recruits to the cause, and to mobilize them for action. Terrorism, to survive and thrive, needs a complicit society, a societal surround sympathetic to its aspirations [*What Terrorists Want* 69].

The point here is that terrorism must be studied in its context, right down to the individual, and although Oz creates Elphaba and other oppressed groups like her who are fighting the government's oppression of the Animals, other groups, such as the Munchkinlanders and Quadlings, or even the Animals, do not fight back.

The Wicked Witch of the West is not a terrorist because of any sense of metaexplanations such as alienation or "nationalism" (she is the only one who is green in a world full of talking animals and other people with "seemingly" magical qualities). Her terrorism, and thus the only sense of evil that she has, is born of empathy for an oppressed group of which she is not a member. In this way, Elphaba finds herself in the company of a John Walker Lindh or an Adam Gahane (both Americans who converted to Islam and worked with the Taliban and Al Qaeda, respectively). In this case, Maguire creates an Elphaba who is not evil in a traditional way because she is not sinful nor is she cruel to others; rather, she is wicked because she chooses to challenge the government violently and the government sees her as a threat to their own plans. The answer to the question of evil as represented in *Wicked* is complicated. It is not that evil is innate; the prerogative of those in power is to define evil for their citizens. The government, who feels its power is threatened, has the power to define evil; however, the storyteller also holds the power to make an opposing case. To avoid relativism, however, which Maguire and I risk (recall, Kakutani criticizes Maguire for this as well), Elphaba is placed in a state in which there is no voice offered to those who are oppressed. The most evil of labels in our age, the most wicked, is that of terrorist — in this way Maguire's text is just as political as Baum's text (Thacker and Webb 86–87). However, Elphaba is *perceived* to have power because of her rebellion against the brainwashing of Madame Morrible, and she protests on behalf of an oppressed group. The novel sets up a definition of evil that is not inherent to the individual; rather, it is inherent to oppression and its effects.

As much time as is spent capturing Elphaba's back story, the reader is constantly reminded of the political situation of Oz. Elphaba is always intertwined with the goings on of the Wizard's laws, troop movements, and massacres. Remember that Elphaba is born green-skinned with a mouth full of razor-sharp teeth. She is born in Munchkinland to a woman who, by blood, is related to the royalty of Munchkinland. Her mother, however, has chosen to live in the poor countryside with Frex, her preacher husband. All of Munchkinland is undergoing a drought, and with agriculture the major staple of the area, people are poor, mostly uneducated, and seeking answers to their plight. The context of the countryside is important, for as Richardson explains, terrorism is likely to occur "in developing countries, especially in countries experiencing rapid modernization. Changing economic conditions are conducive to instability, and traditional means of making sense of the world, such as religion or local power structures, are challenged by the scale of the change" (*What Terrorists Want* 55). The Land of Oz has areas of rapid growth like Shiz and the Emerald City, but it also has greater amounts of land and population who are out of reach of wealth and the promises of modernization, such as Munchkinland, the Vinkus, and Quadling country.

Maguire's text represents the Land of Oz as a land in transition. Readers get the first inkling of the conditions of greater Oz early through Turtle Heart, the Quadling Glassblower. As he reports of his "backward land," he comments that "in Ovvels the houses to float between trees. Crops grow on small platforms ... Quadling country is poor country but beauty rich. It only to support life by careful planning and cooperation" (55). And yet, Quadling country is being plundered, not only for a continuation of the Yellow Brick Road, which cannot be physically supported because of saturated ground, but also because of the discovery of rubies. Elphaba reports of her time in Quadling country that

> the Wizard's men began draining the badlands to get at the ruby deposits. It never worked, of course. They managed to chase the Quadlings out and kill them, round them up in settlement camps for their own protection and starve them. They despoiled the badlands, raked up the rubies, and left. [...] There never were enough rubies to make it worth the effort; we still have no canal system to run that legendary water from the Vinkus all the way cross-country to Munchkinland [135].

The discovery of rubies leads the government of Oz to plunder Quadling country and systematically slaughter and "rendition" the inhabitants.

Elphaba spends her formative years in Quadling country, as her father, Frex, takes the family there, so he can convert the Quadlings to the Unionist faith. However, this is not the only group affected by the government of Oz. The biggest effect on Elphaba's political activities and later reclusive experiments is the treatment of the Animals. The Animals are sentient, animals "with spirit" and Elphaba's first exposure to Animals is Dr. Dillamond (who is a goat), a professor at Shiz. A series of Banns on Animal Mobility are passed at the same time she enters university. These Banns not only prevent Animals from traveling, but also limit where they can stay, their access to public services, and their ability to work professionally or in the public sector (88–89). Slowly, Animals are being eliminated from public life all together.

Elphaba is moved by the discrimination that the Animals face. As Mockaitis writes, "Identifying root causes of terrorism does not explain why some individuals and not others join a terrorist group.... Whatever the precise reason, recruits feel powerless and the group empowers them" (46). Elphaba begins working with Dr. Dillamond as he sets out to prove biologically that there is no difference between Animal and human tissue. As Elphaba says, if Dr. Dillamond proves that human and Animal tissue is similar, "On what grounds could the Wizard possibly continue to publish those Banns?" (111). This question is not answered for we soon learn that the Wizard has dissolved the Hall of Approval which is responsible for passing Banns. Slowly, the Wizard is consolidating power and passing measures that have no basis in any kind of democratic process.

The ultimate reason for the oppression of Animals is finally revealed in the climatic problems in Oz. Munchkinland, the breadbasket of Oz, has undergone a drought for some time. The irrigation of water from the Vinkus to Muchkinland never happens. Elphaba reasons to her friend Glinda: "The Animals are recalled to the lands of their ancestor, a ploy to give the farmers a sense of control over something anyway. It's a systematic marginalizing of populations, Glinda, that's what the Wizard's all about" (135). Elphaba's observation is correct — she sees through the government's actions. She summarizes the actions of the Oz the Terrible in this passage:

> They [the Gale Force] march in those boots all over the poor and the weak. They terrify households at three in the morning and drag away dissenters — and break up printing presses with their axes — and hold mock trials for treason at midnight and executions at dawn. They rake over every quarter of this beautiful, false city. They harvest a crop of victims on a monthly basis. It's government by terror [187].

This is the first time Maguire makes Elphaba do the labeling. It is possibly her most impassioned speech in the book.

Finally, to present even further the case of the government's machinations on a personal level, Madame Morrible, the Head of the University of Shiz, wants to use Elphaba, her sister, Nessarose, and Glinda for political purposes. As Morrible says, "If only people would obey the Wizard absolutely, there would be abundance" (155). By putting a spell on the three girls, Morrible hopes to involve them in helping the Wizard consolidate his power. Elphaba, realizing that she is being magically brainwashed, leaves Shiz. The section of the novel ends, and when we meet her again, she is older and is now embroiled with an Animal Rights Group.

Up to this point in the novel, there is a tension that emerges from finding a root cause, such as something in her childhood, her upbringing, or her schooling that would explain Elphaba's labeling as wicked. Yet, what the reader perceives is a representation of a girl, born with different skin, and exposed to atrocity after atrocity by her government. She develops empathy for the oppressed and a dislike of the human. As she eventually says to her lover, Fiyero, "I never use the word humanist or humanitarian, as it seems to me that to be human is to be capable of the most heinous crimes in nature" (187). Her passion for the Animals and her dislike of the government lead her to be involved with an underground organization that champions Animal Rights. It is all very secretive and the reader is never fully informed of their doings, but at one point, Elphaba is charged to blow up Madame Morrible; however, she does not carry this act out because there are children in the area.

This leads us to a larger question. Because of Elphaba's actions involved with a terrorist plot, does this action (or near action) explain or point to a quality of wickedness, the nature of her evil? Maguire does not answer this question for us. Within the context of his text, he makes it clear that Elphaba is not wicked except to those in the government who see her as a threat. In that case, she becomes a hero, of sorts, to the reader. She is the only one of the three who is initially brainwashed by Madame Morrible who does not succumb to Oz's demands (Glinda and Nessarose both become members of the elite and rule in some capacity just as he wished).

Even though the government of Oz reaches into Elphaba's personal life, Elphaba seeks recovery and seclusion over anger. After Elphaba does not go through with the assassination of Madame Morrible, Fiyero is ambushed in her apartment by the Gale Force, the Wizard's counter-terrorist thugs. Fiyero is soon executed. Elphaba makes her way to the Vinku's where she wants to apologize to Fiyero's widow. While there, she discovers the Grimmerie, which turns out to be a book that Oz had brought with him from Nebraska. Still recognizing the tyranny that is going on in the country, Elphaba tries to find a spell to "overthrow a regime" (293). She is unable to find one.

The last section of the book recreates the one chapter of Baum's book on which Maguire has based his text and retells the murder of the Wicked Witch of the West. Dorothy and the members of her group do not understand why they must kill the Witch, and her eventual death is represented as an accident. But, in the sequel to *Wicked,* and in Che Guevara style, the reclusive Witch, who has not had any contact with anyone for years, reappears again, only this time as a myth, a hero, a symbol. She represents a hope for those who are oppressed by the tyrannical government of Oz (and later the inept government of the Scarecrow) despite that fact that she has lived in seclusion for many years. In Maguire's sequel, *Son of a Witch,* people begin to scrawl "She Lives" and "Elphie Lives!" on the walls of Oz. Despite her desires to overthrow the government and her connections with terrorism, her name is redeemed as she becomes a figure of hope while Oz continues to slide into political disarray.

Maguire's *Wicked* is a political tale. It shows the problem of rhetoric when used by an autocratic power. If the government continues to label an individual or a group as a terrorist, the initial and knee-jerk reaction (as is evidenced from Baum's text) is to believe them. However, as terrorist experts suggest the context must be examined when the label is applied. The context will reveal the nuances of terrorist activity and help to suggest appropriate counter-terrorist solutions. Put simply, the counter-terrorist solution for Oz is to stop oppressing minority groups. Maguire's text also highlights the difficulty of the word terrorism in our culture. If an individual is faced with a government that is systematically marginalizing populations, should she fight? The book suggests that the answer to that is in the affirmative, even if one should face marginalization, as well. In the end, is Elphaba wicked? As they say, one person's wicked witch is another person's freedom fighter.

Notes

1. For a concise history of the politicization of *The Wonderful Wizard of Oz,* see Parker 46–93.

2. For more essays on the political interpretation of Oz, see Eric Gjovaag's *The Wonderful Wizard of Oz* website: <http://thewizardofoz.info/>.

Works Cited

Baum, Frank L. *The Wonderful Wizard of Oz.* New York: Barnes and Noble Classics, 2005.

Kakutani, Michiko. "Let's Get This Straight: Glinda Was the Bad One?" *New York Times.* 24 Oct. 1995: C17.

Littlefield, Henry M. "The Wizard of Oz: Parable on Populism." 5 Apr. 2007. <http://www.amphigory.com/oz.htm>.

Maguire, Gregory. *Wicked: The Life and Times of the Wicked Witch of the West.* New York: HarperCollins, 1995.

_____. *Son of a Witch.* New York: HarperCollins, 2005.

Mockaitis, Thomas. *The "New" Terrorism: Myths and Reality.* Westport, CT: Praeger, 2007.

Parker, David P. "The Rise and Fall of the Wonderful Wizard of Oz." *Journal of the Georgia Association of Historians* 15 (1994): 46–93.

Richardson, Louise. "The Roots of Terrorism: An Overview." *The Roots of Terrorism.* Ed. Louise Richardson. London: Routledge, 2006.

_____. *What Terrorists Want: Understanding the Enemy, Containing the Threat.* New York: Random House, 2006.

Schwarz, Hans. *Evil: A Historical and Theological Perspective.* Minneapolis: Fortress Press, 1995.

Thacker, Deborah Cogan, and Jean Webb. *Introducing Children's Literature: From Romanticism to Postmodernism.* London: Routledge, 2002.

Whittaker, David J. *Terrorism: Understanding the Global Threat.* Harlow, Essex, UK: Pearson, 2007.

Embracing Equality
Class Reversals and Social Reform in Shannon Hale's *The Goose Girl* and *Princess Academy*

SUSAN REDINGTON BOBBY

"It seems like the world has changed and we shouldn't still be talking about things like marrying a prince."
— Shannon Hale, *The Princess Academy*

There is no doubt that the literary fairy tale has explored the divisions of class on a superficial level. Over centuries, fairy tale plots have pitted the "haves" versus the "have-nots", reflecting wish fulfillment for the poor through attainment of wealth, position, and prestige by the happily-ever-after conclusion. Classic tales present characters with scant resources who may come to alter their life circumstances, emerging as members of the aristocracy, suggesting the ease of ascension in socioeconomic group if it is so fated. Tales of "winning the lottery" have implied that wealth and power equal success and happiness. A rarity, though, is the tale that explores in depth the meaning of class distinctions from the perspective of characters who do not wish for jewels and coin, but who hope for social harmony. Perhaps these characters wish to overthrow their oppressors, not to become what they fought against, but to change the face of society and to erase the boundaries of class distinction.

In his preface to the 2002 edition of *Breaking the Magic Spell*, Jack Zipes notes that although there have been various approaches to the study of fairy tales since 1979, "there has been a strange avoidance to discuss social class [and] ideological conflicts" (ix). Zipes focuses on social and economic power in his article "The Struggle for the Grimms' Throne", asserting that contemporary German tales might more accurately be termed "reutilized" versions, for they "[break] down the closure of the original" to offer an innovative interpretation of the source text and to explore "contemporary social conditions" (179). Referencing the work of German authors since 1970, Zipes delineates six groups of tales, adding that many straddle categories. Calling one grouping "utopian fairy tales" (181), he observes,

> Whereas the satirical fairy tale often has a skeptical or cynical viewpoint about social change, the plot of the utopian fairy tale most often maps out the possibility for alternative lifestyles. Implicit is a major critique of the Grimms' tales that are primarily concerned with individual happiness and power: utopian fairy tales depict change through collective action and equal participation in the benefits of such work.... The central theme is the overcoming of oppression [181–82].[1]

Zipes's remarks point to Marxist themes, which are also paramount in the 1972 revision of Snow White by the Merseyside Fairy Story Collective.

In this politically-charged revision, Snow White becomes a revolutionary, leading her people to victory over a corrupt queen who enforces hard labor, seizing the fruits of their toil, permitting them only to possess "what was left over or spoiled" (74). The magic mirror calls for happiness, a byproduct of power and authority, over fairness or beauty. The Queen of the Mountains takes authority by forcing the dwarves to mine jewels that she accumulates in glass jars. Snow White, a skilled jewelry-maker, serves the queen by constructing intricate pieces for her collection. Snow White's conscience is troubled, however, by her quite plush accommodations in the castle. Despite the contrast with the horrid working conditions for her compatriots, Snow White yearns to return to them, missing their sense of community. Having pleased the queen, she is promised a reward, yet she asks only to be returned to her people. Denying her wish, the queen's actions strengthen Snow White's resolve, and the second time she may name her prize, she implores, "Majesty ... take only what you need from the people of the kingdom and let them keep the rest so that they will no longer be cold and hungry and miserable" (76). Calling her a traitor, the queen tries to tempt her allegiance by showing her in the magic mirror a vision of Snow White's future as a bourgeois. Unfazed, Snow White instead contemplates a workers' song which describes how the jewels they mine pale in comparison to the elements of the natural world.

Stating a third time that she wants for nothing, Snow White is banished to the tower for her disobedience. After she is rescued and returns to the working class, the magic mirror declares her the "happiest", enraging the queen who imprisons her and the dwarves in the mine. During a vigil for those trapped, the growing crowd, workers and soldiers, unites against the queen. When the dwarves dig their way out and they are threatened by the few remaining queen's soldiers, Snow White emerges as the leader of the revolt, pledging, "You may kill some of us ... but in the end you will lose for there are far more people than there are soldiers" (79). With the tide of public opinion now against the ruler, she consults her mirror, which declares, "The people cast [her] from their land" (80); in retaliation the queen commits suicide, thus ending the reign of the tyrant and ushering in a new era of equality.

Merseyside's Snow White bridges two of Zipes's categories (feminist and utopian fairy tales), with a Marxist agenda. By contrast, a plethora of tales from the 1970's to the present, both retellings and new creations, highlight issues of gender rather than politics. There seems to be no shortage of contemporary heroines who dominate the narrative landscape as they prefer to take charge of their quests rather than wait on the knight in shining armor to rescue them. Yet a fairly new writer to the genre of fairy tales, Shannon Hale, has broken from this contemporary tradition and focused specifically on class consciousness and social reform in her novels *The Goose Girl* and *Princess Academy*. [2] In "A Conversation with Shannon Hale", when asked about the "female power" motif in her work, Hale responds, "I did not set out to write stories of girl power ... I'm very lucky to be writing after decades of writers have already fought for their genuine, interesting, and varied heroines. I don't have the burden of writing on offense, trying to prove that girls can be main characters." Perhaps these strides for women have encouraged Hale to focus on larger issues of socioeconomic equality that prove relevant in today's social, political, and cultural climate. Hale's novels tend towards social and political allegory in her presentation of a pseudo–Marxist utopia. She explores many integrated themes: one, equality is eventually attainable but rife with difficulties due to prejudice; two, a sense of community is of greater importance than the attainment of wealth; and three, developing one's own gifts is more satisfying than being handed riches. Before a discussion of Hale's contemporary vision of class and reform, we must consider the background of her source text and the minor distinctions from the Grimms' tale that she has brought to the foreground.

Ruth B. Bottigheimer's *Grimms' Bad Girls and Bold Boys* provides an interesting analysis of class distinctions, labor, and reward. Bottigheimer reveals "protagonists are introduced more often by their occupation than by any other characteristic" and their work is demanding and physical, separating it even further from Italian or French collections (124). This phenomena reflected German society, for over 40 percent of children eligible to be schooled were instead employed in factories and mills in the Grimms' era in Berlin, ushering forth much youth exploitation (124). Bottigheimer explains, "Unending labor forms so central a motif in *Grimms' Tales* that it provides the metaphor for the meaning of the span of life for earth's creatures, including human beings" (125). One might assume that hard labor would yield a better existence, but "in tale after tale, honest physical labor ... is a demonstrably unproductive route to financial reward" (123). So how might one escape the socioeconomic circumstances into which he or she is born if the virtue of hard work elicits no results? The answer lies in luck, happenstance, or magic.

A cursory look at the Grimms' tales provides many examples of characters living in poverty who through such avenues emerge as so-called lottery-winners. Perhaps a poor man vanquishes the evil queen and takes her riches for himself. Or the youngest daughter of a peasant is arranged in marriage to a wealthy aristocrat. Ideally those who move from poverty to wealth share their spoils with their families and friends. These events easily lend themselves to the classic fairy tale plotline, for as Bottigheimer says, "Sudden and unanticipated reward after ceaseless labor seems to represent a constant dream ... of eternal release from endless grinding toil" (126). Ashliman concurs, stating that traditional fairy tales reflect superficial Marxist concerns with clashes between proletariat and bourgeoisie, yet such conflicts tend to focus on "one hero over one tyrant", as opposed to entire class rebellions (147). Furthermore, as Zipes states in "Breaking the Magic Spell: Politics and the Fairy Tale," "The change [in tales] reflects the desire of the lower classes to move up in the world and seize power *as monarchs*, not necessarily the desire to alter social relations. The endings of almost all folk tales are not solely emancipatory, but actually depict the limits of social mobility" (124). The message is clear: one cannot earn through labor the right to shift classes: progress either occurs by magic or not at all. One's lot in life is permanent unless one encounters a "fairy-tale" ending.

At first glance, one might find that the Grimms' version of *The Goose Girl* has everything to do with birthright and magical objects and nothing to do with class consciousness. Designated as AT533 "The Speaking Horsehead," Aarne and Thompson identify several key motifs, such as "the treacherous maid-servant" (191), false bride vs. true bride, the enchanted horse, and "marks of royalty" (191), all symbols which only serve to perpetuate a pampered life for the aristocracy, even if the princess must spend some time as a peasant before she is restored to her "rightful" place. Aarne and Thompson also identify a variant, "The Snake Helper," in which a snake plays a similar role to the magical horsehead, becoming the true bride's protector (192). Both versions by name alone allude prominently to the role of an enchanted animal rather than an exploration of rich versus poor.

The Grimms' tale *The Goose Girl* depicts a princess on her way to meet her betrothed, having been given "all manner of precious utensils and vessels, jewelry and goblets, gold and silver" (Tatar 312), and a handkerchief with three drops of her mother's blood. Despite holding a talisman, the princess loses control of her maid who ceases her servitude once they have left the kingdom. The enchanted drops of blood speak to the princess, implying that the maid's defiance and the princess's lowered status would "break her [mother's] heart" (312). Characterizing the princess as forgiving, the Grimms note that she drinks of the river herself after her maid's second refusal to serve; after she loses the handkerchief in the process, the maid notices the missing charm and takes absolute power over the monarch. She steals the princess's horse Falada and her beautiful gowns, forcing her to "swear on a stack of bibles" that she will keep this a secret (313). The imposter is welcomed at the castle, while the true bride is abandoned. Pitied by the king, he entrusts the deposed princess to tend his geese. The pretender, fearing that Falada will "talk," orders its beheading and public mounting for the princess to witness. After death, Falada assumes the role of the handkerchief as the princess's protector. Simultaneously, the goose boy, Conrad, becomes fascinated with the princess's golden locks, a signifier of her royalty. She calls to the wind to blow to keep him from touching her hair; eventually, Conrad asks the king to be released from working with her, citing her talking to the mounted horse head and wind as peculiarities. Wishing to see for himself, the king hides and witnesses the girl's odd behavior. When he asks for an explanation she tells him that she has sworn an oath to remain silent. He convinces her to tell an old stove her secret, and as she complies he listens. Afterward, he tells her to change into beautiful clothes as he reveals to his son that she is the true bride, "both beautiful and virtuous" (320). At the final banquet, she sits by the prince and the false bride who no longer recognizes her. To trap the imposter, the king asks her what she would do if someone were to carry out the heinous acts for which she was responsible; unwittingly, the maid names a very grotesque punishment. The king reveals his secret, and the false bride dies of the penalty she dictated, while the true princess is restored to her place to marry the young king.

As a source text, the Grimms' Goose Girl provided a bit of inspiration for Shannon Hale who expands on those subtle differences of class that the Grimms alluded to but did not fully explore, and her novel-length revision of the tale instead offers a pseudo–Marxist utopia. Class differences articulated by both individuals and larger groups form the core of the novel. In addition, the gifts of nature, happiness, and community become central motifs, replacing the prevalence of magic from earlier versions. As Beth Wright notes in her review of the novel, Hale "has produced a satisfying high fantasy with a thoughtful subtext about persuasion, politics, and power" (40–41).

Born Anidori-Kiladra Talianna Isilee, Crown Princess of Kildenree, Hale's protagonist is destined for rule though wary of the task. Her aunt, who nurtures her and shortens her name to Ani, tells her of three gifts: "people-speaking" (5), held by rulers, a powerful yet potentially dangerous gift; "animal-speaking" (6), an ability to learn an animal's native tongue; and "nature-speaking"(6), the capacity to control aspects of nature, such as wind or water. Ani learns that both her mother the queen and her lady-in-waiting, Selia, have been blessed with the people-speaking ability, and this automatically sets them apart from others. Ani's mother stresses that a ruler will prevail only through "separation, elevation, delegation" (25). Since Ani's mother has only ever sought a crown and power, Ani finds that those who choose an alternative path through animal or nature speak are condemned to a solitary existence, destined to be viewed by many as sorceresses or witches.[3] After Ani's aunt's death, and the discovery that Ani may be refining these gifts, she is secluded and groomed to be the next queen, despite her natural inclination to avoid rule. Hale makes a clear distinction, though, between those seemingly "born" to govern by name or temperament versus those who "grow" into the role legitimately. Selia, Ani's rival and lesser, is said to have been a very badly behaved child who learned how to mimic the airs of royalty (10). By contrast, Ani is a pleasant and agreeable child who tries desperately to please the queen and to fit the role demanded of her. The question of identity surrounds this character; Ani's quest revolves around finding out who she is and discovering her place in the larger community, a much larger function than the Grimms bestowed on their heroine.

After Ani's father's death the divisions between aristocracy and peasantry rise to the forefront through many levels of allegory. For instance, Hale presents two political trajectories via Selia's flawed proletariat vision versus Ani's egalitarian awakening. Hale also focuses on the symbolic characteristics inherent in physical attributes and environmental cues. Furthermore, geese and swans represent two levels of class. All of these elements reinforce Ani's identification with the worker class and her rise as a revolutionary who desires to use her restored position to enact early stages of equality.

When Ani is escorted to Bayern for her arranged marriage to their prince, Selia seizes the opportunity to carry out a proletariat uprising against the monarch who leaves her native Kildenree laden with treasure. Prior to the journey her mother gave Ani a golden cup, saying that "the lips of our honored daughter will never touch the vulgar things" (Hale 43). Selia's anger towards this and other injustices encouraged her to unite with many soldiers before their departure; when Ani drinks from the golden cup and bathes in hot water while they wait on her hand and foot, they are moved to put their revolt into action. Selia's rebellion is strengthened by her words to Ani's defender, Talone, to whom she asserts, "Royalty is not a right, Captain. The willingness of the people to follow a ruler is what gives her power. Here, in this place, by this people, I have been chosen. These men are tired of being told whom to follow. Now they have a choice, and they use that choice to call me Princess" (79). Yet Selia's lower class uprising is flawed: she only wishes to replace the aristocracy with a harsher regime; she lacks the desire to erase class distinctions.[4]

Once Selia's usurpers take power in Bayern, they rule with an iron fist. Just as in the Grimms' version, Ani's horse Falada is killed, but his pain is much more drawn out than his Grimms' counterpart as Ungolad, Selia's partner in crime, torments him into madness before she orders his death. His head is mounted alongside the wall of criminals in Bayern. Notably Selia does not order this punishment inflicted on Falada to stop him from talking; rather, her goal is vengeance against Ani. Further retribution towards Ani comes with an attempt on her life which nearly succeeds when Ungolad delivers a vicious stab wound to her back. Even though Ani was sent to Bayern to forge an alliance by marriage, Selia and her ruthless band deceive Bayern's king into believing Kildenree will attack, suggesting that Bayern must preemptively "head off" an invasion by attacking first. Selia and her band are more than willing to bring bloodshed on their native land to disguise their transgressions and secure their aristocracy. Thus, while Selia might have made a stirring speech about deposing the monarchy, she only becomes a more frightening version of what she seemed to condemn once she holds the power.

By contrast, Ani's appointment as the king's goose girl informs her knowledge of the worker class's plight, leading her to a changed identity, reflected succinctly in Hale's section titles "Crown Princess" vs. "Goose Girl." Hale explores the allegorical meanings of the sensual world, beginning with one's outer physical attributes and their relationship to status. The wealthy from Kildenree are fair-skinned with blond hair, so Ani must hide her hair and blacken her eyebrows with an herb dye to blend with the worker class, made up of Forest-born and Bayern folk, recognized by their dark skin and hair. Gilsa, her rescuer in the forest, immediately notes her "yellow hair" and "soft little hands" (92)—marks of nobility she must take care to hide from others. These physical characteristics compel Gilsa to give up her bed for Ani because they show she is of higher status. Later, the goose boy, Conrad, mistrusts her when he briefly witnesses her golden locks, and Ungolad is only able to recognize her and attempt murder after he sees her unwrapped tresses. Names and accents also distinguish the classes. Ani uses the name Isi (a form of her grandmother's name) with the Forest-born people she meets and later with the workers, for a dual purpose: to help her hide her identity and to break the link to her mother who has betrayed her. To blend in, she also imitates the rough accent of the worker class. Through Ani's/Isi's disguises, she becomes accepted by the worker class and treated as one of their own.

Classes are also separated by scent. On her first trip to seek an audience with the king, Ani notices "a kingdom of smells" (Hale 110) that represent cleanliness, wealth, and power belonging exclusively to the upper class. Later, she contrasts these aromas of parchment, wax, and perfume with "refuse, smoke, food, and people and animals living too close together" (117).[5] Later she wonders if it is possible to eat while smelling "bodies that spent too much time with animals and too little time in a bath" (124). Enna, Ani's worker friend and confidante, later remarks, "We're almost, almost like animals to them" (159) in referencing the condescension of the bourgeoisie. However, Ani learns to identify with the smells and status of the worker class, for when she is eventually captured by Selia, and Selia says she has sunk in rank as the goose girl, Ani defends their position and is pleased to be welcomed "as a fellow laborer" (168).

Furthermore, Hale uses swans and geese to symbolize class status. Ani grows up learning the swans' language, indicating her upper class status. When she first hears the language of the geese, her attempts to communicate are laughable, geese being "smaller and much less grand than the swans she knew" (128), much less refined and noisy. It is only when she puts aside any notion of "separation, elevation, and delegation" by becoming the nurturing goose girl that she is able to learn to their tongue. Just as Gilsa gave up her bed for Ani, she gives up her bed for her goose Jok who has been injured. The metaphoric connection between swans, geese, and identity is evident at Ani's going away banquet, which includes a meal with white swans "roasted in their feathers" (40), symbolizing the end of her status as a nobly-born princess. As she grows to identify with the workers (geese), she hears the call of leadership and altruism, and she is "a strange bird with large, unpredictable wings" (292). Later, as she leads her people to a peaceful revolution, "they rode in formation like a flock of geese" (329).

Ani's initial impression of the workers' existence is conflicted: she is both horrified by their living and working conditions and lesser status, yet she is simultaneously attracted to their social harmony. "Ani listened and tried to piece together what life must be like living in the Forest on the edge of Bayern — difficult, impoverished, backbreaking work and the persistent question if they would last through another winter, she guessed. But she envied their commonality" (Hale 104–05). Having been sent by the King to the workers' west settlement, separated both literally and figuratively by a wall from the royalty, the page boy utters an ethnic slur by calling her "Forest-born" (115). Her room is claustrophobic, food is often in short supply, laborers are not paid adequate wages, and a day off may be a month away. She notes the workers' disdain for the royals by their comments about Selia's "expensive skin," and their calling her a "snooty, lace-necked royal" (134–35). Geric, the true prince who also masquerades in a lesser position, brings her food as a gift; she indicates what he saw as leftovers would "be a feast in the workers' hall"(185). His promise as a compassionate ruler shows when he says, "If I ruled, you'd all dine" (186). Of course Geric, like Ani, is unique: in general, the workers are not accepted by the upper class. Enna describes them as having a marginal, nearly alien-like status which prevents their admittance to the larger community. These truths stir in Ani a hope that the restoration of her rightful position can mean a change in how the workers are treated.

Unlike the Grimms' goose girl who wanted to regain status to marry and allow her husband to rule as monarchs before, Ani wishes to make living and working conditions better for everyone. Her goals are altruistic. The workers become her family, much more so than the one into which she was nobly born. She sees hope for the power of a queen "to better the ugliness she had seen in the city" (Hale 244). In fact, she becomes so self-conscious about the self-serving nature of most monarchs that she maintains a wish to remain the goose girl in her heart even if she regains her position. One of her first speeches as a restored monarch yields this proclamation: "'Did you know that there're workers in your city who aren't allowed into shops and taverns because they're from the Forest ... and areas so crowded that children live on the refuse of others?'" (374–75). She also works to give the city-dwelling male workers their javelins and shields and made part of the king's army, the only way (other than marriage) by which a worker may be able to move in social status. She even convinces the Forest boys now part of the king's army to call themselves "the Forest band," not "the yellow-band" (381), in an effort to accept and embrace their native background as opposed to buying into hers.

Once Ani's transformation is complete, she sees palace life as overdone and excessive, with a "much too comfortable chair" and an "endless pitcher of iced grape juice" (Hale 368) at her disposal. She also finds solidarity with Geric, who has similar feelings about the exploitation of the workers. At the final banquet, Geric insists that the kitchen-hands eat alongside the nobility, as "noble and city-dweller and Forest dweller" share in equal status (382).[6] Free from the trappings of an absolute monarchy, Ani is also at liberty to nurture her gifts as an animal and nature speaker, qualities she develops much more completely in the other Books of Bayern. However, it is clear that by the end of this novel Hale herself has defined a positive nuance of people speak — hailed as a potentially dangerous ability granted to those in power, Ani proves that if given the authority to erase class boundaries, she feels comfortable in her role as a speaker "*of* the people." Like the Merseyside Fairy Story Collective's Snow White, Ani explores the problems of prejudice and class conflict, emerging as the heroine of a utopian fairy tale.

Hale presents concurrent themes in *Princess Academy*, in which a group of girls is taken from the peasant community and schooled to become potential mates for the prince. This text examines conflicts between rich versus poor, city versus mountain folk, and the prejudices inherent with differences in geography and socioeconomic background. While it would seem that every girl would desire to be taken from her life of poverty and back-breaking work and handed a life of luxury, Hale's protagonist Miri faces conflict over such commonly held assumptions. Faced with the prospect of acceptance into the ruling class, she decides that being a member of the worker class brings with it intangible rewards. For one, her relationships with the villagers carry more meaning, and also, it is her "lower" status that opens her to a world of gifts unknown to the upper class. Only the lower status people have the connection with nature required to appreciate the land and its offerings. This allows her to develop a type of nature speak called "quarry speak," and like Ani, she uses it to save her own life and the lives of others. Therefore, while both *The Goose Girl* and *Princess Academy* showcase a protagonist's search for self and a place in the world, and where each begins in a world rife with social inequalities and class divisions, each arrives in a world with somewhat erased class distinctions and an entirely new view of what it means to be part of a "class" of people. In Ani's case, she returns to the aristocracy, but as a changed and compassionate ruler who continues to erase boundaries of class distinction and usher acceptance of different ethnicities in future novels concerning the fictional Bayern. In Miri's case, she has the opportunity to ascend in class but chooses to remain in her current position having made changes that benefit all in the village economically, and her efforts to achieve social reform change the villagers' relationship to the lowlanders (the members of nobility) as the beginnings of equality are ushered in at the novel's conclusion. Both books have the same goal in mind — the beginnings of the erasure of class distinction and acceptance of those different from one another, though the perspective is changed as the two narratives are told by characters from different social strata.

Hale's *Princess Academy* introduces Miri, a member of the worker class who is not permitted to work alongside the others in the quarry due to her fragility. The chief occupation of Mount Eskel villagers is the mining of linder, a stone prized in the lowland country of Danland. Noting that the workers' songs are "unifying" (9), Miri is troubled at her exclusion from community labor. Hale highlights the divisions between mountain folk and lowlanders, referring to something useless as "'skinnier than a lowlander's arm'" (12). The mountain workers are a proud and harmonious people who are the only ones strong and skilled enough to be quarriers. They are united in their ability to quarry speak, a gift which Miri must cultivate as she grows to identify with her people.

Wishing only to serve her village and strengthen her identity, Miri is called to help her people after a divination rite stipulates that the lowlander prince's future bride must come from Mount Eskel. Ordinarily the prince's wife is chosen from nobility, yet because there is no noble class on Mount Eskel, the kingdom of Danland requires that an academy be built between the mountain village and the main territory; all mountain girls between 12 and 17 are forced to leave their homes and attend the academy in case the prince should choose one of them (Hale 23). Showing no sympathy for the hardship caused by a virtual kidnapping of twenty of its female workers, Miri and others are ordered by soldiers to live at the academy and learn both academic subjects and etiquette, taught by the condescending headmistress, Olana Mansdaughter, who brings immediate attention to the class distinction through her unyielding authoritarian rule and rude remarks about their lower status. Just as scent delineates classes in *The Goose Girl*, Olana greets the girls by exclaiming, "'What a stench! Do you people live with goats?'" (*Princess Academy* 41). The answer, of course, is that the mountain girls *do* live with animals — out of necessity and for warmth. Olana refers to the potentials as "dusty goat girls" (43), "unpolished" (43) and "ignorant" (44), with "brains ... naturally smaller" (61), who need to be civilized before the prince will meet them. She punishes them for helping one another out during lessons by locking them in a dark closet with a biting rat or by lashing their hands with a stick. She refuses to allow them to leave when a scheduled vacation occurs, and she often denies them food in retaliation for their inability to act like lowlander girls. Thus, it is Olana's dictatorial rule that inspires Miri to stand up for their rights.

At first Miri is viewed as a trouble-maker by the others who simply want her to step into line (Olana's main tool of aggression and domination is group punishment in retaliation for the acts of one disobedient girl). When the girls grow angry at Miri's defiance because it results in collective castigation, she sows her first seeds as a potential revolutionary, declaring, "I was trying to stand up for all of us. This is another case of lowlanders treating mountain folk like worn-through boots" (Hale 56). The girls are so caught up in the hope of being the next princess that they see her resistance as sabotage, yet Miri insists that "she knew no lowlander would let a crown sit on a mountain girls' head" (57–58). It is this truth she clings to as she decides that she will compete to win the princess academy, not because she really wants to marry a prince — she seems ambivalent about that prospect — but because she sees the title and its trappings as a means to assist the people of her village.

Miri's first accomplishment, learning to read, earns her the ability to aid the village's economy. Once she reads *Danlander Commerce*, she discovers that the workers have been denied their just payments for the linder they have mined for years. Being highly prized and rare, linder is indigenous to Mount Eskel and carries a much higher exchange rate than traders have led the villagers to believe. Since the villagers cannot read, they have had no way of knowing the extent of their exploitation. Miri realizes that "if the traders dealt fairly, her village could benefit from the heaps of wonders the rest of the kingdom seemed to enjoy" (Hale 103). Once she returns to her village, she enlightens the workers, so that when the traders next visit, they negotiate for better compensation. Eventually, her intervention changes the economic picture of her village; her shoes are thicker-soled and the barrels of food storage are full, with no villager going hungry for weeks at a time any longer.

Miri's next accomplishment is her burgeoning knowledge and use of quarry-speak. Just as Hale introduced different types of "speech" in her first novel, the workers in this text are fluent in another type of language, described thusly: "...a quarry worker [said] that all their pounding and singing stored up rhythm in the mountain. . . the mountain used the rhythm to carry the message [to another worker] for them" (Hale 15). Unable to speak this language, Miri hopes to learn it to share with others. She uncovers its power by accident when locked in the closet with a rat tangled in her hair as she sings to herself and pounds the stone floor below to distract herself from her abhorrent surroundings. Gerti, a friend who suddenly perceives that Miri is in trouble, alerts the headmistress to Miri's whereabouts, and later says that she felt a memory that "reminded [her] of quarry-speech" (76). Miri wonders if quarry-speech might be useful even outside the quarry, but her attempts to use it with Britta, an academy friend born outside Mount Eskel, suggest to her that only the mountain folk have the ability to tap into this "talent" or "secret" (86). The first time she uses quarry speak to start a revolution, she directs it against headmistress Olana. When only she and Katar pass their exams, Olana denies all other girls the right to return to their families for a holiday. After she protests the lack of fairness and Olana threatens to keep all the girls imprisoned, Miri uses quarry-speak to urge the girls to run and escape, en masse, which works. The key to quarry-speak is "shared memories" (122). Later, the girls' common experiences bind them together in negotiations; collectively they use the rules of diplomacy to even their status with Olana. Eventually, Miri encourages all the girls from the mountain to use this ability as a means to help others when facing insurmountable odds. Even if the odds are something like oral exams which, if failed, will prevent one girl from meeting the prince, the girls work to help ensure that all will be on equal footing and receive the same opportunities. This gift, though, isn't used frivolously. At a crucial moment in the novel, quarry speak is used in the matter of life or death when Miri must call the villagers to aid them when kept for ransom by a group of bandits.

Eventually Miri learns that being useful to one's people is of greater importance than marrying "up." Once she is chosen as the winner of the princess academy by the united and now supportive group of girls, she wonders how much she really wants the "prize" after all. Interestingly, the once-meek and fragile Miri meets the prince and jokingly declines, then accepts, his offer to dance with her. Rather than turn the conversation back onto him as she has been taught, she speaks quite frankly with him about commerce, saying, "Now we have a real chance of making things better" (Hale 218). She also hampers her own chances to be "chosen" by calling the prince on his indifferent behavior to all of the girls who have worked so hard to please him.

When the prince at first chooses no one, the girls return to Mount Eskel, and Miri is faced with the knowledge that she has the right to become the next princess if she puts her mind to being chosen; however, in a moment of epiphany, she realizes that "'it seems like the world has changed and we shouldn't still be talking about things like marrying a prince'" (Hale 286). Although wearing the princess gown and earning its trappings of wealth and nobility excites her, the prospect of being needed by her father and village intrigue her more. Eventually her friend Britta, who reveals she had a lifelong friendship with the prince, is chosen; Britta offers Miri a future position as a delegate at the court, yet she refuses, saying she wants only to remain in her village where she hopes to begin an academy where she can teach others to read. Declaring that books are "the most valuable things in the world" (307) she insists that what Mount Eskel needed was not a monarch, but an academy where all could learn, because knowledge helps to erase class distinctions between lowlander and mountain folk.

Granted, many of Hale's characters form intimate relationships with those in their own social class after a series of class reversals. Ani, an aristocrat disguised as peasant who returns to nobility, marries Geric, a noble who pretends to be a royal servant before accepting his role as prince. Each character's experience is widened after seeing "how the other half lives," which elicits changes in their own monarchy once they take their position. Miri comes from the opposite end of the spectrum as she learns to masquerade as a member of the bourgeoisie by learning to read, to negotiate, and to charm; however, she rejects the social trappings of the monarchy to return to her own life, free to explore her feelings for the boy in her class whom she has always known. Britta, a noble, impersonates a member of the lower class, because she desires to marry her best friend the prince but is not from Mount Eskel. Having proven herself as a "Mount Eskel girl," she reveals herself to him, marrying a much less aristocratic and stuffy prince who is finally able to let his guard down once he sees that he may marry his confidante. Now rather than suggest that we are all happiest connecting with our own social class, Hale suggests that if we explore options we see that maybe we should not be so class-conscious. In fact, her others novels from the Bayern series and her *Book of a Thousand Days* do examine relationships between social classes that struggle at first but eventually succeed. It is as if Hale saw that interaction between social classes and even marriage is a process that begins in earnest in these two novels, laying the groundwork for a classless society in the future. We also see that these deeper explorations of class affect the compassion and understanding that one person has towards people different from herself. The world Hale envisions has not become entirely egalitarian, but it is moving towards embracing it.

Thus the new trajectory that Hale imagines for her female protagonists in *The Goose Girl* and *Princess Academy* moves far beyond a concept that the Grimms may have introduced subtly in their version of this classic tale. And, in true reflection of our contemporary world, in which so many girls have achieved equality, Hale feels comfortable in moving her heroines into the realm of working towards social justice and class equality. Hale's work suggests that by exploring the boundaries of our own social class and by learning about prejudice and the differences in other groups, we can find there is a common ground. Perhaps the end result, our "happily ever after," should not be tied to winning the lottery, to going from rags to riches, to becoming the princess. Perhaps what we should be trying to attain is a sense of self-worth, a connection to others in our communities, a notion of our place in the world, and a realization that happiness comes from achieving solidarity with others. In "A Conversation with Shannon Hale," Hale remarks that her novel "feel[s] as though it's starting in a distant fairy tale then bursting through into reality." Clearly Hale's contemporary take on the fairy tale indicates that it is only by putting ourselves in another person's shoes that we can grow to understand him or her, that the path we choose for ourselves allows us to write our own fairy tale, and that it is only through empathy and shared understanding that we can achieve equality and social reform.

Notes

1. Zipes analyzes the elements of three contemporary texts here, *Zwei Korken fur Schlienz* (Two Corks for Schlienz) by Basis Verlag, which revises "How Six Made Their Way in the World"; *Tischlien deck dich und Knuppel aus dem Sack* (Table Be Covered and Stick Out of the Sack) by Friedrich Karl Waechter; and *Das Rumpelstilzchen hat mir immer leid getan* (I Always Felt Sorry for Rumpelstiltskin) by Irmela Brender.

2. Political commentary and social reform are themes that run through most of Hale's novels. *The Goose Girl* is the first of *The Books of Bayern*, a series which includes *Enna Burning* and *River Secrets*. *Enna Burning* depicts Enna, a worker class friend and minor character from the first text who is given her own story. *River Secrets* develops the story of Razo, a minor character from *Enna Burning*. Hale's *Book of a Thousand Days*, a retelling/revision of the Grimms' tale "Maid Maleen," also explores the false bride/true bride dichotomy through the lens of social class. For the sake of essay length, I have decided to concentrate solely on the two books in Hale's collection which focus most primarily on Marxist themes, though all deal with political and social commentary on some level.

3. Both *Enna Burning* and *River Secrets* explore in depth how members of society often view those with nature speak abilities as sorceresses or witches when one character learns to control fire and another water.

4. For an interesting take on class consciousness from the maid's perspective, see Donoghue's "The Tale of the Handkerchief," a short story revision of this tale type, in which Donoghue explores the story of the maid in waiting from her perspective. Rather than pit her as a cold-hearted over-achiever, Donoghue provides a more sympathetic view of her character who seems both saddened and jealous at her own lack of royal blood and servant class identity. Donoghue's princess turned goose girl, like Hale's, embraces her life in the open fields and relinquishes her right to the throne, giving her maid the ability to remain as an aristocrat. However, the maid turned princess finds that she still lacks a true purpose or calling in life and does not know if defying the roots of her bloodline will send her down a path to fulfillment or not (61–80).

5. Ani noticed that before her beloved father died, he smelled "more of stables" and "less of parchment wax" (30), suggesting that her father was a more beneficent monarch comfortable with animals and by extension, the lower class, as opposed to her power-hungry mother who wanted only separation from all but her own class.

6. Another reference to Isi and Geric's less class-conscious monarchy is noted in *Enna Burning*, in which Enna reflects on the times that "Isi would have a picnic on the throne room floor and invite all the animal workers" (11).

Works Cited

Ashliman, D.L. *Folk and Fairy Tales: A Handbook*. Westport, CT: Greenwood, 2004.

Bottigheimer, Ruth. *Grimms' Bad Girls and Bold Boys: The Moral and Social Vision of the Tales*. New Haven: Yale University Press, 1987.

"A Conversation with Shannon Hale." Hale, *The Goose Girl*, N. pg.

Donoghue, Emma. "The Tale of the Handkerchief." *Kissing the Witch: Old Tales in New Skins*. New York: Harper, 1997.

Hale, Shannon. *Book of a Thousand Days*. New York: Bloomsbury, 2007.

_____. *Enna Burning*. New York: Bloomsbury, 2004.

_____. *The Goose Girl*. New York: Bloomsbury, 2003.

_____. *Princess Academy*. New York: Bloomsbury, 2005.

_____. *River Secrets*. New York: Bloomsbury, 2006.

Merseyside Fairy Story Collective. "Snow White." *Don't Bet on the Prince: Contemporary Feminist Fairy Tales in North America and England*. New York: Routledge, 1987. 74–80.

Tatar, Maria, ed. "The Goose Girl." *The Annotated Brothers Grimm*. New York: Norton, 2004. 310–21.

Wright, Beth. "Once Upon a Time: A Librarian Looks at Recent Young Adult Novels Based on Fairy Tales." *School Library Journal* Dec. 2004: 40–41.

Zipes, Jack. "Breaking the Magic Spell: Politics and the Fairy Tale." *New German Critique* 6 (1975): 116–35.

_____. Preface. *Breaking the Magic Spell: Radical Theories of Folk and Fairy Tales.* Lexington: University Press of Kentucky, 2002.

_____. "The Struggle for the Grimms' Throne: The Legacy of the Grimms' Tales in the FRG and GDR since 1945." *The Reception of Grimms' Fairy Tales: Responses, Reactions, Revisions.* Ed. Donald Haase. Detroit: Wayne State University Press, 1993. 167–206.

Comprehensive Bibliography

Aarne, Antti Amatus. *The Types of the Folktale*. Trans. Stith Thompson. Bloomington: Indiana University Press, 1964.

Alfer, Alexa, and Michael J. Noble, eds. *Essays on the Fiction of A.S. Byatt: Imagining the Real*. Westport, CT: Greenwood Press, 2001.

Andersen, Hans Christian. "The Wild Swans." *The Complete Fairy Tales and Stories*. Trans. Erik Christian Haugaard. New York: Anchor, 1983. 117–31.

Arlow, Jacob A. "Metaphor and the Psychoanalytic Situation." *The Psychoanalytic Quarterly* 48 (1979): 363–85.

Ashliman, D.L. *Folk and Fairy Tales: A Handbook*. Westport, CT: Greenwood, 2004.

_____, trans. "The Three Billy Goats Gruff." "The Three Goats." "How the Goats came to Hessen." *Folklore and Mythology Electronic Texts*. University of Pittsburgh. 14 June 2007 <*http://www.pitt.edu/~dash/type0122e.html*>.

Bacchilega, Cristina. *Postmodern Fairy Tales: Gender and Narrative Strategies*. Philadelphia: University of Pennsylvania, 1997.

Barrie, J.M. *Peter Pan in Kensington Gardens; Peter and Wendy*. Oxford: Oxford University Press, 1999.

Barthes, Roland. *Mythologies*. 1957. Paris: Seuil, 1970.

Basile, Giambattista. "The Seven Doves." *The Great Fairy Tale Tradition*. Ed. Jack Zipes. New York: Norton, 2001. 641–47.

Baum, Frank L. *The Wonderful Wizard of Oz*. New York: Barnes and Noble Classics, 2005.

Beres, D., and Jacob A. Arlow. "Fantasy and Identification in Empathy." *The Psychoanalytic Quarterly* 43 (1974): 26–50.

Bernheimer, Kate. *The Complete Tales of Ketzia Gold*. Tallahassee: FC2, 2001.

_____. *The Complete Tales of Merry Gold*. Tuscaloosa: FC2, 2006.

_____, ed. "Editor's Note." *Fairy Tale Review*. 2005.

_____, ed. *Mirror, Mirror on the Wall: Women Writers Explore their Favorite Fairy Tales*. New York: Anchor, 1998.

_____, ed. *Mirror, Mirror on the Wall: Women Writers Explore Their Favorite Fairy Tales*. New York: Bantam Doubleday Dell, 1998.

Bettelheim, Bruno. *The Uses of Enchantment: The Meaning and Importance of Fairy Tales*. 1975. New York: Vintage, 1977.

_____. *The Uses of Enchantment: The Meaning and Importance of Fairy Tales*. 1975. New York: Vintage, 1989.

Bhabha, Homi K. *The Location of Culture*. 1994. New York: Routledge, 2006.

Bizzarri, Aldo. *Mauthausen: Città Ermetica (Mauthausen: Hermetic City)*. Rome: OET/Edizioni Polilibraria, 1946.

Blau du Plessis, Rachel. *Writing Beyond the Ending: Narrative Strategies of Twentieth Century Women Writers*. Bloomington: Indiana University Press, 1985.

Boggs, Carl. "Postmodernism the Movie." *New Political Science* 23.3 (2001): 351–70.

Bottigheimer, Ruth. *Grimms' Bad Girls and Bold Boys: The Moral and Social Vision of the Tales.* New Haven: Yale University Press, 1987.

Braudy, Leo. *From Chivalry to Terrorism: War and the Changing Nature of Masculinity.* New York: Knopf, 2003.

Brombert, Victor. *In Praise of Antiheroes.* Chicago: University of Chicago Press, 1999.

Broumas, Olga. *Beginning with O.* New Haven: Yale University Press, 1977.

Brown, Rosellen. "It Is You the Fable Is About." Bernheimer 50–63.

"The Bulger Case: Chronology." *The Guardian* 6 Dec. 1999. 16 June 2008 <*http://www.guardian.co.uk/bulger/article/0,,195274,00.html*>.

Burns, Edward McNall. *The American Idea of Mission: Concepts of National Purpose and Destiny.* Westport, CT: Greenwood Press, 1973.

Butler, Judith. *Bodies that Matter: On the Discursive Limits of "Sex."* New York: Routledge, 1993.

_____. "Imitation and Gender Insubordination." *The Critical Tradition: Classic Texts and Contemporary Trends.* 2d ed. Ed. David H. Richter. Boston: Bedford/St. Martin's, 1997. 1514–25.

Buxton, Jackie. "'What's love got to do with it?': Postmodernism and *Possession*." Alfer and Noble 89–104.

Byatt, A.S. *The Djinn in the Nightingale's Eye: Five Fairy Stories.* 1994. New York: Vintage International, 1998.

_____. "Fairy Stories: The Djinn in the Nightingale's Eye." May 1995. 27 Aug. 2005 <*http://www.asbyatt.com/Onherself.aspx*>.

_____. "The Omnipotence of Thought: Frazer, Freud, and Post-Modernist Fiction." *Passions of the Mind.* New York: Vintage International, 1991.

_____. *On Histories & Stories.* Cambridge, MA: Harvard University Press, 2000.

_____. *Possession: A Romance.* 1990. New York: Vintage International, 1991.

_____. *The Shadow of the Sun.* 1964. San Diego: Harcourt Brace, 1992.

Cadden, Michael. "The Illusion of Control: Narrative Authority in Robin McKinley's *Beauty* and *The Blue Sword*." *Mythlore* 20.2 (1994): 16+.

Carroll, Lewis. *Alice's Adventures in Wonderland and Through the Looking-Glass.* London: Penguin, 1998.

_____. *The Annotated Alice.* Ed. Martin Gardner. Rev. ed. London: Penguin, 1970.

Carter, Angela. "Ashputtle *or* The Mother's Ghost." *American Ghosts and Old World Wonders.* London: Vintage, 1993. 110–20.

_____. "The Bloody Chamber." *The Bloody Chamber and Other Stories.* New York: Penguin, 1979. 7–41.

_____. *The Bloody Chamber and Other Stories.* 1979. London: Penguin, 2006.

_____. Introduction. *Angela Carter's Book of Fairy Tales.* Great Britain: Virago, 2005. xi–xxiv.

_____, trans. *Sleeping Beauty and Other Favourite Fairy Tales.* Boston: Otter, 1991.

Caruth, Elaine, and Rudolf Eckstein. "Interpretation within the Metaphor: Further Considerations." *Journal of the American Academy of Child Psychiatry* 5 (1966): 33–45.

Cavell, Stanley. *The Claim of Reason: Wittgenstein, Skepticism, Morality, and Tragedy.* Oxford: Oxford University Press, 1979.

Chénetier, Marc. "Robert Coover's Wondershow." *Amerikastudien* 1 (1984): 75–85.

Coelsch-Foisner, Sabine. "A Body of Her Own: Cultural Constructions of the Female Body in A.S. Byatt's Strange Stories." *Reconstruction: Studies in Contemporary Culture* 3.4 (2003). 24 June 2006 <http://reconstruction.eserver.org/034/coelsch.htm>.

Cohoon, Lorinda B. "Transgressive Transformation: Representations of Maid Marian in Robin Hood Retellings." *The Lion and the Unicorn* 31 (2007): 209–31.

Cole, Babette. 1987. *Prince Cinders*. London: Puffin, 1997.

Colebrook, Claire. *Gilles Deleuze*. London: Routledge, 2002.

Collodi, Carlo. *The Adventures of Pinocchio*. London: Roydon, 1975.

Connell, Robert W. *Gender and Power: Society, the Person and Sexual Politics*. Stanford: Stanford University Press, 1987.

"A Conversation with Shannon Hale." Hale, *The Goose Girl*, n.pg.

Coover, Robert. *Briar Rose*. New York: Grove Press, 1996.

_____. "The Master's Voice." *American Review* 26 (1977): 361–88.

_____. *Pricksongs and Descants*. New York: Dutton, 1969.

Coppola, Maria Mircea. "The Gender of Fairies: Emma Donoghue and Angela Carter as Fairy Tale Performers." *Textus* 24 (2001): 127–42.

Crew, Hilary. "How Feminist are Fractured Fairy Tales." *Fractured Fairy Tales*. 3 pp. 2 July 2004. <http://www.scils.rutgers.edu/~kvander/Culture/crew.html>.

Cross, Gillian. *Wolf*. London: Puffin, 1990.

Culbertson, Roberta. "Embodied Memory, Transcendence, and Telling: Recounting Trauma, Re-establishing the Self." *New Literary History* 26 (1995): 169–95.

Currie, Mark, ed. *Metafiction*. London: Longman, 1995.

_____. *Postmodern Narrative Theory*. New York: Palgrave, 1998.

de Alta Silva, Johannes. *Dolopathos* or *The King and the Seven Wise Men*. Trans. Brady B. Gilleland. Binghamton: Center for Medieval & Early Renaissance Studies, 1999.

De Certeau, Michel. "On the Oppositional Practices of Everyday Life." Trans. Frederic Jameson and Carol Lovitt. *Social Text* 3 (1980): 3–43.

De Ford, Sara. "The Sleeping Beauty." *Disenchantments: An Anthology of Modern Fairy Tale Poetry*. Ed. Wolfgang Mieder. Vermont: University Press of New England, 1985.

de Mylius, Johan. " 'Our Time Is the Time of the Fairy Tale': Hans Christian Andersen Between Traditional Craft and Literary Modernism." *Marvels and Tales* 20.2 (2006): 166–78.

Dentith, Simon. *Parody*. London: Routledge, 2000.

Deppey, Dick. Interview with Bill Willingham. *The Comics Journal*. 18 Sept. 2006. 15 Apr. 2007 <http://www.tcj.com/index.php?option=com_content&task=view&id=410&Itemid=48>.

Donoghue, Emma. *Kissing the Witch: Old Tales in New Skins*. New York: HarperCollins, 1997.

Dundes, Alan, ed. *Cinderella: A Folklore Casebook*. New York: Garland, 1982.

Eaglestone, Robert. "From behind the Bars of Quotation Marks: Emmanuel Levinas's (Non)-Representation of the Holocaust." Leak and Paizis 97–108.

Fergnani, Enea. *Un uomo e tre numeri (A Man and Three Numbers)*. 1945. Milan/Rome: Avanti, 1955.

Fiander, Lisa M. *Fairy Tales and the Fiction of Iris Murdoch, Margaret Drabble, and A. S. Byatt*. New York: Peter Lang, 2004.

Foote, Jennifer. "Interview: Out from Sister's Shadow." *Newsweek* 21 Jan. 1991: 12. June 2008 <http://newsweek.com/id/121233/page/2>.

French, Fiona. *Snow White in New York*. Oxford: Oxford University Press, 1986.

Freud, Sigmund. "The 'Uncanny.'" *The Complete Standard Edition of the Complete Psychological Works of Sigmund Freud. Vol XVII (1917–1919)*. 1953. Ed. James Strachey. London: Hogarth Press, 1971.

Fussell, Paul. *Wartime: Understanding and Behavior in the Second World War*. New York: Oxford University Press, 1989.

Gaiman, Neil. "All Books Have Genders." *Essays by Neil*. 23 Nov. 2008 <http://www.neil gaiman.com/p/Cool_Stuff/Essays/Essays_By_Neil/All_Books_Have_Genders>.

_____. *Black Orchid*. New York: DC Comics, 1991.

_____. *Fragile Things*. London: Review, 2006.

_____. *Smoke and Mirrors*. London: Review, 2005.

_____. "Snow, Glass, Apples." *Smoke and Mirrors*. London: Review, 2005. 371–84.

_____. *Stardust*. London: Review, 1999.

_____. "Troll Bridge." *Smoke and Mirrors*. London: Review, 2005. 59–70.

Gates, Geoffrey. "'Always the Outlaw': The Potential for Subversion of the Metanarrative in Retellings of Robin Hood." *Children's Literature in Education* 37.1 (2006): 69–79.

Gaudesaboos, Pieter. *Roodlapje*. Tielt: Lannoo, 2003.

Geras, Adèle. *Pictures of the Night*. 1992. London: Red Fox, 2002.

Gilbert, Sandra M., and Susan Gubar. *The Madwoman in the Attic: The Woman Writer and the Nineteenth-Century Literary Imagination*. New Haven: Yale University Press, 1979.

_____, and _____. *The Madwoman in the Attic: The Woman Writer and the Nineteenth-Century Literary Imagination*. 2d ed. New Haven: Yale University Press, 2000.

Gilligan, Carol. *In a Different Voice: Psychological Theory and Women's Development*. 1982. Cambridge, MA: Harvard University Press, 1993.

Gilmore, Mikal. Introduction. *Black Orchid*. New York: DC Comics, 1991.

Gordon, Robert S. "Holocaust Writing in Context: Italy 1945–47." Leak and Paizis 32–50.

Grandstaff, Mark R. "Visions of New Men: The Heroic Soldier Narrative in American Advertisements During World War II." *Advertising and Society Review* 5.2 (2004). Project Muse. 1 May 2007 <http://muse.jhu.edu.spot.lib.auburn.edu/journals/advertising_and_society_review/v005/5.2grandstaff.html>.

Grimm, Jacob, and Wilhelm Grimm. *Little Snow White*. Trans. Margaret Hunt. London: George Bell, 1884. *SurLaLune Fairy Tales*. Ed. Heidi Anne Heiner. 4 July 2007 *<http://www.surlalunefairytales.com/sevendwarfs/index.html>*.

_____, and _____. "The Seven Ravens (Die Sieben Raben)." *Children's and Household Tales (Kinder- und Hausmärchen)*. Trans. D.L. Ashliman. *Folklore and Mythology Electronic Texts*. University of Pittsburgh. 16 Feb. 2005 <www.pitt.edu/~dash/grimm049.html>.

_____. "The Six Swans (Die sechs Schwane)." *Children's and Household Tales (Kinder- und Hausmärchen)*. Trans. D.L. Ashliman. *Folklore and Mythology Electronic Texts*. University of Pittsburgh. 16 Feb. 2005 <www.pitt.edu/~dash/grimm025.html>.

_____. "The Twelve Brothers (Die zwolf Bruder)." *Children's and Household Tales (Kinder- und Hausmärchen)*. Trans. D.L. Ashliman. *Folklore and Mythology Electronic Texts*. University of Pittsburgh. 16 Feb. 2005 <www.pitt.edu/~dash/grimm009.html>.

Haase, Donald. "Feminist Fairy-Tale Scholarship." *Fairy Tales and Feminism— New Approaches*. Detroit: Wayne State University Press, 2004. 1–36.

_____. "Yours, Mine, or Ours? Perrault, the Brothers Grimm, and the Ownership of Fairy Tales." *The Classic Fairy Tales: Texts, Criticism*. Ed. Maria Tatar. New York: Norton, 1999. 353–64.

Hale, Shannon. *Book of a Thousand Days*. New York: Bloomsbury, 2007.

_____. *Enna Burning*. New York: Bloomsbury, 2004.

_____. *The Goose Girl*. New York: Bloomsbury, 2003.

_____. *Princess Academy*. New York: Bloomsbury, 2005.

_____. *River Secrets*. New York: Bloomsbury, 2006.

Hallett, Martin, and Barbara Karsek, eds. *Folk and Fairy Tales*. 2d ed. Peterborough, Ontario: Broadview Press, 1996.

Harries, Elizabeth Wanning. *Twice Upon a Time: Women Writers and the History of the Fairy Tale*. Princeton, NJ: Princeton University Press, 2001.

Hay, Sara Henderson. *Story Hour.* Fayetteville: University of Arkansas Press, 1998.

Heiner, Heidi Anne. "What is a Fairy Tale?" 1999. *Sur La Lune Fairy Tales.* 26 July 2006 <*http://www.surlalunefairytales.com/introduction/ftdefinition.html*>.

Herman, Judith. *Trauma and Recovery: The Aftermath of Violence — from Domestic Abuse to Political Terror.* New York: Basic, 1997.

Hollindale, Peter. "The Professional Child: Performing *Lord of the Flies.*" *Children's Literature and Childhood in Performance.* Ed. Kimberley Reynolds. Lichfield: Pied Piper, 2003. 13–25.

Hutcheon, Linda. *Narcissistic Narrative: The Metafictional Paradox.* New York: Methuen, 1984.

Jaggi, Maya. "Profiles and Interviews: Jeanette Winterson." *The Guardian* 29 May 2004. 1 March 2007 <http://www.jeanettewinterson.com/pages/content/index.asp?PageID=272>.

Jameson, Fredric. "Metacommentary." *PMLA* 86 (1971): 9–18.

Jarvis, Christina S. *The Male Body at War: American Masculinity During World War II.* DeKalb: Northern Illinois University Press, 2004.

Jeffords, Susan. *The Remasculinization of America: Gender and the Vietnam War.* Bloomington: Indiana University Press, 1989.

Johnson, Daniel. "Books Barely Furnish a Room." *The Times* 16 Sept. 1992: 3.

Joosen, Vanessa. "Disenchanting the Fairy Tale: Retellings of 'Snow White' Between Magic and Realism." *Marvels and Tales* 21.2 (2007): 228–39.

_____. "Scene 9, Take 45: Collage and the Postmodern Fairy Tale." *The Journal of Children's Literature Studies* 4.2 (2007): 54–76.

Kading, Terry. "Drawn into 9/11, But Where Have All the Superheroes Gone?" *Comics as Philosophy.* Ed. Jeff McLaughlin. Jackson: University of Mississippi Press, 2005. 207–27.

Kakutani, Michiko. "Let's Get This Straight: Glinda Was the Bad One?" *New York Times.* 24 Oct.1995: C17.

Kantor, Melissa. *If I Have a Wicked Stepmother, Where's My Prince?* New York: Hyperion, 2005.

Kelly, Kathleen Coyne. *A. S. Byatt.* New York: Twayne, 1996.

Kerr, Peg. *The Wild Swans.* New York: Warner, 1999.

Khalifa, Samuel. "The Mirror of Memory: Patrick Modiano's *La Place de l'etoile* and *Dora Bruder.*" *The Holocaust and the Text: Speaking the Unspeakable.* Leak and Paizis 159–73.

Kukil, Karen V., ed. *The Journals of Sylvia Plath, 1950–1962.* London: Faber and Faber, 2000.

Kusnir, Jaroslav. "Subversion of Myths: High and Low Cultures in Donald Barthelme's Snow White and Robert Coover's *Briar Rose.*" *European Journal of American Culture* 23. 1 (2004): 31–49.

Lackey, Mercedes. *The Fairy Godmother.* New York: Luna, 2004.

Lang, Andrew, ed. "Cinderella; or, the Little Glass Slipper." 1889. *The Blue Fairy Book.* New York: Dover, 1965.

Lang, Berel. "Holocaust Genres and the Turn to History." Leak and Paizis 17–31.

Leak, Andrew, and George Paizis, eds. *The Holocaust and the Text: Speaking the Unspeakable.* New York: St. Martin's Press, 2000.

Lederer, Wolfgang. *The Kiss of the Snow Queen: Hans Christian Andersen and Man's Redemption by Woman.* Berkeley: University of California Press, 1986.

Lee, Tanith. *The Green Man: Tales from the Forest.* Ed. Ellen Datlow and Terri Windling. New York: Firebird, 2002.

Levi, Primo. *If this is a Man.* London: Abacus, 1987.

Littlefield, Henry M. "The Wizard of Oz: Parable on Populism." 5 Apr. 2007. <*http://www.amphigory.com/oz.htm*>.

Lodge, David. *The Art of Fiction.* London: Penguin, 1992.

Lothe, Jakob. *Narrative in Fiction and Film: An Introduction.* Oxford: Oxford University Press, 2000.

Lüthi, Max. *Das europäische Volksmärchen: Form und Wesen.* 8. Auflage. Tübingen: Francke Verlag, 1985.

_____. *The European Folktale: Form and Nature.* Trans. John D. Niles. Philadelphia: Institute for the Study of Human Issues, 1982.

_____. "The Fairy Tale Hero: The Image of Man in the Fairy Tale." Hallett and Karsek 295–305.

_____. *Once Upon a Time: On The Nature of Fairy Tales.* Trans. Lee Chadeayne and Paul Gottwald. Bloomington: Indiana University Press, 1976.

Lyotard, J.F. *Heidegger and "the jews."* Trans. Andreas Michel and Mark S. Roberts. Minneapolis: University of Minnesota Press, 1990.

Maack, Annegret. "Wonder-Tales Hiding a Truth: Retelling Tales in 'The Djinn in the Nightingale's Eye.'" Alfer and Noble 123–134.

Maclean, Marie. "Oppositional Practices of Women in Traditional Narrative." *New Literary History* 19 (1987): 37–50.

Maguire, Gregory. *Son of a Witch.* New York: HarperCollins, 2005.

_____. *Wicked: The Life and Times of the Wicked Witch of the West.* New York: HarperCollins, 1995.

Marillier, Juliet. *Daughter of the Forest.* New York: Tor, 2000.

Markey, Constance. *Italo Calvino: A Journey Toward Postmodernism.* Gainesville: University of Florida Press, 1999.

Marriott, Zöe. *The Swan Kingdom.* Cambridge, MA: Candlewick, 2008.

Martin, Rafe. *Birdwing.* New York: Levine, 2005.

McCabe, Joseph. *Hanging Out with the Dream King.* Seattle: Fantagraphics Books, 2004.

McCaffery, Larry. *The Metafictional Muse: The Works of Robert Coover, Donald Barthelme, and William H. Gass.* Pittsburgh: University of Pittsburgh Press, 1982.

McGillis, Roderick. "'A Fairytale Is Just a Fairytale': George MacDonald and the Queering of Fairy." *Marvels and Tales* 17.1 (2003): 86–99.

McKinley, Robin. *Beauty: A Retelling of the Story of Beauty & the Beast.* New York: Harper, 1978.

_____. *Deerskin.* New York: Ace, 1993.

_____. *Dragonhaven.* New York: Putnam, 2007.

_____. *The Outlaws of Sherwood.* New York: Ace, 1989.

_____. *Rose Daughter.* New York: Ace, 1997.

_____. *Spindle's End.* New York: Putnam, 2000.

_____. *Sunshine.* New York: Berkley, 2003.

Meletinsky, Eleazar M. *The Poetics of Myth.* Trans. by Guy Lanoue & Alexandre Sadetsky. London: Routledge, 2000.

Merseyside Fairy Story Collective. "Snow White." *Don't Bet on the Prince: Contemporary Feminist Fairy Tales in North America and England.* New York: Routledge, 1987. 74–80.

Miller, Laura. "Jeanette Winterson: England's Literary Outlaw." *Salon.* Apr. 1997. 22 Nov. 2003 <http://archive.salon.com/april97/winterson970428.html>.

Mishara, Aaron L. "Narrative and Psychotherapy: The Phenomenology of Healing." *American Journal of Psychotherapy* 49 (1995): 180–95.

Mockaitis, Thomas. *The "New" Terrorism: Myths and Reality.* Westport, CT: Praeger, 2007.

Morehouse, Lydia. "SFC Interview: Peg Kerr." *Science Fiction Chronicle* 207 (2000): 13–15.

Morse, M. Joy. "The Kiss: Female Sexuality and Power in J.M. Barrie's *Peter Pan.*" *J.M.*

Barrie's Peter Pan *In and Out of Time: A Children's Classic at 100.* Ed. Donna R. White and C. Anita Tarr. Lanham, MD: Scarecrow Press, 2006. 281–302.

Murphy, Louise. *The True Story of Hansel and Gretel: A Novel of War and Survival.* New York: Penguin, 2003.

Natov, Roni. *The Poetics of Childhood.* New York, London: Routledge, 2003.

Nikolajeva, Maria. *Children's Literature Comes of Age.* New York: Garland, 1996.

Noakes, Jonathan, and Margaret Reynolds. *A. S. Byatt.* London: Vintage, 2004.

_____, and _____, eds. *Jeanette Winterson: Vintage Living Texts.* London: Vintage, 2003.

Noon, David Hoogland. "Operation Enduring Analogy: World War II, the War on Terror, and the Uses of Historical Memory." *Rhetoric & Public Affairs* 7.3 (2004): 339–64.

Nussbaum, Martha. *Love's Knowledge: Essays on Philosophy and Literature.* Oxford: Oxford University Press, 1990.

Oakley, Glenn. "Historical Overview." In *Wolf!* Ed. Wolves in American Culture Committee. Ashland: NorthWord, 1986. 1–7.

Oates, Joyce Carol. "In Olden Times, When Wishing Was Having: Classic and Contemporary Fairy Tales." *Mirror, Mirror on the Wall: Women Writers Explore Their Favorite Fairy Tales.* Ed. Kate Bernheimer. New York: Anchor, 1998. 247–72.

Onega, Susana. *Jeanette Winterson.* Contemporary British Novelists Series. Manchester: Manchester University Press, 2006.

Özüm, Aytül. "Deconstructed Masculine Evil in Angela Carter's *The Bloody Chamber* Stories." *Wickedness.Net.* 2006. 28 Aug. 2008 <*http://www.wickedness.net/Evil/Evil %208/ozum%20paper.pdf*>.

Palmer, Paulina. "Lesbian Transformations of Gothic and Fairy Tale." *Contemporary British Women Writers.* Ed. Emma Parker. Cambridge: D. S. Brewer, 2004. 139–53.

Parker, David P. "The Rise and Fall of the Wonderful Wizard of Oz." *Journal of the Georgia Association of Historians* 15 (1994): 46–93.

Parry, Ann. "Idioms for the Unrepresentable: Postwar Fiction and the Shoah." Leak and Paizis 109–24.

Paxton, Tamara. "McKinley's *Deerskin*: From Passive Princess to Independent Heroine." *The Image of the Hero: Selected Papers of the Society for the Interdisciplinary Study of Social Imagery, March 2004, Colorado Springs, Colorado.* Pueblo: The Society-Colorado State University-Pueblo, 2004. 150–56.

Perrault, Charles. "Cinderella; or, The Glass Slipper." *The Great Fairy Tale Tradition: From Straparola and Basile to the Brothers Grimm.* Ed. Jack Zipes. New York: Norton, 2001. 449–54.

Phillips, Kathy J. *Manipulating Masculinity: War and Gender in Modern British and American Literature.* New York: Palgrave Macmillan, 2006.

Pratchett, Terry. *Witches Abroad.* London: Victor Gollancz, 1991.

Prickett, Stephen. *Victorian Fantasy.* Waco, TX: Baylor University Press, 2006.

Propp, Vladimir. *The Morphology of the Folktale.* Austin: University of Texas Press, 1968.

_____. *The Morphology of the Folk Tale.* 2d ed. Trans. Laurence Scott. Austin: University of Texas Press, 1968.

Pullman, Philip. *I Was a Rat!* Ill. Kevin Hawkes. New York: Dell Yearling, 2000.

_____. "The Republic of Heaven." *The Horn Book Magazine* (2001): 655–67.

Rabkin, Eric S. *The Fantastic in Literature.* Princeton, NJ: Princeton University Press, 1976.

Redies, Sünje. "Return with New Complexities: Robert Coover's *Briar Rose*." *Marvels & Tales* 18.1 (2004): 9–27.

Renk, Kathleen Williams. "A.S. Byatt, the Woman Artist, and Suttee." *Women's Studies* 33 (2004): 613–28.

Reynolds, Richard. *Superheroes: A Modern Mythology.* Jackson: University of Mississippi Press, 1994.

Rich, Adrienne. "Compulsory Heterosexuality and Lesbian Existence." *Signs* 5.4 (1980): 631–60.

_____. "When We Dead Awaken: Writing as Re-Vision." *Adrienne Rich's Poetry.* Ed. Barbara Charlesworth Gelpi and Albert Gelpi. New York: Norton, 1975. 90–98.

_____. "When We Dead Awaken: Writing as Re-Vision." *College English* 34.1: Women, Writing and Teaching (Oct. 1972): 18–30.

Richardson, Louise. "The Roots of Terrorism: An Overview." *The Roots of Terrorism.* Ed. Louise Richardson. London: Routledge, 2006.

_____. *What Terrorists Want: Understanding the Enemy, Containing the Threat.* New York: Random House, 2006.

Rose, Jacqueline. *The Case of Peter Pan or The Impossibility of Children's Fiction.* 1984. Philadelphia: University of Pennsylvania Press, 1992.

Roth, Christine. "Babes in Boy-Land: J.M. Barrie and the Edwardian Girl." *J.M. Barrie's* Peter Pan *In and Out of Time: A Children's Classic at 100.* Ed. Donna R. White and C. Anita Tarr. Lanham, MD: Scarecrow Press, 2006. 47–67.

Rozett, Martha Tuck. *Constructing a World: Shakespeare's England and the New Historical Fiction.* Albany: State University of New York Press, 2003.

Rubinson, Gregory J. *The Fiction of Rushdie, Barnes, Winterson and Carter: Breaking Cultural and Literary Boundaries in the Work of Four Postmodernists.* Jefferson, NC: McFarland, 2005.

Rushdie, Salman. "Angela Carter, 1940–1992: A Very Good Wizard, a Very Dear Friend." *The New York Times* 8 Mar. 1992. 13 May 2008. http://www.nytimes.com/books/98/12/27/specials/carter-rushdie.html>.

Rutledge, Amelia A. "Robin McKinley's *Deerskin*: Challenging Narcissisms." *Marvels & Tales* 15 (2001): 168–82.

Sackelman, Ellen R. "More Than Skin Deep: Robin McKinley's *Beauty: A Retelling of the Story of Beauty and the Beast* (1978)." *Women in Literature: Reading Through the Lens of Gender.* Ed. by Jerilyn Fisher and Ellen S. Silber. Westport, CT: Greenwood, 2003. 32–4.

Schwarz, Hans. *Evil: A Historical and Theological Perspective.* Minneapolis: Fortress Press, 1995.

Sedgwick, Eve Kosofsky. *Tendencies.* Durham: Duke University Press, 1994.

Sellers, Susan. *Myth and Fairy Tale in Contemporary Women's Fiction.* New York: Palgrave, 2001.

Sexton, Anne. *Transformations.* 1971. Boston: Houghton Mifflin, 2001.

Sigler, Carolyn, ed. *Alternative Alices: Visions and Revisions of Lewis Carroll's Alice Books.* Lexington: University of Kentucky Press, 1997.

Silver, Carol G. *Strange and Secret Peoples: Fairies and Victorian Culture.* Oxford: Oxford University Press, 1999.

Sinfield, Alan. *Cultural Politics-Queer Reading.* Philadelphia: University of Pennsylvania Press, 1994.

Singh, Gurbhagat. *Literature and Folklore after Poststructuralism.* Delhi: Ajanta, 1991.

Slabbert, Mathilda. "Inventions and Transformations: An Exploration of Mythification and Remythification in Four Contemporary Novels." Diss. University of South Africa, 2006. <http://etd.unisa.ac.za/ETD-db/theses/available/etd-09222006-1041 34/unrestricted/thesis.pdf>.

Slotkin, Richard. *Gunfighter Nation: The Myth of the Frontier in Twentieth-Century America.* New York: Atheneum, 1992.

_____. *Regeneration through Violence: The Mythology of the American Frontier, 1600–1860.* Middletown: Wesleyan University Press, 1973.

Smith, Kevin Paul. *The Postmodern Fairytale: Folkloric Intertexts in Contemporary Fiction.* New York: Palgrave Macmillan, 2007.

Soucy, Gaétan. *The Little Girl Who Was Too Fond of Matches.* Trans. Sheila Fischman. New York: Arcade Publishing, 2001.

Steiner, George. "The Hollow Miracle." *Literature and the Modern World: Critical Essays.* Ed. D. Walder. Oxford: Oxford University Press, 1990.

Stoffel, Stephanie Lovett. *Lewis Carroll in Wonderland: The Life and Times of Alice and Her Creator.* New York: Wonderland Press, 1997.

Tatar, Maria. *The Hard Facts of the Grimms' Fairy Tales.* Princeton: Princeton University Press, 2003.

_____. *Secrets Beyond the Door: The Story of Bluebeard and His Wives.* Princeton, NJ: Princeton University Press, 2004.

_____, ed. *The Classic Fairy Tales: Texts, Criticism.* New York: Norton, 1999.

_____, ed. "The Goose Girl." *The Annotated Brothers Grimm.* New York: Norton, 2004. 310–21.

_____, trans. "Brothers Grimm: Cinderella." *The Classic Fairy Tales.* New York: Norton, 1999. 117–22.

Thacker, Deborah Cogan, and Jean Webb. *Introducing Children's Literature: From Romanticism to Postmodernism.* London: Routledge, 2002.

Todd, Richard. *A. S. Byatt.* Plymouth, UK: Northcote House, 1997.

Tolkien, J.R.R. "On Fairy Stories." *Tree and Leaf.* New York: HarperCollins, 1965.

_____. "On Fairy Stories." Hallett and Karsek 263–94.

True Caribbean Pirates. Dir. Tim Prokop. The History Channel. 26 Sept. 2006.

Tucker, Nicholas. *Darkness Visible: Inside the World of Philip Pullman.* Cambridge: Wizard Books, 2003.

Vloeberghs, Katrien. "Het kind zonder gezicht: Figuraties van het kind in interferenties tussen het literaire modernisme, de filosofische theorie van Lyotard, Kristeva en Agamben, en de hedendaagse kinder- en jeugdliteratuur." Diss. University of Antwerp (Belgium), 2005.

Walker, Steven F. *Jung and the Jungians on Myth.* New York: Routledge, 2002.

Warner, Marina. *From the Beast to the Blonde: On Fairy Tales and their Tellers.* New York: Farrar, Straus, and Giroux, 1994.

Whittaker, David J. *Terrorism: Understanding the Global Threat.* Harlow, Essex, UK: Pearson, 2007.

Willingham, Bill. *Homelands.* New York: DC Comics, 2005.

_____. *Legends in Exile.* New York: DC Comics, 2002.

_____. *March of the Wooden Soldiers.* New York: DC Comics, 2004.

_____. *The Mean Seasons.* New York: DC Comics, 2005.

_____. *1001 Nights of Snowfall.* New York: DC Comics, 2006.

_____. *Storybook Love.* New York: DC Comics, 2004.

_____. *Wolves.* New York: DC Comics, 2006.

Wilson, Ann. "Hauntings: Anxiety, Technology, and Gender in *Peter Pan.*" *Modern Drama* 43 (2000): 595–610.

Windling, Terri. "Old Wives Tales: An Exhibition of Women's Fairy Tale Art, Old and New." *Endicott Studio.* 12 June 2008 <http://www.endicott-studio.com/gal/gal Wives/wivestales.html>.

Winquist, Charles E. "The Act of Storytelling and the Self's Homecoming." *Journal of the American Academy of Religion* 42.1 (Mar. 1974): 101–13.

Winterson, Jeanette. *Art Objects: Essays on Ecstasy and Effrontery.* New York: Knopf, 1996.

_____. "Books: The PowerBook." *Jeanette Winterson Website.* 25 Feb. 2007 <http://www.jeanettewinterson.com/pages/content/index.asp?PageID=10>.

_____. *Oranges Are Not the Only Fruit.* New York: Grove, 1985.

_____. *The Passion*. New York: Grove, 1987.

_____. *The PowerBook*. London: Vintage, 2001.

_____. *Written on the Body*. New York: Vintage International, 1994.

Wittgenstein, Ludwig. *Philosophical Investigations*. Trans. G.E.M. Anscombe. New York: MacMillan, 1953.

_____. *Tractatus Logico-Philosophicus*. Trans. C.K. Ogden. New York: Harcourt, 1922.

Wolff, Sula, and R.A.A. McCall Smith. "Child Homocide and the Law: Implications of the European Court of Human Rights in the Case of the Children Who Killed James Bulger." *Child Psychology & Psychiatry Review* 5.3 (2000): 133–38.

Wrede, Patricia C. *Dealing With Dragons*. New York: Harcourt, 1990.

Wright, Beth. "Once Upon a Time: A Librarian Looks at Recent Young Adult Novels Based on Fairy Tales." *School Library Journal* Dec. 2004: 40–41.

Wright, Bradford W. *Comic Book Nation: The Transformation of Youth Culture in America*. Baltimore: Johns Hopkins University Press, 2001.

Wullschläger, Jackie. *Inventing Wonderland*. New York: The Free Press, 1995.

Yolen, Jane. *Briar Rose*. New York: Tor, 2002.

_____. *Not One Damsel in Distress: World Folktales for Strong Girls*. New York: Harcourt, 2000.

_____. *Sister Emily's Lightship and Other Stories*. New York: Tor, 2000.

_____. *Touch Magic: Fantasy, Faerie, and Folklore in the Literature of Childhood*. Expanded ed. New York: Philomel Books, 2000.

_____. *Twelve Impossible Things Before Breakfast*. New York: Harcourt Brace, 1997.

Yudkin, Leon. "Is Aaron Appelfeld a Holocaust Writer?" Leak and Paizis 142–58.

Zimmerman, Bonnie. "Perverse Readings." *Sexual Practice, Textual Theory: Lesbian Cultural Criticism*. Ed. Susan J. Wolfe and Julia Penelope. Cambridge, MA: Blackwell, 1993. 135–49.

Zipes, Jack. "Breaking the Magic Spell: Politics and the Fairy Tale." *New German Critique* 6 (1975): 116–135.

_____. *Breaking the Spell: Radical Theories of Folk and Fairy Tales*. Austin: University of Texas Press, 1979.

_____. *Fairy Tales and the Art of Subversion*. New York: Wildman Press, 1983.

_____. *Fairy Tale as Myth, Myth as Fairy Tale*. Lexington: University Press of Kentucky, 1994.

_____. Preface. *Breaking the Magic Spell: Radical Theories of Folk and Fairy Tales*. 1979. Lexington: University Press of Kentucky, 2002. ix–x.

_____. "Spells of Enchantment." Hallett and Karsek 370–92.

_____. "The Struggle for the Grimms' Throne: The Legacy of the Grimms' Tales in the FRG and GDR since 1945." *The Reception of Grimms' Fairy Tales: Responses, Reactions, Revisions*. Ed. Donald Haase. Detroit: Wayne State University Press, 1993. 167–206.

_____. "Towards a Definition of the Literary Fairy Tale." *The Oxford Companion to Fairy Tales: The Western Fairy Tale Tradition from Medieval to Modern*. Oxford: Oxford University Press, 2000. xv–xxxii.

_____. *The Trials and Tribulations of Little Red Riding Hood*. New York: Routledge, 1993.

_____. *Why Fairy Tales Stick: The Evolution and Relevance of a Genre*. London: Routledge, 2006.

About the Contributors

Bethany Joy Bear is a Ph.D. student in literature and religion at Baylor University, where she is an instructor of freshman composition. Her publications and presentations study the works of A.S. Byatt, Lewis Carroll, Hans Christian Andersen, and other writers who create and recreate fairy tales. Her essay comes from an unpublished thesis on cross-cultural variants of AT 451, the "sister-savior" fairy tale.

Susan Redington Bobby, an assistant professor of English at Wesley College, specializes in classic and contemporary fairy tales and adolescent literature. She earned her B.A. and M.A. in English from Millersville University of Pennsylvania. She has published an article on Philip Pullman's *His Dark Materials* in *The Looking Glass: An Online Children's Literature Journal* and has presented papers on Pullman's work at both NEMLA and Popular Culture Association conferences. She has chaired the NEMLA panel *Fairy Tale Visions and (Re) Visions* from which this collection took root.

Marie C. Bouchet, a professor at the University of Toulouse, France, teaches American literature and specializes in 20th and 21st century American fiction and the works of Vladimir Nabokov. Her 2005 Ph.D. dissertation deals with the representation of desire in Nabokov's fiction. She has published various academic articles in international, peer-reviewed journals, such as *Anglophonia/Caliban*, *Transatlantica*, *Nabokov Studies*, *Zembla*, *Moveable Type*, and others. Since 2003 she has presented papers at 14 conferences and published 8 articles. She has two articles forthcoming and is currently at work on translating her Ph.D. dissertation into English for publication.

Lauren Choplin is a graduate student in the M.F.A. program in creative writing at the University of Alabama, where she holds a teaching fellowship. She is currently at work on an autobiographical literary analysis of her childhood diary and a series of essays on the relationship between violence, war, and human rights discourse in twentieth-century literature.

Amie A. Doughty is an assistant professor of English at the State University of New York–Oneonta, where she teaches courses in linguistics, composition, and literature. She received her Ph.D. from the University of Oklahoma in 2000. She has presented papers about various aspects of children's literature at the Popular Culture Association's conferences and is the author of *Folktales Retold: A Critical Overview of Stories Updated for Children* (McFarland, 2006) as well as several articles about folktale revisions and children's literature.

Jeffrey K. Gibson, an associate professor of English and a British literature specialist at Wesley College, received his Ph.D. in English from the University at Albany–State University of New York. He has published on Peter Carey and Chuck Palahniuk, and has delivered papers on historical fiction and the contemporary revision of cultural forms at MMLA, AWP, and the National Humanities Center. Most recently, he presented a paper on Todd Solodnz's *Storytelling* at NEMLA 2007.

Martine Hennard Dutheil de la Rochère is associate dean of the humanities at the University of Lausanne, Switzerland, where she teaches modern English literature and comparative literature. Her research interests include various aspects of colonial and postcolonial fiction, modernism and postmodernism, fairy tale rewritings and translation studies. She is the author of *Origin and Originality in Rushdie's Fiction* (1997) and has published articles in *MFS*, *Dickens Quarterly*, *Dickens Studies Annual*, *College Literature*, *EJES*, *Conradiana*, and, more recently, *The Conradian* (2008) and *Marvels and Tales* (2009). Her current projects are a study of Angela Carter's translations of Perrault and a book on contemporary fairy tale rewritings.

Mark C. Hill is an English instructor at Alabama State University and a Ph.D. candidate in English at Auburn University. This first publication is based on research and work done towards a dissertation on the cultural construction of the post 9/11 soldier, and it was nominated for a writing award at Auburn. He has presented his work at numerous conferences, including the Mythopoeic Society's annual convention. His interests are primarily in cultural imaginings, identity and national mythology, especially as interpreted in fairy tales, graphic novels, and film.

Vanessa Joosen is a postdoctoral researcher at the University of Antwerp, where she is funded by an FWO scholarship. She earned an M.A. in English and German literature from the University of Antwerp and an M.A. in children's literature from the University of Surrey Roehampton. In 2008, she defended her Ph.D. dissertation, "New Perspectives on Fairy Tales: The Intertextual Dialogue Between Fairy-Tale Criticism and Dutch, English and German Fairy-Tale Retellings in the Period from 1970 to 2006." Her publications include *Changing Concepts of Childhood and Children's Literature* and *Uitgelezen jeugdliteratuur* (both with Katrien Vloebergs) and articles in *Children's Literature in Education*, *The Continuum Encyclopedia of Fairy Tales*, *The Journal of Children's Literature*, and *Marvels and Tales*. She currently researches the translation and reception of the Grimm tales in Dutch.

Christa Mastrangelo Joyce is privately editing books of fiction and nonfiction, while collaborating on a poetry translation project with Peter Levitt and continuing to write poems for her second book-length manuscript. She earned a B.A. in English writing from Towson College and an M.F.A. in creative writing from Antioch University, Los Angeles. Her poetry has been published in print and online journals, including *Arsenic Lobster*, *Water~Stone Review*, *Valparaiso Poetry Review*, *Florida English Journal* and *Blue Ridge*. She has published works of nonfiction in *Woman's World*, *Bohemian Bridge* and *Style* magazines. Ms. Joyce has taught in the English department at Dean College, Massachusetts, and American University in Washington, D.C.

Margarete J. Landwehr, an associate professor of German and the German Program Coordinator in the Department of Foreign Languages at West Chester University, holds the Ph.D. in German language and literature from Harvard University. She has published articles on Kleist, fin-de-siècle Vienna (Schnitzler, Roth), and postwar German literature and film. Her articles have appeared in *Monatshefte*, *The German Quarterly*, and *Colloquia Germanica*. Her current book project is *Trauma Narrative in Postwar German Literature and Film* and one chapter of this book, "Maerchen as Trauma Narrative: Helma Sanders-Brahms' Film *Germany, Pale Mother*," has appeared as an article in *Folklore and Film* (Utah State University Press, 2007).

Helen Pilinovsky recently completed her dissertation, "Fantastic Émigrés: Translation and Acculturation of the Fairy Tale in a Literary Diaspora," at Columbia University, and is now a professor at California State University–San Bernardino. Her reviews have appeared in *Marvels & Tales: Journal of Fairy-Tale Studies* and in the *New York Review of Science Fiction*, and she has been published at the *Endicott Studio for the Mythic Arts*, *Realms of Fantasy* magazine, and a selection of academic journals. She has guest-edited issues of the *Journal of the Fantastic in the Arts and Extrapolations*, and she is the academic editor of *Cabinet des Fées*.

Christopher Roman, an assistant professor of English at Kent State University, Tuscarawas, earned his Ph.D. in English literature from the University of Alabama. He teaches courses in medieval literature, Chaucer, composition, creative writing, and technical writing. His book *Domestic Mysticism in Margery Kempe and Dame Julian of Norwich* was published by Edwin Mellen Press in 2005. His articles and reviews have appeared in *Transformations*, *Speculum*, and *Florilegium*. He is currently working on a book tracing the development of the uses of space from the *Ancrene Wisse* to *The Book of Margery Kempe*.

Mathilda Slabbert, a post-doctoral fellow in the Department of English at Stellenbosch University, South Africa, obtained her M.A. in English literature from Johannesburg University in 1998 and holds a D.Litt. et Phil. from the University of South Africa. Her thesis, "Inventions and Transformation: An Exploration of Mythification and Remythification in Four Contemporary Novels" (2006), explores the hypothesis that myths are present, albeit in transformed version, in contemporary fiction. She teaches a course on critical theory and film studies at Vega Brand Communication School in Cape Town. Her research interests focus primarily on storytelling, intertextuality and identity and include approaches to mythopoetics, narratology, and gender and cultural studies.

Joanne Campbell Tidwell, a lecturer at Peace College in Raleigh, North Carolina, earned her Ph.D. from Auburn University in May 2005. She is the author of *Politics and Aesthetics in The Diary of Virginia Woolf* (Routledge, 2007), which explores the conflict of Woolf's aesthetic principles with her political viewpoints. She has published in *a/b: Auto/Biography Studies* and Woolf conference publications. She has presented papers on Woolf's diary and fiction, the diaries of Katherine Mansfield, Vera Brittain, and Anaïs Nin, and Anne McCaffrey's Pern books. Her research focuses primarily on Virginia Woolf, modernism, and the diary genre.

Maureen Torpey is an independent scholar living in Buffalo, New York. She earned her M.A. in English literature from Buffalo State College and her B.A. in English literature from Boston College where she also minored in Irish studies. She has presented papers at Southern Literature conferences at both Methodist and Berry Colleges, as well as the Child and the Book conference in Newcastle, England. She has published her article "Cultural Conservation: The Influence of the Irish Literary Revival on the Harlem Renaissance" in *Crossroads: A Southern Culture Annual*, and she is currently researching further the connection between Irish literature and the literature of the American South.

Index